W9-AAE-151

Mark Attridge, PhD
Patricia A. Herlihy, PhD, RN
R. Paul Maiden, PhD, LCSW
Editors

The Integration of Employee Assistance, Work/Life, and Wellness Services

The Integration of Employee Assistance, Work/Life, and Wellness Services has been co-published simultaneously as *Journal of Workplace Behavioral Health*, Volume 20, Numbers 1/2 and 3/4, 2005.

Pre-publication REVIEWS, COMMENTARIES, EVALUATIONS . . .

"**A** must read for anyone who is providing or purchasing employee assistance, work-life, or wellness programs. Readers will gain insight of the impact employee health and well-being has on organizations. This volume provides the reader with an understanding on how employee assistance, work-life, and wellness programs support organizations in maximizing the return on human capital."

Paul A. Courtois, MSW
Senior Auditor, Corporate Audit Services

More pre-publication
REVIEWS, COMMENTARIES, EVALUATIONS . . .

"A VALUABLE RESOURCE FOR ALL PROFESSIONALS who face the challenge of keeping the worker healthy and engaged. This book breaks down the silo approach an thoroughly investigates the integration of key service providers, employee assistance, work-life, and wellness services. It is well laid out, moving from a conceptual framework to case examples from private and public sectors. Given the globalization of business, the international section ensures the relevancy of this material for today's professional."

Dr. Louise Hartley
President, Employee Assistance Society of North America

The Haworth Press, Inc.

New York • London • Victoria (AU)
www.HaworthPress.com

The Integration of Employee Assistance, Work/Life, and Wellness Services

The Integration of Employee Assistance, Work/Life, and Wellness Services has been co-published simultaneously as *Journal of Workplace Behavioral Health*, Volume 20, Numbers 1/2 and 3/4, 2005.

Monographic Separates from the *Journal of Workplace Behavioral Health*

For additional information on these and other Haworth Press titles, including descriptions, tables of contents, reviews, and prices, use the QuickSearch catalog at http://www.HaworthPress.com.

The *Journal of Workplace Behavioral Health*™ is the successor title to *Employee Assistance Quarterly*™, which changed title after Vol. 19, No. 4, 2004. The *Journal of Workplace Behavioral Health*™, under its new title, begins with Vol. 20, No. 1/2/3/4, 2005.

The Integration of Employee Assistance, Work/Life, and Wellness Services, edited by Mark Attridge, PhD, Patricia A. Herlihy, PhD, RN, and R. Paul Maiden, PhD, LCSW (Vol. 20, No. 1/2/3/4, 2005). *"A must read for anyone who is providing or purchasing employeess assistance, work-life, or wellness programs." (Paul A. Courtois, MSW, Senior Auditor, Corporate Audit Services)*

*Accreditation of Employee Assistance Programs,** edited by R. Paul Maiden, PhD (Vol. 19, No. 1, 2003). Accreditation ensures private or public sector organizations that an employee assistance program (EAP) has acceptable level of experience, advisement, and expertise. Accreditation of Employee Assistance Programs gives you the information you need to get an employee assistance program accredited. Thorough and focused chapters by respected authorities discuss the value of EAP accreditation to future customers, the development of accreditation standards for employee assistance programs, and the smoothest road to travel to your destination of EAP accreditation.*

*Global Perspectives of Occupational Social Work,** edited by R. Paul Maiden, PhD (Vol. 17, No. 1/2, 2001). A broad survey of the development and current practices of occupational social work as practiced in seven countries around the world.*

*Emerging Trends for EAPs in the 21st Century,** edited by Nan Van Den Bergh, PhD, LCSW (Vol. 16, No. 1/2, 2000). "An excellent book. . . . Relevant with respect to contemporary practice and current state of the art for EAPs. A sound disciplinary input for both program development and service delivery." (William L. Mermis, PhD, Professor of Human Health, Arizona State University)*

*Employee Assistance Services in the New South Africa,** edited by R. Paul Maiden, PhD (Vol. 14, No. 3, 1999). Addresses the many issues affecting the development of EAP programs in the new South Africa.*

*Women in the Workplace and Employee Assistance Programs: Perspectives, Innovations, and Techniques for Helping Professionals,** edited by Marta Lundy, PhD, LCSW, and Beverly Younger, MSW, ACSW (Vol. 9, No. 3/4, 1994). "A valuable resource and training guide to EAP practitioners and managers alike. Most importantly, it increases the sensitivity of women's issues as they relate to the workplace." (R. Paul Maiden, PhD, Chair, Occupational Social Work, Jane Addams College of Social Work, University of Illinois at Chicago)*

*Employee Assistance Programs in South Africa,** edited by R. Paul Maiden, MSW (Vol. 7, No. 3, 1992). "The first comprehensive collection of perspectives on EAPs in an industrializing third-world country." (Brian McKendrick, PhD, Professor and Head, School of Social Work, University of the Witwaterstrand, Johannesburg)*

*Occupational Social Work Today,** edited by Shulamith Lala Ashenberg Straussner, DSW, CEAP (Vol. 5, No. 1, 1990). "A well-organized overview of social work practice in business . . . interesting and timely." (Journal of Clinical Psychiatry)*

*Evaluation of Employee Assistance Programs,** edited by Marvin D. Feit, PhD, and Michael J. Holosko, PhD (Vol. 3, No. 3/4, 1989). "The definitive work in the field of program evaluations of EAPs. . . . A must for anyone considering planning, implementing, and most importantly, evaluating employee assistance programs." (Dr. Gerald Erickson, Professor and Director, School of Social Work, University of Windsor)*

*Alcohol in Employment Settings: The Results of the WHO/ILO International Review,** edited by D. Wayne Corneil, ScD (cand.) (Vol. 3, No. 2, 1988). Valuable insights into attitudes about alcohol and the effects of its use with courses of action for educating and treating employees who need help with alcohol problems.*

EAPs and the Information Revolution: The Dark Side of Megatrends, * edited by Keith McClellan and Richard E. Miller, PhD (Vol. 2, No. 2, 1987). *A serious examination of treatment methods that can be used to help working people cope with a rapidly changing economic society.*

The Integration
of Employee Assistance,
Work/Life, and Wellness
Services

Mark Attridge, PhD
Patricia A. Herlihy, PhD, RN
R. Paul Maiden, PhD, LCSW
Editors

The Integration of Employee Assistance, Work/Life, and Wellness Services has been co-published simultaneously as *Journal of Workplace Behavioral Health*, Volume 20, Numbers 1/2 and 3/4 2005.

The Haworth Press, Inc.

New York • London • Victoria (AU)
www.HaworthPress.com

The Integration of Employee Assistance, Work/Life, and Wellness Services has been co-published simultaneously as *Journal of Workplace Behavioral Health*, Volume 20, Numbers 1/2 and 3/4, 2005.

© 2005 by The Haworth Press, Inc. All rights reserved. No part of this work may be reproduced or utilized in any form or by any means, electronic or mechanical, including photocopying, microfilm and recording, or by any information storage and retrieval system, without permission in writing from the publisher. Printed in the United States of America.

The development, preparation, and publication of this work has been undertaken with great care. However, the publisher, employees, editors, and agents of The Haworth Press and all imprints of The Haworth Press, Inc., including The Haworth Medical Press® and Pharmaceutical Products Press®, are not responsible for any errors contained herein or for consequences that may ensue from use of materials or information contained in this work. Opinions expressed by the author(s) are not necessarily those of The Haworth Press, Inc. With regard to case studies, identities and circumstances of individuals discussed herein have been changed to protect confidentiality. Any resemblance to actual persons, living or dead, is entirely coincidental.

Cover design by Kerry E. Mack

Library of Congress Cataloging-in-Publication Data

The integration of employee assistance, work/life, and wellness services / Mark Attridge, Patricia A. Herlihy, R. Paul Maiden, editors.
    p. cm.
    "Co-published simultaneously as Journal of Workplace Behavioral Health, volume 20, numbers 1/2 and 3/4 2005."
    Includes bibliographical references and index.
    ISBN-13: 978-0-7890-3062-7 (hard cover : alk. paper)
    ISBN-10: 0-7890-3062-4 (hard cover : alk. paper)
    ISBN-13: 978-0-7890-3063-4 (soft cover : alk. paper)
    ISBN-10: 0-7890-3063-2 (soft cover : alk. paper)
    1. Employee assistance programs. 2. Work environment. I. Attridge, Mark. II. Herlihy, Patricia A. III. Maiden, R. Paul.
HF5549.5.E42I56 2005
658.3'8–dc22
                                                                        2005022182

Indexing, Abstracting & Website/Internet Coverage

This section provides you with a list of major indexing & abstracting services and other tools for bibliographic access. That is to say, each service began covering this periodical during the year noted in the right column. Most Websites which are listed below have indicated that they will either post, disseminate, compile, archive, cite or alert their own Website users with research-based content from this work. (This list is as current as the copyright date of this publication.)

Abstracting, Website/Indexing Coverage . . . . Year When Coverage Began

- *Business Source Corporate: coverage of nearly 3,350 quality magazines and journals; designed to meet the diverse information needs of corporations; EBSCO Publishing <http://www.epnet.com/corporate/bsourcecorp.asp>* **2002**

- *Criminal Justice Abstracts* . . . . *

- *EAP Abstracts Plus <http://www.eaptechnology.com>* **1994**

- *EBSCOhost Electronic Journals Service (EJS) <http://ejournals.ebsco.com>* **2001**

- *EMBASE.com (The Power of EMBASE + MEDLINE Combined) <http://www.embase.com>* **1985**

- *EMBASE/Excerpta Medica Secondary Publishing Division. Included in newsletters, review journals, major reference works, magazines and abstract journals <http://www.elsevier.nl>* **1985**

- *Entrepreneurship Research Engine <http://www.research.kauffman.org>* **2004**

- *e-psyche, LLC <http://www.e-psyche.net>* **2001**

- *Excerpta Medica . . . . See EMBASE* **1985**

(continued)

- *Family & Society Studies Worldwide (online and CD/ROM)*
  <http://www.nisc.com>................................. 1996

- *Family Index Database <http://www.familyscholar.com>* 2004

- *Google <http://www.google.com>*........................... 2004

- *Google Scholar <http://www.scholar.google.com>* 2004

- *Haworth Document Delivery Center*
  <http://www.HaworthPress.com/journals/dds.asp> 2004

- *Health & Psychosocial Instruments (HaPI) Database (available*
  through online and as a CD-ROM from Ovid Technologies) .. 1999

- *Human Resources Abstracts (HRA)*....................... 1985

- *IBZ International Bibliography of Periodical Literature*
  <http://www.saur.de>.................................. 2001

- *Index Guide to College Journals (core list compiled by integrating*
  48 indexes frequently used to support undergraduate programs
  in small to medium sized libraries) 1999

- *Index to Periodical Articles Related to Law*
  <http://www.law.utexas.edu>........................... 1985

- *Internationale Bibliographie der geistes- und*
  sozialwissenschaftlichen Zeitschriftenliteratur . . . See IBZ
  <http://www.saur.de>.................................. 2001

- *Links@Ovid <via CrossRef targeted DOI links)*
  <http://www.ovid.com>................................ 2005

- *Medical Benefits <http://www.aspenpublishers.com>*.......... 2002

- *OCLC ArticleFirst <http://www.oclc.org/services/databases/>* 1985

- *OCLC ContentsFirst <http://ww.oclc.org/services/databases/>* ... 1984

- *OCLC Public Affairs Information Service <http://www.pais.org>* . 1985

- *Ovid Linksolver (OpenURL link resolver via CrossRef targeted*
  DOI links) <http://www.linksolver.com>.................. 2005

- *Peace Research Abstracts Journal* 2003

- *Personnel Management Abstracts* 1988

- *Psychological Abstracts (PsycINFO) <http://www.apa.org>* 1985

(continued)

- *Social Services Abstracts <http://www.csa.com>* 1999

- *Social Work Abstracts*
  <http://www.silverplatter.com/catalog/swab.htm> 1988

- *SocIndex (EBSCO)* 2003

- *SocioAbs <http://www.csa.com>* 1990

- *Sociological Abstracts (SA) <http://www.csa.com>* 1990

- *Spanish Technical Information System on Drug Abuse
  Prevention "Sistema de Informacion Tecnica Sobre
  Prevention del Abuso de Drogas" (In Spanish)
  <http://www.idea-prevencion.com>* 1999

- *zetoc <http://zetoc.mimas.ac.uk>* 2004

*Exact start date to come.

*Special Bibliographic Notes related to special journal issues
(separates) and indexing/abstracting:*

- indexing/abstracting services in this list will also cover material in any "separate" that is co-published simultaneously with Haworth's special thematic journal issue or DocuSerial. Indexing/abstracting usually covers material at the article/chapter level.
- monographic co-editions are intended for either non-subscribers or libraries which intend to purchase a second copy for their circulating collections.
- monographic co-editions are reported to all jobbers/wholesalers/approval plans. The source journal is listed as the "series" to assist the prevention of duplicate purchasing in the same manner utilized for books-in-series.
- to facilitate user/access services all indexing/abstracting services are encouraged to utilize the co-indexing entry note indicated at the bottom of the first page of each article/chapter/contribution.
- this is intended to assist a library user of any reference tool (whether print, electronic, online, or CD-ROM) to locate the monographic version if the library has purchased this version but not a subscription to the source journal.
- individual articles/chapters in any Haworth publication are also available through the Haworth Document Delivery Service (HDDS).

ALL HAWORTH BOOKS AND JOURNALS
ARE PRINTED ON CERTIFIED
ACID-FREE PAPER

The Integration of Employee Assistance, Work/Life, and Wellness Services

CONTENTS

About the Contributors   xvii

Preface: Welfare Capitalism Comes Full Circle
    Through the Integration of EAPs, Work-Life and Wellness   xxix

CONCEPTUAL MODELS AND MEASUREMENT ISSUES

Chapter 1: Employee Assistance, Work-Life Effectiveness,
    and Health and Productivity: A Conceptual Framework
    for Integration   1
    Mary Ellen Gornick
    Brenda R. Blair

Chapter 2: The Business Case for the Integration of Employee
    Assistance, Work-Life and Wellness Services:
    A Literature Review   31
    Mark Attridge

Chapter 3: Health and Productivity Management: The Integration
    of Health and Wellness into Employee Assistance
    and Work-Life Programs   57
    Michael D. Mulvihill

RESEARCH ON INTEGRATION

Chapter 4: Research on the Integration of Employee Assistance,
    Work-Life and Wellness Services: Past, Present and Future   67
    Patricia A. Herlihy
    Mark Attridge

Chapter 5: Perspectives on the Integration of Employee
  Assistance and Work-Life Programs:
  A Survey of Key Informants in the EAP Field   95
    David A. Sharar
    Edward Hertenstein

INTEGRATION IN ACADEMIC SETTINGS

Chapter 6: University Of Arizona Life & Work Connections:
  A Synergistic Strategy for Maximizing Whole-Person
  Productivity over the Employees' Life-Cycle/Work-Cycle   105
    Darci A. Thompson
    David L. Swihart

Chapter 7: Johns Hopkins University: Diary of Integration   123
    Everett Siegel

Chapter 8: Responding to Deaths of Faculty, Staff
  and Students at UC, Berkeley–An Integrated Approach   143
    Carol Hoffman
    Bruce Goya

Chapter 9: Disaster Consequence Management: An Integrated
  Approach for Fostering Human Continuity in the Workplace   159
    Nancy T. Vineburgh
    Robert J. Ursano
    Carol S. Fullerton

INTEGRATION BY AN EXTERNAL SERVICE PROVIDER

Chapter 10: Ceridian's Experience in the Integration
  of EAP, Work-Life and Wellness Programs   183
    Brian Kelly
    Jean Holbrook
    Ronnie Bragen

INTEGRATION IN INTERNAL PROGRAMS

Chapter 11: Motorola Drives Strategic Initiatives
  Through Collaboration and Interdependence   203
    Nancy K. Lesch

Chapter 12: Wells Fargo's Employee Assistance Consulting
    Model: How to Be an Invited Guest at Every Table   219
    Rick Bidgood
    Arne Boudewyn
    Betsy Fasbinder

INTEGRATION IN HYBRID MODELS

Chapter 13: Ernst & Young's Assist: How Internal
    and External Service Integration Created a 'Single Source
    Solution'   243
    Sandra Turner
    Michael Weiner
    Kate Keegan

Chapter 14: Fairview Alive–An Integrated Strategy
    for Enhancing the Health and Well-Being of Employees   263
    Barbara D. Eischen
    Jessica Grossmeier
    Daniel B. Gold

INTEGRATION IN THE PUBLIC SECTOR

Chapter 15: An Integrated EAP–Defining One's Place
    in the Organization: A Perspective from the Internal
    EAP Side of the Fence   281
    Bernard E. Beidel

Chapter 16. Integration of Occupational Health
    Services in the Federal Sector   307
    Diane Stephenson
    Mark Delowery

Chapter 17. Integrating Employee Assistance Services
    with Organization Development and Health Risk
    Management: The State Government of Minnesota   325
    Stephen P. Birkland
    Adib S. Birkland

INTERNATIONAL PERSPECTIVES OF INTEGRATION

Chapter 18: Australian Perspectives on the Organizational
    Integration of Employee Assistance Services   351
    Andrea K. Kirk
    David F. Brown

Chapter 19: Work-Life and EAPs in the United Kingdom
    and Europe: A Qualitative Study of Integration   367
    Linda Hoskinson
    Stephanie Beer

Chapter 20: A Social Partnership Approach to Work-Life
    Balance in the European Union–The Irish Experience   381
    Maurice Quinlan

A CRITICAL ANALYSIS AND FUTURE PERSPECTIVES OF INTEGRATION

Chapter 21: A Commentary on the Integration of EAPs:
    Some Cautionary Notes from Past and Present   395
    Paul M. Roman

Chapter 22: Perspectives on the Future of Integration   407
    Patricia A. Herlihy

APPENDIX

Resources in the EAP, Work/Life and Wellness Fields   419

Index   425

ABOUT THE EDITORS

Mark Attridge, PhD, is a consultant in the employee assistance field. Since 1994, he has conducted dozens of applied research studies using clinical, survey and claims data for various Fortune 500 employers and health plans. He was the Chair of the Research Committee for the Employee Assistance Professionals Association from 1999 to 2004 and has been on the advisory council for the Institute for Health and Productivity Management. He is a scientific reviewer for several scholarly journals and the National Registry of Effective Prevention Programs, Workplace Division for the U.S. government. Dr. Attridge has taught over 50 undergraduate- and graduate-level classes at the University of Minnesota, the University of Wisconsin and Augsburg College. He has created over 100 publications and conference presentations in the areas of health, social psychology and communication. Mark is also President of Attridge Studios–a family business in the fine arts and personal growth consulting.

Patricia A. Herlihy PhD, RN, is a Research Analyst and CEO of Rocky Mountain Research in Boulder, Colorado. She is a Psychiatric Clinical Nurse Specialist with over 25 years of psychiatric experience. Her range of experience includes Charge Nurse on an Inpatient Adult Psychiatric care unit, Family Therapist in an outpatient child guidance center; Director of an Adolescent Substance Abuse Program; Assistant Professor at Boston University's Graduate Psychiatric Nursing Program; Systems Manager for Digital Equipment Corporations' EAP; and Principal Investigator for three international studies on the topic of integration of services. She received her doctorate from the Florence Heller Graduate School, Brandeis University. Patricia has presented extensively in North America on the topic of integration of EAP, W/L and wellness services and has numerous publications on this topic. Currently she is on the Board of EASNA serving as their Research Chair.

R. Paul Maiden, PhD, LCSW, is Director of the School of Social Work at the University of Central Florida in Orlando and is a faculty member of the Public Affairs PhD program. he is the editor of the *Journal of Workplace Behavioral Health*. From 1986-1999 he was chair of the occupational social work program at the University of Illinois-Chicago. He has been in the EAP field since 1980. He has published, presented, trained, and consulted extensively in teh U.S. and abroad, particularly in South Africa and Russia.

He is the recipient of a Senior Fulbright to Russia and is involved in curriculum development and training in employee assistance and workplace and family and violence. Dr. Maiden is a principal of Behavioral Health Concepts, Ltd. He has consulted with a wide range of numerous domestic and international organizations and employers in the public and private sectors in the development, administration and evaluation of employee assistance and managed care programs, workplace polices and educational programs on drug testing, family medical leave, HIV/AIDS, harassment and disabilities, training and development of treatment providers in managed care, and organizational development and change.

About the Contributors

Mark Attridge, PhD, is a consultant in the employee assistance field. Since 1994, he has conducted dozens of applied research studies using clinical, survey and claims data for various Fortune 500 employers and health plans. He was the Chair of the Research Committee for the Employee Assistance Professionals Association from 1999 to 2004 and has been on the advisory council for the Institute for Health and Productivity Management. He is a scientific reviewer for several scholarly journals and the National Registry of Effective Prevention Programs, Workplace Division for the U.S. government. Dr. Attridge has taught over 50 undergraduate- and graduate-level classes at the University of Minnesota, the University of Wisconsin and Augsburg College. He has created over 100 publications and conference presentations in the areas of health, social psychology and communication. Mark is also President of Attridge Studios–a family business in the fine arts and personal growth consulting. Address correspondence to: Attridge Studios, 1408-1410 Grand Street NE, Minneapolis, MN. 55413 (E-mail: mark@attridgestudios.com).

Stephanie Beer is an independent EAP consultant based in the UK. She has 8 years direct experience with Accor Services as Head of Operations responsible for the delivery of both Psychological and Work/Life Services. Before this she had 7 years experience in the delivery of telephone help lines following social broadcasting with BBC and ITV. She was also a specialist debt advisor with Citizen Advice Bureaux for 10 years. She is the immediate past Chair of EAPA UK and the Chair of the EAPA UK sub-committee responsible for revising and updating the current UK EAPA standards. Address correspondence to: 4 Woodland Rise, London N10 3UG, United Kingdom (E-mail: stephanie.beer@blueyonder.co.uk).

Bernard E. Beidel, MEd, CEAP, is the Director of the Office of Employee Assistance at the U.S. House of Representatives in Washington, DC. He is responsible for the planning, development, management, evaluation, and continued enhancement and integration of the House's employee assistance service. Prior to joining the House in 1991, he developed and directed the EAP for the New Jersey State Police. His initial EAP experience came as an external provider managing an employee assistance consortium in rural Virginia. Address correspondence to: The Office of Employee Assistance, U.S. House of Representatives, H2-140, Ford House Office Building, Washington, DC 20515-6619 (E-mail: bern.beidel@mail. house.gov).

Rick Bidgood, MSW, LCSW, CEAP, is the Vice President and Director of Wells Fargo's Employee Assistance Consulting (EAC) and Work*Ability*. Mr. Bidgood has been involved in the employee assistance field since 1985 having worked at external EAPs and at academic, healthcare and other financial services organizations. He has been with Wells Fargo since 1997. Mr. Bidgood is a graduate of the School of Social Welfare at the University of California at Berkeley and resides in San Francisco. Address correspondence to: Wells Fargo EAC, MACA0163-111, San Francisco, CA 94104 (E-mail: bidgood@wellsfargo.com).

Adib S. Birkland is an advanced doctoral student in the department of Human Resources and Industrial Relations in the Carlson School of Management at the University of Minnesota. His areas of specialization include staffing, training, development, organizational behavior, and organizational theory. Specifically, his research interests include personality and emotion at work and counterproductive work behaviors. Address correspondence to: University of Minnesota 3-300 Carlson School of Management, Industrial Relations Center, 321 19th Avenue South, Minneapolis, MN 55455- 0438 (E-mail: abirkland@csom.umn.edu).

Stephen P. Birkland, MS, is a Licensed Independent Social Worker and a Certified Employee Assistance Professional. He is the principal of Birkland and Associates. He has also worked for nearly 20 years as a senior consultant with the State of Minnesota. Birkland also teaches at Metropolitan State University College of Management (since 1989). Address correspondence to: State of Minnesota EAP, 658 Cedar St. Suite 200, St. Paul, MN 55155 (E-mail: stephen.birkland@state.mn.us).

Brenda R. Blair, MBA, CEAP, is President of Blair Consulting Group, Inc., a consulting firm focused on areas where employee personal concerns and employer productivity concerns overlap. Always on the cutting edge of new thought and opportunity, the company includes a team of first class consultants assisting employers and service providers with EAP, work/life, health and productivity, expatriate support, coaching, resilience, organizational effectiveness, DOT/SAP services, and international service delivery. A sought-after speaker and trainer, Brenda has presented to professional audiences throughout the United States and in the UK, Japan, Trinidad, Canada, Greece and South Africa. An independent consultant since 1983, she was EAPA's first recipient of the prestigious Member of the Year Award in 1988. Other awards include the EAP Hall of Fame, Georgia Tech EAP Leadership Award and North Carolina EAPA President's Achievement Award. She has authored numerous articles, and is a member of EAPA, EASNA, AWLP, IHPM, and SHRM. Address correspondence to: Blair Consultants, P.O. Box 9927, College Station, TX 77842 (E-mail: bblair@blairconsultants.com).

Arne Boudewyn, PhD, is a Lead Business Consultant for Wells Fargo's Employee Assistance Consulting (EAC). Prior to joining EAC, he worked as a clinician, research investigator, teacher and health education project manager. Mr. Boudewyn received his graduate degree in clinical psychology from the University of Massachusetts (Boston). Address correspondence to: Wells Fargo EAC, MACA0163-111, San Francisco, CA 94104 (E-mail: arne.c.boudewyn@wellsfargo.com).

Ronnie Bragen is a Product Manager for Ceridian. She directs activities related to the strategy, development, maintenance, evaluation and support of health promotion and risk management services. Ronnie has authored articles for various EAP industry publications. Address correspondence to: Ceridian Corporation, 930 Commonwealth Avenue, Boston, MA 02215 (E-mail: Ronnie.bragen@ceridian.com).

David F. Brown, PhD, is Professor of Management in the School of Business at La Trobe University, Melbourne Australia. He has specialised for over fifteen years in teaching and research in the areas of knowledge and skills development, training and performance in the workplace, competency evaluation, and occupational health and safety. He has acted in a research capacity and as a consultant to organisations that include Victorian Auditor-General's Office, Queensland Police Service, Sydney Water, BHP, and Rio Tinto. Address correspondence to: La Trobe University, School of Business, Bundoora Campus, Kingsbury Drive, Bundoora, Melbourne, Victoria, 3086, Australia (E-mail: D.Brown@Latrobe.edu.au).

Mark Delowery, DO, MPH, Director for Clinical Services for Federal Occupational Health, is a licensed physician, board eligible in occupational medicine, and holds a master's degree in Public Health. He started his medical career in private family practice and has more than 18 years of occupational health and management experience. Address correspondence to: Federal Occupational Health, 150 S. Independence Mall West, Suite 368 Philadelphia, PA 19106 (E-mail: mdelowery@psc.gov).

Barbara D. Eischen is Director of Health and Benefits Services, in the human resources department for Fairview Health Services. Ms. Eischen has over 25 years experience in various aspects of human resources, including benefits, compensation, operations, employment and health management, primarily in the health care industry. In her current role, she established and oversees the *Fairview Alive* program, an integrated employee health management function, which includes employee benefits, employee assistance program, employee occupational health services and a comprehensive health promotion program. Ms. Eischen was awarded a Bachelor of Arts degree in psychology from Miami University, Oxford, Ohio. Address correspondence to: Fairview Health Services, 2450 Riverside Avenue, Minneapolis, MN 55454 (E-mail: beishe1@fairview.org).

Betsy Fasbinder, MFT, is a Lead Business Consultant at Wells Fargo's Employee Assistance Consulting (EAC) and she has been associated with EAC since 1993. Ms. Fasbinder has a background as a clinician and community educator in mental health, educational and academic settings. She received her graduate degree from San Francisco State University. Address correspondence to: Wells Fargo EAC, MACA0163-111, San Francisco, CA 94104 (E-mail: fasbing@wellsfargo.com).

Carol S. Fullerton, PhD, is Research Associate Professor in the Department of Psychiatry at the Uniformed Services University of the Health Sciences School of Medicine (USUHS), Bethesda, Maryland. She is also Scientific Director of the Center for the Study of Traumatic Stress (CSTS), an interdisciplinary Center with an established international reputation for research, education and consultation on the effects of terrorism, bioterrorism, trauma, disasters, and war on individuals, communities and groups. Dr. Fullerton is widely published in the areas of post-traumatic stress disorder and the behavioral and psychological effects of terrorism, bioterrorism, traumatic events and disasters, and combat. Dr. Fullerton and her group are at the forefront of public health policy planning for terrorism and bioterrorism. Her work has been widely cited in government planning and Institute of Medicine, National Academies of Sciences reports addressing these issues. She was a national consultant for planning research programs following the September 11th terrorist attacks. Dr. Fullerton and her group developed educational materials that were some of the most widely disseminated throughout the nation to assist populations exposed to the September 11th attacks. Address correspondence to: Department of Psychiatry Uniformed Services University of the Health Sciences School of Medicine, 4301 Jones Bridge Road, Bethesda, MD 20814 (E-mail: cfullert@erols.com).

Daniel B. Gold, PhD, is Director of Research for StayWell Health Management, where he is responsible for the design and implementation of cost effectiveness evaluations as well as outcomes measurement for self-insured employers, managed care organizations and other providers. Dr.

Gold has conducted numerous studies in the areas of health promotion, disease prevention, self-care, and disease management. Dr. Gold is a contributing editor to the *American Journal of Health Promotion*, has published several peer-reviewed papers, and is a frequent speaker at professional conferences nationwide. Dr. Gold received his PhD in Social Psychology from the University of Virginia. Address correspondence to: StayWell Health Management, 2700 Blue Water Road, Suite 850, St. Paul, MN 55121-1400 (E-mail: Dan.Gold@StayWell.com).

Mary Ellen Gornick, MA, is Senior Vice President at Workplace Options (WPO), a leading provider of Work-Life solutions for Employee Assistance Programs (EAP). She provides leadership to the Work-Life consulting practice and the National Training Center. The consulting practice assists clients advance work-life effectiveness initiatives through organizational assessments, impact studies, program design and strategy development. The National Training Center includes an inventory of 85 work–life personal and professional development seminars delivered through a national network of trainers in traditional and online venues. Prior to joining Workplace Options, she founded the CPA Group, a nationally recognized work-life consulting and training organization. Ms. Gornick is a founding board member and past President of the Alliance of Work-Life Progress (AWLP). She currently services as a subject matter expert on the EAPA Work-Life Committee. Ms. Gornick earned a master's degree from the University of Chicago, School of Social Service Administration and is currently associated with the Entrepreneurship Center, housed in the School of Management at Purdue University-Calumet. Address correspondence to: Workplace Options, Inc., 161 West Harrison Street, Suite 201, Chicago, IL 60605 (E-mail: maryelleng@workplaceoptions.com).

Bruce Goya, MEd, is a Program Coordinator at the University of California, Office of the President. He provides system-wide coordination for Rehabilitation Programs and Employee Assistance Programs, and serves as program administrator for behavioral health care benefits. He has presented at national conferences for the Washington Business Group on Health, the Employee Assistance Professionals Association, and the Alliance of Work-Life Progress. Address correspondence to: University of California, 300 Lakeside Drive, 12th Floor, Oakland, CA 95612-3557 (E-mail: bruce.goya@ucop.edu).

Jessica Grossmeier, MPH, is a Senior Researcher at StayWell Health Management, where she contributes to program evaluation and research studies that examine the impact of worksite health promotion programs. Since joining StayWell in 2001, she has worked with over a dozen customers on program evaluation and outcomes studies, including Caterpillar,

DaimlerChrysler, Hawaii Medical Services Association, Fairview Health Services, Marathon Ashland Petroleum/Marathon Oil Company, Mack Trucks, and many more. Prior to beginning her career as a researcher, she spent many years developing and delivering health promotion programs in corporate and manufacturing settings. In addition to her work at StayWell, Jessica also serves as an online faculty member for the University of Phoenix, College of Health Sciences and Nursing. Address correspondence to: StayWell Health Management, 2700 Blue Water Road, Suite 850, St. Paul, MN 55121 (E-mail: Jessica.Grossmeier@staywell.com).

Patricia A. Herlihy PhD, RN, is a Research Analyst and CEO of Rocky Mountain Research in Boulder, Colorado. She is a Psychiatric Clinical Nurse Specialist with over 25 years of psychiatric experience. Her range of experience includes Charge Nurse on an Inpatient Adult Psychiatric care unit, Family Therapist in an outpatient child guidance center; Director of an Adolescent Substance Abuse Program; Assistant Professor at Boston University's Graduate Psychiatric Nursing Program; Systems Manager for Digital Equipment Corporations' EAP; and Principal Investigator for three international studies on the topic of integration of services. She received her doctorate from the Florence Heller Graduate School, Brandeis University. Patricia has presented extensively in North America on the topic of integration of EAP, W/L and wellness services and has numerous publications on this topic. Currently she is on the Board of EASNA serving as their Research Chair. Address correspondence to: Rocky Mountain Research, 6255 Red Hill Road, Boulder, CO 80302 (E-mail: p_herlihy@msn.com).

Edward Hertenstein, PhD, is Assistant Professor of Labor and Industrial Relations and Head of the Labor Education Program, Institute of Labor and Industrial Relations, University of Illinois at Urbana-Champaign. His research has been in the area of measuring outcomes of employment decisions. He holds a BS in Labor Studies from Indiana University, and earned his PhD in Labor and Industrial Relations from the University of Illinois. Address correspondence to: University of Illinois at Champaign School of Labor Relations, 504 E. Armory, Champaign, IL 61820 (E-mail: hertenst@ilir.uiuc.edu).

Carol Hoffman, MSW, LCSW, CEAP, is the Manager, Work/Life at UC Berkeley. Prior to this, she founded and directed two employee assistance programs, at Kaiser Permanente Medical Center, San Francisco, and UC Berkeley (for faculty and staff). Carol currently participates on the Employee Assistance Professionals Association (EAPA) Work/Life Committee, College and University Work/Family Association (CUWFA) Board of Directors, and the Advisory Council of One Small Step, the SF-Bay Area

Employer Work/Life Organization. She has presented at many conferences and has been published in a number of publications on various work/life and EAP topics including elder care, trauma, disaster, and deaths. Address correspondence to: Tang Center, 2222 Bancroft, University of California, Berkeley, CA 94720-4300 (E-mail: choffman@uhs.berkeley.edu).

Jean Holbrook is Director of Product Management for Ceridian. Jean has held a variety of leadership roles in the industry and has published various articles related to the integration of EAP, work-life, and wellness programs. Address correspondence to: Ceridian Corporation, 930 Commonwealth Avenue Boston, MA 02215 (E-mail: jean.holbrook@ceridian.com).

Linda Hoskinson, CEAP, is an independent EAP consultant based in the UK. She has 15 years experience in human resources, 10 years as a director of an international EAP/WL provider and is Managing Director of People Resolutions Group providing UK employers with prevention and resolution to workplace disagreements and grievances and offering access to independent mediators and investigators. She was the first UK Chair of EAPA and was responsible for its currently published 'standards' for the delivery of EAPs in the UK. She is a Director of Worklife Support Ltd, part of the Teacher Support Network charity, ensuring tailored support and risk management services to the education sector, including resolution services. Address correspondence to: Hoskinson Associates, 12 Tudor Gardens, Stony Stratford, Milton Keynes, Buckinghamshire, England MK11 1HX (E-mail: linda@hoskinson-associates.com).

Kate Keegan, MSW, has been active in the work/life industry since 1987. As a account executive she has managed many Fortune 100 company accounts, helping them create, implement, and measure successful work/life initiatives according to their specific needs, culture and business objectives. Prior to her career in the work/life arena, Ms. Keegan was the Director of Client Services for Boston Senior Care where she developed innovative programs for elders, and oversaw a staff of 60 people who provided services to Boston's aging population. Ms. Keegan is a graduate of the University of Wisconsin and has a master's degree in social work from the University of Hawaii. Address correspondence to: 8 Cleveland St., Cambridge, MA 02138; (E-mail: kkeegan@lifecare.com).

Brian Kelly is a Product Manager for Ceridian. He has specialized in launching award-winning Web-based services to the industry. Brian has spoken on the issue of Web-based solutions which are accessible and usable to everyone, including those with disabilities. Address correspondence to: Ceridian Corporation, 930 Commonwealth Avenue, Boston, MA 02215 (E-mail brian.kelly@ceridian.com).

Andrea K. Kirk, PhD, is a Senior Lecturer in the Department of Management at Monash University in the areas of Organisational Behaviour and Strategic Management. In addition to her academic career Andrea spent ten years working as a clinical psychologist in the Victorian and New South Wales Public Services. Andrea has a particular interest in researching employee assistance in the Australian context, and developed a postgraduate course in EAPs at Griffith University, Queensland. She has published numerous journal articles and reports on the practice of EAPs in Australia. Address correspondence to: Monash University, Department of Management, Berwick Campus, P.O. Box 1071, Narre Warren, VIC 3805, Australia (E-mail: andrea.kirk-brown@buseco.monash.edu.au).

Nancy K. Lesch has been at Motorola for a total of ten years, most recently as Manger of Corporate Wellness Programs. She has over eighteen years experience in the wellness and fitness fields, including corporate program design and consultation, wellness and work/life project management, fitness instruction and center management, personal training and coaching/mentoring. She is a frequent presenter on the topic of resilience and its impact on employee health and well-being, providing courses and presentations for audiences such as the Institute for Health and Productivity Management, the Alliance for Work-Life Progress, the Conference Board Work/Life Conference, the Art of Health Promotion Journal, Rocky Mountain University of Health Professions, Arizona State University and The University of Texas at Austin. Address correspondence to: Motorola Corporate Wellness, 7700 West Parmer Lane, PL 66, Austin, TX 78729 (E-mail: Nancy.Lesch@Motorola.Com).

Michael D. Mulvihill, MSW, is President of Leade Health, Inc., an Ann Arbor, MI based wellness and disease prevention firm in business for over 14 years. The company specializes in evidence-based health behavior change programs such as smoking cessation, weight management, stress management and heart health. Leade Health has achieved award-winning outcomes in a variety of health and productivity programs. Michael has a master's degree in social work from the University of Michigan and is a member of the Academy of Certified Social Workers. He is an active member of the Employee Assistance Professionals Association Work/life Committee and the Health Enhancement Research Organization known as HERO. Address correspondence to: Leade Health, Inc., 310 Miller Suite, 1 Ann Arbor, MI 48103 (E-mail: mmulvihill@leadehealth.com).

Maurice Quinlan is Director of the EAP Institute. His interest in Employee Assistance Programmes (EAPs) developed when he worked in a semi-state company in 1972. Following a short period studying EAPs in the U.S., he introduced the EAP concept to Europe and hosted the first seminar on this topic in the Clarence Hotel, Dublin, Ireland, in September 1980. He established the EAP Institute to provide seminars, conferences and training on relevant work-related issues, such as work stress, violence, trauma, dignity at work, harassment/bullying, alcohol/drugs and work-life balance. Address correspondence to: EAP Institute, 143 Barrack Street, Waterford, Ireland (E-mail: eapinstitute@eircom.net).

Paul M. Roman, PhD, is Distinguished Research Professor of Sociology and directs the Center for Research on Behavioral Health and Human Services Delivery at the University of Georgia where he has been a faculty member since 1986. He received his PhD from Cornell University in 1968. Current research interests are alcohol and drug abuse in the workplace, employee assistance programs, organizational patterns associated with innovation and change in substance abuse treatment, inter-organizational relations in a clinical trials network, and the organization and management of therapeutic communities. Address correspondence to: Center for Research on Behavioral Health and Human Services Delivery 102 Barrow Hall, D. W. Brooks Drive, University of Georgia, Athens, GA (E-mail: proman@uga.edu).

David A. Sharar, MS, is Managing Director of Chestnut Global Partners, an international provider of employee assistance and expatriate support services and Director in the Employee Assistance/Workplace Services Division of Chestnut Health Systems, a not-for-profit agency based in Bloomington, Illinois. He is also a doctoral candidate at the School of Social Work, University of Illinois at Urbana-Champaign where his academic focus is employee assistance, occupational behavioral health, and managed behavioral health care. He has authored over 25 articles in professional magazines and peer-reviewed journals. Address correspondence to: Chestnut Health Systems, 1003 Martin Luther King Drive, Bloomington, IL 61701 (E-mail: dsharar@chestnut.org).

Everett Siegel, MD, is Assistant Professor of Psychiatry at John Hopkins School of Medicine. He is also Medical Director, Faculty and Staff Assistance Program and Student Assistance Program, and Director, Student Mental Health, John Hopkins School of Medicine. His areas of research include the relationship between psychoanalysis and culture, clinical studies and occupational psychiatry. Address correspondence to: 7511 Stream Crossing Road, Baltimore, MD 21209 (E-mail: esiegel@jhmi.edu).

Diane Stephenson, PhD, CEAP, is an occupational health manager with Federal Occupational Health and a licensed clinical psychologist. She has more than 20 years of healthcare experience in the management and direction of behavioral health programs, organizational and efficiency analysis, quality review, and direct clinical practice. Address correspondence to: Federal Occupational Health, 233 N. Michigan Avenue, Suite 270, Chicago, IL 60601 (E-mail: dstephenson@psc.gov).

David L. Swihart, MC, LPC, is the Employee Assistance Coordinator for the University of Arizona, serving in the integrated UA Life & Work Connections program. Besides providing employee assistance services, Dave is also a frequent presenter to university groups, and at the state and national levels on a variety of topics related to emotional health, wellness, and life cycle balance. Dave's background includes work as a clinician in community and other non-profit mental health agencies. Address correspondence to: UA Life & Work Connections, 1533 E. Helen St., Tucson, AZ 85721 (E-mail: dswihart@email.arizona.edu).

Darci A. Thompson, MSW, LCSW, is Director of UA Life & Work Connections, an integrated employee assistance, wellness, and work/life program at the University of Arizona. Darci has 20 years in higher education, focusing on strategic organizational growth and leveraging interdisciplinary teams. Additionally, she is a business consultant regarding employee life cycle services, a program developer, emphasizing the health resiliency approach to client services, and an educator and field liaison for undergraduate and graduate students in social work. Darci has been a presenter to national, state, and local conferences, and holds a bachelor's degree in communications and marketing from the University of Arizona and a master's degree in social work from Arizona State University. Address correspondence to: UA Life & Work Connections, 1533 E. Helen Street, Tucson, AZ 85721 (Email: darci@email.arizona.edu).

Sandra Turner, PhD, is Director of EY/Assist, Ernst and Young's integrated employee assistance and work/life resource and referral service. Sandra served in numerous capacities for the international Employee Assistance Professionals Association (EAPA). This includes President, founding Member and Chair of the Employee Assistance Certification Commission (EACC), member of the Role Delineation Study, and Chairperson of these committees: Education and Training, EAP and Work/Life Integration, and Awards Restructuring. She is a recipient of the EAPA President's Award, 2002. Dr. Turner is a Mandel Leadership Fellow at the Case Western Reserve University Mandel School of Applied Social Sciences. Her PhD dissertation focused on smoking-cessation treatment in the workplace. Address correspondence to: Ernst & Young, LLP, 1228 Euclid Ave., Suite 350, Cleveland, OH 44115 (E-mail: Sandra.turner04@key.com).

Robert J. Ursano, MD, is Professor of Psychiatry and Neuroscience and Chairman of the Department of Psychiatry at the Uniformed Services University of the Health Sciences, Bethesda, Maryland. He is also Director of the Center for the Study of Traumatic Stress that has over six million dollars in research funding. Dr. Ursano is widely published in the areas of Post-Traumatic Stress Disorder and the psychological effects of terrorism, bioterrorism, traumatic events and disasters and combat. Dr. Ursano and his group are at the forefront of public health policy planning for terrorism, and bioterrorism in particular. Their work has been widely cited in government planning and Institute of Medicine, National Academies of Sciences reports addressing these issues. He was a national consultant for planning clinical care responses and research programs following the September 11th terrorist attacks, providing consultation to New York State Governor's Office, New York City Mayor's Office, Department of HHS, National Capital response teams and the Department of Defense Pentagon response groups. His group developed educational materials that were some of the most widely disseminated throughout the nation to assist populations exposed to the September 11th attack. Address correspondence to: Department of Psychiatry, Uniformed Services University of the Health Sciences, 4301 Jones Bridge Road, Bethesda, MD 20814 (E-mail: rursano@ usuhs.mil).

Nancy T. Vineburgh, MA, is Assistant Professor, Department of Psychiatry, Uniformed Services University of the Health Sciences (USUHS) in Bethesda, Maryland, and Director, Office of Public Education and Preparedness, Center for the Study of Traumatic Stress (CSTS). CSTS is internationally renowned for research, education and consultation on the traumatic effects of disaster, terrorism and bioterrorism. Ms. Vineburgh is a recognized expert in health communications encompassing television, radio and print journalism, and community and employer-based initiatives related to public health and mental health issues. Address correspondence to: Department of Psychiatry, Uniformed Services University of the Health Sciences School of Medicine, Office of Public Education and Preparedness, Center for the Study of Traumatic Stress, 4301 Jones Bridge Road, Bethesda, MD 20814 (E-mail: nvineburgh@usuhs.mil).

Michael Weiner, MA, LMSW, is the Manager of Account Management for MHN, which provides employee assistance services for Ernst & Young. Mr. Weiner has been in the EAP and behavioral health field for more than 12 years. He has been the account manager for Ernst & Young for 5 years. Together with LifeCare, he accepted an award from Ernst & Young, on behalf of MHN, for services provided related to the 9-11 tragedies. Mr. Weiner received his BA from the State University of New York–Binghamton, and earned an MA in social work from Columbia University. Address correspondence to: MHN, 40 Wall St., 6th Fl., New York, NY 10005 (E-mail: Michael.weiner@mhn.com).

Preface:
Welfare Capitalism Comes Full Circle Through the Integration of EAPs, Work-Life and Wellness

It is with great pleasure that I present to you the inaugural issue of the *Journal of Workplace Behavioral Health*. Formerly the *Employee Assistance Quarterly*, the name change reflects the continued evolution in the delivery of workplace human services. This journal will highlight best practices in workplace human service delivery, as well as empirical, outcomes-based research on employee assistance, work-life, health and wellness, emerging technologies, and other major issues impacting the global workplace in increasingly complex societies.

Industrial social services first emerged in the late 1800s and early 1900s with the introduction of social service workers into a rapidly industrializing workplace. These personnel were charged with the development of a wide range of services for employees that had not existed before and were not available in the community (Popple, 1981). Companies such as Pullman Coach Car and H.J. Heinz were among the first to hire "welfare secretaries" who were employed to oversee the development and management of medical care, washing and bathing facilities, lunchrooms, loans, insurance, savings plans, job training, citizenship training for immigrants, housing, recreation, and family care. These employer-sponsored services were often a necessity in the absence of a yet-to-be developed system of public social services. Labor problems

[Haworth co-indexing entry note]: "Preface: Welfare Capitalism Comes Full Circle Through the Integration of EAPs, Work-Life and Wellness." Maiden, R. Paul. Co-published simultaneously in *Journal of Workplace Behavioral Health* (The Haworth Press, Inc.) Vol. 20, No. 1/2, 2005, pp. xxxv-xxxix; and: *The Integration of Employee Assistance, Work/Life, and Wellness Services* (ed: Mark Attridge, Patricia A. Herlihy, and R. Paul Maiden) The Haworth Press, Inc., 2005, pp. xxix-xxxiii. Single or multiple copies of this article are available for a fee from The Haworth Document Delivery Service [1-800-HAWORTH, 9:00 a.m. - 5:00 p.m. (EST). E-mail address: docdelivery@haworthpress.com].

Available online at http://www.haworthpress.com/web/JWBH
© 2005 by The Haworth Press, Inc. All rights reserved.

were also an increasing threat to the paternalistic and autocratic style of the 19th century manufacturing and industrial concerns and these programs serve as a socializing influence and bridge between employer and employee (Fleisher, 1917).

Other programs developed after the turn of the century such as the one at Macy's department store, Department of Social Services (Evans, 1944). Employees who staffed this program had a multifaceted role: informational, societal, and psychosocial. The role of Macy's caseworkers was to provide comprehensive information about social service agencies and community resources. It was also the caseworker's responsibility to recognize conditions in an employee's living situation requiring assistance through financial intervention such as loans and grants. They also provided personal counseling and guidance to workers about problems and solutions (Masi, 1982).

The early corporate social welfare efforts were not sustained, however. Several factors contributed to their decline. As welfare capitalists began to react to the growing threat of organized labor and unionization efforts, these work-based welfare workers were increasingly viewed with distrust by employees, as their primary purpose appeared to be that of socialization agent for the employer. Additionally, the emerging social work profession was ambivalent about the role of social workers in work settings and the field of personnel management was also starting to take shape and was viewed to be a more appropriate venue to deal with workplace issues and worker problems (Maiden, 2001).

As unions gained a foothold and began to advocate for worker concerns and social welfare needs free of the restrictions imposed by employers, the job of the welfare secretary gave way to union-sponsored assistance and counseling programs in the 1920s, many of which remain active today. This was followed by the emergence of occupational alcoholism programs (OAPs) to combat the effects of problem drinking on work performance and productivity in the 1940s, that evolved in the early 1970s into employee assistance programs (EAPs) offering a broader range of services beyond what was perceived as the narrow focus of "alcoholism only" programs. The broader focus of employee assistance programs also served to de-stigmatize the need to seek professional help for personal problems. In the late 1980s and early 1990s the continuum of work-based human services continued its evolution from an intervention model focusing on the "troubled employee" to incorporation of health and wellness programs aimed at prevention and health promotion. This era also saw a major shift in outsourcing what traditionally had been internal, employer staffed EAPs, to external contracted specialty vendors. These firms offered a plethora of services ranging from employee assistance, family specific services such as childcare and elder care, help with troubled teens, violence prevention, trauma debriefing, stress management, health risk appraisals, healthy lifestyle programs including as physical fitness regimes, stress management, smoking cessation, weight management and a full range of concierge services.

The workplace of the 21st century is an increasingly demanding, complex, and stressful environment in which humans spend approximately two-thirds of their lives. Global competition is fiercer than it has ever been and the pressures for performance and productivity have increased exponentially.

From all indications, it appears this notion of welfare capitalism has, in some respects, come full circle. Increased technology requires highly trained, skilled workers. Productivity, performance, retention and cost containment are essential in an increasingly competitive global marketplace.

Occupational alcoholism programs of the '40s, '50s, and '60s proved to be an effective means of dealing with employee whose drinking had become unmanageable, requiring structured intervention and treatment. EAPs of the '70s and '80s also produced desirable measures of cost-effectiveness in dealing with a myriad of personal problems that affected absenteeism, sick leave, accidents, and consumption of health and mental health benefits. It is clear that workplace social programs have reemerged. The range of options now available to purchasers and consumers is substantial and sophisticated and has become key elements in protecting and enhancing human capital.

The 22 articles in this volume provide a state-of-the-art review of current human services programs in the workplace. The editors invited a representative cross section of experienced professionals and asked them to discuss their efforts to create linkages between employee assistance, work-life and wellness. The contributing authors describe strategies they and their organizations have undertaken to integrate and shape the continuum of these three areas of practice into a seamless and holistic circle of work-based human services.

In the first article, Mary Ellen Gornick and Brenda Blair present a comprehensive conceptual framework for the integration of employee assistance, work-life and wellness programs. Mark Attridge and Michael Mulvihill follow with two articles addressing the economics of integration but stress the need to measure the real cost-benefit value of these emerging integrated programs to the sponsoring organizations.

The fourth and fifth articles focus on current research on integration. Patricia Herlihy and Mark Attridge provide a thorough review and analysis of integration research to date and offer their thoughts on future research needs. David Sharar and Edward Hertenstein present their findings from a survey of key informants, a study conducted specifically for this volume.

The next 15 articles represent a cross section of program models and service settings addressing the unique aspects of university-based offerings at Arizona State University, John Hopkins, UC–Berkeley, and the Uniformed Services University of the Health Sciences in Bethesda; internal and external service providers including Motorola, Wells Fargo and Ceridian; internal/external hybrid models developed by Ernst and Young and Fairview; federal and state programs including the U.S. House of Representatives, Federal Occupational Health Services and the State of Minnesota; and several international models developed in Australia, Ireland, Britain and the EU.

In the next to last article, Paul Roman, an eminent scholar of EAPs and the workplace, provides a commentary on the integration of EAPs with other work-based human services. He issues some cautionary warnings, suggesting a need for empirical research similar to that conducted in early occupational alcoholism programs to demonstrate the true effectiveness and real value of these services to the purchaser and the consumer.

Patricia Herlihy offers an insightful wrap-up article on the future of integration and raises questions on areas requiring further investigation on the topic of integration, as well as a challenge to professionals regarding what role they would like to take regarding the future of these services.

I trust this collection of articles will be informative and will serve as a valuable point of reference as you move forward in the development and integration of employee assistance, work-life and wellness in you own organization.

R. Paul Maiden, PhD, LCSW
Editor
University of Central Florida
Orlando

REFERENCES

Evans, E. (1944) A business enterprise and social work. *The Compass*, January, 11-15.
Fleisher, A. (1917) Welfare services for employees. *Annals of the American Academy of Political and Social Science*, 69, 50-57.

Maiden, R. P. (2001) The evolution of occupational social work in the United States. In Maiden, R.P. (ed) *Global Perspectives of Occupational Social Work*. New York: Haworth Press.

Masi, D. (1982) *Human Services in Industry*. Lexington, MA: Lexington Books.

Popple, P. (1981) Social work practice in business and industry. *Social Service Review*, June, 257-269.

CONCEPTUAL MODELS AND MEASUREMENT ISSUES

Chapter 1

Employee Assistance, Work-Life Effectiveness, and Health and Productivity: A Conceptual Framework for Integration

Mary Ellen Gornick
Brenda R. Blair

SUMMARY. As context for the following collection of articles, this article provides a conceptual framework regarding integration of employee assistance, work-life and health and productivity management initiatives. The discussion begins with a description of five societal trends in medicine, business, social work, globalization, and ecology

The authors wish to acknowledge a useful discussion regarding Health and Productivity Management with Tanya Lughermo who reviewed an earlier draft of this article.

[Haworth co-indexing entry note]: "Employee Assistance, Work-Life Effectiveness, and Health and Productivity: A Conceptual Framework for Integration." Gornick, Mary Ellen, and Brenda R. Blair. Co-published simultaneously in *Journal of Workplace Behavioral Health* (The Haworth Press, Inc.) Vol. 20, No. 1/2, 2005, pp. 1-29; and: *The Integration of Employee Assistance, Work/Life, and Wellness Services* (ed: Mark Attridge, Patricia A. Herlihy, and R. Paul Maiden) The Haworth Press, Inc., 2005, pp. 1-29. Single or multiple copies of this article are available for a fee from The Haworth Document Delivery Service [1-800-HAWORTH, 9:00 a.m. - 5:00 p.m. (EST). E-mail address: docdelivery@haworthpress.com].

Available online at http://www.haworthpress.com/web/JWBH
© 2005 by The Haworth Press, Inc. All rights reserved.
doi:10.1300/J490v20n01_01

that lead to ideas of connectedness, interdependence, a systems approach, and the reciprocal interaction between the individual and the whole. An examination of how these societal trends have influenced the current approaches to human resources management and occupational health show that these departments have become strategic, preventive, and population focused. This new thinking has stimulated awareness of the commonalities of employee assistance, work-life, and health and productivity management initiatives. Brief descriptions of the history and evolution of each distinct field are set forth, followed by an identification of commonality in purpose and service delivery. The article concludes with the suggestion that integration of service delivery makes sense and offers recommendations for how organizations can approach the integration of existing services. *[Article copies available for a fee from The Haworth Document Delivery Service: 1-800-HAWORTH. E-mail address: <docdelivery@haworthpress.com> Website: <http://www.HaworthPress.com> © 2005 by The Haworth Press, Inc. All rights reserved.]*

KEYWORDS. Work-life initiatives, health and productivity management, EAP, work-life wellness integration, workplace flexibility, worker resilience, interconnectedness

FRAMING THE DISCUSSION

The workplace today is global, fast paced and under intense pressure to achieve financial results. To survive and thrive in this environment, organizations must marshal resources and design strategies to manage changes in production, distribution, marketing, sales, finance, structure, and governance. Today's business reality dictates that the ultimate success of all these strategies depends on the people who implement them. Forward-thinking employers realize that the success of their organizations is fundamentally linked to how well they maximize the effectiveness of their people.

In response to a variety of needs–performance, employee attraction and retention, productivity, rising benefit costs–employers over the past 20 years have instituted a number of specific programs. Often housed in the company Human Resources or Occupational Health Departments, these programs have addressed issues such as adoption assistance, alcoholism, flexible work arrangements, exercise, depression, weight reduction, telecommuting, lactation support, smoking cessation, dependent care, and stress reduction. Typically, they fall under one of three general program categories: employee assistance, work-life, or health and productivity. Each of these services is defined as follows:

- *Employee Assistance (EA).* Employee assistance is the work organization's resource that utilizes specific core technologies to enhance employee and workplace effectiveness through prevention, identification, and resolution of personal and productivity issues (Employee Assistance Professionals Association, 2003).
- *Work-Life (WL).* The Alliance of Work-life Progress defines work- life effectiveness as a specific set of organizational practices, policies, programs and a philosophy that recommends aggressive support for the efforts of everyone who works to achieve success at home and at work (Alliance of Work-life Progress, 2004).
- *Health and Productivity Management (HPM)* is the integrated management of data and services related to all aspects of employee health that affect work performance, and includes measuring the impact of targeted interventions on both health and productivity (Institute for Health and Productivity, 2004).

The term "integration" is used to describe the recent progression of combining and collaborating among the three areas above. The conceptual framework discussed in this chapter, uses the definition of integration described below:

- *Integration.* Integration involves bringing together, in a synergistic way, the specialized knowledge and trained expertise of professionals in different but related fields to better serve organizations and their employees (Swihart and Thompson, 2002).

The purpose of this article is to provide a framework for understanding the forces behind this movement, how it is occurring, and a general strategy for introducing an integrated approach into an organization. Subsequent articles in this publication deal in more detail with history, measurement, and specific case examples of integration from both the public and private sector.

HOW DID WE GET HERE?
CHANGES IN SOCIETY THAT INFLUENCE THIS DISCUSSION

Trends in the larger, global society have influenced a more holistic and interconnected perception of strategic service integration. These trends have occurred in five areas: medicine, business, social work, globalization, and ecology. Significant changes occurring in each of these domains in the 1970s and 1980s began to coalesce in the 1990s to influence thinking on the strategies and service delivery of the employee assistance, work-life, and health and productivity fields.

Medicine. In the past 20 years, medical researchers have produced a flurry of studies exploring the mind/body connection and seeking to understand stress as a mental/physical phenomenon. Pioneering work by Bensen and Klipper (1975) described the relaxation response as a practical way in which people could be taught specific behaviors and mental processes that would result in a physical relaxation and lowering of the heart rate and blood pressure. More recent work by Thomas et al. (1997) studied psychological factors and survival after heart attacks. They found:

> Among patients who had asymptomatic ventricular arrhythmias after myocardial infarction, psychological status during the period after infarction contributed to mortality beyond the effect of physiological status. The results reaffirm the critical interrelationship between mind and body for cardiovascular health. (Thomas et al., 1997)

The concepts of mind/body interaction are becoming so widespread that primary care physicians regularly receive information about specific techniques and are recommending them to patients as part of treatment plans. The medical establishment now routinely accepts information about alternative medicine therapies, including those designed to promote mental health (Chiarmonte, 1997).

Another major concept in the medical world is the increasing interest in health rather than illness, moving toward the idea of well-being. Building on the approaches of public health, with its focus on populations, both health promotion experts and individual physicians are focusing more on managing risk factors as a first line of defense against treating disease. Further evidence of this trend is the number of hospitals that have opened health productivity management centers to offer fitness classes, health education programs and alternative medicine therapies, such as acupuncture, massage, and chiropractic services. Additional evidence comes from the growing literature on the consequences (both mental and physical) of excessive stress.

Business. In the business world, there has been a shift in understanding the critical factors that lead to success. Authors such as Peter Drucker, Gary Hamel, Tom Peters, and W. Edwards Deming, have identified new paradigms for interpreting how businesses function to achieve financial success. For example, the development of systems for quality management and continuous improvement changed the way businesses organized their daily activities. Measuring the effectiveness of processes became critically important. As part of this increased understanding of business processes, the role of the organization and its members has received greater attention. Hiring and retaining the "best and brightest" became a goal and more attention was paid to attraction and retention of the right people. Business success in today's highly competitive global market requires that investment in knowledge and service workers as assets. Today, organizational leaders have a heightened awareness that knowledge and service workers are a critical ingredient in business success. Those workers make a choice every day to contribute to the organization, and this discretionary effort develops and sells products and services to create customer and brand loyalty.

Social Work. In the 1970s an understanding of family systems transformed the practice of social work. The works of Virginia Satir (1964), Jay Haley (1968), Salvador Minuchin (1974), Murray Bowen (1985) and others sought to understand more precisely how individual personality and behavior is affected by the family system. Extensive research was done on how one member of a family system can alter the behavior of all members within that system. By extension, family systems theory has been applied to the organizational family. Work groups in many ways replicate family systems, and the application of systems theory in groups has become an integral part of organizational development activities.

Globalization. As technology has made communication easier and more rapid and as distribution channels move goods, funds, services around the world, economies have become interconnected and interdependent. While appreciating the opportunities offered by a global economy, many groups have become concerned about the impact on individuals and society. For example, the European community has developed a number of positions on corporate social responsibility. A 2001 Green Paper (European Union, 2001) outlines a number of components to social responsibility, including:

> lifelong learning, empowerment of employees, better information throughout the company, better balance between work, family, and leisure, greater work force diversity, equal pay and career prospects for women, profit-sharing and share-ownership schemes, concern for employability as well as job security

Supported by regulation, employers are nevertheless encouraged to go beyond regulation, for the benefit of the communities they work in, for their employees, and for their enterprises. The EU's approach is to encourage the linkage of workers, their employers, and their larger environment.

Business success now depends on managing the technology and interconnectedness of the global economy. Goods manufactured in one continent are distributed and sold worldwide. How one manages the human beings that perform the work, distribute the products, and sell products in one country can have ramifications for the entire world. The business imperative here is to understand how the pieces fit together and recognize that success depends on global interconnectedness.

One other outgrowth of globalization deserves mention. Some employers are beginning to develop a greater appreciation of the role of culture in organizational effectiveness. Not only does cultural awareness help employers succeed in different countries, but also a positive corporate culture, e.g., a culture of respect for employees, is critical for success. Although viewed by many employers as a "soft" concept, a few have begun to observe the strength brought to teams, work groups, and larger organizations by a shared value system and organizational culture. Many of the discussions about positive work environment, resilience, and diversity emphasize the role of culture and culture change. There is much evidence that enlightened business leaders understand that culture needs to be analyzed at several levels and contexts: work groups, corporate, local, and national (Casner-Lotto, 2000).

Ecology. The study of ecology leads to an understanding of the connection among individuals, groups, their local conditions and the larger environment, and how all components of the system must function well in order for life to thrive. Most recently, the concept of sustainability deals with environmental health, and how resources can be used without being depleted. The 1987 *Brundtland Report* (World Commission on the Environment and Development) stated, "Sustainable development is development that meets the needs of the present without compromising the ability of future generations to meet their own needs." William Ruckelshaus added that "economic growth and development must take place, and be maintained over time, within the limits set by ecology in the broadest sense–by the interrelations of human beings and their works, the biosphere and the physical and chemical laws that govern it" (Ruckelshaus, 1989). In the workplace, the concept of ecology leads one to considerations of how organizations and workers can maintain a sustainable level of effort, one that does not destroy them in the process.

Emerging Themes. Paradigm shifts in medicine, business, social work, globalization, and ecology in the 1970s to 1990 have influenced thinking in the EA, WL, and HPM fields. The three fields (EA, WL, and HPM) started independently, with distinct bodies of knowledge, core skills and service delivery systems, evolved along parallel paths and began to converge throughout the 1990s. The larger societal themes that guided this convergence are systems, connectedness, interconnectedness (or interdependence) and the reciprocal interaction of the individual and the whole. These trends have led to a focus on prevention and a systems focus in the workplace that is drawing together the EA, WL, and HPM fields.

THE IMPACT OF THESE CONCEPTS IN THE WORKPLACE

The societal changes described above have influenced a shift in thinking regarding how people function in organizations. Two key groups responsible for people in the workplace are the human resources and occupational medicine functions, both of which have undergone many changes in recent years.

Human resource professionals are increasingly seated at the executive table in organizations, giving a voice to the alignment of people or human capital strategies with overall business strategies. Issues such as recruitment, retention, deployment and development of healthy and motivated workforce are equally or more important than the more transactional activities of benefits and compensation administration. For the human resource professional the objective is to create the systems and processes to assure that people factors are managed proactively for the benefit of both the employer and employee.

Elevation of the HR function to a senior strategic role in organizations has resulted in a focus on the new employee-employer value proposition "total rewards" that includes compensation, benefits and the total work experience. Employees consider the "total rewards" package when they consider joining an organization, and it is what retains them (World at Work, 2004). While benefits and compensation have always been important, the work experience is now the focal point. Multiple elements to the work experience encompass organization culture, rewards and recognition, career development, work-life balance, and environment. Successful organizations now invest in their people because they are recognized as a capital asset, rather than as a cost to be managed. Managing human capital requires belief in the assumption that for individuals to be effective at work, they need to be able to make their unique contributions to the organization within the context of their own personal circumstances. Today we see more interest in understanding and measuring the nature of the worker's interaction with the workplace, how workers become engaged and committed, and what prompts workers to voluntarily invest discretionary effort in the work they perform. Human resources professionals, redefining their role as key to business success, are also looking for new metrics and value propositions (Beatty et al., 2003).

Similar changes have been occurring in the occupational health arena. Whereas employers used to have "medical departments," focused on occupational injury and illness, as well as compliance with legal requirements, today's occupational health departments have shifted focus to reducing risk and promoting health. Occupational health professionals are also aligning with the company business objectives to help employees be more productive and reduce employer costs. On an individual level, occupational health focuses proactively on overall well-being rather than reactively on treating disease.

Today's proactive occupational health professionals talk about health and productivity, linking risk reduction to greater productivity and reduced costs. While many employers have used health risk appraisals for some years, the interest now is in trying to develop predictive instruments that will identify specific HPM efforts that will have the most direct impact on the worker at risk. If the worker is at risk, the workplace is also at risk. Increasingly there is awareness of the connection between physical and mental health with an emphasis on changing behavior to promote positive HPM.

Historically, responsibility for EAP, work-life and HPM functions typically resided either in the Human Resources (or Benefits) Department or in Occupational Health, and were implemented independently to resolve a number of specific problems. Today, consistent with the shift in human resources and occupational health, all three of these separate services have moved to a more solutions-oriented approach. The concept of service integration is broader than the notion of streamlining a service delivery system. Rather, as each of these initiatives search for strategic solutions, it makes sense to see how they can be integrated to maximize achievement of similar objectives. Human Resource and Occupational Health Departments, with their increasingly strategic focus, are more receptive to facilitating program integration of EAP, WL and HPM services.

A SHORT HISTORY AND THE CURRENT SITUATION: EAPs, WORK-LIFE, AND HEALTH AND PRODUCTIVITY

Employee Assistance Programs (EAP). The EAP concept in the United States developed as a result of employer initiatives to address alcoholism in the workplace. Following upon the founding of Alcoholics Anonymous in 1936 and the American Medical Association's formal recognition of alcoholism as a disease in 1950, there was more acceptance that alcoholism was a treatable illness and that the majority of alcoholics were not unemployed but were at work. With the passage of the Comprehensive Alcohol Abuse and Alcoholism, Prevention, Treatment and Rehabilitation Act of 1970 (commonly called the Hughes Act), in which the U.S. government formally acknowledged a national interest in addressing alcoholism as an illness, Occupational Alcoholism Programs were developed. A key feature of the act provided for 100 "occupational program consultants," known as the "Thundering Hundred," to educate employers about alcoholism and to encourage the adoption of identification and referral programs.

The premise for these Occupational Alcoholism Programs was that supervisors should be trained to identify individuals with problems and refer them for treatment. It was quickly discovered that teaching supervisors to look for alcoholics equated to asking them to diagnose alcoholism and it made them uncomfortable, whereas asking them to look for a pattern of job performance decline was within their normal purview. Not surprisingly, once referrals were made for job performance issues, a number of other conditions were identified, e.g., depression, family difficulties, stress, and marital problems. Services were expanded to focus on a wide range of personal issues and were renamed Employee Assistance Programs in the late 1970s.

From the beginning a key component of EAPs was organizational consultation, assisting management and union in resolving workplace problems caused by the *troubled employee*. Early EA professionals understood that an individual worker's problems had consequences for the entire work group and produced *the troubled supervisor*. This consultative and problem-solving function was critical to the success of EAP interventions. Having been ignored by some EAPs, consultation is receiving renewed appreciation as a valuable service to management, labor, and the organization, whether or not the individual worker ultimately receives service (Blair, 2002 and 2004).

Initially, most EAPs were staffed by employees of the organization, e.g., internal model, but the need for services among smaller employers who could not afford to hire an internal EAP professional fueled the growth of EAP vendors, e.g., external model. Some programs evolved using both internal staff and externally contracted services, e.g., combination model. Some programs were sponsored by organized labor for their members or as joint labor-management programs.

A variety of service configurations evolved from these basic structures. Variations occur in the type of problems covered, whether the services are delivered in person or telephonically, the number of sessions authorized, the way in which supervisory referrals are handled, and the amount of consultations offered to the workplace. The Employee Assistance Professionals Association (EAPA) has developed a list of core functions and program standards that describe the basic features of an EAP (EAPA, 1998). While still meeting those criteria, EAPs may be designed with different numbers of authorized telephonic or face-to-face sessions, with or without an on-site presence at the employer's location, and with a range of service offerings. Unfortunately, some services calling themselves EAP do not meet the basic standards.

Perhaps the most significant "integration" for EAPs in the U.S. occurred with the advent of Managed Behavioral Health Care (MBHC) in the 1980s. The typical MBHC effort includes a number of components including mental health and substance abuse benefit plan design, negotiated rates with a network of preferred providers, referral to those providers (may include screening or direct access through the Internet to an approved list), and case management. When EAPs were perceived as providing access to counseling, and MBHC was perceived as similar, there was a move to integrate service delivery. The goal of simplified access led to involve single call centers, congruent networks, and one set of case managers. Large MBHC organizations, themselves often subsidiaries of larger health care organizations, acquired EAP organizations and the "integrated EAP/MBHC" product was dominant. Unfortunately this integration with MBHC led to a reduction in the traditional EA focus on the workplace (Herlihy, 2000).

Today, however, there is renewed interest among EA professionals in integration with other workplace services, such as work-life and HPM, rather than with health care systems. EA professionals understand that the original twofold mission of EA work, helping individuals and work organizations, needed to be revived. They recognized that while many clinical professionals can help individuals with personal concerns, the unique contribution of EAPs is in connecting the support for the individual to problem solving in the workplace. There is an increasing appreciation of the essence of EAP, defined as follows:

> The essence of EAP work is the application of knowledge about behavior and behavioral health to make accurate assessments, followed by appropriate action to improve the productivity and healthy functioning of the workplace. (Maynard, 2003)

This definition refocuses EA efforts on the dual audiences of individuals and workplaces. It allows for assessments of individuals as well as work teams; it encourages action that may involve traditional EA counseling or a whole range of responses from other arenas. Forward-thinking EAPs have shifted their focus from problem resolution to a more positive, preventive approach. This has led to a natural partnership with work-life and health promotion efforts.

Work-Life. Recognition of the reciprocal relationship between performance at work and responsibilities of personal life has been recognized at several points in U.S. history. Examples exist during the Civil War, industrial revolution and again in World War II (Googins and Godfrey, 1987). Yet the modern day work-life field did not gain traction until the mid 1970s. From that time to the early 1980s, the need for work-life services became evident in response to a dramatic demographic shift in the workforce. As a result of the women's movement in the early 1970s, women entered the workforce in large numbers, taking on professional roles in addition to more traditional clerical and support roles. These women remained in the workplace after their children were born, or they entered the workforce when their children were enrolled in elementary school. Communities were not prepared to care for the influx of the children of working parents. As a result, childcare emerged as a critical issue for families, communities and the workplace. Employers, wishing to retain talented female employees, had to address the need for quality childcare. Without quality childcare, these female employees would not be able to remain in the workforce. Thus, while employer-sponsored childcare was the visible trigger that launched the field of work-life, the underlying momentum came in response to two questions:

- For the individual: How can I manage work and personal life so that I can perform most effectively at work while also maintaining a personally fulfilling life outside of work?
- For the organization: How do we engage a workforce to effectively meet our business objectives in the midst of a competitive and chaotic business climate?

For the past quarter of a century, the work-life field has attempted to ease the tensions between work and home, provide tools, remove barriers and implement solutions that answer those two questions. Dependent care opened the door to the dual focus of workers, yet the programs quickly expanded beyond childcare to include life management issues at all stages of the life cycle. Today, a robust work-life program will address a wide range of personal issues (including dependent care), time and work schedules, work processes and work environment–in effect the total work experience. According to The Alliance for Work-life Progress (AWLP), work-life effectiveness now encompasses seven categories of focus listed below:

1. Workplace flexibility
2. Paid and unpaid time off
3. Health and well-being
4. Caring for dependents
5. Financial support
6. Community involvement
7. Management involvement/culture change interventions

The AWLP suggests that the above categories "have a proven track record in helping organizations create a collaborative relationship between employers and employees in order to optimize business outcomes. These categories of support for work-life effectiveness address the most important intersections between the worker, his or her family, the community and the workplace" (AWLP, 2004).

The Families and Work Institute described the evolution of a work-life program as a four-stage process:

- *Stage One: Programmatic.* In the initial stages, organizations implement programs to address specific workforce and business needs.
- *Stage Two: Integrated.* Programs linkages are made, to related services, such as EA, HPM, diversity and safety. At this stage the ba-

sic principles and assumptions of work-life are woven into the fabric of the organization at all levels.

- *Stage Three: Culture Change.* Employers move beyond programs to focus on creating a culture of "respect" for employees and their contribution to the organization. This stage is marked by culture change that comes from top leadership and penetrates through all levels of the organization. Leaders deliver messages that clearly acknowledge the value of workers. The beliefs and values of the organization are lived on a daily basis.
- *Stage Four: Community Sustainability.* Organizations expand from a single internal focus to include a dual external focus. In this stage organizations visibly and actively acknowledge their interconnectedness with the larger community and their role as corporate citizens of the communities in which they operate.

There is a substantial body of research to support the effectiveness of work-life initiatives in organizations: Baxter Healthcare moved from being a stage two employer to a stage three employer through a corporate strategic initiative (Campbell and Kolbe, 1997). They reported that the reach of work-life issues is broader than previously thought. Employees at all levels of the organization and all life stages experience conflicts between their work and their personal lives. While each conflict results in a different level of pain, all "pain" influences job behavior; when the "pain" is not addressed, individuals tend to behave in ways that may not be aligned with business objectives. This study concluded that programs alone are not enough and must be implemented with an underlying respect for workers. When integrated within the context of a culture of respect, workers take greater advantage of the programs and services; become more engaged in their work and perform more effectively.

The National Study on the Changing Workforce conducted by Bond in 2002 of the Families and Work Institute indicates a positive correlation to worker satisfaction for those companies that offer targeted work-life programs in a supportive work environment. However, the study also reports work-life programs are needed more than ever before. Results of this study indicated that individuals are working longer hours (43 hours in 1977 vs. 47.1 hours in 1997). The work hours of dual earner couples has also increased, by 10 hours a week (81 hours in 1977 vs. 91 hours in 2002). It is no wonder that almost half (45%) of wage and salaried employees with families (spouse/partner and/or children) report significantly higher levels of interference between their jobs and their family lives (Bond et al., 2003).

Perhaps increased work-life interference over the past 35 years has resulted from increased work demands–working longer hours, working faster and harder, not having enough time to get everything done on the job, having longer commutes, and more often bringing work home from the job. (Bond et al., 2003)

Today's work-life practitioners are responding to the increase in work hours and the increase in work-life interference with a renewed focus on wellness programs. Worker stress is at an all time high. The obvious consequence of sustained stress is increased health risks and higher rates of depression and mental illness. Thirty years after their inception, work-life programs, which began as independent responses to a demographic trend, today are connecting with both EA and HPM programs to more completely address the work-life issues of both workers and organizations.

HEALTH AND PRODUCTIVITY MANAGEMENT

Employer efforts regarding health and productivity in the U.S. began with a relatively narrow focus on fitness and limited health promotion efforts, such as smoking cessation and nutrition information. These initiatives were based on two basic tenets:

- Common wisdom that healthy individuals perform at higher levels
- Concerns about escalating health insurance costs for both current employees and retirees

Employers in the U.S. began to enhance their health education and health promotion efforts by using Health Risk Appraisals (HRA). The development of HRAs was key to linking individual behavior, risk factors, and mortality (Foxman and Eddington, 1987). Based on both self-report information and baseline physical data (such as height, weight, blood pressure and cholesterol), they provided individual, confidential results that could encourage individuals to adopt more healthy behaviors. Often a health professional was present to interpret the results. The employer received aggregate data to help identify risk factors and to set clearer priorities for health education initiatives.

Today HPM has evolved into a much broader focus on the health of populations of workers as that health status is related to productivity. Although EA and WL services also address issues of productivity, the

HPM research is the most interesting in terms of defining and measuring impact of interventions on productivity. From studies that document reductions in health benefit costs due to lifestyle changes (Eddington, 1998) to studies that demonstrate change in health risk and productivity over time (Pelletier, Boles, and Lynch, 2004), the HPM research is rapidly amassing substantial evidence about the relationship between health risks in populations and overall productivity.

The field of HPM has introduced the concept of predictive modeling to differentiate risk factors. This research enables employers to identify population groups with specific risk factors and to predict the costs that may result from letting those risk factors develop into disease conditions. Interestingly, these models use self-report information, and have determined that individuals' assessments of their own health status and personal productivity appear to be quite accurate in predicting their use of health care benefits. Using predictive models, employers may then design targeted interventions for those population groups with the highest risks. As researchers have developed more evidence concerning the direct impact of health in the workplace, supported by extensive data about the connection between selected health risk factors and specific disease states, HPM professionals can design very precise interventions, such as smoking cessation or exercise promotion, for selected target groups.

A number of recent studies have focused on two key aspects of health and productivity: absenteeism and presenteeism. Presenteeism results when an individual is physically present at work but is not fully contributing at a normal standard of performance. Presenteeism can occur because of chronic diseases, emotional problems, or short-term situations, such as the worker who comes to work with a cold instead of staying at home. The costs of presenteeism are the direct losses of productivity by the "presentee" person, as well as indirect costs, such as passing on that cold to several co-workers (Hemp, 2004).

As health care costs continue to rise, employers are increasingly interested in the relationship among health care costs, absenteeism, workers compensation costs, short-term and long-term disability. HPM initiatives now involve a wide range of interventions, including structural approaches (such as redesigning health benefits), population-based interventions (such as promoting exercise), and individual strategies (such as disease management). Some of the specific programs include:

- Complex care management.
- Health care consumer education.
- Nurse lines for inquiries and health education.
- Disease management: catastrophic, chronic, as well as assistance in decision-making for acute situations.
- Triage of risk into low, medium, and high, and design of programs to address specific behavior change for each category.
- Education programs to assist with demand management, especially for prescription drugs.

As noted above, employers with occupational medical departments are becoming increasingly strategic in terms of their approach and services offered. While assuring any regulatory compliance that may be required, they are focusing on employee health and well-being, health care risks and costs, and the needs of populations, e.g., an aging workforce. The focus on the health needs of selected populations, such as aging or pregnant workers, brings HPM close to WL concerns that also focus on needs of populations as they move through the life cycle. As HPM research links depression and stress to 3-year increases in health care costs (Goetzel, 1998), HPM initiatives move into the arena typically occupied by EA initiatives. Driven by demographics and data, HPM initiatives are leading the way in measuring the connection between individual needs and behaviors and productivity in the workplace.

GLOBAL PERSPECTIVE

While this article focuses mainly on the U.S., programs in other countries have experienced a very different history and evolution. Some countries have led their initiatives with childcare or information services, some with an occupational welfare focus, and others with a health promotion emphasis. Today, there is increasing interest in understanding how these diverse, but related, programs can be integrated into a comprehensive approach to enhancing the effectiveness of people at work. Many U.S.-based employers have a tendency to look only to each other for examples of creative approaches to complex issues of work environment and well-being. The justification for this approach is the extent to which law and regulation in different countries defines an organization's management of its employees. However, a truly global perspective requires employers throughout the world to assess the impact of action in one country on all other parts of their organizations. As employers worldwide seek economic success, the importance of managing the human part of that success equation is increasingly evident. Examples of good ideas and creative approaches to a variety of services (services that may resemble but not be called EAP, work-life and Health and Productivity initiatives) abound in many countries. Other articles in this publication present specific examples from Ireland, United Kingdom, Australia and Latin America.

SERVICES AND SERVICE DELIVERY SYSTEMS: EMPLOYEE ASSISTANCE, WORK-LIFE, HEALTH AND PRODUCTIVITY

Services and Service Delivery Systems. As each of the services has evolved, the list of specific offerings provided under the rubric of EA, WL or HPM has started to show similarities. A quick review of Figure 1 shows a convergence of the three services in terms of alignment, area of influence, and impact. Regarding service delivery systems, all three initiatives have implemented expanded technologies to make maximum access for the end user. New technologies are used in Internet service delivery systems and telephonic approaches as well as face-to-face services. Technology plays a major role in service delivery design and is one of the factors that contribute to ease of integration. For example, Websites can offer articles, self-assessments, and contact information topics related to EA, WL, and HPM. Call centers can be configured to respond to inquiries about a variety of issues and can make referrals to a range of specialists. While the focus of this article is not specifically on service delivery, the potential for enhanced service integration and efficiency of service delivery are improved significantly by the technologies currently available.

Overlaps. There is growing evidence of overlap among the three initiatives. For example, consistent with an awareness of the mind/body connection, smoking cessation classes are offered by both EA and by HPM; stress is addressed in programs sponsored by WL, EA, and HPM. HPM experts have realized that even with the best health education, people sometimes do not make changes in their behavior. The influence of psychologists in developing change models for health educators (Prochaska, 1984 and 1994) is but one example of how an increased knowledge of the mind/body connection is being used by multiple programs. The behavioral health knowledge of the EA team can address the addictive components of some unhealthy lifestyles and assist in dealing

FIGURE 1. Convergence of EAP, Work-Life and Health and Productivity: Alignment–Influence–Impact

Employee Assistance	Work-Life	Health and Productivity
Origin Employer initiative to address alcoholism in the workplace (1950s); supported by Hughes Act 1972	**Origin** Employer-sponsored childcare initiatives in late 1970s-early 1980s	**Origin** Employer initative to reduce health care costs and improve the health of workers
Purpose Provide individual and organizational solutions to the problems caused by mental health issues and personal problems at work	**Purpose** Maximize personal effectiveness and well-being to contribute to business growth	**Purpose** Maximize the individual health and well-being to lower health care costs and increase workforce productivity
Area of Direct Influence Organization Individual	**Area of Direct Influence** Organization Individual Community	**Area of Influence** Individual Organization
Aligned with • Human Resources • Work-Life • Diversity • Occupational Health • Safety • Benefits-Health Care • Benefits-Disability Management • HPM Programs • Training and Development • Organizational Development	**Aligned with** • Human Resources • Employee Assistance • Diversity • Occupational Health • Safety • Benefits-Health Care • Fitness • HPM Programs • Training and Development • Community Relations • Organizational Development	**Aligned with** • Human Resources • Employee Assistance • Work-Life • Diversity • Occupational Health • Safety • Benefits-Health Care • Benefits-Disability Management • Fitness • Training and Development
Services Individual Assessment Individual Short-Term Problem Resolution Consultation with Managers, Unions, HR Crisis Response Education Disability Management Disease Management HR Consultations	**Services** Education Consultation and Referral (Dependent Care, Parenting, Education, Adoption, Convenience Services) Flexible Work Arrangements Work Re-Design Lactation Programs	**Services** Health Risk Assessments Health Screenings Education Health Fairs Fitness and HPM Programs Message Lactation Programs Disability Management Disease Management
Impact Individual Performance Work Group Performance Absenteeism Health Care Cost Containment Worker Productivity Violence Prevention Workplace Safety Manager Development Improved Labor-Management Relations Resilience Presenteeism	**Impact** Individual Performance Work Group Performance Absenteeism Engagement and Commitment Worker Productivity Recruitment and Retention Recognition-Employer of Choice Work Environment-Culture Manager Development Resilience Presenteeism	**Impact** Individual Performance Work Group Performance Absenteeism Health Care Cost Containment Worker Productivity Workplace Safety Resilience Presenteeism

with the emotional aspects of change. Likewise, EA professionals are increasingly recommending that clients get a comprehensive physical, begin to exercise, and eat better as ways to deal with emotional problems. WL professionals understand that the realities of working longer hours while managing life events lead to high stress levels, and self-care is often ignored. To create a healthier workforce, WL is reaching out to HPM and EA to offer more wellness-based services during the workday.

Vendors who offer an integrated WL and EA model have been tracking the number of crossover issues between the two programs. While most identify less than 10% of inquiries that require both services, this may be because of limited staff capability to identify the need for a full range of services. Specific examples of the need for multiple services abound.

- An EAP clinician who recognizes that a single mother needs Saturday afternoon childcare in order to attend a counseling session can contact the work-life consultation and referral service.
- A work-life professional helping an employed caregiver find new living arrangements for her aging parents assesses that she may also benefit from the emotional support of the EAP.
- An HPM professional advising someone in the middle of a divorce about ways to quit smoking may suggest that the person seek assistance from EA to increase the likelihood of successful smoking cessation.
- The anxious and overwhelmed client can be referred for counseling, to a fitness program, and also to a community yoga program or to a home organizer for help with a home management issue, enlisting the services of EA, HPM, and work-life.

Ideally, no matter how the individual first accesses services, a comprehensive plan would include all relevant support mechanisms. Individuals are complex and have interconnected needs that can be best addressed simultaneously or at least in a coordinated fashion. As all three professions (EA, WL, and HPM) have evolved, each field has adapted to the workplace by expanding services traditionally provided by the others, resulting in overlap.

INTEGRATION EFFORTS IN THE U.S. WORKPLACE

Integration efforts in the U.S. have occurred in several directions. As noted earlier, EAPs have integrated with Managed Behavioral Health

Care, and some EAPs have expanded into disease management and disability management. Although generally limited to mental health disease and disability management, these efforts enter territory more commonly occupied by HPM professionals. Early efforts at integrating EA with HPM services were documented by Erfurt and Foote, who described a project to address hypertension using EAP-style intervention and follow-up techniques (Erfurt and Foote, 1990). It has been noted that employers offer EA, HPM, and WL services for some of the same reasons, e.g., health care cost containment, employee retention, and increased employee morale (Derr and Lindsay, 1998). EA integration with WL occurred as professionals realized that both approaches addressed individual as well as organizational issues. In the early 1990s the concept of EAP and work-life integration met with resistance from both groups, as each was unsure how a new model might affect service delivery and the key skills of each profession (Herlihy, 1997).

Current research continues to support the logic of integration. A 1997 National Study of the Changing Workforce hinted at the potential for integrating EA, work-life and HPM in response to the phenomenon of overwork (Bond et al., 1997). Confirmed in a 2002 National Study of the Changing Workforce, these results showed that employees with more demanding jobs and less supportive workplace experience more stress, poorer coping mechanisms, worse moods, and less energy off the job–all of which jeopardize their personal and family well-being. This study also found the reverse effect: when employees' personal and family well-being is compromised by work, they experience more negative spillover from home to work which diminishes their job performance (Bond et al., 2003).

Employers that consider the reality of work in the U.S. today find themselves asking questions such as:

- With WL programs already in place, why are workers still experiencing stress, anxiety?
- As the cost of stress-related and behavior-related illness becomes clearer, what strategies should HPM services pursue?
- How can EA knowledge of human behavior and behavior change be leveraged to address issues of health and work-life effectiveness?

The answer is a strategic approach that will of necessity involve the integration of these services. Reinforced by the medical focus on mind/body interaction, the need for global effectiveness, and a general recognition of the reciprocal interaction between the individual and organization, employers are trying to think strategically about integrating EAP, work-life, and health and productivity services. The business need for productivity and worker retention is reinforced by societal trends that emphasize systems and connectedness. In this context, service integration is a logical result.

Integration efforts have focused on several key variables. Among these are the key competencies of the different services that are translatable from one to the other. It has been suggested that the core skills and approaches of each should be maintained while finding the commonalities. For example, joint steering committees addressing both EAP and HPM (Derr and Lindsay, 1998).

Service integration efforts are also being driven by the practical realities of the marketplace. Initially, integration efforts were motivated by the intention to streamline programs with a similar focus on employee behavior. The idea was to provide a single point of contact for employees and a single contract for employers to administer. Cost was definitely a factor; bringing similar programs together was thought to reduce duplicative administrative costs. The timing of these efforts coincided with very strong pressure in the marketplace to reduce the prices of services. By defining these efforts as "benefits" rather than as strategic programs, they became commoditized. The strategic and consultative value to the organization, most often appreciated by human resources, occupational health, and line management, was sometimes lost when services were purchased as a benefit for workers and the lowest cost option was preferred. Both EAP and WL vendors were forced to cut costs because of market pressure and intense price competition; some employers reduced or eliminated selected HPM services.

Current efforts at integration occur in response to the intense price pressure plus a new way of thinking about programs and services. To some degree, integration efforts are driven by a philosophical premise that this "makes sense," based in the trends mentioned at the beginning of this article. On the other hand, an employer's effort to integrate services may be due to a desire to cut costs, resulting in downward price pressures on vendors that essentially devalue the services. In today's environment, it is very difficult to determine the degree to which either philosophical and/or market place forces are driving integration efforts. However, looking at these three aligned services within the context of the larger societal framework, there appears to be a unique opportunity to see the interconnectedness and implement a new model.

The nexus of the interconnectedness among WL, EA, and HPM programs is the focus on individual well-being in a workplace context. The positive impact on the work organization is an essential driver of each of these efforts. Although each program addresses a different aspect of individual and organizational need, the goal is the same: to help individuals to be productive at work and live personally fulfilling lives outside of work.

FINDING THE COMMONALITIES

This review of EA, work-life and health and productivity services has identified several key commonalities that are encouraging the need for integration of concepts and service delivery. Flowing from the societal trends, the changes in the workplaces brought about by those societal trends, and the unique history of each of these services, these commonalities are described below.

Focus on the Nexus of the Individual and the Work Environment. All of the programs that fall under the rubric of EAP, work-life, and health and productivity share a common interest in promoting individual well-being as well as organizational effectiveness. Although some have criticized this dual focus as *making people stronger so they can work harder*, the most enlightened employers see these efforts as true investments in people. Indeed they are looking to determine the value by a higher degree of employee commitment and engagement to the workplace. By contrast, because individuals can choose each day how much energy they wish to invest in their work, it behooves the employer to make certain that the work experience component of the employee-employer value proposition is strong. EAP, work-life, and health and productivity initiatives all provide value to the individual and organization.

Concern with Productivity and Performance. While many professional groups are concerned with the same issues addressed by EA, WL, and HPM professionals, the programs discussed here are all sponsored by the workplace. Whether sponsored by management, by joint labor-management agreements, or by labor unions, these programs exist at the junction between the individual worker and his/her job. They have a responsibility to those workplaces to be sure that their interventions are not frivolous in terms of improved productivity and performance. For example, if EAP counseling improves a person's symptoms of depression but he continues to cause conflict in his work group, then the EAP may have been effective for the person but not for the employer. As another example, if a work-life program helps someone locate good childcare, but she continues to be absent from work, then she may be satisfied, but the workplace is not. A solutions-focused approach to serving both the worker and the employer will address the nexus between the individual and the whole.

It is important to know what impact the workplace expects from these different services. Some employers view them as "benefits" and neither appreciates nor requires the added value of impact on performance. Successful programs will clarify the expectations of their sponsoring organizations to determine the desired outcome and how to measure it.

Identify Common Metrics. To avoid being seen as "just a benefit" or a "soft" program, all three initiatives seek to quantify the results of their programs or services in metrics that are meaningful to the work organization. All three have the common need to ask:

- What are the indicators of success?
- Are those indicators measured?
- What do the current measurement indicators demonstrate?
- What do we need to measure that we are not measuring?
- How do we demonstrate value on behalf of the individual and the organization?

EA, HPM, and WL programs are measured in various ways and look at a variety of different outcomes. Both EA and HPM programs have been linked to lower health care cost and indicate a direct link between program utilization and use of health care. The current trend is to push further to see the impact of EA and HPM programs on disease management, disability management, workers compensation, and similar programs. WL programs have traditionally focused on increased recruitment opportunities, reduction in turnover, absenteeism, and improved productivity. All three programs increasingly see themselves in terms of risk reduction or risk management and try to measure their impact on absenteeism, "presenteeism," health care cost savings, and retention.

Desire to Interact Strategically with Related Programs. All three are increasingly interested in working with still other "programs" or initiatives, such as safety and diversity. For example, HPM strategies understand that diverse populations will have different health risks that need to be identified and addressed for maximum results. The work-life profession has had a major emphasis on diversity–understanding that diversity means not only ethnic and gender diversity, but also generational diversity and differences in family configuration. Employee assistance programs understand that the diversity of the EA staff needs to reflect the diversity of the employers they serve. Employers that seek effective worker attraction and retention of a diverse work force will look to WL, EA, and HPM services to assist in that effort. There is great opportunity to expand the current triad to include diversity as a partner.

Similarly, safety professionals have come to appreciate the human factor in reducing accidents and promoting a safe workplace. They understand that safe machinery can only be operated safely if the workers are concentrating properly. Lack of concentration can be due to many causes, including emotional problems, concerns about family, or health problems. Maintaining safety also requires inculcating the habits of safe behavior. Because EA, work-life, and HPM professionals understand different aspects of human behavior and behavior change, they can provide useful support to safety programs.

In order to influence both employee and organizational well-being, reaching out to diversity, safety, and other organizational partners can reinforce messages about the value of employee and organizational well-being. The idea that the well-being of people in organizations has a wide reaching effect on organizational performance appeals to employers concerned with risk management, operational efficiency, and financial success. If the nexus of WL, EAP, and HPM programs is personal effectiveness, then it is easy to find alignment with other functions within the business that have similar goals. Fully integrating EAP, work-life and HPM services in the organization by looking for commonalities and interconnectedness is crucial to the sustainability of all three services.

Influence by Culture, e.g., National, Local, Company, and Leadership. Because all of these programs live at the crossroads of the individual, the family, and the workplace, they are extremely influenced by the cultures in which they operate. Company culture, and especially the actions of leadership, can either reinforce or undermine efforts to provide a comprehensive array of support for employees and their employers. In those companies where the relationship of HPM, work-life and EAP is seen by the organization's leaders as part of a strategic people plan, those leaders foster integration through carefully crafted messages and leading by example.

Culture also plays a significant role outside the company. Local and national cultural differences must be understood in order to design integrated systems. Views about health, mental health, and the role of the family all contribute to employee and organizational receptivity to HPM, EAP, and work-life services. Global employers must pay special attention to how programs are designed in different locations to be consistent with local cultures.

THE WAY FORWARD

Organizations must be nimble and flexible to survive in an era of global competition and rapid change. Creative and forward-thinking organizations will continue to refine their human capital management strategies, and these efforts will lead to further interest in integrating disciplines and functions to help individuals and organizations perform.

Assuming that turf issues could be overcome, new programs designed to benefit workers while improving performance and productivity would focus on a comprehensive approach to well-being. Such an approach would address the physical, emotional and personal adjustment issues facing individuals, their families, and their workplaces. This service would consult with organizations and individuals to make certain that the people within the organization were in a position (trained, supported, resourced) to grow the business. It would be designed and would continue to develop based on a belief that both employees and organizations must be resilient, balanced, and healthy in order to succeed and thrive. The premise would be a big picture, long-term view of individual and organizational health, balance, and emotional well-being.

Organizations that already have one or more established EA, work-life, and HPM initiatives may find them located in a variety of organizational silos with valid internal reasons to resist change and integration. Each group has a legitimate concern to protect the core elements of its respective approaches. Attempts at integration must be done carefully to maintain the unique knowledge, skills and perspective represented by each field. Integration can be designed with a fresh perspective to leverage the unique features of each program in order to create a more robust model for the organization.

Organizations can use the following principles to integrate programs and services strategically using the eight-step strategy outlined below. They key to success will be collaboration, communication, and respect as the integration plan is implemented.

1. Examine the commonalities in goals, objectives and services.
2. Review all programs to ensure alignment with each other and with business objectives.

3. Determine where in the organization to position the integrated services and activities.
4. Select the organizational area that will have sufficient "clout" both formal and informal–to assure that these efforts are seen as a business imperative–not a "nice to have" employee benefit.
5. Determine the measures of success. Identify the outcomes that will demonstrate that goals have been met. How will they be measured? Are measurement systems in place?
6. Craft the message and a communication plan that ensures the message will be delivered throughout the organization.
7. Proactively anticipate and resolve "turf" issues as the functions merge.
8. Develop general guidelines and standards, but allow for regional and international differences due to culture and/or legislation.
9. Create an operational model (outsource options, internal management) consistent with business realities and with the goals and objectives in Step 1.

CONCLUSIONS

The societal trends in medicine, social work, business, globalization and ecology will continue to encourage an awareness of systems, interconnection, and the reciprocal effects of the individual upon the whole. Employers in this environment will actively look for solutions that enhance the work experience for their employees. Employers will look to maximize the core elements and unique features from each program area to match their particular requirements for an optimal work environment for employees. For the triad (EA, WL, and HPM), coexisting in this environment will require enormous flexibility and creativity. In fact, the visible lead may change depending on the organization; sometimes one of the three will be in the lead and the other two will be supportive partners.

The need for strategic responses to the demands of a global and changing work world will expand, and the identification of those responses will require creativity and flexibility. The EAP, work-life, and health and productivity management programs that want to be effective in meeting the needs of both work organizations and individual workers will follow these trends by finding solutions through collaboration and refinement of existing service delivery models. The benefits will be operational, in terms of cost-effective service delivery, and strategic, in terms of helping organizations to become resilient and to thrive in the years ahead.

REFERENCES

Alliance for Work-life Progress. (2004). *The Categories of Work-life Effectiveness, Successfully Evolving Your Organization's Work-life Portfolio.* Alliance for Work-life Progress.

Anderson, D., Whitmer, R., Goetzel, R., Ozminkowski, R., Wasserman J., and Serxner, S. (2000). *The relationship between modifiable health risks and ground-level health care expenditures; Health Enhancement Research Organization (HERO) research.* St. Paul, Minnesota: in *American Journal of Health Promotion*, 2000: Vol. 15. 45-52.

Beatty, R., Huselid, A., and Schneier, C.E. (2003). *The New HR Metrics: Scoring on the Business Scorecard.* New York: Elsevier Science Inc., Vol. 32, No. 2 pp. 107-121.

Bensen, H. and Klipper, M.Z. (1975). *The Relaxation Response.* New York: Morrow.

Blair, B. (2002). "Consultative Services: Providing Added Value to Employers," *EAPA Exchange*, March/April, 2002.

Blair, B. (2004). "EAPS in the World of Work," *EAPA Exchange*, 2nd Quarter, 2004.

Bond, J, Galinsky, E., and Swanberg, J. (1997). National Study of the Changing Workforce. *Families and Work Institute.*

Bond, J., Thompson, C, Galinsky, E., and Prottas, D. (2003). Highlights of the National Study of the Changing Workforce. *Families and Work Institute*, No. 3.

Bowen, M. (1985). *Family Therapy in Clinical Practice.* Lanham, Maryland: Jason Aronson.

Brundtl and Report (World Commission on Environment and Development), *http://www.ecy.wa.gov/sustainability/definition.htm*

Burud, S. and Tumolo, M. (2004). *Leveraging the New Human Capital, Adaptive Strategies, Results Achieved, and Stories of Transformation.* Davies Black.

Campbell, A. and Koblenz, M. (1997). *The Work and Life Pyramid of Needs: A New Paradigm for Understanding The Nature of Work and Life Conflicts.* Baxter Healthcare Corporation.

Casner-Lotto, J. (2000). *Holding a Job, Having a Life: Strategies for Change, a Work in America Institute National Policy Study.* Scarsdale, NY: Work in America Institute.

Chiarmonte, D.R. (1997). "Mind-Body Therapies for Primary Care Physicians." Maxton, North Carolina: Maxton Family Practice. Primary Care. Dec., 24(4): 787-807.

Davidson, B. and Herlihy, P. (1999). The EAP and Work-Family Connection. *The Employee Assistance Handbook.* pp. 405-419.

Derr, W. and Lindsay, G. (1999). EAP and Wellness Connection. *The Employee Assistance Handbook.* pp. 305-318.

EAPA (Employee Assistance Professionals Association). (1998). EAPA Standards and Professional Guidelines for Employee Assistance Programs.

Eddington, D. (1998). *The Steelcase Wellness Study: 1984-1997*, The University of Michigan Health Management Research Center.

Erfurt, J. and Foote, A. (1984). Cost Effectiveness of Worksite Blood Pressure Control Programs. *Journal of Occupational Medicine.* 12, 892-900.

Erfurt, J and Foote, A. (1990). A Healthy Alliance: Ford Motor and the UAW Endorse wellness Program Through their EAP. *Employee Assistance*. pp. 41-44.

European Union 2001, Promoting a European Framework for Corporate Social Responsibility. Green paper. European Union: Employment and social affairs. Luxembourg: Office for Official Publications of the European Union, July 2001. *http://europa.eu.int/comm/employment_social/soc-dial/csr/greenpaper_en.pdf*

Families and Work Institute. (2004). *Generation and Gender in the Workplace*. The American Business Collaboration.

Faught, L. (1992). One-Stop Shopping for Expanding Family-Care Benefits. *Journal of Compensation and Benefits*. July-August (40-43)

Foxman, B. and Eddington, D. (1987). The Accuracy of Health Risk Appraisal in Predicting Mortality. *American Journal of Public Health*. Vol. 77: 971-974.

Friedman, S.D., Christensen, P., and DeGroot, J. (1998). "Work and Life: The End of the Zero-Sum Game." *Harvard Business Review*. November-December.

Galinsky, E., Kim, S., and Bond, J. (2001). *Overworked: When Work Becomes Too Much*. Families and Work Institute.

Goetzel, R., Anderson, D., Whitmer, R., Ozminkowsky, R., Dunn, R., and Wasserman, J. (1998). The Relationship Between Modifiable Health Risks and Health Care Expenditures: An Analysis of the Multi-Employer HERO Health Risk and Cost Database. *Journal of Occupational and Environmental Medicine*. Vol. 40 No. 10, 843-854.

Googins, B and Godfrey, J. (1987) *Occupational Social Work Today*. New Jersey: Prentice Hall.

Haley, J. (1968). *Techniques of Family Therapy*. Boston: Harvard University Press.

Hamel, G. and Valikangas, L. (2003). The Quest for Resilience. *Harvard Business Review*. September.

Hamel, G. and Prahald, C.K. (1994). *Competing for the Future*. Boston: Harvard Business School Press.

Hemp, P. (2004). Presenteeism: At Work–But Out of It. Boston: *Harvard Business Review*. October.

Herlihy, P. (1997). Employee Assistance Programs and Work/Family Programs: Obstacles and Opportunities for Organizational Integration, *Compensation and Benefits Management*. Spring (22-30).

Herlihy, P. and Davidson, B. (2000). Work-life and Employee Assistance Programs: Collaboration or Consolidation. *Work-life Effectiveness, Programs, Policies and Practices*. 12.3-12.31.

King, A. (2002). Integrated EAP-Work-life Partnerships. *Behavioral Health Management*. September/October. Volume 22, Number 5 pp. 34-35.

Lindsay, G. (1998). *Worksite Health Promotion and Employee Assistance Programs*.

Maynard, J. (2003). The Essence of Employee Assistance Programs. *EAPA Exchange*.

Minuchin, S. (1974). *Families and Family Therapy*. Boston: Harvard University Press.

Parus, B. (2004). Back to School: Educating Employees About Health Care Cost Containment, World at Work, Arizona: Workspan. May, Volume 7, Number 4.

Pelletier, B., Boles, M., and Lynch, W. (2004). Change in Health Risks and Work Productivity Over Time. *Journal of Occupational and Environmental Medicine*. 46: 746-754.

Peters, T. (1987). *Thriving on Chaos*. New York: Perennial.

Pitt-Catsouphes, M. and Bankert, E. (1998). "Conducting a Work-life Assessment." *Compensation and Benefits Management*. Summer.

Prochaska, J. (1984). *The Transtheoretical Approach: Crossing Traditional Boundaries of Therapy*. Homewood Illinois: Dow-Jones Irwin.

Prochaska, J. (1994). *Changing for Good: The Revolutionary Program That Explains the Six Stages of Change and Teaches You How to Free Yourself from Bad Habits*. William Morrow and Co.

Rose, Karol.*Work-life Effectiveness–Program Policies and Practices*. Darien, CT: Kubu Communications.

Rucci, A.J., Kirn, S.P., and Quinn, R.T. (1998). The Employee-Customer Profit Chain at Sears. *Harvard Business Review*. January-February.

Ruckelshaus, W. (1989). Toward a Sustainable World. *Scientific American*. September.

Satir, V. (1964). *Conjoint Family Therapy*. Palo Alto, California: Science and Behavior Books.

Sullivan, S., (2003). *Productivity: Absolute Advantage*. Wellness Councils of America.

Swihart, D. and Thompson, D. (2002). Successful Program Integration: An Analysis of the Challenges and Opportunities Facing an EAP That Integrated with Other Programs Reveals the Keys to Successfully Servicing the Systemic Needs of Employees and Work Organizations, *EAPA Exchange*, Sept./Oct., 10-12.

The Boston College Center for Work and Family. (1999). *Metrics Manual: Ten Approaches to Measuring Work-life Initiatives*.

Thomas, S.A., Friedmann, E., Wimbush, F., Schron, E. (1997). Psychological Factors and survival in the Cardiac Arrhythmia Suppression Trial (CAST): A Reexamination. *American Journal of Critical Care*. Mar. 6(2): 116-26. Siegel and Thomas Healthcare Group, Ellicott City, MD, USA.

Watson, W. (2002). *Human Capital Index: Human Capital as a Lead Indicator of Shareholder Value*.

Yost, C.W. (2004). *Work+Life*, Riverhead Books: New York.

RESOURCES: PROFESSIONAL ORGANIZATIONS

Alliance for Work-life Progress
www.awlp.org
Employee Assistance Professionals Association
www.eapassn.org
Employee Assistance Society of North America
www.easna.org
Institute for Health and Productivity Management
www.ihpm.org
Wellness Councils of America
www.welcoa.org

Chapter 2

The Business Case for the Integration of Employee Assistance, Work-Life and Wellness Services: A Literature Review

Mark Attridge

SUMMARY. Employee assistance programs (EAP), work-life programs and wellness programs are three commonly provided kinds of interventions that have the goals of reducing healthcare costs, improving employee performance and fostering a healthier workplace culture. The integration of these kinds of programs is a recent trend that has the potential to offer additional synergistic benefits. New studies have linked comprehensive delivery services that support human capital needs with bottom-line financial success of the company. This evidence can be used to make the business case for offering EAP, work-life and wellness services in an integrated capacity. However, while promising, the scientific evidence thus far in this area has methodological limitations and there are critical aspects that require further study. *[Article copies available for a fee from The Haworth Document Delivery Service: 1-800-HAWORTH. E-mail address: <docdelivery@haworthpress.com> Website: <http://www.HaworthPress. com> © 2005 by The Haworth Press, Inc. All rights reserved.]*

[Haworth co-indexing entry note]: "The Business Case for the Integration of Employee Assistance, Work-Life and Wellness Services: A Literature Review." Attridge, Mark. Co-published simultaneously in *Journal of Workplace Behavioral Health* (The Haworth Press, Inc.) Vol. 20, No. 1/2, 2005, pp. 31-55; and: *The Integration of Employee Assistance, Work/Life, and Wellness Services* (ed: Mark Attridge, Patricia A. Herlihy, and R. Paul Maiden) The Haworth Press, Inc., 2005, pp. 31-55. Single or multiple copies of this article are available for a fee from The Haworth Document Delivery Service [1-800- HAWORTH, 9:00 a.m. - 5:00 p.m. (EST). E-mail address: docdelivery@haworthpress.com].

Available online at http://www.haworthpress.com/web/JWBH
© 2005 by The Haworth Press, Inc. All rights reserved.
doi:10.1300/J490v20n01_02

KEYWORDS. Human capital, health and productivity management, employee assistance program, work-life, wellness, healthcare, absenteeism, presenteeism

The ultimate goal of any business is to sustain profitability. Managing the organization's most important resource, its human capital, is never easy. Keeping that asset healthy and at work is a challenge. (Kate Winn-Rogers, 2003)

INTRODUCTION

Companies today face the challenges of paying for unprecedented increases in employee healthcare costs and benefits, maximizing the performance of their workers and managing the risks to the organization. This article argues that the integration of the three major kinds of health and productivity management (HPM) services–employee assistance programs (EAP), work-life programs, and health and wellness programs–offers a potent combination of tools for meeting these business goals. The use of these kinds of HPM programs in a comprehensive fashion can yield significant return on investment (ROI) for the company and improve the lives of the employees as well.

Part 1 of this article summarizes the costs of doing business that are relevant to HPM practices. Part 2 examines the drivers of these business costs with an emphasis on human capital. Part 3 addresses certain ways to improve human capital and focuses on the core practices and outcomes for EAP, work-life and health promotion/wellness. The business case for the integration of these three HPM services is presented in Part 4. The final section discusses critical issues, such as the limitations of the research literature and the key success factors for implementing an integrated program to achieve business outcomes.

PART 1: THE COSTS OF DOING BUSINESS

To run a profitable company, one of the fundamental tasks is to understand and manage the costs of doing business. Many of these costs are related to employees and their care. There are three main areas of costs relevant to HPM. These are employee healthcare and benefits, workplace performance costs, and organizational risks. Each of these is reviewed next.

HEALTHCARE AND BENEFITS COSTS

Medical Costs. Annual increases in healthcare premiums have risen in the 8 to 14% range for the last 5 years and are expected to continue at that rate in the future as well. This is compared to overall annual inflation rates in the 3% range. More specifically, recent industry data (cited in Gold in this volume) shows a change from $4,355 in year 2000 to $7,009 in 2004 per employee health insurance premiums paid by employers–this is a staggering cumulative increase of over 60% in just five years. Companies are rightly concerned about healthcare costs and looking for healthcare programs and services that can help save money by reducing the medical cost trend.

Mental Health Costs. Mental health, particularly depression, is an increasingly large component of total healthcare costs. According to National Institutes of Mental Health (NIMH), about 22% of adults in the U.S. suffer from a diagnosable mental disorder. A recent national survey found that more than 1 in 4 Americans received some form of treatment for a mental health issue during the past two years (Harris Interactive, 2004). Pharmaceutical use and their costs for mental health conditions are at record high levels in the U.S. society. The landmark study on the Global Burden of Disease found that the impact of mental illness on overall health and productivity is substantial–ranking second only to cardiovascular conditions in loss of disability-adjusted life years (Murray & Lopez, 1996). According to the Surgeon General's report on mental health, the significance of mental illness is "profoundly under recognized" (U.S. Department of Health and Human Services, 1999). In the HERO studies, depression and stress were found as the two leading modifiable risk factors for healthcare expenditures (Goetzel et al., 1998).

Disability. Employees can also have health consequences that can result in missing enough time away from work to qualify for paid benefits in the form of short-term and long-term disability (Contie & Burton, 1999). During the disability period, the employer typically pays a major portion of the employee's normal level of compensation as well as paying for the medical care costs. Due to rising disability costs, total absence management programs are becoming more popular among large employers (Brunelle, 2004). These kinds of programs take an integrated approach and feature efforts to coordinate a disability manager with staff from areas of safety and injury prevention, wellness staff, and EAP and work-life and emphasize pro-active processes to speed the return to work process.

Workers Compensation. When a worker's physical or mental health is damaged due to their work or job environment, the employee can file a workers compensation claim. In such cases, when legitimately experienced, the company must pay wage replacement to the employee as well as the healthcare costs required for treatment. Indirect costs are also incurred, including lost productivity, increased hiring and training costs, supervisor time demands, overtime pay, and possibly product quality issues generated by less skilled replacement workers. Recent research by consultants at Milliman U.S.A. estimated that the dollar value of these indirect costs is three or more times greater than the direct costs of wage replacement and healthcare (Gallagher & Morgan, 2002).

WORKPLACE PERFORMANCE COSTS

Unscheduled Absenteeism. In addition to the costs of longer absences from work that qualify for disability or workers compensation benefits, are the substantial but often unmeasured costs of casual or unscheduled employee absence. These figures are typically smaller than STD in dollars per event but are experienced by a much larger segment of the employee population and therefore can be very costly. When employees are not at work, they are not producing what their job requires and this can also negatively affect the performance of their work team and result in many indirect costs as well. Recent trends in HR data management can make it even more difficult to track unscheduled absence in a careful manner. Paid Time Off (PTO) record systems, which feature a variety of reasons for employee absence (including vacation) that are all rolled into one measurement bucket, can obscure health-related absences.

Productivity and "Presenteeism." One of the most basic contributions of an employee is his or her ability to be productive on the job. However, employee productivity is not always at a consistently high level and can vary according to many reasons. When health and personal or work-life problems interfere with an employee's ability to perform at normal levels of high productivity, this is considered a "presenteeism" problem. The person is on the job but "out of it," as noted in recent feature article in the *Harvard Business Review* (Hemp, 2003).

Although medical costs tend to get the most attention from employers, innovative recent studies reveal that direct medical costs actually account for only a minor portion of the total health and productivity-related costs faced by businesses. For example, one study examined archival cost data from medical claims, pharmacy, absence, short-term disability (STD) and employee-reported productivity on validated survey instruments that assess presenteeism (Goetzel et al., 2004). The results, based on over 370,000 employees, found that presenteeism losses accounted for the *majority* of per person annual total costs for 9 out of the top 10 most expensive health conditions (only heart disease had the majority of total costs accounted for by medical claims).

Turnover. In addition to the costs of absenteeism and presenteeism are losses from worker turnover. National data shows that employee turnover is frequent–21% for companies with 1,000 to 5,000 employees and 24% for firms over 5,000 employees, according to the 2000 Society of Human Resources Management (SHRM) Retention Practices Survey. The full dollar cost of turnover can vary by many factors, but some estimates range from $25,000 per case and a range of 75% to 150% of a worker's annual salary depending on the type of job (Johnson, 2001).

ORGANIZATIONAL RISKS

A third area of business costs concerns the somewhat intangible area of risk. For many organizations, there can be severe costs associated with large-scale organizational changes (mergers, downsizing, and such). There also can be significant legal liability and direct costs when there are crisis events at work (such as violence, accidents and harassment). Companies must also contend with the consequences of natural disasters and terrorism incidents and help their employees cope with these kinds of critical incidents. EAPs have historically been a valued resource for companies to help plan effective organizational change, to help managers address workforce issues, and to better prepare for and respond to critical incidents (Ginzberg, Kilburg, & Gomes, 1999). While there are few research studies that document the specific financial costs to employers for these kinds of risk-management problems, their potential for large losses is real nonetheless.

PART 2:
THE DRIVERS OF BUSINESS COSTS AND THE ROLE
OF HUMAN CAPITAL

It is clear that there are many costs of doing business that are a source of serious concern for employers. One of the ways to try to control these cost increases is to identify and understand the principal causal factors (drivers) of these costs. If the drivers are identifiable, then it may be possible to implement intervention programs and services to help improve these conditions and avoid or reduce their costs. So, what are the main drivers of healthcare benefit costs and of employee performance costs?

Epidemiological research indicates that healthcare costs are in part escalating in response to certain demographic and societal trends (Gold, 2004). The current U.S. workforce is characterized by increasing age, poorer overall health status, greater obesity, and "baby boomer" generation workers begging to retire and the "sandwich generation" workers (those with both child care and elder care needs) moving into their prime work years with a full plate of responsibilities at home. One can add to this demographic profile the larger societal influences of a faster pace of life and work, rapid technological advances, globalization, and just more time spent working (Lewis & Dyer, 2002). These conditions are all associated with increased health risk, illness burden and stress-related responses and thus can lead to greater demand for healthcare services.

Human Capital. While it is difficult for a business to directly influence these kinds of demographic and larger societal factors, a company can determine how it treats its employees. Indeed, business success today requires more than just the effective management of physical capital (such as machines, inventory, and property); it also demands the effective management of human capital. A cover story in *Workforce* (February 2001) notes a company's success is "embedded in its people and what's in their heads."

One of the most cogent arguments for the business value of human capital is presented in *Leveraging the New Human Capital*. In this new book, Burud and Tumolo (2004) offer an extensive review of the literature that addresses the business case for providing comprehensive and integrated work-life, mental health, wellness and organizational culture kinds of services. Their analysis, involving review of findings from over 50 studies, suggests that human capital performance practices have "overwhelmingly positive effects on business objectives that are pivotal to success: employee creativity, commitment, productivity, health, recruitment and retention" (p. 216). In the book, they also review 13 studies on the link between human capital practices and customer satisfaction and loyalty. Also reviewed are 21 other studies that correlate human capital practices positively with the financial success of the organization. Although most of the research reviewed in their book is not conducted with experimental scientific methods, the sheer number of applied studies with consistent findings is encouraging.

THE HUMAN CAPITAL INDEX RESEARCH BY WATSON WYATT

Also encouraging is the recent work by international consulting firm Watson Wyatt. These studies examined human resources practices of companies and tracked their actual financial performance as a business over several years (Watson Wyatt, 2002). The first study was conducted in 1999 and included data from more than 400 U.S. and Canadian firms that were publicly traded, had three years of shareholder returns and a minimum of 100 million in revenue or market value. Interviews were conducted around more than 30 kinds of HR practices relating to people management. These were coded into a Human Capital Index, a composite single measure that could range from 0 to 100. Results showed that use of these HR practices were significantly correlated with a 30% increase in market value.

The second WWHC study was conducted in 2000 and targeted global businesses. The survey featured over 200 questions and the data was collected in six languages. The sample included more than 250 companies from 16 countries, representing all sizes and sectors of the economy. The findings showed that improvements in 19 key HR practices were associated with a 26% improvement in market value.

The third WWHC study, conducted in 2001, assessed more than 500 North American companies. This sample included some larger companies, with average market value of over $8 billion and over 18,000 employees. The analyses combined the European data with new data to create a study pool of more than 750 firms from the U.S., Canada and Europe. The results of the aggregated study showed the same pattern as the two previous studies. The higher the Human Capital Index score, the higher the financial performance of the company. A total of 43 key HR practices accounted for an increase of 47% in stock market value. More specifically, when the 5-year shareholder return was examined in each of three subgroups, a clear pattern emerged. Those companies with the lowest one-third of HC Index scores had a 21% shareholder return; the medium group averaged 39% return. The highest scoring companies had a 64% average return. Thus, a threefold difference was found between the low and high scoring groups of companies. Of the top five HR practices most strongly associated with business growth, "a collegial and flexible workplace" and "excellence in recruitment and retention" are both associated with work/family, EAP and wellness kinds of services.

Perhaps the most compelling finding was from analysis of the time over time data from the 51 companies who were in both the 1999 and 2001 studies. Results showed that the Human Capital Index score from 1999 was significantly correlated with future financial performance, at $r = .41$. Similarly, the company financial performance record from 1999 was positively correlated with future financial performance, at $r = .19$. However, the human capital correlation was significantly stronger than the financial performance correlation. Thus, future business success was relatively better predicted by how the company treated its people than by its own past financial performance.

These three studies are quite interesting, but it must be noted that they are correlational in nature and offer no direct proof that when a company does the kinds of HR practices that are human capital friendly, they will be more financially successful. It could be that some companies have the kind of organizational culture (or some other factors) that contributes both to business profits and to having management practices and benefits that take good care of their employees. The causal chain is not clear from these studies.

THE HUMAN CAPITAL AND HEALTH AND PRODUCTIVITY MOVEMENTS

There are a number of larger movements in the business world and in academia during the past decade that endorse a human capital model and emphasize the role of health and productivity management.

Consulting Companies. In his 1999 book *Human Capital*, Towers Perrin consultant Thomas Davenport provides a compelling case for how companies can benefit financially from taking an active interest in the welfare and success of their employees. Towers Perrin has a human capital consulting group and features an integrated health model for understanding the bigger picture of how various health and benefits services are interrelated (Winn-Rogers, 2003). Most of the other major human resources and healthcare benefits consulting firms such as Anderson, Aon, Deloitte & Touche, Mercer, Milliman U.S.A., and Watson Wyatt also have a formal business focusing on human capital management services.

Institutes. The Institute for Health and Productivity Management (IHPM) has been gaining momentum during the past few years. IHPM is an organization of employers, health providers, researchers, and pharmaceutical companies that is dedicated to establishing the value of employee health as a business asset and an investment in corporate success. It holds a number of specialized conferences each year and publishes a magazine featuring new research in this area. A similar role is performed by the Integrated Benefits Institute (IBI–see Parry, 2003). IBI focuses on collecting benchmark data from medical claims as well as from disability, workers compensations, absence management and productivity areas. The data is then linked together at the individual employee level and analyzed to reveal opportunities for identification of high-cost/high-risk employees and thus for more coordinated health interventions. IBI has participated in a number of case studies of companies that have saved millions of dollars (compared to projected trend increases) after adopting more integrated health management practices.

Academic Research. The American Psychology Society has produced a series of detailed white paper for its Human Capital Initiative. This academic-based organization has pulled together a great deal of theory and high-quality empirical research findings on how psychological processes and services can help individuals cope with a variety of basic issues, including aging, literacy, productivity, substance abuse, health, and violence.

Taken together, there is a movement taking place in the U.S. and to a lesser extent in other countries as well that features recognition of the health cost savings, workplace performance gains and personal outcomes that are generated from a wide range of human capital management practices.

PART 3:
WORKPLACE PROGRAMS AS A DRIVER OF HUMAN CAPITAL

The evidence reviewed so far in this article suggests that the costs of business are increasing and that a significant portion of these costs are driven by human capital problems. The next question, then, is what are the drivers of human capital? More specifically, what kinds of interventions are effective at addressing and improving the various health, work and personal life problems faced by employees and their families? The following sections address this question by reviewing the practices and outcomes from employee assistance/mental health, work-life and workplace wellness programs.

EAP AND MENTAL HEALTH

The primary job of an EAP professional is to identify and resolve workplace, mental health, physical health, marital, family, personal addictions or alcohol, or emotional issues that affect a worker's job performance (Collins, 2000). Most EAPs also offer consultative and educational services around legal and financial issues that affect employees. Other aspects of EAP include services that support individual supervisors with their management and work team problems. Some EAPs also lead more strategic consulting around organizational change and development issues. EAPs typically offer preventative and reactive services for critical incidents (Everly et al., 2001).

Prevalence and Use. Employees at most large businesses today have access to an EAP. A survey of Fortune 500 companies in 1997 found that 92% of firms offered EAPs–a historic high level of market penetration among large employers (Sciegaj et al., 2001). Similar findings come from a 2000 Society for Human Resource Management Benefits Survey. It found a majority of businesses offering EAP services ranged from 48% for small employers to over 90% for the largest employers. However, many very small employers only have access to EAPs through their health plan medical benefits package and that was only for 17% (based on Mercer/Foster Higgins National Survey of Employee Sponsored Health Plans) (Teich & Buck, 2003).

Effectiveness and Outcomes. There has been only a handful of high quality experimental research work completed in the field of EAP. A recent review of over 30 workplace mental health research studies conducted in the UK found varying levels of methodological rigor to the studies, but consistent evidence of clinical effectiveness, workplace performance improvements and very high client satisfaction from EAP counseling (McLeod & McLeod, 2001). Most of the best research conducted in the U.S. was prior to 1990 and focused largely on issues of alcohol prevention and treatment referral in workplace settings (Roman

& Blum, 2002). When including studies with less rigorous scientific designs, there are several dozen empirical case studies of EAPs that show high levels of outcomes in areas of client clinical change, workplace improvements in absenteeism, productivity and turnover, and a few that document savings in medical, disability or workers compensation claims (see reviews by Blum & Roman, 1995; EAPA, 2003). More typical of EA measurement practices in the business side are non-experimental studies based on follow-up surveys of clients. These studies show high levels of personal health improvements and self- reported workplace performance improvements after use of the EAP (Attridge, 2003).

Clinical Effectiveness and Medical Cost-Offset from Mental Health. One of the functions of an EAP is to appropriately refer employees to mental heath treatment providers. The value of this assess and refer model depends on the success of the therapeutic services provided by the mental health colleagues. This raises the question of whether mental health treatments generally produce positive clinical outcomes. The answer is yes, according to a landmark review study that examined over 300 meta-analysis articles (each article itself a review of other many original studies; see Lipsey & Wilson, 1993). Large-scale survey research of lay consumers of mental health services in the U.S. has also found generally positive outcomes (Seligman, 1995; Harris Interactive, 2004). The appropriate use of mental health services is often associated with lower overall medical costs. This "medical cost-offset" effect has been demonstrated in many studies (Shemo, 1985), although it is not without some debate on the subject (Miller & Magruder, 1999). Some employers–as noted in a recent special report in *HR Magazine* (Tyler, 2003)–are starting to understand that savings in total healthcare costs can come from providing comprehensive mental healthcare benefits.

WORK-LIFE

Modern work-life programs include a wide range of services (Gornick, 2002). Typically, these services include: Workplace flexibility policies, paid and unpaid time off, caring for dependents (child and aging parents), financial education and support, and community involvement (Lingle, 2004).

The increased demand for work-life programs started in the 1970s and comes from both the changing demographics of the workforce that included more women and recognition from employers that to attract and retain valuable employees it was good to offer a climate that sought to balance work and life. Authors of a recent national study of the stressful lives of U.S. workers concluded that "companies should have comprehensive work/life balance initiatives to support their personnel" (Hobson et al., 2001, p. 38). Human resources managers are also advocates of work-life programs for a number of reasons. One is the increasing need to respond to elder care issues (Grillo, 2004). In addition, as more employers are shifting the costs of health insurance coverage to the employee (what has been called "healthcare consumerism"), employee use of work-life balance programs can be promoted as an integral part of a self-care approach. A Watson Wyatt consulting survey of U.S. employers found that 77 of respondents believed that work-life programs improve employee satisfaction; 54% believe that they enhance employee health and productivity and 39% say they reduce healthcare costs (cited in Sherman, 2004). Indeed, according to the Director of the Alliance for Work-Life Progress, in many companies "work-life strategies are taking root in response to evidence that it pays to treat employees like external customers" (Lingle, 2004, p. 37).

Effectiveness and Outcomes. The relatively recent development of work-life as an applied industry has not allowed the opportunity for high quality scientific investigations of the best practices or the outcomes of its core services. Most of the research conducted in this area has featured sociological surveys (for example, see the Families and Work Institute), case studies of major employers, or client outcome studies from the major vendors in the work-life field. Unfortunately, the field has not enjoyed the kind of federal government research support that other more developed fields have had. Despite these obstacles, there have been over 100 studies and reports on the use and impact of work-life practices (reviewed in Work & Family Connection's annotated bibliography, 2003). The book by Burud and Tumolu (2004) also reviews many of the key studies in work-life.

HEALTH PROMOTION AND WELLNESS

The core practices of worksite wellness programs include (Mulvihill, 2003): (1) strategic planning to prevent disease, decrease health risks, and contain rising healthcare costs; (2) health screenings and risk stratification; (3) risk-related health management interventions (exercise, behavior change programs, educational newsletters, Web, self-care books, nurse advice lines, and health coaching, disease management; (4) evaluation and metrics.

Health Risks and Work Problems. One of the foundational tenets of this field is that it is better to prevent health problems than to treat them later on. Thus, there has been a serious effort to understand the relationship between the risks for certain health problems and other outcomes. This focus has led to the development and widespread use of health risk appraisal (HRA) survey instruments to measure risk and target appropriate interventions. Research from StayWell Health Management's database of over 100,000 employees with HRA data shows a consistent pattern of findings. The greater the number of health risks, the greater the level of absenteeism and work productivity loss (Gold, 2004). Similar associations are consistently found between the number of chronic health conditions a person has and also for worse perceived health status and greater days missed from work and productivity losses.

Wellness Programs. Reviews of published research studies have generally found supportive empirical evidence that comprehensive worksite wellness programs can improve employee health and improve work productivity problems (Aldana, 2001; DeGroot & Kiker, 2003; Pelletier, 2001; Riedel et al., 2001). The scientific evidence to date offers documented correlations between: (1) multiple risk factors and lower productivity; (2) chronic illness and lower productivity; and (3) participation in health management programs and improved work performance (Lynch, 2003). Indeed, in his presentation "Making the Business Case for Worksite Wellness," StayWell researcher Dan Gold (2004) notes that there are over 100 published research studies of comprehensive worksite health promotion efforts, with the majority finding positive clinical and cost savings outcomes.

Nurse Lines. When employees call a 24-hour nurse advice line with acute health issues, various research studies have shown results in areas of savings in medical costs from avoided unnecessary use of the ER and doctor office and also from reduced workplace absenteeism and presenteeism (Otis, Attridge, & Harmon, 2003). A randomized controlled experimental study found evidence of dollar savings in medical healthcare claims from implementation of telephonic nurse advice lines (Otis et al., 1998). Follow-up surveys of over 77,000 employee users of a nurse advice line service indicated that about a third reported avoiding missing a day of work and about half reported improvements in their productivity at work (Attridge, 2004).

In sum, the major components of worksite wellness programs and related health management services have been evaluated in many studies.

The results of these studies have generally been positive for the clinical effectiveness, improvements in workplace performance outcomes and healthcare cost savings. Of the three kinds of HPM programs reviewed in this article, wellness and worksite health promotion has the most empirical support.

PART 4:
THE INTEGRATION OF EAP, WORK-LIFE AND WELLNESS

Since the early 1990s, companies have begun to offer more comprehensive preventive services that better address the psychological and social needs of employees as well as their physical health needs (Bergmark et al., 1996). Recent industry surveys suggest trends toward integration between EAP and work-life and there are expectations of even greater formal and informal business integration in the future (Herlihy, Attridge, & Turner, 2002). It is common for many companies now to offer some form of integrated EAP-work/life partnerships (King, 2002). The inherent collaborative nature of the modern work-life function has been described as: "Not all of these programs, policies and practices typically reside in one neatly organized and appropriately resourced department or function. Nor does the work-life professional independently 'own' much of the terrain in which it operates. The work-life function is, therefore, a highly collaborative endeavor that helps connect the dots between many other human resource efforts" (Lingle, 2004, p. 37). Although EAP and Work-life have already become more closely aligned, there are emerging opportunities for their greater integration with both health and wellness programs. "Perhaps one the most exciting developments in the health and wellness field are the migration toward integration and coordination with other employee benefit services" (Mulvihill, 2003, p. 15). EAPs have already been successful at collaborating with disability and workers compensation (Brunnelle & Lui, 2003; Handron, 1997; Smith & Rooney, 1999).

The research to date suggests that there are a number of advantages to integration both for the employer and for the employees.

Integration Is Good for the Employer. When EAP, work-life and wellness programs are integrated there can be advantages for the company. These include the areas of greater efficiencies in overall program management, less administrative costs from only working with one or with fewer vendors, and a greater emphasis on preventive services and early detection across providers. Another area for added value is the opportunity for increased program participation from cross-referral of employees from one service to another program. This process can lead to a boost in overall utilization for the individual programs when integrated (Herlihy, 2000). Integration can offer some operational cost savings and thus a better ROI. Ceridian, a provider of EAP stand-alone and a combined EAP and work-life product, estimates that their employer clients receive a higher ROI from the combined service than from the EAP-alone service (Stein, 2002). These ROI outcome measures include increased employee retention and productivity, reduced healthcare costs and the reduction of redundancies in program management. One key area of potential benefit to employers from integration is the opportunity for better risk management and more effective delivery of crisis prevention services. The more that different areas can work together who have contact with employees and family members at times of need, the sooner the company can respond to a critical situation.

Integration Is Good for the Employee. There can also be several advantages of integration for the employee. Increased employee satisfaction can come from making the combined program use more pleasant and practical to use. Employees have one point of contact and don't have to repeat their problems over and over to different people. The EAPA studies of professionals and vendors also noted several advantages of integration for the employee. For one, for employees with a mental health concern, it can be less stigmatizing to first contact an integrated program or a work-life office than to directly go to the EAP. It can also lead to greater awareness of the full range of services available to employees across the various program offerings. For example, an employee who calls a nurse about a respiratory issue can be introduced to a smoking cessation program offered through the wellness program and also work with an EAP counselor to figure out how to get the level of family support needed for successfully completing the stop smoking plan.

THE INTEGRATED VALUE MODEL

In a previous article, a conceptual model was described that defined the business value for EAPs as having five levels (Attridge, 2001B). According to this model, EAPs should strive to document their value to the company through client-specific activity that (1) establishes the need for EAP services, (2) profiles the use of the EAP, (3) measures the outcomes from users of the program, (4) translates these outcomes into business dollar value metrics, and (5) connects the EAP outcomes and mission to the "big picture" of the organization's interest in managing risk and creating a healthy workforce. This model was developed from analysis of over 200 studies of EAP and other kinds of health services.

More recently, this model has been extended to better specify the major kinds of outcomes from EAP services and their financial and business value (Attridge, Amaral, & Hyde, 2003; Amaral & Attridge, 2004). This Business Value Triad model focuses on three major kinds of outcomes of importance to most companies. The first outcome area is health claims costs, the second is human capital costs, and the third is organizational costs. The health claim cost value component includes the impact of EAP and related services on medical, mental health, disability and workers compensation claims. The human capital value component includes the value of improvements in employee absenteeism and productivity/presenteeism and enhanced employee recruitment and retention (avoided turnover). The organizational value component includes behavioral risk management, liability risk prevention savings, better organizational culture and increased morale and secondary impacts on human capital gains and health claims savings.

For the present article, the Triad model has been further revised to reflect the synergistic added business value potential from the integration of EAP, work-life and wellness (see Figure 1). In this new conceptual

FIGURE 1. The Business Value Model for the Integration of EAP, Work-Life and Wellness

model each of the three service delivery areas can contribute independently to all three kinds of outcomes–healthcare claims, human capital and organizational. This part of the model is based on the research literature already reviewed as generally supportive of these kinds of outcomes for each program type. But in addition, when the services collaborate and work together in an integrated fashion there is the potential for even greater business value to the company (as represented visually by the overlapping circle section in the middle of the figure). This new part of the model remains to be empirically validated, but it suggests the areas of outcomes than can be examined in evaluation opportunities ahead.

Thus, the scientific evidence for making the business case for health and productivity is promising, but it is by no means conclusive. What is interesting about the critical reviews of the literature is that the *nature of how the program is implemented* appears to be the most significant driver of getting results. This suggests the need to identify and focus on the high-risk employees within a company and to use a comprehensive intervention program that is embedded with a supportive "healthy-company" culture (Attridge & Gold, 2004). Yet, this is *not* easy! But it can be done.

Model Programs. Some of the best examples of such programs are listed in the National Registry of Effective Programs (NREP). There are currently four workplace-based programs that have been reviewed and deemed "model programs" by the U.S. Government. These include the following programs: "Coping with Work and Family Stress," "Wellness Outreach," "The Healthy Workplace," and "Team Awareness." Each of these evidence-based programs has a multidisciplinary emphasis that crosses the boundaries of health and wellness, work and home, and the awareness of alcohol and workplace performance issues common to EAP (Bennett, 2003). These programs have been shown in controlled experimental research conducted in workplace settings to be effective at a number of significant outcomes such as greater awareness and treatment seeking for alcohol issues, reductions in binge drinking, and overall health outcomes.

Success Factors. These kinds of integrated services require high-level organizational commitment to both get started and then to promote it well enough to drive a high enough level of participation to create the outcomes that in turn result in an ROI that justifies continuation of the enterprise (Anderson et al., 2004; Lewis & Dyer, 2002). David Hunnicutt, the President of the Wellness Councils of America (WELCOA), considers seven factors that are critical for the success of worksite wellness efforts (Hunnicutt, 2003). These include: getting senior level leadership support, creating cohesive wellness teams from diverse parts of the company, collecting baseline data to assess needs and outcome impact potential, crafting an operating plan with a multiyear agenda, choosing appropriate interventions, creating a company culture that supports health, and consistently evaluating outcomes (including participation rates, changes in employee knowledge, attitudes and behavior, and financial ROI). Program success comes from a high level of collaboration between the company and the providers of the health and wellness programs.

Case Examples. This collaboration issue is illustrated by a study of America Online (AOL). High levels of employee participation in an integrated EAP and nurse advice line program along with the provision of self-care books and newsletters had an estimated \$5:\$1 ROI, based on net cost savings from healthcare and workplace outcomes (Fuller, Attridge, & Doherty, 2001). High program use came in part from a well-managed and internally directed promotional campaign involving all health and wellness partners working together (participation increased over a six-year period from one-third to over half of employees). Similar success was achieved and documented in the award-winning Fairview Alive! program (see this volume, pp. 263-279). Burud and Tumolo (2004) also profile four companies (DuPont, Baxter International, SAS, and FTN) that exemplify how different kinds of adaptive work-life/wellness strategies, when implemented in a systematic organizational fashion, can result in dramatic bottom-line success.

PART 5:
CRITICAL ISSUES

The evidence reviewed so far has the following logic chain: (1) there is a strong need to control rising business costs in areas of healthcare, employee performance and risk management; (2) human capital factors are a significant driver of these kinds of business costs; (3) human capital management programs based in EAP, work-life and wellness traditions are widely available and have been shown in most research to be effective at reducing these kinds of business costs; and (4) these programs have the potential to be even more effective when offered in combination and included in a comprehensive integrated model. The points, if valid, support a general business case for the integration of EAP, work-life and wellness programs (and possibly other allied services).

So then why do many of the providers of these kinds of services tend to have a difficult time convincing their purchasers (HR leaders, company medical directors, benefits managers) that these programs have business value–that there is a positive return on their investment (ROI)? To answer this, one must consider several "reality factors" that can limit the opportunity for being able to make the business case.

Healthcare Data. The irony in this field is that although most employers and healthcare benefits purchasers want to know if health intervention programs have a measurable business value, the hard data available to answer this quite reasonable question is rarely available for such an analysis. One primary data source is healthcare claims records (often considered the gold standard) and yet this system was designed to pay medical bills and is simply not well suited to evaluation purposes. The reason is that most of it is stored in transactional databases and aggregated around the kind of benefit, or the place of service (ER, MD office, hospital, etc.), or type of medical diagnosis. In contrast, one of the requirements for effectively evaluating the impact of these kinds of programs is to collect data at the person or patient-centric level, versus the typical benefit-centric model that aggregates data across people or benefits (Otis, Attridge, & Riedel, 2000). Thus, in day-to-day business, healthcare data usually is either not available, is inaccurate, or is too costly to obtain retrospectively.

Workplace Data and Self-Report Tools. The evaluation of workplace outcomes is even more difficult than healthcare claims outcomes. The first issue is a general lack of workplace performance data to even study. Less than a third of businesses routinely measure workplace outcomes (productivity and absenteeism) in enough detail to be able to accurately study the data (IBI, 2002). The lack of company administrative records of workplace outcome data has necessitated a shift toward self-report measures. A variety of validated self-report measures are now available to businesses (see Goetzel et al., 2004). Fortunately, the validity of some self-report measures in this area is now supported by empirical research. For example, a recent study of over 5,000 employees found that self-report measures of work limitations (based on a 15-minute survey assessed retrospectively, concurrently or prospectively) were correlated with company administrative data on adverse events in terms of absenteeism hours, workers compensation claims, short-term disability claims, group health claims dollars and pharmacy claims dollars (Allen & Bunn, 2003). A number of published, validated survey tools of health and work factors are now in the public domain. Many of these instruments are profiled in the 2004 *Platinum Book* by IHPM. One of the most popular tools is the *Health and Productivity Questionnaire* (see www.HPQ.org), developed by Ron Kessler of Harvard University and based on normative data from over 200,000 respondents around the world.

Research Design Limitations. Another limitation is that even if there is good data available on health or workplace measures, the data often cannot be interpreted because of ambiguity around the causal nature of the forces at play other than the program or service of interest to the evaluation. Applied research on evaluation of workplace health outcomes often suffers from inherent limitations imposed by the business settings in which the programs are implemented (for EAP field see Attridge, 2001A; for work-life field see Nord et al., 2002; for wellness field see Anderson, Sexner, & Gold, 2001). The manner in which the delivery of these programs is set up is often inappropriate to scientifically test their impact. Programs are commonly offered to all covered employees as part of a broader constellation of benefit services and without a control group (or even a matched comparison group), it is difficult to test the unique causal role of the program versus other factors. This same problem affects almost all benefit-related programs (such as general medical procedures, pharmacy management programs, disease management). The other problematic design issue is the instability of the context. There are frequent changes to benefits design and to company and vendor data management systems that can render data from one period incomparable to other periods.

CONCLUSIONS

Employers are faced with tight budgets and increasing costs in many aspects of their business. The use of employee assistance, work-life, and health and wellness programs can be effective tools to care for the human capital of the company–its employees. When these kinds of HPM programs are designed in a comprehensive fashion, employers can expect to see a business return on their investment in the areas of reduced healthcare costs, reduced losses in workplace performance costs, and in managing the human risks to the organization. Although there is a great deal of research in this area to support these ideas, the scientific rigor of the evidence base is just beginning to yield quality findings that can be used to build a solid base from which to build the business case. However, if the early returns from the pioneers who have taken the lead in this area are accurate, then one of the ways toward greater profitability and financial success is found in fully embracing the stewardship of their human capital.

At the most basic level, for companies in the U.S., the underpinning of the business case for offering these kinds of health and benefits services has been capitalistic in nature. It is based on the goal of making the company more competitive in its ability to attract and retain employees and to better manage the mandated costs of doing business associated with healthcare (Georgia Tech Human Resources Department & WorkLifeBalance.com, 2004). Yet, considering the larger societal need for these kinds of services, the employee-sponsored delivery channel now in place in the U.S. is a rather limited solution. Macro-level historical analysis of societal factors in the U.S. suggests that despite the progress by some leading employers to provide comprehensive work/family programs, the present piecemeal approach to offering such programs is "woefully inadequate" (Grosswald, Ragland, & June, 2001). Perhaps there is a need for a much larger-scale model in which the government– rather than employers–is responsible for providing. This kind of "socialistic" approach for offering human capital support services is more akin to the basic funding and delivery models found in the UK and other industrialized countries. While such a model is thought provoking, perhaps the best that can be done today in the U.S. is for more employers to appreciate the value–the business case–for providing these kinds of services and embrace the opportunity to invest more in their human capital, one company at a time.

REFERENCES

Aldana, S.G. (2001). Financial impact of health promotion programs: A comprehensive review of the literature. *American Journal of Health Promotion*, 15(5): 296-320.

Allen, H.M., & Bunn, W.B. (2003). Validating self-reported measures of productivity at work: A case for their credibility in a heavy manufacturing setting. *Journal of Occupational and Environmental Medicine*, 45(9): 926-940.

Amaral, T., & Attridge, M. (2004, November). Communicating EAP business value: Successful strategies for measurement, reporting, and presentations. Presented at Employee Assistance Professionals Association Annual Conference, San Francisco, CA.

Anderson, D.R., Sexner, S.A., & Gold, D. (2001). Conceptual framework, critical questions, and practical challenges in conducting research on the financial impact of worksite health promotion. *American Journal of Health Promotion*, 15(5): 281-288.

Attridge, M. (2001A). Can EAPs experiment in the real world? *EAPA Exchange*, 31(2): 26-27.

Attridge, M. (2001B). Making the business case for EAPs: A conceptual framework. *EAPA Exchange*, 31(4): 37-38.

Attridge, M. (2003, March). EAP impact on work, stress and health: National data 1999-2002. Presented at *Work Stress & Health Conference (APA/NIOSH)*, Toronto, Canada.

Attridge, M. (2004). New research on health outcomes and workplace performance among NurseLine callers. *Health & Productivity Management*, 3(1): 35.

Attridge, M., Amaral, T.M., & Hyde, M. (2003). Completing the business case for EAPs. *Journal of Employee Assistance*, 33(3): 23-25.

Attridge, M., & Gold, D. (2004, October). Improving employee performance by improving health: Secrets of successful health and productivity management (HPM) programs. Presented at Institute for Health and Productivity Management 4th Annual Conference, Phoenix, AZ.

Bennett, J. B. (2003). Using evidence-based workplace training. *Journal of Employee Assistance*, 33(2): 12-14.

Bergmark, R.E., Dell, P., Attridge, M., & Parker, M.K. (1996). Creating an integrated healthcare system: The health and human risk management model. *Managed Care Quarterly*, 4: 36-42.

Blum, T., & Roman, P. (1995). *Cost-Effectiveness and Preventive Implications of Employee Assistance Programs*. Rockville, MD: U.S. Department of Health and Human Services.

Brunnelle, A. (2004). Out of action: Absence management strategies can help keep workers on the job. *Benefits and Compensation Solutions*, 28(15): 39-41.

Brunnelle, A., & Lui, J. (2003). Disability management programs and EAP. *Journal of Employee Assistance*, 33(2): 7-8.

Burud, S., & Tumolo, M. (2004). *Leveraging the New Human Capital: Adaptive Strategies, Results Achieved, and Stories of Transformation*. Davies-Black: Palo Alto, CA.

Collins, K. (2002). The EAP core technology. *EAPA Exchange*, May/June, 11.

Contie, D.J., & Burton, W.N. (1999). Behavioral Health Disability Management. In J. Oher (Ed.), *The Employee Assistance Handbook* (pp. 319-336). NY: Wiley.

Davenport, T.O. (1999). *Human Capital*. San Francisco: Jossey-Bass.

EAPA. (2003). *The Dollar$ and Sense of Employee Assistance*. Employee Assistance Professionals Association, Washington, DC.

Everly, G., Flannery, R. Jr., Eyler,V., & Mitchell, J. (2001). Sufficiency analysis of an integrated multi-component approach to crisis intervention: Critical incident stress management. *Advances in Mind-Body Medicine*, 17: 160-196.

Fitzenz, J. (2000). *The ROI of Human Capital: Measuring the Economic Value of Employee Performance*. NY: AMACON.

Fuller, J., Attridge, M., & Doherty, W. (2001, October). You've got ROI: AOL's winning initiatives. Presented at Benefits Management Forum and Expo, Atlanta, GA.

Gallagher, P.A., & Morgan, C.L. (2002). Defining the intangible: Measuring the indirect costs related to workers' absence. *Health and Productivity Magazine*, 1(3): 26-27.

Georgia Tech Human Resources Department and WorkLifeBalance.com. (2004). Work-life balance: Competitive advantage or social responsibility? *Benefits and Compensation Solutions*, 28(12): 38-39.

Ginzberg, M.R., Kilburg, R.R., & Gomes, P.G. (1999). Organizational counseling and the delivery of integrated human services in the workplace: An evolving model for employee assistance theory and practice. In J.M. Oher (Ed.), *The Handbook of Employee Assistance* (pp. 439-456). NY: Wiley.

Goetzel, R.Z., Anderson, D.R., Whitmer, R.W., Ozminkowski, R.J., Dunn, R.L., & Wasserman, J. (1998). The relationship between modifiable health risks and health care expenditures: An analysis of the multi-employer HERO health risk and cost database. *Journal of Occupational & Environmental Medicine*, 40(10): 843-54.

Goetzel, R.Z., Long, S.R., Ozminkowski, R.J., Hawkins, K., Wang, S., & Lynch, W. (2004). Health, absence, disability, and presenteeism cost estimates of certain physical and mental health conditions affecting U.S. employers. *Journal of Occupational and Environmental Medicine*, 46(4): 398-412.

Gold, D. (2004, November). Making the business case for worksite health promotion. Presented at 2004 Midwest Worksite Health Promotion Conference, Bloomington, MN.

Gornick, M.E. (2002). Work-life core competencies. *EAPA Exchange*, May/June, 11.

Grillo, J. (2004). When the time comes: Elder-care programs are increasingly important. *Benefits and Compensation Solutions*, 28(14): 44-47.

Grosswald, B., Ragland, D., & Fisher, J.M. (2001). Critique of U.S. work/family programs and policies. *Journal of Progressive Human Services*, 12(1): 53-81.

Handron, K. (1997). Managing workplace disabilities: How EAPs can help put the cap on rising costs. *EAPA Exchange*, May/June, 21-23.

Harris Interactive. (2004, May). Therapy in America 2004. Cited in *Open Minds*, July 2004, 16(4): 11-12.

Hemp, P. (2003, October). Presenteeism: At work–but out of it. *Harvard Business Review:* 49-58.

Herlihy, P. (2000). EAPs and work/family programs: Different paths, same purposes? *EAPA Exchange*, Sep/Oct, 24-26.

Herlihy, P., Attridge, M., & Turner, S. (2002). The integration of EAP and work/life programs. *EAP Exchange*, 32(1): 10-12.

Hobson, C.J., Delunas, L., & Kesic, D. (2001). Compelling evidence of the need for corporate work-life balance initiatives: Results from a national survey of stressful life-events. *Journal of Employment Counseling*, 38(1): 38-44.

Honnicutt, D. (2003). Understanding the seven critical benchmarks of worksite wellness success. *Health & Productivity Management*, 2(3): 18-19.

Hyworon, Z., & Colombi, A.M. (2004). The ROI challenge: Evaluating return on investment from pre-loss indicators. *Health & Productivity Management*, 3(4): 7-9.

Integrated Benefits Institute. (2002). On the brink of change: How CFOs view investments in health and productivity. White article by IBI, San Francisco, CA.

Johnson, W.G. (2001). Economic analysis of health and productivity: An integrated approach to health. White article for IHPM. Scottsdale, AZ: Institute for Health and Productivity Management.

King, A.S. (2002). Integrated EAP-work/life partnerships. *Behavioral Health Management*, 22(5): 32-41.

Lewis, S., & Dyer, J. (2002). Towards a culture for work-life integration? In C.L. Cooper & R.J. Burke (Eds.), *The New World of Work: Challenges and Opportunities* (pp. 193-210). Williston, VT: Blackwell.

Lingle, K.M. (2004). Work-life. *Benefits and Compensation Solutions*, 28(12): 36-37.

Lipsey, M.W., & Wilson, D.B. (1993). The efficacy of psychological, educational, and behavioral treatment confirmation from meta-analysis. *American Psychologist*, 48(12): 1181-1209.

Lynch, W. (2003). Trusting that the truth will be good enough. *Health and Productivity Magazine*, 1(3): 10-11.

McLeod, J., & McLeod, J. (2001). How effective is workplace counseling? A review of the research literature. *Counselling and Psychotherapy Research*, 1(3): 181-191.

Miller, N.E., & Magruder, K.M. (Eds.). (1999). *Cost-Effectiveness of Psychotherapy: A Guide for Practitioners, Researchers and Policymakers.* New York: Oxford.

Molmen, W. (2005). Health and productivity management. *Benefits and Compensation Solutions*, 28(12): 38-39.

Mulvihill, M. (2003). The definition and core practices of wellness. *Journal of Employee Assistance*, 33(3): 13-15.

Murray, C.J.L., & Lopez, A.D. (Eds.). (1996). The global burden of disease and injury series, volume 1: A comprehensive assessment of mortality and disability from diseases, injuries, and risk factors in 1990 and projected to 2020. Cambridge, MA: Published by the Harvard School of Public Health on behalf of the World Health Organization and the World Bank, Harvard University Press.

Nord, W.R., Fox, S., Phoenix, A., & Viano, K. (2002). Real-world reactions to work-life balance programs: Lessons for effective implementation. *Organizational Dynamics*, 30(3): 223-238.

Otis, J., Attridge, M., & Harmon, R. (2003, November/December). Nurse call centers extend their reach. *HealthPlan*, 34: 37-38.

Otis, J., Attridge, M., & Riedel, J. (2000, September). Managing human capital for organizational success. Presented at the Benefits Management Forum and Expo, Chicago, IL.

Otis, J., Kelly, B., Jacobs, A., & Attridge, M. (1998). Two-year effect of a demand-side management program on outpatient utilization: Applied research brief–A summary of findings to date. In J. Burns & M. Sipkoff (Eds.), *Guide to Managed Care Strategies* 1998 (pp. 49-64). Faulkner & Gray, New York.

Parry, T. (2003, May). The business case for managing health & productivity. Presented at Ingenix Health Care Information Summit, Las Vegas, NV.

Pelletier, K.R. (2001). A review and analysis of the clinical- and cost-effectiveness studies of comprehensive health promotion and disease management programs at the worksite: 1998-2000 update. *American Journal of Health Promotion*, 16(2): 107-116.

Pratt, D. (2003). Driving breakthrough business and health strategies. *Health and Productivity Magazine*, 1(3): 12-13.

Riedel, J.E., Baase, C., Hymel, P., Lynch, W., McCabe, M., Mercer, W.R., & Peterson, K.W. (2001). The effect of disease prevention and health promotion on workplace productivity: A literature review. *American Journal of Health Promotion*, 15(3): 167-191.

Roman, P.M., & Blum, T.C. (2002). The workplace and alcohol problem prevention. *Alcohol Research and Health*, 26(1): 49-57.

Sciegaj, M., Garnick, D.W., Horgan, C.M., Merrick, E.L., Goldin, D., Urato, M., & Hidgkin, D. (2001). Employee assistance programs among Fortune 500 firms. *Employee Assistance Quarterly*, 16(3): 25-35.

Seligman, M.P. (1995). The effectiveness of psychotherapy. *American Psychologist*, 50(12): 965-974.

Shemo, J.P. (1985). Cost-effectiveness of providing mental health services: The offset effect. *International Journal of Psychiatry in Medicine*, 15(1): 19-31.

Sherman, B. (2004). Work-life balance: Key component of an integrated HPM strategy. *Health & Productivity Management*, 3(3): 19-20.

Smith, G.B., & Rooney, T. (1999). EAP intervention with workers' compensation and disability management. In J. Oher (Ed.), *The Employee Assistance Handbook* (pp. 337-360). NY: Wiley.

Stein, S.A. (2002). Why work/life and EAP should be integrated. *Behavioral Health Management*, 22(5): 32-41.

Teich, J.L., & Buck, J.A. (2003). Mental health services in employee assistance programs, 2001. *Psychiatric Services*, 54(5): 611.

Tyler, K. (2003, August). Mind matters: Reducing mental health care today may cost you more tomorrow. *HR Magazine*, 48(8): 54-62.

U.S. Department of Health and Human Services. (1999). *Mental health: A report of the Surgeon General*. Rockville, MD: U.S. Department of Health and Human Services, Substance Abuse and Mental Health Services Administration, Center for Mental Health Services, National Institutes of Health, National Institute of Mental Health.

Winn-Rogers, K. (2003). In sickness and in health. *Health and Productivity Magazine*, 3(4): 23-25.

Work & Family Connection. (2003). The most important work-life-related studies. Minnetonka, MN.

Chapter 3

Health and Productivity Management: The Integration of Health and Wellness into Employee Assistance and Work-Life Programs

Michael D. Mulvihill

SUMMARY. This article focuses on the emergence of Health and Productivity Management (HPM) as a context for understanding the integration of health and wellness into employee assistance and work-life programs. Major factors influencing the growth of HPM are raising medical costs as well as the rising incidence of obesity. The Wake-up Call to Corporate America underscores the need to manage these costs and improve health through the proactive alignment of health-related benefits and programs. HPM is described as an integrated approach to capture direct medical costs as well as the indirect costs associated with poor health and lost productivity. Critical design and implementation features that are likely to contribute to a successful integrated approach are described and highlighted. An HPM case example of a large pharmaceutical company examines a unique cross referral program including considerations for continuous improvement. Finally, the article concludes with key challenges related to marketplace competition, pricing pressures, concerns regarding the sub-optimization of programs and the influence of current health care system changes. *[Article copies available for a fee from The Haworth Document Delivery Service: 1-800-HAWORTH. E-mail address:*

[Haworth co-indexing entry note]: "Health and Productivity Management: The Integration of Health and Wellness into Employee Assistance and Work-Life Programs." Mulvihill, Michael D. Co-published simultaneously in *Journal of Workplace Behavioral Health* (The Haworth Press, Inc.) Vol. 20, No. 1/2, 2005, pp. 57-66; and: *The Integration of Employee Assistance, Work/Life, and Wellness Services* (ed: Mark Attridge, Patricia A. Herlihy, and R. Paul Maiden) The Haworth Press, Inc., 2005, pp. 57-66. Single or multiple copies of this article are available for a fee from The Haworth Document Delivery Service [1-800-HAWORTH, 9:00 a.m. - 5:00 p.m. (EST). E-mail address: docdelivery@haworthpress.com].

Available online at http://www.haworthpress.com/web/JWBH
© 2005 by The Haworth Press, Inc. All rights reserved.
doi:10.1300/J490v20n01_03

<docdelivery@haworthpress.com> Website: <http://www.HaworthPress.com>
© *2005 by The Haworth Press, Inc. All rights reserved.]*

KEYWORDS. Health and Productivity Management (HPM), integration, health and wellness, employee assistance, work-life, rising medical costs, health enhancement and disease prevention

INTRODUCTION

As a new partner in the integration dance, health and wellness presents new growth opportunities and perspectives for service integration. A key challenge regarding the migration toward integration amongst EAP, work-life and health and wellness programs is how to create a genuine, proactive integration while maintaining the integrity and impact of the different disciplines involved. While the concept of integration continues to prompt debate, there are ways to begin to understand genuine, proactive integrated programs.

The integrity of proactive integration, this author contends, resides in the design of the program, determination of key goals and metrics, the implementation process, ongoing follow-up and evaluation of the initiative/program. From a health and wellness (H&W) perspective, key issues and challenges will be discussed in this article along with the emergence of Health and Productivity Management (HPM).

GROWING CONCERNS ABOUT HEALTH CARE COSTS AND EMPLOYEE PRODUCTIVITY

In an editorial published in *the Journal of Environmental Medicine*, a Wake-up Call for Corporate America states that, "past attempts to control increases in health care costs have failed in the long term and that health care costs are on target to double in the next five years." Furthermore, an employee health care crisis is on the horizon unless funding is directed toward health enhancement programs and services that optimize employee health, which can reduce health care use, moderate cost increases, reduce illness absenteeism, and improve work performance (Whitmer, 2003).

The "wake-up call" is finally beginning to be heard. Soaring medical and productivity costs due to lifestyle/chronic disease have become well documented as a major influence on rising medicals costs. The growing obesity epidemic is costing employers billions. It is well known that obesity is a serious health risk linked to Type 2 diabetes, heart disease, breast and colon cancer, musculoskeletal disorders, depression and other psychological problems (NIH, 1998). There is a growing recognition that disease prevention and disease management programs can manage and contain the rise of health care costs.

In addition to rising health care costs, there is increasing concern about employee productivity. The workplace is undergoing significant changes and many employees in the new economy are no longer engaging in the physical labor of the past. "In this rapidly 'dematerializing' economy of knowledge work, 'intangible' capital is supplanting physical capital as the critical asset" (Sullivan, 2003). Knowledge workers in this paradigm, then, are increasingly viewed as human capital. Accordingly, investments made in "human capital" produce healthy returns. The key challenge is that the transfer of knowledge into performance depends heavily on "people's capacity and functionality, which is to say their health!" (Sullivan, 2003). Recent studies on presenteeism have become instrumental in illustrating the cost implications of lost employee productivity. Presenteeism costs are higher than medical costs in most cases by 18% to 60% for 10 health conditions (Goetzel et al., 2004). It is increasingly obvious that when an employee is at work but not engaged in their work, bottom line losses for employers occur.

The "wake-up call" therefore is not only about rising medical costs but also about the increasing costs associated with presenteeism and lost productivity. Employers are finally beginning to take serious steps to address these issues through Health and Productivity Management strategies and programs.

WHAT IS HEALTH AND PRODUCTIVITY MANAGEMENT (HPM)?

Health and Productivity Management (HPM) has grown out of considerable research over the past 10 years. This body of work documents the connection between health and productivity and its impact on corporate costs and profitability. Much of this research relates to the cost of poor health and lost productivity. HPM is specifically defined as:

> The integrated management of health and injury risks, chronic illness, and disability to reduce employees' total health-related costs

including direct medical expenditures, unnecessary absence from work, and lost performance at work. (IHPM, 2003)

Critical to an understanding of HPM is that the concept of productivity has been expanded to include presenteeism, absence management, and disability. Health-related productivity loss is therefore defined as unnecessary absence from work as well as "presenteeism." Presenteeism is understood as lost productivity because of health problems while at work and is a key focus in the HPM efforts.

An important dimension of the HPM field is the adoption of a person-centric rather than benefit-centric approach (Sullivan, 2003). That is to say, that the HPM model has sharpened its focus on the individual and their related health needs rather than a corporate benefit viewpoint. So, rather than "carving out" benefit programs like mental health, etc., the HPM strategy is to manage employees' total health and align various benefit programs together. This represents a major trend toward a more holistic view of a person and all their health-related conditions as well as supporting the trend towards integration of programs.

A CRITICAL MASS OF SUPPORT IS DEVELOPING FOR HPM INITIATIVES

According to the second annual employee benefits survey conducted by the Integrated Benefits Institute, 56% of employers have current or planned HPM initiatives. They also found that there is a shift in emphasis from post-absence disability management to disability prevention and health promotion (Risk and Insurance, 2004). Taking into account these developments, strong growth opportunities exist for HPM given the current commitment to HPM initiatives, the shift to prevention and a growing understanding of the value of integrated HPM programs.

In terms of the marketplace, clearly, the employees/purchasers are one of the major drivers for HPM. Typically, it is the Human Resources Dept., Corporate Benefits or Finance or Occupation Medicine who lead the charge on behalf of the employers. Supporting the employers, the major consulting firms such as Mercer, Towers Perrin and Wyatt Watson. The consulting firms are also encouraging health plans to begin providing coverage for these programs as well; however, they are moving at a somewhat slower pace.

Predictive modeling and data management firms are beginning to present powerful data, which documents both the direct and the indirect costs associated with poor health. HPM programs are using this data to not only design programs but also to develop and deliver tailored, proactive messages to high-risk individuals as well as individuals who make excessive use of the health care system. Key associations and membership groups that many providers belong to are also encouraging the migration toward integration along with HPM (IHPM, HERO, Integrated Benefits Institute, EAPA, EASNA, World at Work/AWLP, and SHRM–see Appendix).

The provider community (EAPs, work-life, health and wellness, disability) itself is beginning to strategically align their services in order to prepare for market changes with predicted health care consolidation. Many of the providers are beginning to develop strategic partnerships with a view toward providing seamless behavioral health interventions. The move toward strategic partnerships is seen as an important business strategy in terms of capturing market share and ultimate survival. Sparking controversy is that some of the larger behavioral companies have also made a strategic decision to build all of these programs internally. Important questions have been asked challenging whether the quality and integrity of programs will be maintained with internally built models by large corporate conglomerates.

PROGRAM DESIGN: GOALS, INTEGRATION CONTINUUM, AND KEY METRICS

Currently, much of the program design activity is centering around the integration of health and wellness into employee assistance and work-life, however, HPM initiatives broadly speaking include many employee benefit players like disability, disease management, workers compensation and so on. As the number of players increase, design issues become more complex. Clearly, in order to manage an increasing number of players, it is critical to clarify goals and objectives from a management perspective in order to sustain long-term top support. Resistance from supervisory staff as well as other people with key roles in the organization must be recognized and defeated.

One critical design feature of an integrative program is the degree to which it is proactive as opposed to reactive. Reactive integration can be characterized as loosely affiliated programs standing side by side with little or no connections. While reactive may sound a little pejorative, it could be argued that aligning related programs is the beginning step to an integrated effort. It could be further argued that this could represent the early identification of key issues. However, most would agree that serious integration efforts are ambitious and aim to be proactive.

Early research in the 1990s on program design introduced the concept of an Integration Continuum with three main stages, "Stand-Alones, Partnerships, and One-Stop Shopping" (Herlihy, 2000). The "Stand-Alone" stage would be viewed in this context as the more reactive whereas Partnerships and One-Stop Shops would generally be more proactive and integrated. The proactive model is viewed by most as having greater health outcomes and eventual return on investment (ROI).

Integration and closely tied core employee benefit programs are central to the person-centric approach and the realization of a true health and productivity initiative. Benefits design must be structured to prevent disease and disability. The goal is to offer preventive maintenance on people (not just on machines) through wellness and health promotion programs, preventive care (screenings), and EAPs and other work-life programs.

Finally, one must determine up-front, what the key metrics should be. Such measures allow employers/sponsors to determine the effect of health problems on employee functionality and performance. Two important metrics include the ability to calculate the equivalent "lost time" from this reduced capacity to work and to be able to "dollarize" the time loss using average pay rates. The most popular metrics involve measures of absenteeism and presenteeism. Ultimately, establishing key metric sets the stage for evaluating the program design and determining a return on investment.

SUCCESS WILL ULTIMATELY RESIDE IN THE IMPLEMENTATION!

It has been said that "knowledge is power" but in this case the power of integration will reside in implementation. Implementation that is tied to and supported by corporate mission and objectives sets the stage for a successful health and productivity initiative (Attridge and Gold, 2004). The difficult issues, however, revolve around stakeholder and staff training, roles, communication systems, and turf/boundary issues. Leadership is required around these critical issues when designing and implementing an integrated effort.

HPM CASE STUDY: PFIZER

One case example that illustrates key implementation issues was the development of a cross referral program at the pharmaceutical company Pfizer. This large company operates in a dynamic and competitive marketplace. They have developed a major organizational health and benefits initiative to ensure employees are fully engaged in their work. It is important to stress the point of developing employees who are "fully engaged" in their work. This alludes to the trend discussed earlier on the "dematerialization" of labor and the need to develop "human capital" in an environment, which relies so heavily on intellectual capacity. Accordingly, Pfizer requested that the EAP and wellness programs integrate their services. A cross referral program was created which required intensive design meetings, staff training and continuous follow-up. Many of the design meetings dealt with helping the EAP counselors and the health coaches become comfortable in their screening roles. Without a strong continuous focus on staffing and training issues, there is no question but that the effort would fail.

Operationally, in this case, the health and wellness program screens for depression, anxiety and other mental health issues and the EAP screens for tobacco cessation, weight management and stress management. Two majors assumptions supported the cross screening initiatives from the health and wellness perspective.

1. Health behavior change is thwarted by depression, anxiety, other mental health/substance abuse problems,
2. Change is further diminished by the lack of social and emotional support.

Cross screening is a proactive integrative strategy but it remains a challenge due to the labor intensity of it and the many assessment tasks that must be completed under usual circumstances. Therefore, strong leadership and consistent follow-up have been deemed vital.

It remains too early to evaluate the program as there are still too few enrollments in the cross referral program to establish any valid and reliable data. We found that the number of cross referrals was too low and it will require more access points if we are to improve participation. Tracking of the data remains difficult, which makes it hard to evaluate outcomes and satisfaction. Despite these measurement limitations, the program has been well received by the providers as well as by the end users and it continues to enjoy top management support. (Editors' Note:

see other case study of HPM in this volume–the Fairview Alive Program, pp. 263-279).

FINAL CONSIDERATIONS:
THE IMPACT OF THE HEALTH CARE SYSTEM
ON INTEGRATION AND KEY CHALLENGES

The "integration movement" is picking up steam. There is strong interest and positive collegial relationships between strategic providers and vendors. There is general agreement on integration goals and there is a willingness to experiment. Health and productivity initiatives and integration strategies are gaining exposure and experience. The fault lines are beginning to be identified and the strategic quality improvement process is well underway. However, there are extremely important trends to follow. As service providers integrate, will program quality be maintained, what impact will changes in the health care system have and who ultimately will lead integration efforts?

THE SUB-OPTIMIZATION OF PROGRAMS
AND COMMODIZATION

There is intense pressure between competing vendors and service providers "to get to market first." Purchasing decisions are highly scrutinized, competitive and have prolonged due diligence. For those service providers who developed strategic partnerships, there is additional scrutiny to show value and strong vendor synergy. There is also tremendous pressure to document short-term results and long-term return on investment (ROI). These pressures will threaten the scope and integrity of different fields and disciplines.

As one example shows, historically there was a great deal of misunderstanding about health and wellness as a field and its clinical applications. Health and wellness, in fact, has a very distinct set of powerful interventions aimed at improving health, controlling health care costs and improving employee productivity (Mulvihill, 2003). These interventions are evidence-based comprehensive programs that are based on solid research. Many programs have a strong ROI. However, the pressures to keep pricing low and bundle a variety of programs together will challenge the retention of robust programs and discipline integrity. Leaders in all fields need to rally and resist the threats of commodization and sub-optimizing of programs.

INFLUENCE OF THE HEALTH CARE SYSTEM ON HPM AND INTEGRATION

One need only follow the "yellow brick road" of risk to understand that eventually the health care system will become involved and have an impact on how Health and Productivity Management and integration initiatives will evolve. Mounting health care system changes including consumer-driven models of health care will alter the financing of health care and the employee will become more involved in health care purchasing and decision-making. A variety of strategies will expand including value purchasing of health care, consumer-driven health care, health savings accounts/high deductible plans, cost shifting, incentive-based health promotion programs and proactive health screening/ preventative medical plan design.

Finally, as the migration toward more integrated programs gains momentum the players will expand beyond health and wellness, EAP, disease management, disability and work-life. Integration will further evolve toward "higher levels" which will not only include employers and health plans but also large insurers and, yes, even the government. True sustained integration will require strong leadership and where will that come from and who will step up?

REFERENCES

Attridge, M., and Gold, D. (2004, October). Improving employee performance by improving health: Secrets of successful health and productivity management (HPM) programs. Presented at Institute for Health and Productivity Management 4th Annual Conference, Phoenix, AZ.

Goetzel, R.Z., Long, S.R., Ozminkowski, R.J., Hawkins, K., Wang, S., Lynch ,W. (2004). Health, Absence, Disability, and Presenteeism Cost Estimates of Certain Physical and Mental Health Conditions Affecting U.S. Employers. *Journal of Occupational Environment Medicine*, 46(4): 398-412.

Herlihy, P. (2000). Work-life and Employee Assistance Programs: Collaboration or Consolidation. In Karol Rose's *Work-life Effectiveness: Programs, Policies and Practices*. CT. KUBU Communications. Chapter 1.

Mead, P. (2004). Who Will Manage Employee Health? *Risk and Insurance: Emerging Strategies for Risk*, November, 1-3.

Mulvihill, M. (2003). The Definition and Core Practices of Wellness. *Journal of Employee Assistance.* October,13-15.

National Institutes of Health (1998). *Clinical guidelines on the identification, evaluation, and treatment of overweight and obesity in adults.* Bethesda, Maryland: Department of Health and Human Services, National Institutes of Health, National Heart, Lung, and Blood Institute.

Sullivan, S. (2003). The Power of Productivity. *Absolute Advantage, WELCOA,* August, 1-4.

Whitmer, W., Pelletier, K., Anderson, D., Baase, C., Frost, G. (2003). A Wake-Up Call for Corporate America. *Journal of Occupational Environmental Medicine.* September 45(9): 916-925.

APPENDIX

Organizations with Health and Productivity Management Focus

ALWP. Alliance for Work-life Progress. *www.awlp.org*
EAPA. The Employee Assistance Professionals Association. *www.eap-association.org*
EASNA. The Employee Assistance Society of North America. *www.easna.org*
HERO. Health Enhancement Research Organization. *www.the-hero.org*
IBI. The Integrated Benefits Institute. *www.ibiweb.org*
IHPM. The Institute for Health and Productivity Management. *www.ihpm.org*
SHRM. Society for Human Resource Management. *www.shrm.org*
World at Work. *www.worldatwork.org*

Chapter 4

Research on the Integration of Employee Assistance, Work-Life and Wellness Services: Past, Present and Future

Patricia A. Herlihy
Mark Attridge

SUMMARY. This article will focus on the research exploring the degree to which organizational integration of Employee Assistance, Work/Family and Wellness Programs has evolved since the early 1990s. The first study reviewed is the *National Study of EAP and Work/Family Programs* conducted in 1994 by Boston University's Center on Work and Family in which 100 of the top family friendly companies were inter-

[Haworth co-indexing entry note]: "Research on the Integration of Employee Assistance, Work-Life and Wellness Services: Past, Present and Future." Herlihy, Patricia A., and Mark Attridge. Co-published simultaneously in *Journal of Workplace Behavioral Health* (The Haworth Press, Inc.) Vol. 20, No. 1/2, 2005, pp. 67-93; and: *The Integration of Employee Assistance, Work/Life, and Wellness Services* (ed: Mark Attridge, Patricia A. Herlihy, and R. Paul Maiden) The Haworth Press, Inc., 2005, pp. 67-93. Single or multiple copies of this article are available for a fee from The Haworth Document Delivery Service [1-800-HAWORTH, 9:00 a.m. - 5:00 p.m. (EST). E-mail address: docdelivery@haworthpress.com].

Available online at http://www.haworthpress.com/web/JWBH
© 2005 by The Haworth Press, Inc. All rights reserved.
doi:10.1300/J490v20n01_04

viewed. Two major studies conducted under the guidance of the Employee Assistance Professional Association (EAPA) are then reviewed. The Phase I research conducted in 2001 was a large-scale survey of the professionals in fields of EAP and Work-life (N = 950). The Phase II research conducted in 2002 was comprised of two stages: A pilot study surveying vendors in the EAP and Work-life fields (N = 213) and a qualitative study consisting of in-depth interviews with vendors from all three professions (N = 79). The overall theme from this body of research is one of dramatically increasing movement and market demand for some form of collaboration/integration of service delivery. Finally, the chapter offers recommendations for further research regarding integration of services as well as implications for the professional fields. *[Article copies available for a fee from The Haworth Document Delivery Service: 1-800-HAWORTH. E-mail address: <docdelivery@haworthpress.com> Website: <http://www.HaworthPress.com> © 2005 by The Haworth Press, Inc. All rights reserved.]*

KEYWORDS. Integration, differentiation, collaboration, organizational integration, employee assistance programs, work-life and wellness programs, market demand and research

The future is already written. All we need is the confidence to accept it.

–Roger Cass (2001)

INTRODUCTION

The conceptual study of "organizational integration" originated back in the early 1960s when two Harvard Professors, Paul Lawrence and Jay Lorsch, conducted an industrial research study on collaboration (Lawrence & Lorsch, 1967). These researchers were aligned with the "contingency" school of organizational theory, but their work focused specifically on refining the concepts of integration and differentiation particularly from the perspective of functional managers. Lawrence and Lorsch posed the question of "what kind of organization does it take to effectively deal with various economic and market conditions." Their study conducted in 1963 examined 10 departments within 10 different corporations focusing on the level of integration or differentiation within each company. The researchers identified four specific dimensions, which accounted for the managerial difference in thinking and activity. It is this part of their research, which has relevance to the question of integration of Employee Assistance Programs (EAPs), Work-life (WL) and Wellness Programs. Each of these three programs has arisen on a separate track with a very specific ideology and skill sets. Attempts to integrate these services have met with resistance and road-blocks despite the positive economic reasons for streamlining services. Lawrence and Lorsch's earlier research provides some hints about both the decisions for integrating services within an environment as well as reasons why a differentiated model of service delivery might better fit certain organizations.

The first application of the concept of integration in the Employee Assistance field arose from Jack Erfurt, Andrea Foote and Max Heirich's pioneering research at the Ford Motor Company conducted through the University of Michigan's Industrial Relations Center. These researchers put forward the concept of "Mega brush"–Integrating Employee Assistance and Wellness (Erfurt, 1992). It is interesting to note that these researchers also discussed the issue of paying attention to tasks in various environments. They noted that both EAPs and Wellness Programs were focused on behavioral change; utilizing strategies for overcoming denial and reducing relapse; and both required organizational knowledge and skills. These researchers also noted some of the reasons for differentiating these two services, mainly that EAPs were problem focused on the so-called "walking wounded" and dealt with only approximately 15% of the workforce, while Wellness programs were targeted for the whole work-force in an attempt to provide preventative treatment to individuals with risk factors that might lead to serious illness in the future. In retrospect, this study provides a fascinating precursor of current trends in that it evaluated the interrelationships between EAPs and Worksite Wellness Programs from the context of the EA Core Technology.

This article will focus on the research since the early 1990s that focused initially on the interrelationship between EAPs and Work/Family Programs and then expanded in the late 1990s to incorporate the Wellness field. Specifically, this chapter briefly reviews the initial survey: *National Study of EAP and Work/Family Programs* conducted in the early 1990s and then the focus moves to a review of two major studies conducted under the Employee Assistance Professional Associations' (EAPA) guidance in the late 1990s. Finally, the chapter identifies potential future research projects and recommendations for the field. But first, it is helpful to understand the historical background for this research by examining the parallel developments of the EAP, Work-life and Wellness fields.

HISTORICAL BACKGROUND

EAPs

Early EAP services arose out of a need for a stable and skilled workforce during WWII. The severe shortage of male workers in New York City prompted some corporations to recruit workers from the Bowery district, resulting in the hiring of numerous alcoholics. Corporate medical directors postulated that it might be more cost effective to rehabilitate these problem drinkers than to have a revolving door employment policy (Trice, Harrison & Schronbrunn, 1981). This corporate approach led to the emergence of Occupational Alcoholism Programs (OAPs). These workplace-based programs grew in acceptance and number throughout the 1950s and 1960s. In the early 1970s, the U.S. government established the National Institute on Alcohol Abuse and Alcoholism (NIAAA) with the mission of promoting the growth and diffusion of EAPs throughout the United States. Also emerging at this time was the Association for Labor-Management Administrator and Consultants on Alcoholism (ALMACA).

During the mid 1970s, private EAP consulting firms such as Human Affairs International and Personnel Performance Consultants began to offer an alternative option for the delivery of EAP services from an internal model to an external model. In 1985, Blum and Roman reported that approximately 68% of EAPs were provided through internal programs. By 1988, this number had decreased to 58% (Blum & Roman, 1988). Data from 1994, estimates the number of internal EAP programs in the U.S. to be less than 20% (French et al., 1997). Unfortunately, there is no more recent empirical data that has addressed the question of the prevalence of EAPs. Another trend that began in the late 1980s was the expansion of EAP services to family members (Burden, 1987; Jankorski, 1988). A bit later in the early 1990s, Managed Mental Health Care made its entrance into the health care arena. Some credit the Managed Mental Health Care Movement with EAPs' decrease in focus on family issues during that time period. Meanwhile Work-life Programs were evolving in strength and popularity to deal with a range of family concerns. For a more detailed history of EAPs, refer to Davidson and Herlihy (1999).

WORK-LIFE PROGRAMS

Although there are reports of on-site child care programs during the Civil War and over 3,000 child care centers during World War II (Friedman, 1990), Work/Family Programs themselves trace their development to the Great Society policies of Lyndon Johnson. During the 1960s, the U.S. federal government sponsored the formation of county-based "child care coordinating councils" (4-Cs). These programs were specifically designed to coordinate childcare resources for preschool children so that Head Start Centers would be in close physical proximity to targeted children. The 4-Cs spawned the formation of childcare resource and referral programs that emerged in the corporate sector during the early 1980s. The creation of these employer-sponsored childcare resource and referral services is credited with the beginnings of the Work/Family and later the Work-life industry (Burud, 1984). By 1985, several private companies began administering referral networks for large multisite employers. This field grew throughout the early 1990s and eventually evolved into offering services focusing on helping today's workers deal with the multiple demands of careers, care of their children, and care of their aging parents.

Today, the Work-life field continues to evolve in two main areas: First, programmatic focus on supporting workers to balance the demands of both their work and personal life; and second, consultation to corporations on how to provide a family friendly supportive environment aimed at increasing creativity and productivity in the workplace (Gornick, 2002). For a more detailed history of work/family, refer to Rose (2000).

WELLNESS

Wellness Programs began in the 1970s as worksite-based offerings that focused on physical fitness centers and related health activities. One of the first fitness-oriented books, Kenneth Cooper's *Aerobics* (1968), had a major influence on this movement. The healthy living focus led to the spread of corporate fitness centers and then to modern, state-of-the-art corporate fitness facilities. Many of these now offer a range of occupational, physical therapy, rehabilitative, and alternative medical services. Another major development occurred when Erfurt, Foote and Heirich (1990) began conducting cardiovascular-oriented blood pressure screenings of employees in the auto industry. They were among the first to promote annual health screenings and to coordinate linkages between wellness programs and EAPs. These researchers illustrated the potential health care costs savings, and employee productivity when effective follow-up programs were put in place. The U.S. government, through the Department of Health and Human Services, has also played a major role in the spread of wellness and health promotion programs through its series of "Healthy People" reports. Together, these developments and influences set the stage for today's portfolio of comprehensive health management services, including fitness centers, health screenings, health risk appraisals, educational activities, behavior change programs, and high-risk interventions. The focus of health and wellness programs is expanding toward a total population approach including high-risk individuals, low-risk individuals and the chronically ill. Increasingly, health and wellness programs will become integrated with a variety of health and productivity programs including disease management, demand management (self-care), disability management, EAPs, Work-life initiatives, health care coverage and other key employee benefit programs. Health and productivity initiatives are becoming a major corporate strategy to improve employee health and to engage employees at a high level of workplace functioning. For a more detailed history of the Wellness field, refer to Mulvihill (2003).

The next section of this article focuses on the three major studies conducted over the last 15 years that have explored the relationships between EAP, Work-life and Wellness Programs. A brief overview will be given of the 1994 Boston University study and then a more detailed description will follow of the first two phases of EAPA's three-phase research endeavor that began in the late 1990s.

INTEGRATION RESEARCH STUDIES

National Survey of EAP and Work/Family Programs (1994)

In 1994, Boston University's Center on Work and Family conducted the *National Survey of EAP and Work/Family*. This study was funded by the Center's Work/Family Roundtable (Herlihy, 1997). At that time, the nation was experiencing a booming economy both nationally and internationally. Employee Assistance Programs, although battling with managed care, had already enjoyed a history of providing valuable service to the corporate bottom line. On the other hand, Work/Family Programs were a newer benefit and although popular with the media, were fighting desperately for funds and recognition in corporate boardrooms. Wellness, which was not included in this initial Boston University survey, was simultaneously taking hold in many corporations across North America. It was an interesting time to examine the interplay between EAP and Work/Family Departments in the corridors of corporate America.

Methodology

A national study group consisting of 100 corporations with employee populations of 1,000 or more was selected from established lists of family friendly companies. A total of 126 companies were approached and 96 completed the entire survey giving the study an overall response rate of 76%. A detailed survey instrument was designed with 157 different items divided into the following three sections: Section I–Basic Company Information; Section II–EAP Information and Section III–Work/Family Information. Both the EAP and Work/Family Manager were approached in the participating companies and asked to fill out their respective sections.

Results

This exploratory study was examining the nature and extent to which EAP and Work/Family Programs, individually and as intertwined functions, provided services to employees and their families. The specific research question was: Which factors inhibit or promote the integration between EAP and Work/Family Programs. A bivariate analysis was conducted to examine the association of seventy-five key independent variables that were organized according to Lawrence and Lorsch's theoretical framework. The sole variable that predicted integration from both the EAP and Work-life respondents was the use of interdepartmental committees to gain consensus on important policy decisions.

The other noteworthy response from this earlier research is that when respondents were asked if their organizations' EAP and Work/Family Programs were integrated in any fashion, the overwhelming response (75%) was no. And the respondents' comments further indicated that EAP and Work/Family were two separate, distinct services. Only 10% of the responding companies had "integrated" programs for EAP and Work-life services. This was a surprising finding given the sample selection of family friendly companies with populations over 1,000.

Summary

The major finding of the key predictor for integration being *the use of interdepartmental committees for important policy decisions* prompted a larger policy discussion about the future of these two services. It was an interesting time in the life development of both the EAP and Work/ Family field, and the question remained whether there would be any further collaboration down the road or if each profession would remain differentiated. The consensus at the time was that integration of services in any form was highly dependent on the corporate culture of the organization.

EAPA'S WORK-LIFE COMMITTEES' RESEARCH PROJECTS

During the time of the Boston University study, the Employees Assistance Professionals Association (EAPA) had also been tracking the development of the EAP and WL fields. In the late 1990s, with a dramatic downturn of the economy, EAPA felt that it was time to revisit the issue of whether collaboration or integration of EAP and WL benefits might be advantageous for both employers and employees. These events led to the creation of a Work-life Committee for EAPA (see Appendix) and significant collaboration between EAPA, leaders from the Employee Assistance Society of North America (EASNA), and the Alliance for Work-life Professionals (AWLP–now the Alliance for Work-life Progress). This committee began a three-phase research effort to empirically study three primary perspectives on the issue of integration–each with its own phase of research activity.

Phase I of the National Survey of EAP and Work-life Professionals (2001) focused on the individual professionals' perspective and involved a self-report survey of members from the three major associations (listed above). Phase II, the International Survey of EAP, Work-life and Wellness Vendors (2002), was conducted in two stages and assessed the perspectives of the specialized external vendor companies. The first stage of Phase II consisted of a brief mailed survey to the universe of EAP and Work-life vendors in North America. The second stage of Phase II followed up with an in-depth phone interview with a select representative group of EAP, WL and Wellness vendors. Phase III that was originally planned to replicate the earlier Boston University study is still under consideration at the time of this writing.

PHASE I–NATIONAL SURVEY OF EAP AND WORK-LIFE PROFESSIONALS (2001)

The first phase of the EAPA Work-life Committee Studies explored the breadth and depth of services provided by EAP and WL practitioners in the workplace. The organizational settings represented in this sample included both private and public sector practitioners across North America. While the survey primarily focused on programmatic aspects of both fields, questions were also asked about future integration opportunities.

A distinguishing feature of the Phase I study was the degree of collaboration of the three major professional associations in the EAP and Work-life fields–AWLP, EASNA and EAPA. This was the first time these organizations had ever collaborated on such a large project. A major factor in the success of Phase I was the process of gaining support and cooperation from these three associations in the exploration of the topic of integration of services.

The research question for this initial study was: "What are the current practices and future directions of the Employee Assistance and Work-life fields in relationship to the integration of services?" Integration was defined as "the collaboration among departments to achieve unity of effort" (Lawrence & Lorsch, 1967).

Methodology

Over 6,000 survey instruments were mailed and/or e-mailed when possible to members of all three professional organizations. A total of 950 completed surveys were returned giving the study an overall response rate of 15%. Interestingly, the response rate for the electronic method of data collection was 30% compared to the 7% for the postal method. It is important to note that while professionals from all three organizations responded, there were six times as many EAP respondents as there were Work-life respondents. This difference reflects the size variation in the membership levels of the three associations. Figure 1 displays the sampling and response rates for the study.

Sample

The sample was comprised of a diverse mix of professionals from both large and small organizations. Almost 40% of the sample worked at organizations with less than 100 employees, whereas 15% of re-

FIGURE 1. Survey Sampling Frame for Phase I 2001 Study of Professionals

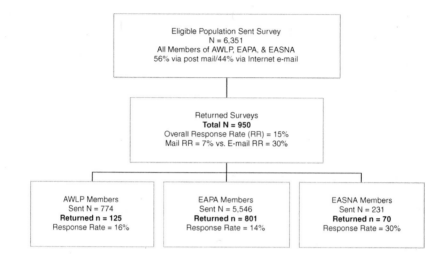

spondents were employed at organizations with a population over 20,000. This was also a seasoned group of professionals who reported their median years of experience in the field as 12 years for EAPs and 6 years for WL. About half of the respondents were from external programs, another one-third from internal programs and the remainder of respondents were from Human Resources, union, or consultant/research areas.

Results

For the purposes of this historical review of integration research, only two of the main findings of this study will be addressed: Professional Identity and Level of Collaboration of Services. The following is the first key result from Phase I:

Professional Identity

When respondents were asked directly about their professional identity, about 1 in 6 members characterized themselves as having a dual professional identity that was affiliated with "Both EAP and Work-life."

Respondents were asked whether they identified themselves as primarily an EAP professional, primarily a Work-life professional, both or "other." Seventeen percent of the total sample considered themselves *both* an EA professional and a Work-life professional. This result was somewhat consistent across the three professional associations: 16% of AWLP members, 19% of EAPA members, and 24% of EASNA members identified themselves as "Primarily both an EAP and WL professional."

The second key finding of the Phase I study revolved around collaboration of efforts at the service level. Respondents were given a list of 30 services, derived from a complete list of Work-life initiatives (Friedman & Wald, 2000) and EAPA's Core Technologies. For each listed service, survey respondents could select if it was offered by the EAP, Work-life, Other department, or any combination of these, or not offered at all at their company (for internal programs) or offered by the vendor they worked for (for external providers). A somewhat arbitrary cut-off level of 50% (offered by a majority) was used to determine a service as characteristic of that respondent's professional identity grouping. The responses led to the following key finding:

Services Provided

There is a significant level of collaboration/integration at the service level. The overlap of services in general tends to be in the non-core areas of each profession. In addition, there is an emergence of a "New Breed" of professional who seems to provide services across core areas of both professions.

A Venn diagram was created to visually identify both the cleavage and the common ground between EA and Work-life professionals in their service offerings (see Figure 2). The left circle shows the services characteristic of EAP professionals and the circle on the right shows the services characteristic of Work-life professionals. In the middle, where the two circles overlap, are the services offered by a majority of both professional groups. The pictorial rendition shows both groups offer various kinds of training, evaluation, information, and consulting services, with each group also offering certain services unique to their own individual field. What is more important to underscore is that the dual-identity professionals offer services from all three areas of the Venn diagram.

But to take this same data a bit further note in Table 1 that the top 11 services were considered characteristic of EAP and separate from

FIGURE 2. Venn Diagram of Services Offered (Phase I 2001 Survey of Professionals)

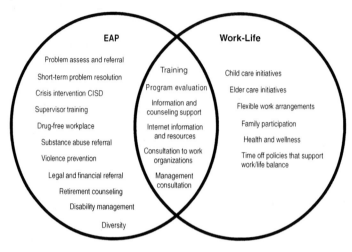

NOTE: Left Side of Diagram = Services offered by most EAP professionals but not by most Work-Life professionals. Middle = Services offered by most EAP professionals *and* by most Work-Life professionals. Right = Services offered by most Work-Life professionals but not by most EAP professionals.

Work-life. Most of these services are well known in the EA field as Core Technology functions. Conversely, the next six services listed are distinctly characteristic of Work-life's Core Competencies. The surprise in this section of Table 1 is Health and Wellness Promotion being in the Work-life categories. But perhaps the most significant finding related to the exploration of integration of services was the next seven items that were common to all three groups. The services common to both professions included consultation to work organizations, management consultation, training, information and counseling support, Internet information/resources and program evaluation. Table 1 also lists other services that were not offered by a majority of the primarily EAP or Work-life groups. These services nonetheless add to the profile of services available in the market in 2002.

Summary

This groundbreaking national survey of EAP and WL professionals offered a clear profile of an industry in transition. Although most of the professionals were aligned with only one of these fields, about 1 in 6

TABLE 1. Services Offered by Group: 2001 Survey Study of Professionals

Area	Service	EAP Primarily (n = 575)	Work-Life Primarily (n = 92)	Both EAP and Work-Life (n = 160)
EAP	**Problem Assessment and Referral**	97	29	**96**
EAP	**Critical Incident Stress Debriefing**	96	13	**90**
EAP	**Supervisor Training**	96	48	**88**
EAP	**Substance Abuse Treatment and Referral**	95	9	**93**
EAP	**Short-Term Problem Resolution**	93	9	**94**
EAP	**Drug-Free Workplace**	91	7	**89**
EAP	**Violence Prevention**	86	22	**88**
EAP	**Legal and Financial Referral**	78	41	**83**
EAP	**Retirement/Outplacement Counseling**	60	32	**69**
EAP	**Diversity**	57	29	**63**
EAP	**Disability Management**	51	12	**56**
Work-Life	**Child Care Initiatives**	26	**79**	**62**
Work-Life	**Elder Care Initiatives**	48	**76**	**71**
Work-Life	**Flexible Work Arrangements**	15	**71**	33
Work-Life	**Family Participation**	17	**62**	44
Work-Life	**Health and Wellness Promotion**	35	**57**	**52**
Work-Life	**Time Off Policies that Support Work-Life Balance**	26	**53**	41
Both	**Consultation to Work Organizations**	**94**	**73**	**93**
Both	**Management Consultation**	**92**	**55**	**88**
Both	**Training**	**87**	**72**	**86**
Both	**Information and Counseling Support**	**73**	**55**	**84**
Both	**Program Evaluation**	**74**	**80**	**68**
Both	**Internet Information and Resources**	**62**	**67**	**68**
Other	**Risk Management/Loss Reduction**	46	4	**53**
Other	**Career Development**	40	29	**50**
Other	**Strategic Alignment**	33	23	43
Other	**Community Involvement**	28	44	39
Other	**Welfare to Work Programs**	15	27	36
Other	**Internet Counseling Services**	14	25	24
Other	**Convenience Services**	5	46	18
	Total Offered (> 50%)	17	12	22

Note: Number indicates the percentage of the group who offers the service at their company. Bold indicates majority of group offers the service.

felt affiliated with both on a day-to-day working basis. Integration between EAP and Work-life is also occurring in the ways that both internal and external programs are structured–particularly in the use of vendor partnerships to augment primary services. This evolution toward greater integration has engendered ambivalent emotional reactions among professionals about their futures. It has also led to concerns about how to best structure collaborative efforts in order to retain the unique advantages of each field while maintaining the delivery of high quality services. Respondents generally commented that integration of EAP and Work-life is a "good thing" for the employee and for the company, but what remains less clear are the repercussions of this movement on the future of each of these professions.

PHASE II–INTERNATIONAL SURVEY OF EAP, WORK-LIFE AND WELLNESS VENDORS (2002): PILOT SURVEY

Overview

Phase II of the research project was broken down into two stages. The first stage involved distributing a brief written survey to the universe of all EAP and Work-life vendors. The main purpose of this pilot stage, conducted during the summer of 2002, was to identify the field of EAP and Work-life vendors in North America as well as pre-test certain questions for the more in-depth phone interviews conducted in the second stage during the fall and winter.

Methodology

The universe of EAP and Work-life vendors was established by consulting three noted lists in the industry: EAPA, AWLP and EASNA members, Monica Oss's Behavioral Health Management list, and Sue Seitel's Work/Family Connections Membership List (see Figure 3). This process yielded 1,225 vendors. A brief two-page questionnaire asking about current practices and future directions regarding integration of services was mailed out to each vendor company. A total of 213 usable surveys were returned for a response rate of 17%.

FIGURE 3. Survey Sampling Frame for Phase II 2002 Pilot Study of Vendors

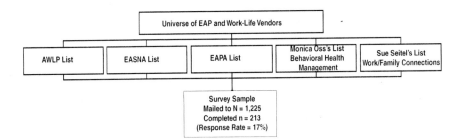

Sample

The overwhelming majority of the sample was from the United States (95%) and the remainder of the respondents was from Canada. Vendors classified themselves based on scope of market reach as local (89), regional (83) or national/international (39). Median totals of employees served by the vendors for these three markets were 26,000, 68,000 and 455,000, respectively.

Key Findings

There are two key findings from this pilot stage of the International Survey of EAP and Work-life Vendors that are worth noting. The first revolves around the notion of business models of service delivery, and the second involves predictions for the future of service delivery. Please note that in stage one of this study Wellness vendors were not included in the sampling. The following is the first key finding from this pilot study.

Business Model

About one-third of vendors have a business model with integrated offerings of some combination of services from EAP, Work-life and Wellness. The surprise here was the inclusion of Wellness.

The respondents most often cited two kinds of organizational business approaches. The "Focused" vendors offered services primarily in one field whereas the "Integrated" vendors offered services from more than one field (see Table 2). The Focused vendors comprised about two-thirds of the respondents and represented those companies offering primarily EAP, primar-

TABLE 2. Characteristics of Focused and Integrated Vendors: 2002 Pilot Study

Descriptive Characteristics	Type of Vendor	
	Focused (n = 143)	Integrated (n = 65)
Kinds of Services Offered	93% Primarily EAP 6% Primarily Work-Life 1% Primarily Wellness	43% EAP and Work-Life 37% EAP, WL and Wellness 14% EAP and Wellness 9% Work-Life and Wellness
Location: USA/Canada	97% / 3%	95% / 5%
Market Served:		
Local	50%	25%
Regional	37%	46%
National/International	13%	30%
Size (Median Number of Total Covered Employee Lives)	78,105	200,711
Annual Utilization Rate for Typical Customers	7.4%	8.1%
Clinical Service Delivery Channel:		
Face-to-Face	83%	81%
Telephone	15%	15%
Internet	2%	4%

ily Work-life, or primarily Wellness services. Integrated vendors comprised about one-third of the respondents and offered one of the following combinations of services: EAP and Work-life, EAP, Work-life and Wellness, EAP and Wellness, or Work-life and Wellness. The two business delivery models were quite similar on factors of location, annual customer utilization rate, and mix of service delivery channel. The major differences were that the Integrated vendors were more than twice as large and were in larger markets than the Focused vendors.

The second major finding of this pilot survey was the vendors' predictions for the future of possible integration. This was another surprise finding and greatly helped with the development of the survey instrument for the in-depth phone interviews. This second finding is described below:

Future Projections for Integration

Vendors reported that the market demand for integrated services had already doubled in the previous 5 years and was expected to double again in the next 5 years into the future.

When vendors were asked about current market demand for combined EAP,WL and Wellness Services, they reported a 50% increase in demand for integrated services compared to 5 years ago. However, when asked about anticipated Future Demand (defined as the market in 5 years), this number increased to 65%. In addition, when the parameters were widened to include EAP, WL and Human Resources and benefit functions, the Current Demand compared to 5 years ago was reported at a 48% increase while Future Demand spiked to 72%. Clearly, a strong perception exists among vendors for the programmatic and organizational integration of a wide variety of services.

Summary

The pilot vendor survey showed increased movement in the industry towards integration of employee services with a third of vendors offering integrated services. The market demand for integrated products had already increased since 5 years ago and was expected to more than double in the next 5 years. Clearly, the results indicated a shift toward a more integrated approach for service delivery. The personal reactions from respondents expressed a cautionary tone and some ambivalence about the general direction away from specialization and toward integration and increasingly complex vendor arrangements.

PHASE II–INTERNATIONAL SURVEY OF EAP, WORK-LIFE AND WELLNESS VENDORS (2003): IN-DEPTH INTERVIEWS

Overview

The self-report survey of vendors was intended largely as a pilot to refine the sampling targets and questions to be used in the in-depth qualitative interviews. Up to this point in time, the emphasis of the research had been on closely examining the extent of interaction between EAP and Work-life Programs and did not formally include Wellness vendors. However, results from the pilot study led to the discovery of ongoing collaboration between EAP and Wellness Programs, and to a smaller degree between Work-life and Wellness. Thus, Wellness was added to the sampling frame for the interview study. The goal of the in-depth interviews was to replicate the self-report vendor survey findings and explore in more detail the nature of integration between EAP, Work-life and Wellness Programs as experienced by vendors.

Methodology

A convenience sample was derived from the pilot phase list of EAP and Work-life vendors (n = 91) and an additional 10 Wellness vendors were added (see Figure 4). All of the 101 vendors on this list were initially contacted by letter and then with a follow-up phone call. Phone interview sessions were then scheduled and ranged in duration from 15 minutes to 2 hours. Interviews were completed with 79 vendors. A detailed instrument guide was used for each interview, but there was a great deal of freedom for the interviewer to deviate when necessary. This study was a time-consuming undertaking and resulted in over 400

FIGURE 4. Sampling Frame for Phase II 2002 Interview Study of Vendors

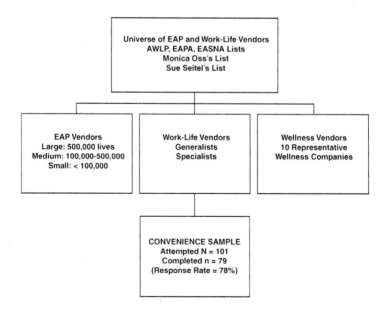

hours of interviews conducted by three researchers. The high response rate (79%) reflected the vendor's interest in the topic and a desire to tell their side of the integration story.

Sample

The sample was constructed to gather a balanced representation of perceptions on the issue of integration from three types of vendor ships. Thus, the sample featured 26 companies classified as Integrated, 23 as Primarily EAP, 24 as Primarily Work-life and 6 as Primarily Wellness from across the United States (86%) and Canada (14%). There was a range of market size among the companies interviewed, with 17 local, 24 regional, 30 national, and eight international vendors.

Results

While an abundance of data exists from these in-depth interviews, for the purposes of this summary chapter, the authors only highlight several key findings: the breadth of services provided, the emergence of Health and Wellness, the expected future of integration, and the personal reactions of vendors about what integration and collaboration means for quality of services.

Service Offerings

A list of 17 services was used to capture the range of offerings by each vendor (see Table 3). The average Integrated Vendor offered 13 distinct services with nearly 90% offering the following core services: EAP, financial, legal, health and wellness, risk management, elder care, program development and measuring program effect. The services offered by a majority of the Primarily Work-life vendors but not by the majority of EAP vendors included: childcare assistance, organizational, community outreach, administrative contracts, adoption, and convenience. In contrast, the only services offered by a majority of the Primarily EAP vendors but not by a majority of WL vendors were EAP services and risk management services. Indeed, of the 10 services offered by a majority of EAPs, seven were also offered by a majority of WL vendors. Among the Integrated Vendors, the majority offered the entire services characteristic of EAP and most of the services characteristic of Work-life.

TABLE 3. Percentage of Services Offered by Type of Vendor: 2002 Interview Study

Does your company offer this service?	Type of Vendor			
Product or Service:	Integrated	EAP Primarily	Work-Life Primarily	Total Sample
Sample size:	*n = 26*	*n = 23*	*n = 24*	*N = 79*
Measuring program effect	**92%**	**78%**	**79%**	**82%**
Health and wellness	**96%**	**74%**	**67%**	**81%**
Financial	**100%**	**91%**	**50%**	**79%**
Legal	**100%**	**74%**	**54%**	**75%**
Older/disabled adult care	**89%**	**61%**	**71%**	**73%**
Program development	**89%**	**57%**	**71%**	**72%**
EAP	**100%**	**100%**	21%	**72%**
Child care assistance	**81%**	39%	**92%**	**70%**
Risk management services	**89%**	**100%**	13%	**66%**
Policy development	**77%**	**65%**	**50%**	**65%**
Organizational	**50%**	44%	**75%**	**57%**
Adoption	**81%**	30%	**58%**	**57%**
Community outreach	46%	39%	**75%**	**56%**
Convenience	**65%**	30%	**54%**	48%
Executive coaching	**73%**	**52%**	13%	44%
Administrative contracts	23%	26%	**63%**	37%
Concierge	**50%**	17%	21%	28%
Average offered from 17 possible services	13.00	9.78	9.25	10.61

Note: Bold indicates the service is offered by a majority of that group. Total sample includes additional 6 Wellness vendors.

This overlap among the kinds of services provided suggests a clear expansion from the origins of both the EAP and Work/Family fields. While there are a few key differences between the kinds of services uniquely offered by the Primarily EAP and Primarily Work-life vendors, considerable overlap exists. This pattern of findings is very similar to what was found earlier in the professionals' survey and again in the vendor's survey.

Health and Wellness

As can be seen in Table 3, Health and Wellness services was the second most frequent offering of all 17 services (81%). Virtually all of the Integrated vendors (96%) claimed that they provided a Health and Wellness offering, while EAPs at 74% and WL at 67% were also strong proponents of the health awareness movement. Respondents were given the following breakdown of potential wellness services: smoking cessation, health education, consultation on nutrition and health issues, referrals to health and wellness providers, health fairs and screenings, health risk assessments, telephonic nurse advice lines, fitness discounts and disease management. This linkage with the physical or medical side of employee health reflects a growing awareness in the corporate sector for increased attention to all health issues. The spiraling costs of health care benefits, currently 15% GNP (NYT), is forcing corporate executives to take a closer look at this area and to provide a more preventative health focus in the workplace.

Future Predictions

The third major finding from the interview study revolved around the anticipated future direction of the field. Vendors were asked to estimate if market demand would be less, the same, or more for various kinds of services. Key results are presented in Figure 5. Clearly, the growth in the industry is expected to be in products and services that feature some form of integration. While approximately three-fourths of vendors expected growth in various forms of partnership arrangements, only 1 in 4 vendors expected business growth for stand-alone EAP or Work-life products.

Vendors also made the following predictions about general market trends:

- 62% of the marketplace would be integrated in the next 5 years (by 2007)
- 66% of those integrated programs would be provided by a single vendor

Thus, 2 out of 3 vendors in the near future were expected to offer integrated service delivery with a majority controlled by a single vendor. This latter result is interesting and perhaps troubling in that the sample

FIGURE 5. Percentage of Vendors with Predictions of *Greater* Market Demand in Next 5 Years (versus Same or Less Demand) for Integrated and Stand-Alone Services

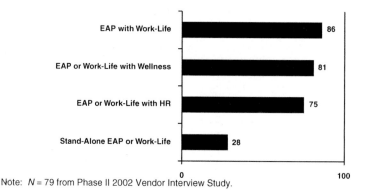

Note: *N* = 79 from Phase II 2002 Vendor Interview Study.

population interviewed was comprised of 22% local vendors; 30% regional vendors; 38% national vendors and 10% international vendors. Thus the results make one wonder whether these respondents truly had a crystal ball or were overly concerned about their companies outsourcing to larger national vendors. It is also unclear what this type of consolidation and therefore lack of competitive alternatives might mean for the quality and range of services offered.

Qualitative Comments

The final area of the in-depth interview study results focused on a range of qualitative responses. Three areas seemed to raise the most interest and concern amongst the vendors: The expansion of Web services; size issues; and quality of service delivery.

Respondents were asked what changes in products will come about in the future as a result of new technologies. The overwhelming response was expansion of Web services (77%). This finding in itself was not a surprise, but it was interesting to note that the EAP vendors commented on this development significantly more often (85%) than either Work/Family (67%) or Wellness (60%). Integrated vendors also claimed this as a major wave of the future (83%).

The issue of "company size" arose from a question inquiring about what their company might look like in five years. While over half of the vendors raised this as a concern, a surprising difference was that 69% of the Work-life respondents were very concerned versus 20% of the Wellness respondents. The Wellness respondents also answered this question differently than the other groups. When asked about the future of their company, Wellness vendors tended to comment on anticipated integration and partnerships with other fields far more often (80% versus 33% for total sample), and with a more positive tone. For example: one Wellness respondent commented that "integration of services will increase across needs and interests and have a cascading effect." This respondent used the example of the Quit Line–Smoking Cessation Program as an example of how one employee services falls into another.

The last significant qualitative finding was the overarching worry among vendors that quality is being sacrificed for cost-cutting efficiency. Respondents over and over again verbalized their concern that changes in the marketplace–whether integration of services, economy, downsizing or globalization of efforts–were all decreasing the quality of service to both the employee and the employer. Two telling quotes from both the WL and EAP field exemplify this concern. "Work-life professionals are an important voice in Corporate America, and because of the economy and many lay offs . . . we will hear less of their voices." And "the loss of the original concept of EAP–the identification of the troubled employee–has led to this service being relegated to merely a gatekeeper function. . . ."

CONCLUSIONS AND FUTURE DIRECTIONS

The research challenge of these studies was to capture an accurate snapshot of current practices, as well as emerging visions of future trends based on the self-reports of professionals, vendors and corporate managers. As the research evolved, it became clear that the concept of organizational integration was even more complex than initially thought. Lawrence and Lorsch's earlier work on integration simply defined the concept as collaboration or unity of effort. These researchers found it hard to quantify that concept. Structural forms of integration such as EAP and WL programs residing in the same department, or reporting to the same manager were often taken to mean a program was integrated. Clearly there exists a great diversity in reported methods of delivery of services. This research revealed numerous combinations of internal staffing arrangements for both areas, internal staffing with services contracted from external vendors, and partnerships between external vendors. But it was the voice of concern of many respondents that probably truly captured the complexity in sorting out the true process of integration.

One dramatic illustration of the integration movement over time, no matter how one defines true integration, is captured in Figure 6. The percentage of companies claiming an integrated service has gone from 10% in 1994 (BU Study) to 33% in 2002 (Vendor Study) to a projected 62% in 2007 (Vendor Study). Whatever is learned from the many detailed findings of this series of research studies, the most important result is simply that integration is poised to be the dominant business approach for this industry by the end of decade, if not sooner.

FUTURE DIRECTIONS

Many questions remain unanswered in the area of integration of services. The actual definition of integration despite the early work of Lawrence and Lorsch and the more recent definition by Swihart and

FIGURE 6. Percentage of Companies with Integrated Services: By Year

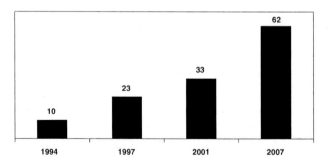

Note: 1994 = Study of Employers. 1997 = Study of Employers. 2002 = Study of Vendors. 2007 is projected in next 5 years from 2002 Vendor Study.

Thompson (Chapter 6, this volume) still remains elusive to many professionals and thus requires further exploration. Many models of integration exist in today's marketplace as can be seen in the various articles in this collection, but there is still a need to operationalize a measurable definition of this concept. Specifically a clear definition is needed to further the study of effectiveness and efficiency of this collaborative approach to employee benefits.

There has been discussion about replication of the original Boston University study in order to obtain longitudinal data concerning the integrated approach to service delivery. One of the main findings of the original research was that corporate culture was the main predictor of whether a company would pursue an integrated approach. It would be interesting to revisit this question in order to facilitate business decisions about what type of approach best fits specific employee populations and business interests. In addition to the interest of replicating the earlier employer study new questions have arisen. The following is a list of recommended areas to be included in future research endeavors on this topic of integration of services:

- Documentation of existing prevalence of integrated programs
- Rationale for choice of integrated programs–ideological vs. cost effectiveness
- Definition of integration–operationalize the definition
- Predictors for success of integrated programs
- Identification of measurement tools for integrated programs
- Relationship to health and productivity movement
- Development of quality measure for integrated programs

Finally, the whole arena of workplace benefits and service delivery is driven by two often conflicting needs: the employers and the employees. Employers focus primarily on benefit cost and efficiency of delivery while employees struggle with the complexity of life's demands at home and work. Therefore, questions of whether to and how to best provide certain services can be expected to remain under constant scrutiny.

The movement towards organizational and structural integration of service delivery programs, which is well documented in the aforementioned studies, continues to raise difficult questions. Considerable work remains to identify demonstration models of integration that can be studied for their differing levels of programmatic effectiveness and efficiency. The concern over the quality of services looms large in the minds of many professionals, particularly in the EAP and WL arenas. Lastly, and of growing concern and importance, is the evolving convergence of three previously separate professions: Employee Assistance, Work-life, and Wellness. Competitive turf wars between these professional groups still abound in some companies while others embrace the notion of collaboration of effort. According to Roger Cass, the future may already be written but the professional fields are struggling for the confidence on how to best accept it.

REFERENCES

Burden, D. and Googins, B. (1988). *Balancing job and home-life survey.* Unpublished Report: Boston University.

Burud, S., Aschbacher, P., and Mcroskey, J. (1984). *Employer sponsored day care: Investing in human resources.* Boston, MA: Auburn House.

Davidson, B. and Herlihy, P. (1999). The EAP and work/family connection. In J. Oher (Ed.), *The Employee Assistance Handbook* (pp. 405-419). New York: Wiley.

Erfurt, J., Foote, A. and Heirich, M. (1992, Summer). Integrating employee assistance and wellness: Current and future core technologies of a Mega brush program. *Journal of Employee Assistance Research*, 1-31.

French, M.T., Zarkin, G.A., Bray, J.W. and Hartwell, T.D. (1997). Costs of employee assistance programs: Findings from a national survey. *American Journal of Health Promotion*, 11(3): 219-222.

Friedman, D. (1981). *Management by parent objectives.* Unpublished doctoral dissertation, Harvard University, Cambridge, MA.

Friedman, D. and Wald, R. (2000). *Work-life Initiative.* William M Mercer Study and Bright Horizons Survey Report.

Gornick, M.E. (2002, May/June). Work-life core competencies. *EAPA Exchange*, 11-13.

Herlihy, P. (1997, Spring). Employee assistance programs and work/family programs: Obstacles and opportunities for organizational integration. *Compensation and Benefits*, 22-30.

Herlihy, P., Attridge, M. and Turner, S. (2002, January/February). The integration of employee assistance and work-life programs. *EAPA Exchange*, 10-12.

Jankorski, J., Holtgraves, M. and Gerstein, L. (1988). A systematic perspective on work and family units. In E. Goldsmith (Ed.), *Work and Family Theory, Research and Implications*. Sage Publications.

Lawrence, P. and Lorsch, J. (1967). *Organization and Environment: Managing Differentiation and Integration.* Illinois: Richard D Irwin, Inc.

Mulvihill, M. (2003). The definition and core practices of wellness. *Journal of Employee Assistance*, 33(3): 13-15.

Roman, P. and Blum, T. (1988). The core technology of employee assistance programs: A reaffirmation. *The Almacan*, 18(8): 17-22.

Rose, K. (2000). *Work-life Effectiveness: Programs, Policies and Practices*. CT: Kubu Communications.

Rubin H. (2001, July). Roger Cass: The last optimist. *Fast Company*, 48: 88.

Swihart, D. and Thompson, D. (2002, September/October). Successful program integration. *EAPA Exchange*, 10-12.

Trice, Harrison and Schronbrunn. (1981, Spring). A history of job-based alcoholism programs 1900-1955. *Journal of Drug Issues*, 171-198.

Chapter 5

Perspectives on the Integration of Employee Assistance and Work-Life Programs: A Survey of Key Informants in the EAP Field

David A. Sharar
Edward Hertenstein

SUMMARY. A recent qualitative study explored perceptions of critical issues and challenges from the point of view of experts and key informants working in diverse roles in the Employee Assistance Program (EAP) field (Sharar & Hertenstein, 2005). One of the central themes that came out of the study is that EAPs have become a type of platform for the expansion of integrated collateral services, chiefly work-life (WL) programs. This paper presents a variety of perceptions and opinions from experts in the EAP field, both pro and con, on the growing convergence of EA and WL programs, including the rationale to integrate, segregate, and concerns regarding the diffusion of traditional and core EAPs. The paper concludes with the authors' perspectives on implications for the EA field, along with the need to find ways to measure if and when integration leads to employee and organizational improvement. *[Article copies available for a fee from The Haworth Document Delivery Service: 1-800-HAWORTH. E-mail address: <docdelivery@haworthpress.com> Website: <http://www.HaworthPress. com> © 2005 by The Haworth Press, Inc. All rights reserved.]*

[Haworth co-indexing entry note]: "Perspectives on the Integration of Employee Assistance and Work-Life Programs: A Survey of Key Informants in the EAP Field." Sharar, David A., and Edward Hertenstein. Co-published simultaneously in *Journal of Workplace Behavioral Health* (The Haworth Press, Inc.) Vol. 20, No. 1/2, 2005, pp. 95-104; and: *The Integration of Employee Assistance, Work/Life, and Wellness Services* (ed: Mark Attridge, Patricia A. Herlihy, and R. Paul Maiden) The Haworth Press, Inc., 2005, pp. 95-104. Single or multiple copies of this article are available for a fee from The Haworth Document Delivery Service [1-800-HAWORTH, 9:00 a.m. - 5:00 p.m. (EST). E-mail address: docdelivery@haworthpress.com].

Available online at http://www.haworthpress.com/web/JWBH
© 2005 by The Haworth Press, Inc. All rights reserved.
doi:10.1300/J490v20n01_05

KEYWORDS. Collateral services, employee assistance, work-life, integration

INTRODUCTION

A recent qualitative study explored perceptions of critical issues and challenges from the point of view of experts and key informants working in diverse roles in the Employee Assistance Program (EAP) field (Sharar & Hertenstein, 2005). One of the central themes that came out of the study is that EAPs have become a type of platform for the expansion of integrated collateral services, chiefly work-life (WL) programs. The study suggests that while EAPs are a dynamic and growing field of practice, there is tension arising out of the dissipation of EAP as a specialized field. At the same time, there is also recognition that EAPs need to adapt to the changing needs of employers and the workforce as a whole by combining with WL. This article will briefly review the methods of the study, followed by a presentation and analysis of the data relative to the integration of EAP and WL services.

SAMPLING

This emergent sample was not entirely determined in advance but began with the identification of key informants and leaders in the field in order to interview a diverse and representative sample. Purposive sampling, with a mix of stratification and snowballing, was employed to achieve a high variation of multiple perspectives. The initial list of participants contained 30 "experts" with varied and long-tenured leadership roles in the EA field, including:

- Executives in external national/international EA firms (mostly investor-owned companies that offer EAP along with specialty insurance products and other services).
- Executives in external local/regional EA firms (EAPs based in not-for-profit health systems or proprietor-owned practices).
- Directors or labor representatives for internal programs (EAPs based within a company or government entity as a department).
- Researchers, consultants, or program auditors (participants who do not operate an EAP but conduct research or evaluate EAPs).
- Board members or staff for EA's professional associations.

The initial list was called at random until at least one participant from each stratum agreed to be interviewed. Access to these participants was enhanced via collegial networking and introductory e-mails and letters that described the study, along with appropriate informed consent materials. Participants were used to identify other potential participants with extensive experience in the EA field, and they in turn others, until the data seemed redundant. This type of sampling, to the point of saturation, yielded a more convincing description of events and issues. The sampling methodology allowed for mainstream cases as well as atypical cases in order to understand the depth and range of issues. A total of thirty participants were interviewed in all regions of the continental United States and Canada. Nine participants were Canadian and the remaining twenty-one were from the U.S.

INTERVIEW GUIDE

A simple interview guide was developed that contained an agenda for the conversations as well as some prepared questions. The agenda was open-ended and viewed as a way to generate dialogue rather than a packaged approach to gather information. The interview guide posed the following three questions:

- What are the three most critical issues facing the EA field?
- What steps should the field take to address these issues?
- What are your predictions for the future of the field?

Analysis of Themes

Data was evaluated through a process of content analysis and the identification of emerging themes. Open-ended questions served as the conceptual framework and guide for this analysis. A template was constructed by examining field notes and responses to the set of questions, probes, and prompts used by each interviewer. By examining sentences or word segments in response to questions or probes, particular themes were identified and attached to a section of field notes. Chunks of data were sorted and clustered around non-redundant themes.

The study revealed four major themes: (1) Commodification and Pricing; (2) Demonstrating Effectiveness Through Research; (3) Elevating Quality Through Standards Enforcement; and (4) Dilution of Service from Expansion and Integration with WL. The balance of this paper will focus on the fourth theme, the Diffusion of Core EAP and Integration with WL. The following analysis represents a synthesis of qualitative participant data, and where applicable, citations from the literature. The analysis also represents a variety of mixed opinions and observations, both pro and con on the subject of integration, grounded in participant data. The closing section expands on the analysis by discussing implications for the EA field based on the authors' interpretation and perspective.

DIFFUSION OF CORE EAPs

Participants generally shared an appreciation of the concept of integration, that there are opportunities to attain a better match between clients' needs and services rendered. They recognize that creating a more coordinated continuum for delivering services can result in a "whole" that is greater than the sum of its parts. Their concern mainly lies in the array of expansive activities now embraced in many EA contracts, and that this expansion has made EAPs less understood by employers and clients and even harder to define. Several participants believe that the typical benefits purchaser would have a difficult time describing, with any clarity, what services their EAP actually provides, and descriptions would vary considerably from one company to another. Participants identified numerous services that are now integrated or added to program features broadly labeled EAP:

- Managed behavioral health care
- WL services (dependent-care resource and referral)
- Legal consultation and assistance
- Credit counseling, debt management, financial, and retirement planning
- Wellness screenings and corporate health education
- Organizational development, training, and executive coaching
- Drug-free workplace and drug testing services
- Critical incident intervention and planning
- Web-based, online counseling and education

The original workplace mission of EAP–to identify impaired workers, get them into treatment, and back to work–is giving way to a range of mutated products and services. Figure 1 represents the territorial ex-

FIGURE 1

Territorial Expansion

On-line Assistance

Coaching and Organizational Development

Work-Life/Dependent Care Services

Critical Incident Stress Management

Workplace Violence/Threat Management

Behavioral Health Benefits Management

Legal and Financial Issues

Wellness and Health Promotion

Short-term
Counseling Models

Drug-free Workplace
Movement

Broad Brush
EAP's

Occupational
Alcoholism

pansion of EAP from its incubation in the occupational alcoholism field to its current plethora of products and services. One participant stated:

> We don't know when these complementary products actually integrate with a core EAP or when they devour an EAP. Some EAPs are now so diffuse and tangential we can't really call them an EAP.

A majority of participants were concerned that a profession born out of a conviction to help troubled employees, usually alcoholics and addicts, has entered a period when Human Resource (HR) professionals and labor representatives are involved in fewer company referrals to EAP. HR professionals and labor representatives seem to be increasingly losing direct knowledge of and participation in successful recoveries of addicted workers. Participants generally suspect that substance abuse referrals to EAP have dropped and are continuing to drop, even though the percentage of employees who are problem drinkers and substance abusers has changed very little over the past several years. According to these participants, if the EAP is not the employer's primary strategy of intervention to help restore substance abusers to productivity, then perhaps the field has eroded an important and core function.

Recognizing the need for the field to adapt to changing workforce demographics and employer problems, these participants are not arguing against integration and expansion. They want the EA field to find ways to grow and adjust without abandoning the needs of workers with substance abuse and other serious behavioral health issues. A few were also quick to mention the proliferation of disease management initiatives designed to intervene with employees who are at-risk of a chronic or costly illness (such as clinical depression or post-traumatic stress disorder). Disease management type initiatives have been practiced by "true" or "core" EAPs for decades, albeit it in a less systematic fashion. The point is the targeted identification, intervention, and monitoring of high-risk employee "outliers" should remain a central element of any concerted and serious program. Disease management, as a model, is being embraced by purchasers as the way to manage the costs of long-term or co-morbid, complex illnesses. The approach that integrates WL, these participants argue, may inadvertently distract EA providers away from the important task of identifying and following high-cost or high-risk employees and dependents. As integration between EA and WL is currently structured, there is simply not enough emphasis on employees with substance abuse and moderate to serious mental health problems.

RATIONALE FOR INTEGRATION WITH WORK-LIFE

Although there has been considerable debate in the EA field as to where to draw the lines between EAP and WL (Herlihy, 2000), the most common form of integration supported by the majority of participants is with WL services. WL services assist employees with elder/child care resource and referral needs, as well as the broader issue of helping employees balance work and family obligations.

Participants generally argued that both WL and EAP share a common mission–to help employees with personal and family issues that hinder and interfere with productivity and concentration on the job. Even though the foci of the two fields are different, with EAP concentrating more on behavioral health and WL dealing with normal developmental life-events, the rationale to integrate these services on the surface appears compelling, and among many of the larger EAP/WL vendors, has, in theory, already occurred.

Consider a case example put forth by a participant: A multiproblem employee who, in addition to going through a divorce, has an elderly, frail parent in need of assisted-living, a child without reliable day care, mounting credit card debt, and increased occupational stress with changes at work. An employer-sponsored benefit and resource, with a single access point and integrated EA and WL model, could take all of these adverse circumstances into account and quickly arrange for information, educational materials, counseling, and customized referrals for each of these problems. All of these issues can affect job performance, and are well suited for a variety of blended EA and WL interventions that require coordination via a single point of access. These interventions could include short-term counseling for adjustment to divorce and job stress, assistance in identifying and navigating the network of elder care and child care resources, and concise, educational information available online and through mail about all of these issues. Under the traditional separate program model, an EA practitioner would help with the adjustment to divorce but not necessarily the child/elder care problem, and the WL consultant would not address the divorce issue.

Participants also mentioned that employers seem to welcome this convergence of EAP and WL, as evidenced by the many EA providers that have either merged or collaborated with WL vendors (Herlihy, Attridge, and Turner, 2002). Employers who value the reduction in purchasing, implementation, and communication costs increasingly view this integration as an all-encompassing benefit (Williman, 2001). Both EA and WL providers also like the efficiencies that result when similar operational infrastructures are combined (call centers, education and referrals, reporting systems, etc.). Another benefit cited by participants for integrating these two programs is the reduction of social stigma that is sometimes associated with using an EAP. Under combined programs, employees can call for assistance with normal adaptation issues (i.e., WL) and seamlessly receive assistance for issues that could be associated with mental health or family dysfunction, without necessarily enduring the psychological stress of contacting an EAP and presenting with a "clinical" type mental health issue.

One participant summed up with the following rationale:

Combining EAP and WL into a comprehensive service suite to handle all of life's big and small hurdles is a patently sensible and obvious concept that is silly to reject. I can see a possible case for not integrating EAP with managed behavioral health care, since these two programs may have conflict of interest issues. But EAP and WL have similar goals and infrastructure requirements, and ultimately offer a greater capacity to help employees and families.

RATIONALE TO SEGREGATE

Despite the compelling case to fully integrate EAP and WL, some participants contend the sustainability for the future of merging these programs remains unknown and not grounded in evidence-based practice. WL and the behavioral-health professions (i.e., clinical social work, clinical psychology, psychiatry, marriage and family therapy, mental health and substance abuse counseling) are traditionally two separate areas of professional socialization and training. Both fields have separate histories, professional associations, conferences, trade journals, and intervention approaches.

Even the historical and predominant delivery mediums are different. EA providers are accustomed to face-to-face intervention, usually through a network of subcontracted professional clinicians or employed EAP staff. Conversely, WL tends to rely upon Internet-mediated and telephone-based mediums provided from a distance. Consensus in the EAP field regarding the validity and efficacy of telephone and online counseling versus face-to-face is hard to find, in part due to the paucity of empirical evidence on the comparative effectiveness of various mediums. Despite the lack of evidence, the number of expressive opinions and unfounded claims continues to explode (Ragusea and Vandecreek, 2003). A recent review of the literature by Copeland and Martin (2004) concerning Web-based interventions reports a descriptive feast with scientific famine.

A few participants criticized integrated call centers that combined the intake, triage, and phone intervention process for using EA practitioners, who do not possess an adequate skill repertoire to be of service to employees with dependent care needs. Conversely, WL professionals who have no knowledge of behavioral health assessment and treatment are handling EAP cases. The two sets of professionals do not know enough about the other's training, practice, and skill set to be of value to the multiproblem client with both WL and EAP issues. Davidson and

Herlihy (1999) have also discussed this concern about inadequate and divided skill sets.

In addition to these differences, some participants noted that integration of EA and WL tends to be virtual than actual. For example, does the telephone transfer of an EAP client to a WL vendor in another state really constitute an integrated service? This participant subgroup cautions that true integration requires new structures, relationships, procedures, and training experiences that are time consuming and resource intensive to make truly functional. These participants point to the large number of failed integration initiatives in health care as evidence that true integration is hard work and requires exceptional skills in management and collaboration. Moreover, as stated by one participant:

> Many partnerships among managed behavioral health, EAP, and WL vendors tend to exist mainly on paper and can be diagnosed with the failure to thrive syndrome. They maintain the appearance of functionality for marketing purposes but in reality provide less focused service than was historically provided by the single entity. The actual results of integration don't match up to the claims.

TO INTEGRATE OR NOT?
IMPLICATIONS FOR THE EA FIELD

Perhaps the real measure of success of the EA field's integration with collateral products such as WL is whether the act of integration has produced a coordinated "whole" continuum better than actions undertaken by separate single agents. On a practical basis, the success of the integrated EAP and WL model may be very dependent on how well a vendor partnership or merger actually functions. In the general health care arena, estimates suggest up to half of all partnerships that form do not survive the first year; of those that do, many falter when they attempt to implement a new combined system or intervention (Lasker, Weiss, and Miller, 2001).

The combined EA-WL field cannot simply declare that integration is working because purchasers are requesting or buying the integrated product. We need to find ways to measure if and when integration leads to employee and organizational improvement, not just the provider's desire for growth, market share, and the testing of new products. Validating the logical theory of integrating EAP and WL requires marshaling evidence from existing research, which is all too often deemed "proprietary," and conducting new research on the relative effectiveness of an integrated model. This requires collaboration among EA-WL providers and HR benefits purchasers in a way that translates our cause above the daily noise of competitive jargon, low rates, new products, and embellished claims of success. One participant advocated for new partnerships between employers, EA-WL vendors, and academic researchers in the hopes of linking science and research to processes, large secondary databases and actual measurements of outcomes. This participant also suggested the following research study to examine the outcomes associated with integrated versus non-integrated programs: Clients who are served in integrated programs could be compared with similar clients who are served in non-integrated EA-only programs. These two groups could be compared across multiple productivity outcome measures (absenteeism, workers' compensation claims, medical and disability claims, other productivity measures). If better outcomes arise from integrated programs, such findings would provide evidence that integration contributes to outcomes valued by employers. In order to accomplish this type of research, the EA and WL field needs to acknowledge that a full understanding of the impact of an integrated or stand-alone service on organizational productivity has been lacking and will not emerge without a stronger research base.

REFERENCES

Copeland, J. & Martin, G. (2004). Web-based interventions for substance abuse disorders: A qualitative review. *Journal of Substance Abuse Treatment*, 26, 109-116.

Davidson, B. & Herlihy, P. (1999). The EAP and work-family connection. In J. Oher (Ed.), *The employee assistance handbook*. New York: John Wiley & Sons.

Herlihy, P. (2000). Employee assistance and work/family programs: Friends or foes? *Employee Assistance Quarterly*, 16 (1/2), 33-51.

Herlihy, P., Attridge, M., and Turner, S. (2002). The integration of employee assistance and work-life programs. *EAPA Exchange*, January/February, 10-12.

Lasker, R., Weiss, E., & Miller, R. (2001). Partnership synergy: A practical framework for studying and strengthening the collaborative advantage. *Milbank Quarterly*, 79, 179-203.

Ragusea, A. & Vandecreek, L. (2003). Suggestions for the ethical practice of online therapy. *Psychotherapy: Theory, Research, Practice, Training*, 40 (1/2), 94-102.

Sharar, D. & Hertenstein, E. (2005). Critical issues in EAP: A survey of key informants. *Benefits Quarterly* (Scheduled for publication in January).

Williman, M. (2001). Work-life and EAP convergence: A matter of economics. *Employee Benefit News*, October, 1-4.

Chapter 6

University of Arizona
Life & Work Connections:
A Synergistic Strategy for Maximizing
Whole-Person Productivity
over the Employees'
Life-Cycle/Work-Cycle

Darci A. Thompson
David L. Swihart

SUMMARY. The concept of integration has emerged in recent years as a strategy considered by providers of employee assistance, wellness and work-life services to meet the changing needs of the organizations they

[Haworth co-indexing entry note]: "University of Arizona Life & Work Connections: A Synergistic Strategy for Maximizing Whole-Person Productivity over the Employees' Life-Cycle/Work-Cycle." Thompson, Darci A., and David L. Swihart. Co-published simultaneously in *Journal of Workplace Behavioral Health* (The Haworth Press, Inc.) Vol. 20, No. 1/2, 2005, pp. 105-121; and: *The Integration of Employee Assistance, Work/Life, and Wellness Services* (ed: Mark Attridge, Patricia A. Herlihy, and R. Paul Maiden) The Haworth Press, Inc., 2005, pp. 105-121. Single or multiple copies of this article are available for a fee from The Haworth Document Delivery Service [1-800-HAWORTH, 9:00 a.m. - 5:00 p.m. (EST). E-mail address: docdelivery@haworthpress.com].

Available online at http://www.haworthpress.com/web/JWBH
© 2005 by The Haworth Press, Inc. All rights reserved.
doi:10.1300/J490v20n01_06

serve. There continues to be much discussion, however, about what exactly integration is, and how to do it. Beginning with a definition of integration, this article seeks to contribute to the discussion by describing the University of Arizona (UA) Life & Work Connections, a program that was conceived from its development to be an integrated service model. The theoretical and philosophical backgrounds of the program are presented and translated into the UA Life & Work Connections model. Advantages of the model and challenges to integration are discussed, and a detailed case study of a critical incident response is presented. *[Article copies available for a fee from The Haworth Document Delivery Service: 1-800-HAWORTH. E-mail address: <docdelivery@haworthpress.com> Website: <http://www.HaworthPress. com> © 2005 by The Haworth Press, Inc. All rights reserved.]*

KEYWORDS. Integration, health and productivity management, employee assistance, EAP, work-life, wellness, academe, domains, life-cycle, work-cycle, whole-person

INTRODUCTION

Integrating employee assistance, work-life, and wellness programs has become one of the dominant topics of discussion among EAPs at the present time. At issue are three questions: What is integration; how does it work; and will it really offer employers more robust services that enhance employee health and productivity? *UA Life & Work Connections*, on the campus of the University of Arizona, has had a unique opportunity to create an integrated program from inception over the past 14 years. Exploring ways the program developed and is operated provides one example of how these key questions are answered.

The University of Arizona (UA), located in Tucson, is a major academic research institution with a large health sciences campus and teaching hospital. As of fiscal year 2003 to 2004, the UA has 37,000 students and nearly 11,500 FTE employees. The UA has a number of world-renowned research and academic departments, including Astronomy, the Lunar and Planetary Laboratory, Optics and Medicine. The 2004 fiscal year total revenue was slightly over $1 billion, of which nearly $400 million came in the form of research grants and contracts (University of Arizona Office of Decision Planning and Support, 2004).

UA Life & Work Connections was created in 1990 and developed as the result of remarkable foresight on the part of many university employees. Originally associated with the campus health service as "Employee Wellness," it soon became part of the human resources department when an employee assistance feature was added. Over the next ten years, child care, elder care, and work-life support components were added and the program became known as UA Life & Work Connections (LWC).

Remarkably, LWC's creators recognized the value of building an "integrated" program. Long before it was the subject of much discussion, integration was envisioned as a means to carry out LWC's strategic plan. Since its inception, the program's plan has been to provide, within the domains of worksite wellness, employee assistance, and work-life support, as many services as are feasible (without sacrificing quality) to as many employees as possible, while maximizing available resources. The risk was that the program was a sink or swim proposition; fortunately, LWC swam well.

Starting in 1999, the LWC staff team began meeting to document LWC's operational model and to articulate their concept of integration. This process led to the following definition of integration as used by LWC:

> Integration: Bringing together, in a synergistic way, the specialized knowledge and trained expertise of professionals in different but related fields in order to better serve the organization and its employees. (Swihart & Thompson, 2002)

PHILOSOPHY BEHIND LWC'S INTEGRATION

Five concepts are incorporated within LWC's definition of integration: *Systems Theory, whole-person, synergy, differentiation and resiliency and life-cycle/work-cycle.*

Systems Theory

Systems theory examines interactions between an individual and his systemic environment. Its application within LWC's model is to identify interactions between an employee and his environment that negatively affect the individual's productivity. Multiple environmental systems are involved within the general realms of work and family.

One systems theory application to the health field is called the "social ecology of health" (Grzywacz & Fuqua, 1999). This theory describes how to maximize the effect of health resources by focusing them on four "leverage points" (socioeconomic status, family, work, and school), so named because of their disproportionate influence on individual health (Grzywacz & Fuqua, 1999; Grzywacz, 2000; Grzywacz & Marks, 2000). By focusing resources on these leverage points, this disproportionate influence becomes an advantage by multiplying the power of the resources. The social ecology of health perspective places equal focus on both the person and the environment as influencing factors on health. Certain qualities of an individual influence his health, while his environment influences health as "a set of nested, interacting systems" (Grzywacz & Fuqua, 1999). Environmental systems commonly consist of partner relationships, children, extended family, networks of friends, churches (examples associated with the family leverage point); immediate work culture, supervisor and co-worker relationships, and the broader work environment (work leverage point).

Some of these "nested, interacting systems" became evident in 2004 when half of the United States' anticipated influenza vaccine turned out to be tainted and unusable. The ensuing reactions reverberated from the international level down to the individual level as elderly people across the country scrambled to get vaccinated before the supplies were exhausted.

The vaccine disruption is also a good example of a systemic phenomenon called spillover. Spillover occurs when events or conditions in one system cannot be contained, and thus, affect other systems. When news of the vaccine shortage broke, individuals became worried and stressed. From one system to the next, the effects "spilled over," disrupting people, agencies, and institutions.

Individual factors are on the other side of the health influence equation. The social ecology of health asserts that a person's disposition, resources, and characteristics are mediating factors in health (Grzywacz & Fuqua, 1999). Self-care habits, physiology, emotional traits, priorities, self-image, thought patterns, genetic makeup, social skills, and their mutual interactions differ from person to person, leading to idiosyncratic influences on personal health. Consequently, the form and degree of spillover will also be unique, and so intervention efforts must then also fit the individual.

The social ecology of health model applies systems theory to public health issues in a general population; LWC has applied this same framework to productivity issues in the workplace. In the former case, spillover affects health and population-wide epidemiology. In the LWC case, spillover diminishes an employee's performance, affecting the overall performance in the workplace. In this context, the same two leverage points are relevant: family and work. It should be noted here that, technically, spillover can be a positive force also. In the context of this article, spillover specifically refers to negative spillover.

When spillover occurs, the disruption that carries over from one system to another is transmitted through the employee, and can be thought of as waves that pass through the person. Many "domains" of life can therefore be affected when this happens: emotions, thoughts, psychological health, physical health, spirituality, relationships, etc. So when spillover prompts an employee to seek assistance, the most comprehensive approach is to provide assistance from a "whole-person" perspective.

Whole-Person

Having a whole-person view of human beings is the primary driving force behind an integrated service format. In the real world, nobody can completely lay aside their roles in home relationships, forget about health problems, or ignore the needs of their children when they walk through the door at work. Recognizing this, many employers give employees access to an EAP counselor for stress and psychological problems, access to a worksite wellness program to try to address physical problems, and access to some sort of child care vendor to address child care problems. Tying these programs together administratively and calling the package a whole-person, integrated approach barely scratches the surface of what is possible.

Whole-person philosophy goes beyond simply acknowledging the existence of many domains in a person's life, to recognizing the *interactions* between domains. In LWC's whole-person approach, assessment of an employee's situation may uncover spillover effects in several domains, on top of which may be issues caused by the multiple effects together. For example, an employee who is also a parent will worry when his child is sick, and may take time off to care for the child. Between the slowdown from worrying and his time away from work, he falls behind. Stress and a sense of powerlessness give way to burnout and depression. A child care referral program can perhaps help him find assistance with caring for his child. A work-life program may help him explore telecommuting possibilities. Employee assistance can work with him on depression.

A whole-person approach, however, will look for other things also. What's happening physically, and what risks may be involved? Are there mid-life developmental issues? How are these events affecting how he sees himself? The follow-up question is, "Why?"

These different domain areas roughly correspond to different specialty fields (e.g., EAP, wellness). Addressing the domain interactions programmatically produces ongoing multidisciplinary discussions among service staff. Conducted well, these discussions foster cross-discipline understanding, mutual trust, and creativity with collaboration in providing service. An integrated program should produce *synergy*.

Synergy

If a whole-person view of human beings is the primary driving force behind an integrated service format, then synergy should be one of its distinguishing features. Synergy is usually defined by the phrase, "the whole is greater than the sum of its parts." (LWC has adopted the unofficial motto, "The whole person working is better than just some of their parts.") Bringing program pieces together under one roof, physically and/or administratively, is one matter; integrating them operationally is quite another. Programs where EAP, wellness, and work-life are connected administratively, but function independently, are not truly integrated. Synergy is created when staff with different but related domain expertise come together with the common purpose of exploring and creating new services or programs. It spills over into service offerings that provide more broad-based knowledge, are often unique, and have a tighter, better fit to equip employees to manage their real-world life and work situations.

Differentiation and Resiliency

As mentioned previously, systems theory addresses the interactions between an individual and the system(s) of which he is a part. Figure 1 illustrates the case of an individual as part of two systems, symbolized by springs. When one person acts in a way that affects the group, it can be pictured as reverberations that move around the system. Given the characteristics, personalities, context, etc., of the different people in the system, the group will develop unique patterns in the way that they vibrate together. These patterns have a single purpose: to return the system to the stability of its previous state or structure. This characteristic is called homeostasis.

"Differentiation," a concept developed by Murray Bowen (Kerr & Bowen, 1988) and built upon by David Schnarch (Schnarch, 1997), works

FIGURE 1. An Individual as Part of Two Systems

against homeostasis. Differentiation is the degree to which an individual can resist a system's pressure to make him vibrate in the old pattern, back to homeostasis. In relational terms, a highly differentiated individual determines his own role, identity, and behavior independent of the group rather than allowing the group to dictate these factors. A well-differentiated person is able to maintain a sense of self-identity and self-directedness without overwhelming or withdrawing from the larger group.

Differentiation is also a developmental concept, which means that resisting the system's strongest pressures to conform is a natural challenge for the individual to grow up to the next level of differentiation. This requires that the person develop more effective self-soothing and self-validating skills in order to hold his or her ground.

Resiliency is closely related to differentiation and is a quality that increases as differentiation develops. It is, in part, the ability to bounce back, survive, grow, and even thrive in adverse circumstances. Other traits include playful curiosity (Siebert, 1996; also see *www.resiliencycenter.com*). While differentiation is about a person's ability to maintain self-directedness and self-identity in a system, resiliency provides the self-motivation and efficacy to make the person able to "stay the course" while increasing his or her differentiation. Being a developmental concept also means that employee problems are framed in a positive growth perspective, instead of the negativity of "pathology."

Life-Cycle/Work-Cycle

As life brings circumstances that challenge people to increase their differentiation, it often does so in somewhat predictable ways. Transitional events such as marriage, parenthood, and mid-life reevaluation help define a common "life-cycle." In a sense, the life-cycle concept is akin to "leverage points": There are times and events in life that have a disproportionately greater power to challenge people to differentiate to a higher level. Consequently, focusing program offerings on these common times and events promotes broader utilization and optimal use of resources.

Note that most life-cycle events transcend work, even though they can create spillover at work. In contrast, work-cycle events–a subset of life-cycle events in LWC's philosophy, are those that are defined within work. Promotions, job changes, layoffs, pre-retirement and post-retirement adjustments are examples of work-cycle challenges. Just as life-cycle events can create spillover at work, so also can work-cycle events. Operating in the work environment makes integrated programs like LWC especially well-equipped to identify, understand, and assist employees facing these challenges.

Because life-cycle and work-cycle events are generally common life experiences, employee assistance, wellness and work-life programs can anticipate them and prepare services for assisting employees.

LWC'S ADAPTATIONS

UA Life & Work Connections' mission is to build resiliency in the individual and in the organization. Employees are seen as assets that should be able to flourish as much as possible, instead of budget lines whose compensation is a "cost of doing business." Building and maintaining resilient employees leads to a much healthier, stronger organization (Hope & Hope, 1997).

Applying the terms, "systemic," "whole-person," "synergy," "differentiation" and "resiliency," and "life-cycle/work-cycle," as defined above, to this mission leads to two guidelines for assessment and intervention. First, the issues that bring a client in for help generally contain some embedded developmental challenge for that employee. More than just problem solving, the goal is to facilitate a developmental process that helps the employee not only resolve the problem at hand, but better equips him to manage future issues. Growth eases the grip that past stressors have had on him.

The second guideline is that building resiliency leads to longer lasting behavioral change. Self-efficacy and self-motivation are core elements in resiliency, and when they are the basis for an employee making changes in his life, the changes tend to "stick" and are longer lasting.

Drawing on an employee's intrinsic motivation is more powerful than trying extrinsically, or externally, to motivate him.

STRATEGIC AND TACTICAL SERVICES

Recall that a systemic view considers both the individual as well as his environment, which is the group of systems around him. LWC's efforts to build resiliency in the organization (the employee's work environment) take the form of "strategic" services. Departmental consultations, presentations, classes, and committee involvement are examples of these. LWC's services to individual employees (i.e., counseling, consultations, etc.) are considered "tactical" services, because they involve the individual "battles" that employees face, which are only a small part in shaping the whole picture.

PUTTING IT ALL TOGETHER

Figure 2 is a depiction of UA Life &Work Connections' model. From left, LWC, composed of its integrated components, with its mission, goals, contract, and partnerships, markets itself and offers strategic services to the University of Arizona workplace, where the individual employees and the institution interact. The combination of unique, indi-

FIGURE 2. UA Life & Work Connections' Model

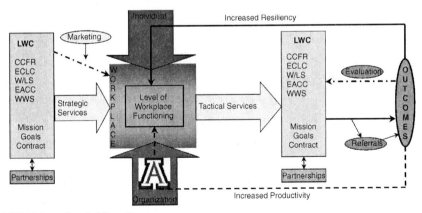

© 2004 Arizona Board of Regents
Diagram created by Lynne Smiley, PhD

vidual employees and organizational factors creates a certain level of functioning.

When the level of functioning in a particular workplace drops below a certain threshold (i.e., negative spillover within the unit reaches some subjective level of critical mass), the individual(s) and/or supervisor(s) involved may request specific tactical services from LWC. With the integration of five areas of service and the availability of partnerships to assist, LWC can provide a tailored set of services to meet the need, including referrals as appropriate. These services lead to one or more outcomes, which are intended to increase the individual's resiliency while at the same time increasing the organization's productivity. Regular evaluations help LWC make certain of its effectiveness and reveal any gaps missed in the service.

CASE VIGNETTE

One of LWC's more popular and visible services is the Worksite Wellness Heart Health Screening, usually conducted in the participants' workplace. The screening offers participants an opportunity to have their blood pressure taken, total cholesterol (TC), HDL cholesterol, the ratio of TC to HDL, long-term blood glucose level, weight, body fat percentage, and a perceived exertion exercise recovery test. At the next station in the screening, participants meet with a fitness and nutrition expert on LWC's staff, where their test results are explained in detail, their responses to a fitness and nutrition questionnaire are discussed, and recommendations are made. Finally, participants meet with an employee assistance counselor, who discusses with them their responses on a questionnaire about sleep and stress.

The counselor is an integrated part of the screenings for several reasons. First, it provides exposure to employee assistance services in an upbeat, non-stigmatizing setting. Meeting and getting acquainted with the counselor eliminates one of the barriers to those who may not otherwise seek help. Another reason is the whole-person approach. Employees who are struggling with weight gain in spite of their best efforts to manage it are often also experiencing excessive stress, depression, or other conditions. In many of these cases, eating habits are a minor issue compared to what else may be going on in the client's life. Having a more comprehensive picture can provide more effective strategies to build resiliency. If an employee so chooses to seek help, it now has a name, a face, and a personal connection.

Yet another reason to include employee assistance in the health screening is exposure to EAP as a supervisory resource. For example, some employees in a department that was being screened chose to reveal to each other their (confidential) blood pressure readings, and expressed surprise that many of them were high. As the group talked more, including the supervisor, it dawned on them that there may be a common denominator for the surprise readings. This generated conversation about the work environment, and with EAP assistance, the supervisor and employees began making adjustments to help relieve department-wide stress.

ADVANTAGES OF LWC'S INTEGRATED MODEL

The mission of building resiliency is the means of maximizing productivity and minimizing health care costs in LWC's systemic, whole-person, life-cycle approach. It is designed to be as comprehensive as possible, as a promotion-prevention-intervention-post-intervention model. Along each of the three dimensions (systemic, whole-person, life-cycle) lie a range of possibilities, which, singly, and in combination with each other, affect productivity and health care costs. LWC's model has some advantages:

- *The Capability to Identify a Broader Range of Risk Factors.* The more risk factors an employee has, the greater his overall probability of experiencing a spillover condition. By identifying more of these risk factors to an employee, they can be reduced by preventive education and/or effective intervention.
- *Future Scanning.* The systemic, whole-person, life-cycle nature of LWC's approach allows a broader awareness of new developments, trends, and research (e.g., paucity of skilled workers, rise of depression impact). Through this awareness, LWC can anticipate some shifts and prepare service offerings guided by relevant research.
- *Lower Overhead and Administration.* Because it is an internal model housed under one roof, LWC does not have to negotiate with other vendors and the client. The five components of LWC answer to a single administrator (the director), who makes the necessary networking contacts.
- *Flexibility and Collaboration.* Service offerings can be creatively combined to meet the unique needs of a particular client or group.

There are also occasions where any of several LWC staff can cover one type of presentation leading to quicker response times.

- *Synergy.* Frequent informal and lively discussions occur among staff about some research topic or societal trend. Mutual respect and trust develop. These interactions not only keep the team members sharp and in touch, but they also provide opportunities to brainstorm and think "outside the box."
- *Reduced Costs.* Having a broad, multidisciplinary base, the model is designed so that losses of productivity and health care costs increases are minimized.
- *Enhances Risk Management.* In January 2004, the Arizona Board of Regents released an audit of the University of Arizona's Loss Prevention Program. The UA Life & Work Connections program was specifically cited as a positive benefit to the UA and its employees through ". . . reduced loss of life, hours, and property through substance abuse training for supervisors; reduced absenteeism, illness and employee recruitment costs through teaching of stress management and assisting employees with stress reduction."

CHALLENGES TO THE INTEGRATED MODEL

- *Metrics.* Establishing reliable metrics is difficult due to the difficulty in establishing outcome definitions, measuring prevention, and overcoming privacy issues. There is also the added difficulty of measuring how integrated services are more effective than "silo" approaches.
- *Personnel.* Much of the value of synergy and integration will be lost if the staff refuses to cooperate with each other. Beyond effectively resolving conflict, synergy will be compromised when there is not a general sense of being part of the team. Playful curiosity, and the ability to learn quickly and be mentally and emotionally flexible are critical to success of each individual and the integrated team as a whole (Siebert, 1996; also see *www.resiliencycenter.com*).

DETAILED CASE APPLICATION

The following true story is presented in detail to illustrate the complexity of the many systems and groups of people affected by tragic events that recently occurred at the university, and to demonstrate how integration made LWC's response to these events effective.

The Events

On the clear, chilly Monday morning of October 28, 2002, fourth semester nursing student Robert Flores walked into the College of Nursing building on the University of Arizona campus with five guns and 150 rounds of ammunition in his backpack. Several individuals recalled saying "Hi" to him as he passed by. He went first into the 2nd floor office of Robin Rogers, a nursing instructor who taught his class the previous semester, closed the door, and shot her twice, killing her. Flores then proceeded upstairs to the 4th floor, where the class he was currently enrolled in was taking a test. He walked into the room, asked Cheryl McGaffic, one of the course's two instructors, if she was ready to meet her Maker, and when she replied, "Yes," he shot her several times at pointblank range, killing her. The 46 students in the class screamed and dove for cover behind desks, tables, chairs, whatever they could find. Flores then curtly dismissed them from the classroom. After a moment's fearful hesitation, they rushed to the doors to get out. When the room cleared, he shot and killed Barbara Monroe, the other course instructor, before finally turning the gun on himself.

One of the fleeing students, not knowing that Flores was dead, ran into a nearby office and told the occupants to call 911. As word spread through the building, many chose to run while others locked themselves in their offices. By amazing coincidence, a Tucson Police Department SWAT team was at a nearby park, already geared up for a training exercise. They were at the College of Nursing in seven minutes and began a floor-by-floor search for potentially several gunmen (with the dead on two different floors, some concluded that there was more than one gunman). Those who had locked themselves in offices were afraid to open their doors. The pounding, shouting people in the hallways, who were demanding they unlock the doors, could be the police (who had no keys) or gunmen. When doors were not opened, the SWAT team blew them open and stormed the room. Terrified occupants were told to get out of the building as quickly as they could. By ones and twos they ran out, huddling together in small groups in the parking lot.

In other nearby buildings on the Arizona Health Sciences Center campus, including University Medical Center hospital, occupants received diverse and often conflicting instructions about what they should do. Some ended up needlessly enduring an anxiety-filled six-hour wait in their darkened, locked offices before someone remembered to inform them that the danger was over.

The media, of course, immediately picked up on the event, and were on scene almost as quickly as the SWAT team. Local television stations cut into regular programming and carried live reports from the scene, becoming the first source of information for many in the campus community, including family members of students, faculty, and staff.

Flores' final act of defiant revenge was a 22-page letter that he had written and mailed to a local newspaper before the shootings, timed to be received the day after the shootings. The paper printed part of the letter but posted its entirety online. The letter was a long, rambling recital of perceived wrongs that had been inflicted on him, which he used to justify the killings. The letter sparked a good deal of anger and only added to the follow-up work for LWC.

THE RESPONSE

Many people and different units on campus got involved to assist students and employees in the immediate aftermath. LWC led the recovery effort because of its ability to work with individuals as well as layers of organizational systems. Systemically, progress on both sides is intertwined, and therefore the best recovery outcomes required working on both sides simultaneously. Other campus units collaborated with LWC, including Risk Management, Campus Health Services, CAPS, the student counseling center, and Human Resources. Those people who had been closest to the shootings–several hundred people–were herded into a nearby building away from the media. A systemic approach was used so that the eyewitnesses (the "hot" group) were separated from the rest (the "warm" group) and moved to a separate room; Critical Incident Stress Management ("CISM") interventions were begun for both groups. In the coming days and weeks, there would also be interventions for groups in other health sciences colleges, in a number of other specific departments on the main campus, and two "Town Hall" meetings for the entire campus community.

LWC's integrated response began with the worksite wellness coordinator assisting the organizing efforts at the request of employee assistance. By mid-morning planning discussions were taking place with upper administration from the Arizona Health Sciences Center and from the university proper. During these discussions, the worksite wellness coordinator called attention to the fact that the physiological effects of traumatic stress were soon going to put people in urgent need of sustenance. Food, drinks and water were ordered immediately.

Integration led to other contributions and task assignments. LWC's administrative associate became a "gopher," taking care of rescheduling clients and arranging for materials, rooms, and other needs. The Human Resource Specialist working in the child care component shifted her duties to cover the phones, while the child care component coordinator pulled together and posted guidelines for families about responding to children's fear and questions on its Web site.

Calls from external CISM vendors offering their services began pouring in and had to be assessed. College of Nursing and university administrators needed assistance from someone familiar with trauma to make decisions about next steps: How long a wait is appropriate until resuming classes? How should faculty be involved in making these decisions? What kind of memorial service would be appropriate and helpful for grieving people? What should be done about the victims' offices and the classroom where the murders took place? How are these decisions made when the decision makers themselves are in shock and grief?

In response, LWC began providing ongoing consultations to work with administrators both as humans responding to a traumatic event and as professionals struggling to make business recovery decisions. These consultations, which addressed workgroup dynamics, reclaiming the working and learning environment, student responses and concerns, and more, continued throughout the following year.

LWC decided to partner with a volunteer CISM network sponsored by the Northwest Fire and Rescue District. The volunteers were made up of firefighters, hospital, and ER nurses, and school counselors who were all trained and experienced with CISM. Sixteen volunteers showed up the next day, some coming from nearly 200 miles away.

The integrated response and partnerships with Northwest Fire and Rescue District's CISM team and other campus groups led to three remarkable outcomes. First, every one of the students who witnessed the murder of their teacher graduated on time, having passed the full curriculum requirements. Second, not one employee of the College of Nursing resigned because of the shootings. On the contrary, over the following year, some fifteen new faculty were added without questioning the security of the college. Finally, as of this writing two years after the shootings, there have been no lawsuits against the university stemming from the shootings.

This scenario, and a handful of others like it, represents an extreme in the intensity and scale of problems encountered by LWC. They are not the norm of everyday functioning. The bulk of the work takes the form of small day-to-day breakthroughs; an employee learning to say "no" and set better boundaries, another learning to have a hard conversation with an aging parent, and another learning self-care regarding diabetes.

CONCLUSIONS

Recognizing that spillover has many sources and takes many forms, integration, as LWC has defined it, was a strategic innovation to address employees as whole people. The strategy of integration is intended to develop whole-person resiliency.

This is a very critical time for EAPs, wellness and work-life programs. In today's context of depleted budgets, a shrinking force of skilled workers, and skyrocketing health care costs, employee assistance, wellness and work-life services must fully realize their value and innovatively step forward. A mountain of research has been piling up, demonstrating, in terms of dollars lost, just how shockingly costly spillover is–likely in the tens of millions of dollars for an institution like the University of Arizona (Goetzel, 2003; Kessler, 2001). The development of accurate, *meaningful* metrics is crucial in order to connect outcomes with dollars saved; demonstrating how integrated programs contribute in terms of reducing health care costs, productivity costs, and meeting recruitment and retention goals.

> Not everything that matters can be measured, and not everything that can be measured matters.
>
> –Einstein

REFERENCES

Goetzel, R.Z. et al. (2003). The Health and Productivity Cost Burden of the "Top 10" Physical and Mental Health Conditions Affecting Six Large US Employers in 1999. *Journal of Occupational and Environmental Medicine*, 45:5-14.

Gryzwacz, J. (2000). Work-Family Spillover and Health During Midlife: Is Managing Conflict Everything? *American Journal of Health Promotion*, 14:236-243.

Grzywacz, J. & Fuqua, J. (1999). The Social Ecology of Health: Leverage Points and Linkages. *Behavioral Medicine*, 26:3.

Grzywacz, J. & Marks, N. (2000). Reconceptualizing the Work-Family Interface: An Ecological Perspective on the Correlates of Positive and Negative Spillover Between Work and Family. *Journal of Occupational Health Psychology*, 5:1, 111-126.

Hope, J. & Hope, T. (1997). *Competing in the Third Wave*. Boston: Harvard Business School Press.

Kerr, M. & Bowen, M. (1988). *Family Evaluation: An Approach Based on Bowen Theory*. New York: W.W. Norton.

Kessler, R.C. et al. (2001). The Effects of Chronic Medical Conditions on Work Loss and Cutback. *Journal of Occupational and Environmental Medicine*, 43:218-225.

Office of Decision Planning and Support, University of Arizona (2004). "The University of Arizona FAQ, 2003-2004" Brochure.

Schnarch, D. (1997). *Passionate Marriage*. NY: Henry Holt and Co.

Siebert, A. (1996). *Survivor Personality*. NY: Ley Publications.

Siebert, A. (2004). The Resiliency Center Web site. *www.resiliencycenter.com*.

Swihart, D.L. & Thompson, D.A. (2002). Successful Program Integration: An Analysis of the Challenges and Opportunities Facing an EAP That Integrated with Other Programs Reveals the Keys to Successfully Serving the Systemic Needs of Employees and Work Organizations. *EAP Association Exchange*, 32 (5): 10-13.

Chapter 7

Johns Hopkins University: Diary of Integration

Everett Siegel

SUMMARY. This article discusses the need for integration between different models of mental health, as seen through a "diary" of the events in a typical week of EAP supervision. Clinical and supervisory examples are offered as an example of integrating perspectives in the clinical setting. The overall process of integration in a clinical setting is discussed from both a philosophical and psychoanalytic perspective, and several examples of integration are related for the sake of discussion. Complementarity is invoked as a central theme of key importance for integration. *[Article copies available for a fee from The Haworth Document Delivery Service: 1-800-HAWORTH. E-mail address: <docdelivery@haworthpress. com> Website: <http://www.HaworthPress.com> © 2005 by The Haworth Press, Inc. All rights reserved.]*

KEYWORDS. Integration, mental health, Johns Hopkins, clinical, psychoanalytic

The significant problems that we face can not be solved at the same level of thinking we were at when we posed them.

–Albert Einstein

[Haworth co-indexing entry note]: "John Hopkins University: Diary of Integration." Siegel, Everett. Co-published simultaneously in *Journal of Workplace Behavioral Health* (The Haworth Press, Inc.) Vol. 20, No. 1/2, 2005, pp. 123-142; and: *The Integration of Employee Assistance, Work/Life, and Wellness Services* (ed: Mark Attridge, Patricia A. Herlihy, and R. Paul Maiden) The Haworth Press, Inc., 2005, pp. 123-142. Single or multiple copies of this article are available for a fee from The Haworth Document Delivery Service [1-800-HAWORTH, 9:00 a.m. - 5:00 p.m. (EST). E-mail address: docdelivery@haworthpress.com].

Available online at http://www.haworthpress.com/web/JWBH
© 2005 by The Haworth Press, Inc. All rights reserved.
doi:10.1300/J490v20n01_07

INTRODUCTION

Integration is a process of reconciling different frameworks. It is well-known that Employee Assistance (EA), Work-life (WL) and Health and Productivity Management (HPM) have different knowledge bases, models and areas of expertise. These different areas of competencies and skills need to be brought together in a fashion that allows each model to be used fully and effectively. This process of integration occurs across a "macro" picture between organizations or on a "micro" level within each person's mind. It is well-known in individual psychotherapy or in observations of groups that bringing together different ideas or belief systems causes conflict.

By understanding how individuals approach joining differing frameworks, and by looking at the problems and obstacles of integrating different models, insight will be gained as to how different ways of thinking can be integrated by organizations. Psychoanalysis studies the mind in conflict, and thus offers unique insights for integration. This article will examine clashing frameworks within individuals through the lens of psychodynamic theories. Through the examples of a psychiatric resident struggling to integrate different mental health perspectives in treating a patient, a coaching process, and finally through the supervision of a client who is operating with limited resources, we will see some of the difficulties surrounding reconciling different perspectives. The author will then examine how these difficulties can be formulated and resolved.

The assumption is that integrating on a "micro" level is analogous to a "macro" level, and that insights gained from examining specific instances of integration can be carried over to the reconciling of different organizations. We begin by looking at a psychiatric resident struggling with integrating different models of patient care in the following brief vignette of a clinical case treated by a psychiatric resident. Towards the end of a supervision session with the resident it was clear that she was in some turmoil. When asked what was going on, she responded, "I'm torn between sympathy for my patient's (a graduate student) plight, yet I feel compelled to talk to him about the frame of treatment. How can I set limits and encourage expressive techniques when he is so obviously suffering? And, how can I use the techniques you are teaching me when I should be focusing on finding the right medications?" These sorts of tensions, so palpable in mental health and psychiatry, speak to the clash between frameworks viewed as incompatible. The models available to understand the patient are seen as mutually exclusive and ultimately as not amenable to integration. How can we approach integration in ways that allow meaningful synthesis between different frameworks?

These struggles to integrate are part of our daily practice. Johns Hopkins University and Hospital made an effort to connect the EA program with the department of psychiatry. The EA program hired the author, a psychoanalyst in training and a member of the psychiatry department, as psychiatric consultant. The goal was to integrate psychiatric and psychodynamic perspectives with the EA core technologies, and to draw bridges between clinical perspectives, programs and departments. As time has passed, psychoanalytic theory and practice have played a crucial role in facilitating bringing together the departments, programs and ideologies. The size and scope of the EA program at Johns Hopkins Hospital and University provided ample opportunities for integration. Since the original goal of integration was formulated, the author's role has expanded and the challenges presented by integration have increased. The author is currently the Medical Director of the Faculty and Staff Assistance Program (FASAP), the Student Assistance Program (SAP), and Director of Student Mental Health (SMH). The SAP functions as the EA program for the School of Medicine, while SMH is a traditional mental health evaluation and treatment program. Our SMH serves well over 1,000 students and dependents, and performs treatment and over 150 new evaluations per year.

BACKGROUND

The Johns Hopkins Hospital and the Johns Hopkins University launched the Faculty and Staff Assistance Program as a joint enterprise in 1986. In the seventeen and a half years since its inception, FASAP has provided services to about 11,500 clients and the work-life program to about 3000 clients. Furthermore, FASAP and the work-life program serve approximately 33,000 faculty members, staff, students and their dependents (B. Fowler, personal communication, July 26, 2004). The founding Director of the EAP, Dr. Dick Kilburg, notes the following key concepts that have underwritten FASAP:

1. Awareness of the progressive development across the life span.

2. Developing programs and services to meet the needs associated with different developmental phases (emphasizing times stress and transition).
3. Prevention of the individual, group or organization impairment and regression and the promotion of resilience.
4. Encouraging individual and group autonomy and competency and supporting key values (integrity, wisdom, justice).
5. Promoting an inclusive organizational culture that respects the valuation of individuals in their various aspects of diversity.
6. Focusing and creating an environment of collaboration both inside and
7. Outside the organization. (R. Kilburg, personal communication, July 26, 2004)

These concepts and values have led seamlessly to the development of the work-life program. Begun unofficially in 1989, Organizational Development was formalized and expanded to the Organizational Health Services (OHS) in 1992, under the directorship of Dr. Richard Kilburg. The OHS initially combined FASAP and a small Training and Education program in Human Resources (Chart 1).

In 1992-1993, the next step was taken, and the work-life and Organizational Development and Diversity Programs were begun, and in 1993-1994 Career Management was added. Work-life offers a number of services to employees, focusing on employees' family and home needs, financial planning and other needs across their lifespan (K. Giuirceo, personal communication, July 23, 2004) (Chart 2).

Dr. Kathleen Beauchesne, originally the assistant director of FASAP, became the first director of the work-life program in 1992. When Dr.

CHART 1. Organizational Health Services Chart 1989

CHART 2. Occupational Health Services Chart 1994

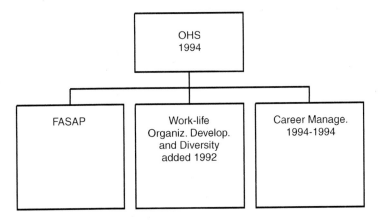

Beauchesne was appointed joint director of both FASAP and the work-life program in 1998, she envisioned and began to implement the long-range goal of merging the programs (K. Beauchesne, personal communication, July 22, 2004). The FASAP and work-life program have begun integrating the models of the work-life program: psycho-education and services spanning life stages with the core technology model of FASAP. The integration has begun with the coordination of the infrastructure of FASAP and work-life programs. This process has continued with cross training of both personnel in the different models, shared retreats and advisory committees, as well as coordinated HIPPA and confidentiality policies and procedures, and shared access, information and administrative support (M. Heitt, personal communication, July 23, 2004; K. Beauchesne, personal communication, July 27, 2004).

The author's involvement with FASAP began when the program first started at Hopkins in 1987, where he was hired at a psychiatric consultant. Initially, FASAP clinicians presented all of their evaluations to the medical director at a case conference, where history taking, evaluation, brief treatment, coaching, organizational dynamics and referral were discussed. As time passed, the author's role evolved. In addition to hearing individual case presentations, a new case conference was formulated whose goal was to discuss clinical and organizational issues in more depth. In addition to supervising clinicians, the author provided clinicians with perspectives on integration through clinical feedback and during performance reviews. The author supervised the clinical directors on clinical issues, and worked jointly on administrative matters. The author and Dr. Beauschesne have met weekly for years for an extended collaboration focused on the integration of clinical, administrative services in the program. The author undertook a key role in developing and implementing a program on workplace violence and mental health disaster planning, performed extensive teaching and set standards for evaluative and progress notes and formulations, as well as fine-tuned clinical skills of our clinicians to be congruent with EAP standards and core technology as well as the Hopkins culture. Because of the author's expanded supervisory and consultative role, he was appointed medical director of FASAP in 1998.

The culture of Johns Hopkins both facilitates and hinders integration across disciplines and clinical and administrative models. There is an overriding interest in quality that shapes the FASAP and the work-life programs' efforts to learn new perspectives and incorporate them into practice. Also, the academic environment of Johns Hopkins presupposes openness to ideas and to theories. Thus, when confronted with new frameworks for viewing experience, the culture encourages rational consideration of the costs and benefits. However, Johns Hopkins is a large institution, encompassing two main campuses as well as several important satellite institutions and over 30,000 employees. With the bustle and complexity of the institution, it sometimes is problematic to have close and continuous communication. This complexity sometimes causes a sense of urgency, and can implicitly encourage sticking to what's safe and familiar. It is in this setting that the author undertakes to bridge ideas and models and to facilitate integration.

The author functions at the boundary of several worlds (psychoanalytic and psychiatry department, psychiatry department and EAP, clinical and administrative duties at FASAP, SAP and SMH). The author has found that most of the roadblocks in the day-to-day situations that are encountered necessitate thinking about integration across models, disciplines and perspectives. Like the Chinese character that represents both danger and opportunity, the author has found that these integrative knots can be cut through and represent tremendous opportunities for shifts in thinking and personal growth, as well as solving problems. Cutting through these knots is like an "aha" moment of insight in therapy; what before had seemed an impossible deadlock suddenly becomes light and clear.

Operating at the boundaries between worlds, the author has come to view himself as an ambassador, whose job is to teach people to see and work with different models at the same time. The process of integration is defined as a reconciling of different models, frameworks or perspectives so that the whole is greater than the sum of the parts. This process of restoring complexity adds to the quality of the work and the challenge of fostering integration makes alive the author's sense of being an ambassador, and his ideals of questioning. To provide examples of the daily struggle with integration, the author kept an "integration" diary of a week at Hopkins this past spring. These examples will be used as starting points to illustrate the concepts and process of integration. The cases are fictional, and represent an amalgam of the examples the author has encountered over the years that are similar to the ones seen during the diary week. The primary example will be a clinical one. Examining the process of integrating the different perspectives of psychiatry will point to more general lessons in an individual's process of integration. Since organizations integrating different perspectives are comprised of individuals assimilating different models, these individual lessons on integration are applicable when different entities assimilate their different cultures and perspectives.

CONCEPTS OF INTEGRATION

Paradigms

Since integration involves the reconciliation of different models, to understand the difficulties in integration necessitates an examination of the nature of models. It is a well-known fact that the field of mental health uses multiple models to understand human behavior. These frameworks range from the disease model of biological psychiatry, the behavioral model, family, group and organizational models, cognitive and psychodynamic theories. These frameworks are necessary to make sense of the vast amount of information in the field yet the frameworks are incomplete. Just like integrating EAP and work-life programs, each of which function within different models, in clinical/supervisory, coaching and organization work, one is always trying to integrate different perspectives from the mental health field.

So, for example, the disease perspective would be used to understand the symptoms of the depressed graduate student presented earlier, while the psychodynamic perspective might be used to formulate the graduate student's self-criticism or resistance to treatment. A systems viewpoint helps us understand an instance of a threat in a workplace or an employee who wasn't performing to the standards of the organization, while a behavioral perspective might be advantageous in focusing on substance abuse in the workplace.

Sometimes using more than one model can be problematic to put into practice. Why is that? In part, the answer resides in the nature of the models themselves. Kuhn (1970) introduced the concept of paradigms. Kuhn believed that we see the world mediated through paradigms or models. These models are maps that tell us what to expect in a given situation, and allow us to make sense of phenomena that we observe or encounter (Covey, 1989; Westen, 1999). Paradigms serve as interpretive frameworks for phenomena. Gestalt psychology adds that perception is an active process that imposes order in our experiences. Simple perceptual observations do not exist by themselves, but perceptions actually are part of the interpretation of the world that occurs within a paradigm. In other words, we actually allow ourselves to see certain perceptions based on our paradigms, and we actively exclude others. There are famous Gestalt psychology experiments in perception that confirm this principle. For example, the experimenter presents someone with an ambiguous picture, such as a vase or two faces in silhouette, or a young vs. an old lady. The experimenter can prime the subject to see one of the two pictures (for example, showing the subject the vase first). The viewer will then catch the picture that they have been primed to see. The priming acts as a filter that dictates which features of the pictures are noticed and used to form a gestalt of the entire picture (Covey, 1989; Westen, 1999). The priming that occurs in our mental life is the paradigms or models that are used to "catch" experiences and make sense of them. Paradigms are lenses or nets that aide us in focusing on certain elements of experience, while excluding others. So, paradigms have a cognitive component (the informational content of the model), as well as a perceptual aspect that both focuses and narrows the field of vision to fit it into a preexisting map.

Experience in our own particular paradigms causes an emotional investment in their use and validity. The "reality" that we study in human behavior does not exist out there, but rather is only possible to see through the lenses we wear. And it is difficult, like with the experiment in perception, to see more than one paradigm at a time, and sometimes even to realize that we are wearing lenses.

Our familiar paradigms become embedded in our minds and affect our ability to learn new ones in ways that we are unaware of. This sense of being part of the fabric of the way we see the world extends to our loyalty to the teachers of our familiar paradigms. Like parents who have taught us how to make our way in the world, our mentors and their paradigms have guided us in understanding and working within our work worlds.

In conclusion, paradigms are the models that we use to understand experience. They exist both in the mental health field, as well as within EAP and WL. Paradigms are powerful. They allow us to understand and apply theory to our experience. Yet, this very power makes it difficult to appreciate how they are embedded within our minds; they affect our very perceptions of the world, and engender a personal implicit emotional investment and loyalty to them.

Complementarity

Integration involves reconciling two or more frameworks or paradigms. Sometimes this process is difficult because of the hold that paradigms exert over us. When presented with two or more models we may experience them as being in conflict.

Psychoanalysis is in a unique position to talk about reconciling opposing forces. In fact, psychoanalysis is the study of the mind *as* conflict (Pray, 2001; Wurmser, 1987). The opposing forces range from instinctual drives fighting against internalized societal constraints, or fights for independence clashing with wishes for dependence, etc. People are always trying to integrate their Jekyll and Hyde personalities: as a patient recently laments, "My Hyde takes over and I lie. I wish I could stop." Psychodynamic therapists try to avoid an either-or approach. They encourage both sides of the conflict to have their "say in court." Because of their extensive theoretical and practical experience, psychoanalysis is in the position to offer us some concepts in reconciling (and thus integrating) opposing paradigms in conflict.

One important goal of psychodynamic theory, both on the level of the individual patient, is to promote complementary thinking. Wurmser (2000) describes this philosophy of complementarity as one that "reunites again and again the seemingly contradictory viewpoints and to see them as mutual conditions of each other." This integration through complementary thinking occurs not only in psychoanalysis, but also in the interplay of the various perspectives in mental health and organizational dynamics. In clinical mental health this synthesis must occur between the biological and psychodynamic models. Both of these paradigms are mutually exclusive yet necessary components to treatment. As Frattaroli (2001) observes, the problem arises when the medical model imperiously claims that it is the sole truth.

Frattaroli (2001) advocates cultivating the ability to choose between two perspectives in the way we understand our patients on a moment-to-moment basis. Wurmser (1987) suggests balancing between opposites, not an either-or approach but a more-of-this and less-of-that, and a judicious weighing of utility in the immediate context of a here and now.

Splitting

Pray (2001) claims that the physicist Bohr's use of complementary thinking is closely allied with psychoanalytic notions of splitting. Whereas Bohr raised the mind's capacity for dualities to an epistemological principle, psychoanalysis deals with the mind's capacity to split in a clinical context. Splitting, or keeping mutual ideas or trains of thought apart, is the reverse of integration. To understand how to work with splitting would enlarge our capacity to integrate mutually exclusive theories.

People manage conflict between different, incompatible ideas or perceptions by splitting them apart. One observation, one perception, one train of thought at a time is emphasized, and then the focus shifts to a contrasting perspective. According to Pray (2001), "the ego's regulatory success depends on this ability to disavow, to 'split' attention away from one conscious mental perception to another, always establishing the last as 'true' for the moment." Attention becomes diverted, and clashing ideas are kept separate by focusing on one at a time and forgetting or relegating the other idea to lesser status.

The underlying problem is our reluctance to recognize the truth of complementarity; that mutually exclusive paradigms can both be true. This lack of recognition causes the splitting that keeps the paradigms apart and maintains the resistance towards integration.

Anxiety and Guilt Out of Loyalty to a Paradigm

There can be other reasons for our reluctance to integrate two paradigms. Kris (1982, 1985) studies resistances to free association in psychoanalysis and has identified two types of conflict. The first one, he calls convergent conflict, and it fits the usual psychodynamic model of a conflict between an impulse or a feeling and the ego or superego. The result is anxiety and defenses. This type of conflict can cause a failure in integration. For example, if someone considers a new model they may feel guilty and anxious and stop themselves from thinking about it. They may have a sense of loyalty to their teachers so that learning a new way of thinking may seem like betrayal. At this point, the anxiety and guilt would result in stopping "free associating," or thinking creatively about the model. In this type of conflict, the goal is to express both sides of the conflict, in this case the assertiveness related to thinking of a new model as well as the guilt involved.

Conflict of Ambivalence

The second type of conflict is called a conflict of ambivalence (Kris, 1985). We could recognize the previous instances of failures in conflict and problems with integration by the appearance of anxiety and difficulties continuing to think about the model. The second form of conflict has a fundamentally different form. The conflict appears as a rapid alternation between wishes, moods, associations, or thoughts in two divergent directions. Someone is unable to follow a train of thought, idea (within a model) without switching to another perspective. There is a hurrying away from thinking in a certain direction and onto the alternative one. This hurrying away repeats, so the process appears like a pendulum swing, with alternations between opposite stances. It is as if someone rapidly switched between the face and vase or the old lady and young lady pictures, without looking at either of them long enough to define what was in the pictures and to study them.

The typical way of recognizing this type of conflict is a lack of fulfillment and resolution in thinking along both directions (models). There will be incomplete formulations, an inability to carry through and to prioritize. One experiences the two models or trains of thoughts as mutually exclusive, as an either-or situation. The impetus for the continued lack of resolution is a fear of proceeding further in any course because it would imply a loss of the other perspective. So, the hallmark of the conflict of ambivalence is the anticipation of loss. This sense of loss occurs through the activity of continued thinking and attention along the same direction. It is important to note that it is not the content of the thoughts themselves that causes the pendulum to swing, but rather it the process of thinking and reflecting itself that implies a threat of loss.

ADDRESSING THIS TYPE OF CONFLICT BY EXAMINING SELF-CRITICISM

Kris (1985) offers several ideas. It is striking that self-criticism often underlies the reluctance to proceed. The self-criticism has several sources and forms, and it is difficult to observe, but it is a fundamental cause for the pendulum swings. If you are the one trying to integrate paradigms and are having difficulty, then perhaps introspection could reveal guilt or self-criticism, and your awareness of it could increase your satisfaction in thinking through a model. If you are acting as a consultant, supervisor or educator, then it is important to remember that self-criticism is often projected onto authorities. In that case, you may be "baited" or "tempted" to be critical, or you may feel angry towards the person, system or organization. Recognizing these actions and feelings usually help you in stepping back and reflecting that there is another process going on. At that point, consciousness itself of the self-criticism is helpful, and sometimes a gentle comment about the feeling will help decrease its intensity.

LIVING WITH TWO MODELS

Kris (1985) offers several other suggestions in working with conflicts of ambivalence. We must remember that there are two paradigms needed for integration. Refusing to accept partial resolutions or partial formulations, each side must be expressed for as long as possible, paying attention to anxiety, self-criticism or shifts away from the model. The natural inclination would be for increased tension and withdrawal from thinking about both of the models. To counter the increased vulnerability of our supervisee/student/client to anxiety and self-criticism, the supervisees are pushed to hold both models in their mind. Keeping both paradigms present in mind, and not backing off of one because of discomfort allows for a more complete integration.

Gradually, by gentle and persistent encouragement, they will be able to think about each side for longer periods and allow the pendulum to swing as far as it can go. The process of supporting the supervisee to hold both models at once takes time. As someone develops the ability to think through and integrate two models, then this process becomes satisfying in itself. As this satisfaction increases, the rapid alterations should slow down. The two sides of the conflict, or two models, need to be integrated or brought together consciously in terms not dictated by anxiety.

CASE VIGNETTES

This section will apply this theoretical approach to actual cases requiring integration. It will become apparent that large-scale integration between EAPs and WL are analogous to small-scale integrations involving individuals. This analogy holds true, because synthesizing large scale programs and clinical settings both involve individuals integrating two or more paradigms. To examine integration in individuals, three examples from clinical, supervisory and organization work have been chosen.

CLINICAL CASE EXAMPLE

A resident is treating a 29-year-old graduate student with recurrent major depression and low self-esteem. The resident presents the case to the author by relating both the patient's symptoms and story. The history consisted mostly of frustrated attempts to perform at work and to deal with family conflict. The graduate student has suicidal ideation and labile mood that is directly reactive to events in his family. The patient is a perfectionist and intensely self-critical. He feels like his life is like jogging uphill; the patient is always tired, late and somehow a failure. In treatment, the patient is extremely resistant to any suggestion that his suicidal ideation and his extreme self-criticism have anything to do with the events in his life.

At end of the supervisory session, after discussing this patient's reluctance to come to sessions, including not calling to cancel, or else canceling the session virtually without notice, the resident asks me a question going out the door. When supervisees ask questions when they are leaving, it is just like a patient who asks for help or makes a comment with their "hands on the doorknob." These are crucial questions that must be addressed. The resident said that he is torn between sympathy for the student's plight (depressed, anxious) versus talking to him about the frame. The trainee asks, can I set limits and encourage expressive techniques when he is so obviously suffering? And shouldn't I be focusing more on medications?

Individual Case Discussion

The resident's difficulty treating the graduate stemmed from several sources. The resident had not been readily exposed to psychotherapy paradigms, and she was having trouble assimilating the cognitive component of the mode. She was unaware of how much her choice of paradigms was dictating her observations of the clinical situation; how using a paradigm to understand a patient is also being trapped in the paradigm. It was thus difficult for the resident to think that she could use both psychodynamic therapy and give medications/set limits. This led her ultimately to the splitting between models that are often observed with difficult integrations.

Using our knowledge of paradigms and splitting, the supervisor can work with the clinician in this situation, and foster her capacity to integrate. For example, the following scenario might unfold. The patient is afraid and very resistant to any meaning to his mood shifts and suicidal ideation. "It's all illness." The patient begins to talk about the events during the week that led up to his suicide ideation, and then suddenly he shifts over to talking about his disease causing the suicidal thoughts. The patient elaborates the details of the suicide fantasy; it arose quickly then went away a few hours later. The patient then relates his frustration that his "disease" pops up out of nowhere. The resident seems as trapped in the patient's thinking, alternating between thinking of medication changes or meaningful explanations. In supervision, the author asked the resident to notice how rapidly she shifts from one model to another, seemingly forgetting that she was just talking about a different framework. This process of changing repeatedly was just what the patient was doing, and that knowledge led us to consider bringing it to the patient's attention.

It turned out the resident had difficulty in employing a psychodynamic model. Through reflecting on the reasons for her difficulty, it turned out that the resident was afraid that if she became too immersed in a perspective other than the disease model, then she would be either disloyal to (conflict of defense) or else lose (conflict of ambivalence) the disease model that she was used to. The resident said, "I'm interested in learning more about psychodynamic principles, but I'm afraid that I will have to give up what I'm comfortable in and what works for me." These conflicts of ambivalence, the fear of either being disloyal to or else losing the previous model often prevent integrations between models or organizational entities.

Understanding the dynamics of conflicts of ambivalence provided a means to aid the resident to achieve integration between the two models. Remembering that the way to work with these conflicts is to continue reflecting on both models, the author encouraged the resident to think through a formulation of the patient's difficulties using both perspectives. This process allowed us to hone in on a disease formulation (partially treated depressive disorder vs. bipolar disorder, type II), and discussed a treatment plan using that perspective. If the resident became hesitant or anxious about "missing the other perspective," the author still persuaded her to continue thinking along the same line and reassured her that the psychodynamic contribution wouldn't be forgotten. Considering the patient from a psychodynamic perspective, and the resident and author focused particularly on the patient's sense of self-hatred and its manifestations in his present life and the transference.

The author sensed the resident became anxious and was self-critical in thinking along these lines. Knowing that self-criticism was often present in conflicts of ambivalence between two paradigms highlighted that this was an important area to explore. So the author enquired more about her self-criticism, the resident said explained she felt she was "disloyal" to what she had learned, and that some other psychiatrists would be judgmental of her of thinking this way. The author emphasized that the resident wasn't wrong in reflecting on psychodynamic issues, but instead she was helping the patient. Her using psychodynamic theory was not "giving up" the other approach, and that she was actually adding to it. We decided that whether or not she added any specific new medicine was not as important as reflecting on how does adding medicine fit into both perspectives; in other words, was adding medicine part of a reasonable treatment plan, and how could the psychodynamic issues be kept in sight? In other words, was medicine being used in place of discussing the psychological issues, or as a mechanism to facilitate their processing? And if the resident did not add medications, were we making it more difficult for the patient to process psychodynamic interventions?

Finally, the resident and the author arrived at a metaphor that bridged both paradigms. The patient experienced his life like an uphill mountain climb. He was fighting the weight of his self-criticism, a quality he would not lose even when the disease was fully treated. Using only the disease approach would make his climbing muscles work more efficiently, but the patient still would still only be walking uphill. The goal of therapy was to give the patient a more varied terrain (one that was less self-critical). However, ignoring medications would make the uphill climb steeper and more dangerous, and the patient would be too out of breath to look for the new (inner) terrain. The resident finished the supervision energized, came up with a reasonable medication plan and psychodynamic formulation.

SUPERVISORY CASE EXAMPLE

A senior research member of a medical school department was asked to meet with me because of difficulties in career advancement. The author has permission to speak to her supervisor as well.

The supervisor relates the problem. The researcher had accomplished a great deal in her field, but seemed unable to advance. She was not publishing enough, nor applying for grants, and at times would speak impulsively at departmental and research meetings.

The client and the author met to talk about her difficulties. She could see her supervisor's points, but she had a counter-argument for each instance. She also talked about the dilemma of grant writing. She said that she did not have enough time. Yet, she thought there might be other reasons, but to search for them would be like scuba diving. It would be endless and metaphorically dangerous for her (she has asthma). Her statement revealed a sense of her feelings about exploring some of the issues. She then brings up her problems with assertiveness with her peers, to whom she will sometimes speak impulsively and bluntly, thus losing her message. She also brings up the inconsistency of her supervisor, who tells her to prioritize one thing one week, and another the second week. Which directive should come first?

Supervisory Discussion

The main difficulty with the researcher who was having difficulties with her performance was her belief that the problem was exclusively with the system. She seemed caught in a paradigm that it was the organization's inconsistency that was responsible for her troubles.

Prior conditioning with paradigms affects our perceptions and ability to synthesize new information. Ultimately, paradigm shifts and integrative efforts cannot be imposed from without, but, as psychoanalytic theory claims, they must start from within (Covey, 1989). As I coached the senior researcher and struggled to help her see that the problem was also within her, and not just the way the "system" had been organized, the author realized that in order to help her consider another paradigm coaching needed to start with the "surface." The surface was the presenting concerns of the researcher, and starting with these concerns allowed us to delve deeper into the sources of her anxiety.

The researcher eventually acknowledged issues of power and control. After encouraging her to approach these issues like a research problem, it became clear to the senior investigator that her concerns with control were very powerful filters that limited her perceptions of her experience. With an "aha" moment of insight, she realized there were alternative frameworks to view her experience. Thus, she integrated her "control" paradigm and her new framework. Her understanding was tentative; there was more work to be done.

As the coaching process continued, it became apparent that she experienced rapid alternations between blaming her supervisor for unreasonable and contradictory exams, and admitting that she had a role in her difficulties. Her thoughts in either direction would continue for a few minutes, and then she would veer off onto the opposite direction. Recognizing that this form of thinking was a typical example of a conflict of ambivalence pointed the coaching towards an intervention to help her integrate the opposing sides. First, the conflict was outlined. Her thinking seemed to reflect a conflict between a wish to externalize her difficulties within the context of a systems perspective versus a psychodynamic view in which she was taking responsibility. Gradually, she was able to understand that while the organization and the supervisor did have some role in her dilemma, she could effect the most change by looking at her part. As she became able to focus for longer and longer periods on understanding her role, she was able to work through her conflict of ambivalence and see new available strategies.

SYSTEM CASE EXAMPLE

A challenging resource problem occurred. One of the organizations consulted us because their supervisory management mandated a certain type and level of clinical and administrative service. The consulting organization was concerned about the complexity of the cases and the potential for bad outcomes, and required a certain investment in resources that were unavailable. The next day, the organization, the supervisory management and the consultant met, and management related the history of the mandate, as well as both the external and internal reasons for it. Our client organization presented counter-arguments, but to no avail.

Discussing the new requirements with the consulting group, the consultant advised them to get out of the middle of the dilemma between a need to fulfill the mandate and to provide quality services versus recognizing the limitations inherent in the management of the resources. The consultant discussed various options, including informing this organization's supervisors of the difficulties with the goal of either garnering additional resources or clarifying the problem. The group was encouraged to discuss the dilemma with other bosses. Although sympathetic, there was no immediate help coming. The consulting organization still felt trapped between a desire to fulfill the mandate and to prove to various administrators that more resources were needed. There are also the systemic issues of resource difficulties. They feared that it would be impossible for their staff to fulfill the mandate while maintaining the same quality of work. The situation seemed to be going around in circles.

Systems Example Discussion

In advising the organization with the mandate for services and the difficulty obtaining resources, the team would try hard to solve the problem by first stretching the system to accommodate the demands placed on them, and then rapidly shifting to feeling overwhelmed and distressed. After enough oscillations, they would haphazardly try to figure out ways to obtain resources. The organization would swing wildly back and forth between the two positions without significant movement in either path. They were stuck.

In addition to the conflict of ambivalence, which caused them to shift back and forth between models, the organization was fixated on the unfairness of the system's requirements. It was hard for the group to see the system's perspective.

The author noticed that there was an edge of self-criticism in the organization's self-presentation. Their franticness and sense of implied impotence did not mesh with their previous accomplishments and competence. Remembering that self-criticism is a feature of conflicts of ambivalence (Kris, 1985), we began to highlight the implicit self-criticism in the organization's manner of dealing with the mandate. In psychotherapy, projecting blame to authorities often defends against self-criticism. Then, the authority or the consultant/supervisor/therapist/integrator may be "baited" or "tempted" to be critical, or they may identify with the patient/supervisee/client and feel angry towards the person or system. Being able to observe this process allows the consultant/supervisor to reflect that there may be alternatives to being trapped in anger. At that point, consciousness itself of the self-criticism is helpful, and can decrease it.

The organization was vacillating between trying to prove that their need for additional resources was valid versus trying to solve the problem by fighting the mandate. They went to additional supervisors for support, and had their staff document meticulous records of their time and efforts, and made counter-proposals to the authorities making the demands. Feeling trapped, it seemed to them that either way they had a target painted on their back. It was a losing proposition in either side of the conflict. The client (leader of the organization under the mandate) then reported a dream whose meaning was apparent to them. The client had let some ominous appearing birds go free, but instead of fear, the dreamer had experienced a sense of relief. This was an exciting turn of events. The author wondered whether the birds were the client's experience of the problem they faced. Letting the birds go was dangerous, but freeing, and a necessary step. The organization's integration of the two conflicting demands (the mandate vs. scarce resources) was realizing they couldn't be responsible for problems and resources that they were unable to allocate. A burden was lifted, and like the dream, the executive client felt lighter.

This attitude was reflected throughout the organization. The conflict was there, but the client was able to take another step in working through a conflict of ambivalence. Kris (1985) describes a process similar to mourning; that each side of the conflict of ambivalence (the model) has to be mourned and let go. Although they needed to collect data, the organization could never ultimately be responsible for proving that they needed the resources, nor for changing the mandate. The situation was the organization's to deal with, and they could accomplish a lot, but not more than they were allocated. It seemed that a burden had been lifted from both the client and his entire organization's shoulders, and they could think more clearly.

The organization approached the system giving them the mandate with a request for additional funds. Because of the factual and non-blaming nature of the presentation, their request was received favorably. Although the steps were only a further extension of the organization's previous efforts, they were thought through more strategically and completely, and it seemed true to Einstein's quote mentioned in the beginning of the chapter, that the clash of perspectives could only be solved at a different level in which they had been presented to them.

CONCLUSIONS

Integration involves the melding together of paradigms or perspectives so that the result is greater than the sum of parts. We have looked at how integration occurs in clinical mental health and coaching, relying on clinical examples because the variety of models used in mental health requires us to experience integration intensely and frequently. Since the integration of EA programs and work-life also involves differing models and also must ultimately occur within the individuals of the organization, it is expected that the examples of this chapter will be relevant to the EAP/WL setting.

Invoking the concepts of paradigms and complementarity helped us understand some of the challenges and difficulties of integration. Understanding is mediated through paradigms, which act as perceptual and cognitive maps of the phenomena that are being studied. These maps are guides that can be used to help us see and navigate complex information more clearly, but the map-user can forget that they are only maps and not the real territory. Integration occurs when viewing experience across several paradigms. Complementary thinking considers both alternatives and perspectives to a problem as mutually conditioning each other. Looking at some of the obstacles towards complementary thinking, as manifested in clashing, non-integrated perspectives, has enabled developing tools to facilitate integration.

Just like clinicians train their patients to consciously observe their shifts in attention and how they limit themselves in continuing a train of thought, EAP/WL employees can train ourselves, our organizations or our supervisees to notice when they are stopping thinking along a certain model and shifting to another. Organizations can also notice, on a larger scale, how they appear to have difficulty considering that both models might be true. As our clients and EAP/WL employees become trained in this practice, organizations and employees can become more adept in entertaining more than one paradigm at a time, and become more skillful at integration.

REFERENCES

Covey, S.R. (1989). *The 7 habits of highly effective people.* New York: Simon & Schuster.

Fingarette, H. (1963). *The self in transformation.* New York: Basic Books, Inc.

Fowler, B. (2004). Personal communication, July 26.

Frattaroli, E. (2001). *Healing the soul in the age of the brain.* New York: Viking.

Kris, A.O. (1985). Resistance in convergent and divergent conflicts. *The Psa. Q.,* 54:527-568.

Kris, A.O. (1982). *Free association: method and process.* New Haven: Yale University Press.

Kuhn, T.S. (1970). *The structure of scientific revolutions.* (2nd Ed.). Chicago: University of Chicago Press.

McHugh P.R. & Slavney, P.R. (1998). *The perspectives of psychiatry.* (2nd Ed.). Baltimore: Johns Hopkins University Press.

Parsons, M. (1984). Psychoanalysis as a vocation and martial art. *Int. R. Psycho-Anal.,* 11:453-462.

Pray, M. (2001). *The classical-relational schism and psychic conflict. The use of complementarity and complementary thinking.* Unpublished manuscript.

Siegel, E. (in press). Psychoanalysis as a traditional form of knowledge: An inquiry into the methods of psychoanalysis. *Journal of Applied Psychoanalytic Studies.*

Watts, A. (2000). *What is tao?* Novato, CA: New World Library.

Westen, D. (1999). *Psychology. Mind, brain, & culture.* (2nd Ed.). New York: John Wiley & Sons, Inc.

Wurmser, L. (1987). Flucht vor dem Gewissen (Flight from Conscience). Heidelberg: Springer. Unpublished manuscript in English.

Wurmser, L. (2000). *The power of the inner judge. Psychodynamic treatment of the severe neurosis.* Northvale, N.J.: Jason Aronson, Inc.

Chapter 8

Responding to Deaths of Faculty, Staff and Students at UC, Berkeley– An Integrated Approach

Carol Hoffman
Bruce Goya

SUMMARY. This article describes an important initiative designed to address the deaths of faculty, staff, and students at the University of California at Berkeley. Work-life and EAP practitioners can play a significant role in reducing the distress and lost work time associated with workplace deaths by helping employers to plan a response to employee and client deaths, and by participating in implementing that response. A model framework is presented to demonstrate the vital need for coordination and integration among many of the employers' programs, services, and activities in order to address deaths. *[Article copies available for a fee from The Haworth Document Delivery Service: 1-800-HAWORTH. E-mail address: <docdelivery@haworthpress.com> Website: <http://www.HaworthPress. com> © 2005 by The Haworth Press, Inc. All rights reserved.]*

KEYWORDS. Death, grief, employer response to death, workplace death, program evaluation matrix, work culture evaluation, workplace integration, program integration, program evaluation measures

[Haworth co-indexing entry note]: "Responding to Deaths of Faculty, Staff and Students at UC, Berkeley–An Integrated Approach." Hoffman, Carol, and Bruce Goya. Co-published simultaneously in *Journal of Workplace Behavioral Health* (The Haworth Press, Inc.) Vol. 20, No. 1/2, 2005, pp. 143-157; and: *The Integration of Employee Assistance, Work/Life, and Wellness Services* (ed: Mark Attridge, Patricia A. Herlihy, and R. Paul Maiden) The Haworth Press, Inc., 2005, pp. 143-157. Single or multiple copies of this article are available for a fee from The Haworth Document Delivery Service [1-800-HAWORTH, 9:00 a.m. - 5:00 p.m. (EST). E-mail address: docdelivery@haworthpress.com].

Available online at http://www.haworthpress.com/web/JWBH
© 2005 by The Haworth Press, Inc. All rights reserved.
doi:10.1300/J490v20n01_08

AN INTEGRATED APPROACH TO DEATH
IN THE ACADEMIC SETTING

Many working people may experience at least one death of someone they know during their working lives. This someone could be a coworker who died on site at the workplace or from an accident or illness away from the workplace. The deceased could also be a client or customer of the workplace or known to employees through some work-related activity.

Work-life and EAP practitioners can play a significant role in helping to reduce the distress and lost work time associated with workplace deaths by assisting to plan a response to employee and client deaths, and by participating in implementing that response. This article will demonstrate the vital need for coordination and integration among many employer programs, services, and activities, including work-life and EAP, using the University of California at Berkeley as a model.

DEATH IN THE WORKPLACE

The time following a death of someone whose life was spent in the workplace, or as a significant client of the workplace, can be of critical importance. Having a clear plan involving the necessary departments and outlining key roles and expectations can assure that the response to the death is comprehensive and effective, comforting those adjusting to the loss and attending to issues both personal and practical.

Establishing the anticipated death rate for employees and customers or clients ("clients" will be used in this article to indicate both) can help employers to prepare for this inevitable life cycle event. To estimate the number of deaths per year in your workplace, simply apply the death rate of the appropriate demographic group in the general population (available through census data) to your population of employees and clients.

In the university setting the faculty and staff are the employees, the students are the clients, and all are integral to the workplace community. A death of a faculty, staff, or student can have a far-reaching impact on other members of that community. Nationally, many factors contribute to the importance of examining the way in which deaths and bereavement are handled in the workplace, including:

- Increasing diversity of the population, with varying views, beliefs, and practices regarding death.
- Increased use of guns, resulting in more sudden, violent deaths.
- Greater awareness of the causes of deaths, such as alcohol and drugs, eating disorders, domestic violence, smoking, and other conditions that make it more difficult to minimize and cover up how colleagues and families die.
- More chronic, life-threatening illnesses such as cancer and AIDS that can be treated medically, allowing the affected individual to continue participating in the workplace, sometimes up until the day they die.
- Location of the workplace in a region with natural disasters such as earthquakes, fires, floods, and mudslides.
- Deaths occurring geographically far from the workplace, as employees work and vacation in other parts of the nation and the world.
- Increasing numbers of elderly relatives of employees, sometimes with chronic and terminal conditions, who die after years of caregiving by the employee.
- More immediate awareness of the deaths of colleagues and family members who live and work far away from the workplace due to increased communication technologies.
- Terrorism, war, and violence, which can affect any worksite, locally or internationally, at any time.

INTEGRATION OF EAP AND WORK-LIFE WITH OTHER PROGRAMS

Comprised of approximately 15,000 employees and 35,000 students, University of California (UC)-Berkeley is one of the largest employers in the east bay area, across the bridge from San Francisco. UC Berkeley's EAP and work-life programs are organizationally situated in the University Health Services, which provides primary medical and mental health care to students as well as health and wellness programs for faculty and staff. Along with employee assistance and work-life programs, the University Health Services faculty/staff programs consist of wellness, ergonomics, vocational rehabilitation, workers' compensation, disability management, and occupational health services for UC Berkeley employees.

Each of these programs operates independently, with a program manager reporting to the assistant vice chancellor, University Health and Counseling Services. Program planning and development are coordinated by a team comprised of the managers of each program. While intake for each program and its components is separate, publicity for workshops, brown bag presentations, and other activities are integrated. This model of separated but coordinated services is designed to preserve the integrity of each program, promote trust in the confidentiality of the EAP, increase awareness and support for all programs, and avoid both overlaps and gaps in services.

UC Berkeley experiences about 20 faculty and staff deaths each year. In addition, there are approximately 10 students and over 100 emeriti/retiree deaths.[1] As many as thirty to fifty different units or departments may be involved in responding to a single death at UC Berkeley.

To address this, in 1999 the Chancellor sponsored a major effort to develop death response guidelines for employees and other members of the university community. Before the guidelines were established, each time a UC Berkeley employee died the supervisor or manager would call many departments in the workplace to seek guidance on what to do and how to do it. The need to continually reinvent a death response protocol led to great waste and inefficiency, as well as unnecessary discomfort for all involved. Moreover, discrepancies in the response to each death often left survivors feeling hurt and disrespected.

The first step towards developing the university's new Guidelines for Responding to Death was to identify gaps and duplications in the response process. Now, employees can turn to the Guidelines for a single, reliable reference that assures greater ease and consistency in responding to campus deaths.

BEYOND EAP AND WORK-LIFE

Both EAPs and work-life programs may be called on to address issues related to a death. Employee assistance programs typically are charged with addressing the emotional aftermath of death. Work-life programs focus on life-cycle issues that impinge on work, from birth to death, though most work-life programs have not yet embraced death as an issue in their purview.[2] It is easy to see how these two programs could benefit from a coordinated, integrated approach to dealing with a campus death. But integration can go much further.

While these two programs are important cogs in the wheel, a successful response to a campus death will involve numerous roles and departments. UC Berkeley has developed a collaborative approach to campus deaths that doesn't stop with EAP and work-life programs. By taking a broader approach, UC Berkeley has been effective and efficient in its responses, simultaneously benefiting the university and the bereaved. Gaps and duplication of efforts have been reduced or eliminated, families are relieved of multiple requests for the same information, and the bereaved no longer receive an impersonal form letter following a loss. Some of the many departments involved in the university's integrated death response include benefits, human resources, payroll, information systems and technology, library, public affairs, and parking and transportation.

Integration of death response services is also an issue in non-academic settings. In any workplace, a death is likely to touch many individuals and affect diverse functions beyond those that will be addressed by EAP and work-life programs. Below is a Program Integration Model that visually demonstrates how program integration can improve overall program effectiveness. Here the model is applied to the death of a member of the campus community.

THE PROGRAM INTEGRATION MODEL

The University of California (UC) environment is decentralized and diverse, with ten campuses (one being UC Berkeley), three national laboratories, and five medical centers. Although they share most policies and benefits, each setting has a somewhat different array of services and programs and its own organizational culture. The Program Integration Model developed at UC is part of an effort to bring order to a sometimes chaotic system of responsibilities and services. It helps by creating an integrated, effective model to facilitate the discussion at UC among various programs such as employee assistance, work-life, vocational rehabilitation, workers' compensation, human resources, and benefits. The model provides a useful structure for plotting the collaboration among multiple entities addressing events in the life of an employee or client that have ramifications for the workplace.

In *Integral Psychology*, Ken Wilber (2001) posits the value of a matrix comparing individual and societal concerns with subjective and objective measures. His framework was adapted to help identify a broader context in which to assess program integration across campuses within

UC and across departments within the campus. While Wilber uses the matrix to demonstrate the integration of an individual within a larger universe, the Program Integration Model[3] is an adaptation that demonstrates individual and program integration within the workplace, or in this instance, the University.

The Program Integration Model offers a means of organizing programs and activities within four major categories or quadrants. This model has broad utility for individual program planning and evaluation, or to establish an employer profile of employee-related programs. Plotting programs in the four quadrants highlights the importance of balanced program planning in addressing the needs of both the employee and the employer.

By plotting its programs within the proposed quadrants, an organization will develop a profile that can serve as a road map for improving its balance and addressing programmatic needs at all levels. For example, comprehensive work-life efforts should address the need for leadership support to affect the corporate culture, help with HR policy and benefit design, and include programs such as employee assistance programs to support individuals and families. A complete picture of work-life initiatives within the model will identify gaps and opportunities for future program planning. By plotting program components into the quadrants, an organization can begin to identify individual program strengths and weaknesses, leading toward strategies for improvement.

The premise for this model is that both subjective and objective measures are important to assess program effectiveness for an individual or an organization. While all organizations and programs impact all four quadrants, not all program development intentionally includes in its planning the desire to effectively impact all quadrant areas. For example, the only credible way of measuring a human resources program's "return on investment (ROI)" is to measure its objective elements. However, it has always been difficult to measure the importance, objectively, of employee values, morale and psychological well-being. Therefore, the model distinguishes between subjective and objective programs or program components and also distinguishes between individual and group attributes.

Subjective programs identify and measure values. Objective programs measure specific, identifiable outcomes. For example, when an employer establishes for itself "Principles of Community"[4] initiatives the measure of impact upon the workplace is subjective and difficult to assess, whereas the success of an on-site child care program may be more easily assessed through objective measures. Each company will have different quadrant profiles, and while programs within two different companies may have the same name (e.g., work-life), their program quadrant profiles are likely to be very different.

Using separate descriptive categories of "corporate" and "individual" to intersect "subjective" and "objective" value measures, the resulting grid allows for an assessment of program integration within the work environment. As illustrated in Figure 1, this model serves as an effective program planning and analysis tool.

The first two quadrants of the model focus on issues from the organization's perspective. *Quadrant #1* (Figure 2) focuses on the *organization's culture* and how that culture impacts those working within the organization.

Quadrant #2 (Figure 3) focuses on the *organization's infrastructure*. It represents the framework that supports the workforce and the culture of the organization.

Clearly drawing a hard line between Quadrants 1 and 2 is artificial. Indeed, some of the organization's infrastructure results from its culture. For example, academic cultural values very much affect the development of administrative protocol within the University. Likewise, some infrastructure decisions are made for the express purpose of effecting changes in the organization's culture. For example, the early affirmative action plan was established within the University to facilitate the development of a workplace culture more accepting of diversity within the workforce. The third and fourth quadrants are focused at the individual level, identifying program characteristics related to individual values and activities, as well as the individual's response to the organizational culture and administrative systems.

FIGURE 1. Program Integration Model

Quadrant #1: *Corporate Subjective*	Quadrant #2: *Corporate Objective*
• Organizational culture • Cultural values • Corporate vision statement	• Organizational infrastructure • Systems • Product lines
Quadrant #3: *Individual Subjective*	Quadrant #4: *Individual Objective*
• Individual psychological well-being • Individual values	• Individual physical well-being • Individual work

FIGURE 2

Quadrant #1: Organizational Subjective Measures

This quadrant includes statements and values that identify the organization's world view and defines the context and values of the organization. The culture's communal values, shared language, and perceptions are all plotted in this quadrant. In the UC culture, this quadrant holds the shared values of academic excellence, research, teaching, collegiality, and public service.

An organization's culture is a subjective measure. Every organization has a culture that influences how the work gets done and how the organization relates to its employees. The culture represents communal values, shared perceptions, and meanings. This quadrant defines the background context and values of an organization as well as the overall employee morale. In many instances a company's vision statement will reflect the company's cultural values.

FIGURE 3

Quadrant #2: Organizational Objective Measures

This quadrant identifies an organization's infrastructure, systems, and product lines. An organization's infrastructure includes all corporate programs that are objectively measured. At the University, this infrastructure includes finance administration, personnel policies, labor relations, insurance benefits, the physical plant, and systems (information technology).

Quadrant #3 (Figure 4) focuses on an employee's *individual psychological well-being, values, and morale* as they affect job performance.

Quadrant #4 (Figure 5) focuses on the employee's *individual physical well-being and productive capability.*

Historically, it appears that most employers have focused their efforts on improving quadrants 2 and 4, representing corporate and individual programs that may be objectively measured. As a result, there is an effort to measure subjective programs and initiatives solely by objective measures which often fail to capture their impact on the workplace. Measuring an employee assistance program by the number of employees seen, for example, would miss the point of the program. Work-life

FIGURE 4

Quadrant #3: Individual Subjective Measures

This quadrant includes the individual's sense of self, well-being, and values. Individual morale may dictate the level of engagement in work and productivity. At the university, programs impacting this quadrant might include stress reduction seminars, conflict resolution, and employee assistance programs.

FIGURE 5

Quadrant #4: Individual Objective Measures

This quadrant includes programs such as nutrition classes, disease management, on-site medical services, and wellness programs. Examples related to productivity may include employee training programs, ergonomic workstations, and work tools.

program elements that are selected to support a "return on investment" are different from those that are concerned with the subjective climate of the organization, even though both ultimately influence productivity.

Plotting workplace or program components within the quadrants makes us acutely aware of the ways in which all aspects of work–culture, infrastructure, and psychological and physical well-being–affect, and are affected by each other. To be effective, a comprehensive program must address not only its own area of purview, but must coordinate with other programs, and if located primarily within one quadrant area, coordinate with programs in the other quadrants.

Plotting the University's EAP and work-life programs components identified within the quadrants of the Program Integration Model revealed interesting inter-program working relationships.

- First, it was noticed that most UC EAP and work-life programs emphasized program activities in one quadrant rather than in all four quadrants. For instance, one UC campus' work-life program focused on developing program initiatives that would be identified within Quadrant 2 whereas another work-life program focused more on organizational culture (Quadrant 1). It was discovered that most EAP activities within UC would be located within Quadrant 3 and most work-life activities would be located in Quadrant 2. Quadrant 2 activities may include coordinating/providing child

care support, lactation support, and HR policy coordination supporting work-life initiatives.
- Second, viewing the programs plotted into the quadrants helped to
make it clear why there has been historic difficulty in making com-
parisons among programs across the UC campuses and medical
centers–most programs initially attempt to address specific campus issues rather than to achieve balance among the four quadrants.
- Finally, it was noticed in plotting the university's diverse programs, there were many that, while not traditionally defined as
work-life or employee assistance programs, had an important impact on an employee's work and life relationships, and psychological health. The model reinforced the need for better integration of
EAP and work-life programs with other departments such as human resources, safety, benefits, risk, and legal.

It is within this context that the UC Berkeley initiative on responding
to death is now reviewed. This initiative is an example of a program developed to address the concerns identified across all four of the model's
quadrants. Plotting the program components has helped to identify program strengths and weaknesses, and has provided a road map for future
strategic program planning.

RESPONDING TO A DEATH AT UC BERKELEY

In order to comprehensively address employee issues, work-life programs address life issues from cradle to grave. Yet many organizations
have no process in place for responding to an employee death. Some
employers may not recognize the need for such a program, while others
may be uncomfortable planning for this difficult life transition.

An inadequate or absent response to an employee death can weaken
or break the ties of trust and loyalty that enable other employees to remain engaged and productive in their work. Employees may not remember all of the baby showers, birthdays, and other life events of
coworkers, but they can relay as if it were yesterday what the employer
did or did not do when someone died. The response to death does not
seem to leave the institutional memory.[5]

In order to improve its response to campus deaths, in 1999 UC Berkeley began developing a nationally recognized program that includes
guidelines, a Website, a virtual memorial, and an annual memorial

event. The program's target audience includes faculty and staff, students, emeriti, and retirees.

The objective of the UC Berkeley death-response program is to build a sense of community by addressing the most difficult of life events: the death of a member of the campus community. The program supports the community by simultaneously addressing the needs of the organization and of its employees. Responding to deaths effectively and compassionately assures more efficient operations while addressing the emotional needs and functioning of staff and faculty. The employer may benefit by greater loyalty, increased retention, improved productivity, and enhanced morale.

UC Berkeley's death-response program helps employees navigate a host of campus death-related benefits, policies and programs, including family sick leave, bereavement leave, personal leave, catastrophic leave-sharing, flexible work arrangements, telecommuting, health benefits, domestic partner benefits, disability benefits, accidental benefits, life insurance, dependent care, employee assistance, emergency loans, long-term care insurance, group legal services, and elder/adult dependent care.

The death-response Website [http://death-response.chance.berkeley.edu] functions as the program's hub. It provides a link to the campus Guidelines for Responding to Death, which offers tools to help the campus respond thoroughly and consistently to the needs of family and colleagues following a death. Because each life and death is unique, individual judgment is always necessary. The guidelines help users respond to those judgment calls.

The Website includes detailed guidance for handling the response to every aspect of a campus member's death, with a step-by-step outline of actions to be taken when a death occurs, including:

- How to choose who will be responsible for coordinating the response to a death and an explanation of that role,
- A timeline with detailed information on communications, condolences, survivors' emotional needs, memorial events, and other issues, and
- A list of specific considerations for each population (students, faculty, staff, emeriti, and retirees).

A feature on the site enables users to automatically e-mail a form with pertinent information to all required parties on campus. The automated e-mail program assures that necessary information gets to the right departments, such as the benefits and human resources offices, in a timely and convenient manner.

Information for members of the campus who have lost loved ones also is available on the Website. This includes what the workplace can do when a family member dies and another section on how to deal with grief and loss. There is also a section on preparing for one's own death; putting financial, legal, and medical documents in order in advance eases the burden on survivors. Campus resources, such as an emergency loan program that can be used for death-related expenses, are also listed.

University visitors to the site may create a virtual memorial–a Web page in memory of a family member, friend, or other, either within or outside of the university. Finally, the program established an annual public memorial event honoring members of the campus community who have died during the previous year. This ceremony gives equal weight to the memory of those who were lost in the past year, no matter what their workplace stature or role during their lifetime. This helps to balance the memorial services offered at the time of death for distinguished faculty (such as Nobel Laureates) with the same recognition for other employees such as custodians.

Created by a Chancellor-appointed work group, Berkeley's progressive program for responding to campus deaths has been recognized nationally. Universities and corporations around the country have inquired about Berkeley's death-response procedures, and the program has been referred to in journals and periodicals.

THE PROGRAM INTEGRATION MODEL AND THE RESPONSE TO DEATH INITIATIVE

The Program Integration Model emphasizes the need for balanced program planning that addresses the needs of both the employer and the employee. Though the model was not used in the development and implementation of the death initiative at UC Berkeley, it can now be used for assessment and review of the current program to evaluate program efficacy. Establishing a model profile of the Response to Death Initiative provides the framework that allows for discussion of programmatic balance, resources, and coordination.

A simple listing of Initiative programs and benefits within the respective quadrants of the model creates an "Initiative" profile. The completed model (Figure 6) shows all the programs and benefits coordinated

FIGURE 6. Model Profile of UC Berkeley's Response to Death Initiative

Quadrant #1: *Organizational Subjective*	Quadrant #2: *Organizational Objective*
• Community memorials • Condolences • Obituaries • Diversity	• Group life insurance • AD&D benefits • Survivor benefits • Emergency leaves • Emergency loans • Survivor notification • Inter-program coordination • Integrated Web resource for family members and coworkers
Quadrant #3: *Individual Subjective*	Quadrant #4: *Individual Objective*
• EAP • Dependent care assistance • Personal leave • Bereavement leave • Family sick • Virtual memorials	• Health benefits • Catastrophic leave sharing • FMLA • Flexible work arrangements

for an effective response to a death at the Berkeley campus, providing support for survivors, coworkers, and the employer community.

Balance. Programs and benefits assembled together for this Initiative are comprehensive and provide significant effort in each of the quadrants within the model. Individual and work community values are enhanced; employee and survivor resources are identified and readily accessible. In addition to improving a coordinated response to death, UC Berkeley demonstrates that it values a compassionate response to death, further reinforcing work-culture values of honoring people and their ideas, critical for an academic institution.

Coordination. Program and benefit coordination with the identified goal of establishing an effective and coordinated response to death allows each program to participate in identifying a process and role in supporting the desired outcome.

Effectiveness. Improving program effectiveness by supporting a comprehensive and coordinated response to death in the workplace is the goal. Codifying identified process improvements (see *http://death-reponse.*

chance.berkeley.edu) creates a new base upon which future improvements may be made. Periodic process evaluations including placing programs in all quadrants are required to ensure the Initiative continues to be responsive and current.

The UC Berkeley *Response to Death Initiative* is a premier model of effective program coordination that promotes corporate and individual values while delivering enhanced services and improved program efficiencies. Family members, coworkers, managers, and customers all benefit from comprehensive programming in response to this significant life event. From reinforcing a common value within the workplace to the reduction of program duplication and inefficiency, from providing emotional support for coworkers to the efficient delivery of benefits to family members, the *Response to Death Initiative* provides an example of enhancing objective and subjective values within the workplace. A comprehensive, effective and well-integrated response to a significant event, such as death, demonstrates respect for both individuals and the community.

NOTES

1. Anticipated death rates are based on review of census death rates data based on age and numbers of people in each age group at UC Berkeley. (Thank you to Jon Bain-Chekal, MBA, for this data collection and other work on this project.) These estimates have proven correct over the last four years that the data has been collected.

2. The statement that most work-life programs do not address death-related issues is based on the author's informal discussions with university and other industry work-life professionals, the topic areas covered in workshops, etc., at work-life conferences, and a review of work-life literature.

3. This model was developed in 2000 for the University of California by Judy McConnell, Kris Lange, and Bruce Goya. Judy McConnell, Director of Health & Welfare Administration, has since retired from the University. Kris Lange and Bruce Goya work in the Human Resources and Benefits Department at the University of California Office of the President. This Model was presented to the Alliance of Work-Life Progress (AWLP) conference in February 2002.

4. "Principles of Community" provide stated values of community interaction. See the UC San Diego Principles of Community at *http://www.ucsd.edu/principles/* for an example.

5. Based on feedback from workshop participants and EAP clients plus observational experience.

APPENDICES

Responding to deaths Website, including the virtual memorial, *http://death-response. chance.berkeley.edu*

One article in the employee newspaper about the updated and improved website and memorial event, *http://www.berkeley.edu/news/berkeleyan/2002/09/memorial.html*

Communication to all employees from the Chancellor announcing the Website and memorial event 9/10/04, *http://www.berkeley.edu/news/media/releases/2004/09/memoriam. shtml*

The Berkeley response to deaths program has been highlighted in:

- HR Magazine, *Giving Time to Grieve*, November 1999, *and Helping Employees Cope with Grief*, September 2003, published by the Society for Human Resource
- Management The Robert Wood Johnson Foundation Last Acts Coalition in their materials on end of life issues.
- One Small Step *Newsteps*, Summer 2003, Vol. 2, No. 3

Wilber, Ken (2000) *Integral Psychology*, Shambhala Publications, Inc. USA

Chapter 9

Disaster Consequence Management: An Integrated Approach for Fostering Human Continuity in the Workplace

Nancy T. Vineburgh
Robert J. Ursano
Carol S. Fullerton

SUMMARY. The critical element in a workplace approach to consequence management for disaster, terrorism and other critical incidents is the integrated planning and response across numerous workplace functions including human resources, employee assistance, security and facilities, medical, occupational health, wellness and work-life. These corporate functions ensure the performance, health, safety and human continuity of the workplace. In this model, workplace professionals charged with the human capital and continuity of their organizations play new crucial roles that require an understanding of (1) the integration of mental health into a public health approach for managing the psychological and behavioral implications of terrorism; (2) the integration of operational continuity planning with human continuity resources; and (3) the integration of workplace preparedness into the larger sphere of population health interventions for the 21st century. This new role of workplace health and productivity professionals is necessary to the

[Haworth co-indexing entry note]: "Disaster Consequence Management: An Integrated Approach for Fostering Human Continuity in the Workplace." Vineburgh, Nancy T., Robert J. Ursano, and Carol S. Fullerton. Co-published simultaneously in *Journal of Workplace Behavioral Health* (The Haworth Press, Inc.) Vol. 20, No. 1/2, 2005, pp. 159-181; and: *The Integration of Employee Assistance, Work/Life, and Wellness Services* (ed: Mark Attridge, Patricia A. Herlihy, and R. Paul Maiden) The Haworth Press, Inc., 2005, pp. 159-181. Single or multiple copies of this article are available for a fee from The Haworth Document Delivery Service [1-800-HAWORTH, 9:00 a.m. - 5:00 p.m. (EST). E-mail address: docdelivery@haworthpress.com].

Available online at http://www.haworthpress.com/web/JWBH
© 2005 by The Haworth Press, Inc. All rights reserved.
doi:10.1300/J490v20n01_09

health and resiliency of our global community and its citizens in the workplace and at home. *[Article copies available for a fee from The Haworth Document Delivery Service: 1-800-HAWORTH. E-mail address: <docdelivery@ haworthpress.com> Website: <http://www.HaworthPress.com> © 2005 by The Haworth Press, Inc. All rights reserved.]*

KEYWORDS. Workplace, critical incidents, terrorism, preparedness, employee health, employee assistance, security, integration, business continuity, resilience, population, disaster preparedness

INTRODUCTION

The events of 9/11 and the anthrax attacks that followed constituted a wake up call in the United States–across government (federal, state and local), public health, the health care industry and academia. Some 76% of Americans, two years after 9/11, are concerned about terrorism in the United States (NCDP, 2003). However, most do not believe that the U.S. health system can respond effectively to a biological, chemical or nuclear attack. The most prevalent concern of Americans (66%) is the need to account for the whereabouts and safety of family members yet less than one in four families (23%) actually have a basic emergency plan (NCDP, 2003). The integration of previously separate and often unrelated functions, services and resources are needed to address the unprecedented impact of terrorism.

As a primary target, the workplace was no exception to this call. The importance of human capital–individual employees and their collective needs–took on new meaning to corporate America. Employers from diverse corporations and industries recognized anew the value of their people and their wellness and resiliency (Coutu & Hyman, 2002; Greenberg, 2002; Mankin & Perry, 2004). In the words of Ray O'Rourke, managing director for global corporate affairs at Morgan Stanley, "We knew within the first day that, even though we are a financial services company, we didn't have a financial crisis on our hands; we had a human crisis. After that point, everything was focused on our people" (Argenti, 2002).

While workplaces differ in size, industry and employee populations, the human impact of terrorism is predictable, expectable and requires organization-wide preparedness that includes both general and worksite specific interventions. Responsibilities for employee health and productivity also vary within corporations, but these functions (human resources, employee assistance programs, security and facilities, medical, occupational health, wellness and work-life) can play an essential role in equipping workers and organizations to prepare for and respond to the threat and/or actuality of terrorism.

The critical element in this workplace approach to preparing for and responding to the threat of terrorism is integrated planning and response across the above-mentioned functions. These corporate functions ensure the performance, health, safety and human continuity of the workplace. In order to effectively address critical behavioral preparedness needs, the integration and coordination of these activities is necessary. Such an approach can better protect corporate security, employees and the citizens of the nation.

This article addresses an integrated workplace terrorism, disaster and critical incident response plan. In this model, workplace professionals charged with the human capital and continuity of their organizations play new crucial roles in preparedness and consequence management for disaster, terrorism and other critical incidents. This perspective requires an understanding of: (1) the integration of mental health into a population public health approach for managing the psychological and behavioral implications of terrorism in communities, including vertical communities of the corporate world; (2) the integration of operational continuity planning with human continuity resources; (3) the integration of workplace preparedness into the larger sphere of population health interventions for the 21st century. This new role of workplace health and productivity professionals is necessary to the health and resiliency of our global community and its citizens in the workplace and at home.

THE PREPAREDNESS ROLE OF THE WORKPLACE

The most prestigious science organization of the USA and one of the most prestigious in the world, the National Academies of Science, Institute of Medicine (IOM), recently issued a timely and essential report for workplace planning. *Preparing for the Psychological Consequences of Terrorism: A Public Health Strategy* (IOM, 2003a) identifies ". . . the workplace as a new and important area in which to address public health planning for the psychological consequences of terrorism." Because most acts of terrorism in the U.S. have occurred where and when people work, it is essential that interventions for preparedness, response and recovery occur in occupational settings. Sustaining the workforce–its organizational health and the well-being of workers–is central to protecting the economic and social capabilities of a nation. In addition, the workplace provides one of the most important avenues to go "from the employee to the citizen" to provide community knowledge and resources.

The public is generally not knowledgeable about preparedness within their own workplace (NCDP, 2003). Only 36% of citizens report being familiar with emergency plans in their workplace (Council for Excellence in Government, 2004). Nearly half of U.S. workers feel their employer is not prepared for a terrorist attack (Comp Psych Survey, 2004). In addition, although 70% of people working in companies mandated to have an emergency evacuation plan were aware of such plans, only 42% were familiar with the details (NCDP, 2003).

The work of organizations must continue after terrorist, disaster or other critical incidents despite high levels of anxiety and possible future attacks. Banks, groceries, schools as well as government workplaces of military (e.g., the Pentagon) and services (e.g., the U.S. Postal Service) must continue regardless of the risk of new attack whether that is an explosive or a bioterrorist event such as the anthrax attacks. The IOM report also recognizes that preparing for the psychological consequences of terrorism will have important benefits for dealing with other violent events and critical incidents in the workplace.

A population level approach (rather than individual care, treatment and services) is the core of the public health approach recommended for workplace communities. In this model, screening, early detection, health education, service access, and health promotion and prevention are central. Likening terrorism and the fear it propagates to a disease transmission model, the IOM report points to the need for pre-event, event and post-event interventions to protect the health and sustain the performance capacity of individuals and groups, including the workplace.

'Population health,' a perspective familiar to all workplace services directed to helping employees as a whole, is a term that refers to 'the health of the population' or 'the population's health' (Federal, Provincial and Territorial Advisory Committee on Population Health, 1999 as referenced in IOM, 2003b). Perhaps one of the most universal examples of a population health intervention is automobile seat belts. Seat belts modify the risk of automobile accidents and therefore reduce the risk of injury and psychological disease due to injury after accidents. Similarly, fluoride in drinking water is a population level intervention to modify the risk of tooth decay, and influenza vaccination is a population intervention to reduce the incidence and spread of influenza. Workplace interventions that are to prepare as well as respond to terrorism may use a population health perspective to prevent and/or modify the risk of injury and morbidity from exposure to terrorism. From practicing fire drills to planning for leave policies, emergency hires and depression screening and ensuring adequate health benefits for mental health care for trauma exposure, the population health perspective prompts thinking on the large scale for needed services, behaviors and interventions before, during and after a terrorist or disaster event.

Many workplace professionals, however, lack training in the services and program needs for mental health interventions for the pre-event, event and post-event phases of disaster including terrorism. With training, workplace health and service professionals can make significant contributions to sustaining, protecting and restoring the mental health of employees and the operational continuity of the workplace after terrorist and disaster events (IOM, 2003a; Ursano, Fullerton, & Norwood, 2003). They can also complement the disaster response role of the federal government that is geared to immediate needs at the directly affected site, rather than pre-event planning and longer-term responses that may occur in areas (workplaces or communities) not directly involved but nonetheless affected.

PSYCHOLOGICAL AND BEHAVIORAL IMPLICATIONS OF TERRORISM FOR THE WORKFORCE

It is important to realize that the primary goal of terrorism is to spread terror around a nation and in this way to destabilize trust in public institutions, to change peoples' beliefs, sense of safety, and behaviors (Holloway et al., 1997). The deaths that may occur in the process are, sad to say, only the mechanism for the spread of terror. These psychological effects are especially deleterious in the workplace. They can undermine the economic, intellectual and social capital of a nation, its industries, as well as the health and routine of its citizens, their families and communities.

While not the first terrorism on American soil, the events of 9/11 were the first to have such a profound and pervasive impact on the nation (Silver et al., 2002; Vlahov et al., 2002; Stein et al., 2003). One longitudinal study (Stein et al., 2003) documented that amongst those Americans (16%) who experienced persistent stress two months after 9/11, this distress disrupted their work (65% reported accomplishing less), their social life (24% avoided public places) and led to increased health risks (38% using alcohol, medication or other drugs to relax, sleep and reduce terrorism-related worries).

At a 2003 global symposium on workplace mental health held at the International Labour Organization in Geneva, Switzerland, attendees, including medical directors from multinational corporations, EAP providers and ministers of health, expressed concern about terrorism as an extreme form of workplace violence with global consequences. Recommendations included preparing employees through workplace drills in evacuation, shelter-in-place, as well as training for employee health and productivity professionals in disaster mental health (Vineburgh, 2003).

Immediate responses to disasters and terrorism involve knowledge about "disaster behavior," a term and concept that may be unfamiliar, but can be extremely useful in communicating the value of preparedness to employers, management and employees. Renowned Norwegian disaster psychiatrist Lars Weisaeth (1989) was one of the first to use the term, which refers to behaviors in the face of disaster such as spontaneous reactions like fear and panic, or planned reactions such as evacuation, shelter-in-place and quarantine. These reactions are of critical importance in the workplace (Hall et al., 2003; Ursano & Norwood, 2003). During the 1993 World Trade Center explosion, 32% of individuals had not begun to evacuate by over one hour, 30% decided not to evacuate and only 36% had participated in a previous emergency evacuation (Aguirre et al., 1998). Importantly, large groups (greater than 20 people) took 6.7 minutes longer to initiate evacuation, a time frame of life or death in many disasters. In addition, the higher the location, the greater the delay in initiating evacuation, and the more people were known to one another, the longer the group took to initiate evacuation (Aguirre et al., 1998). These findings may be familiar to anyone who has taken part in a fire drill in the workplace during which often one hears: "Are you going?," "Maybe," "Shall we ask Mary?," "Sure, want to do lunch?," "We better bring our umbrellas," etc. Our wish to affiliate, to join is a danger in these settings because such behaviors delay critical decisions to protect our safety and health. For workplaces, this behavior can be life threatening.

Similar findings from a recent study emphasize the importance of addressing the behavioral issues of preparedness. The study of a representative sample of the United States found that 90% of Americans say they will not evacuate immediately if directed to do so by officials citing concern by 66% of those to account for the whereabouts of family and loved ones (NCDP, 2003). Whether human resource planning includes adequate personnel locator planning for disasters and terrorist events, and "meet up stations" after evacuation to allow for counting heads, may make the difference between knowing who is injured and appropriately notifying families, and minimizing the anxiety that accompanies hours or days of delay in knowing the whereabouts of loved ones. The implications and knowledge of these disaster behaviors is critical to inform interventions around terrorism, bioterrorism and infectious diseases like SARS that pose risks in vertical communities (the workplace) as well as global industries where travel, travel policies and sick leaves are critical to the continuity of infrastructure and people.

Disaster mental health care must address both the psychological and behavioral responses to the traumatic events (Ursano et al., 2004a). These may be evident in distress responses such as changes in perceived safety or the willingness to fly in airplanes or altered behaviors such as increased smoking or alcohol consumption (Fullerton et al., 2003; North et al., 1999; North et al., 2002) or the more traditional illnesses and diseases that may result from trauma exposure including post-traumatic stress disorder and depression (Galea et al., 2002; North et al., 1999; Pfefferbaum & Doughty, 2001; Ursano et al., 2003; Vlahov et al., 2002).

Disasters are either naturally occurring (earthquakes, hurricanes, floods) or human made (industrial and environmental accidents). Terrorism is a human made disaster. Human made disasters, similar to intentional traumatic events such as robbery or rape, carry a potentially greater mental health impact than other disasters because of their malicious intent. Like other human made disasters, terrorism generates a loss of trust in the world, an altered sense of safety and belief in the just world, and disbelief, anger, and feelings of lack of control. In addition, terrorism can open the "fault lines" that are always present in groups of individuals related to differences in ethnicity, race, religion and socioeconomic status. Such fault lines can become major divides that separate labor and management or may result in scapegoating and stigmatization of fellow employees (Ursano, 2002; Ursano, Fullerton, & Norwood, 2003). These behaviors and disorders can be costly in the workplace in terms of safety, productivity and morale, all factors that affect the health and productivity of a corporation.

INTEGRATION:
ADDRESSING WORKPLACE BARRIERS
AND OPPORTUNITIES FOR ORGANIZATIONAL
AND EMPLOYEE PREPAREDNESS

In the USA, the events of 9/11 and the anthrax attacks that followed reinforced in the minds of employers the value of an organization's people and the importance of sustaining their well-being (Argenti, 2002; Coutu & Hyman, 2002; Greenberg, 2002; Mankin & Perry, 2004; Schouten et al., 2004). Addressing the psychological and behavioral effects of terrorism to protect workplace employees and business continuity requires integration across a number of areas previously unaccustomed to collaborating. A number of barriers to preparedness exist within the workplace: (1) a corporate focus on operational versus human continuity (Mankin & Perry, 2004; Ursano, Vineburgh, & Fullerton, 2004; Ursano & Vineburgh, 2004a); (2) corporate silos that prevent the collaboration and coordination essential in facilitating employee preparedness (Vineburgh, 2004; Ursano & Vineburgh, 2004a; Ursano & Vineburgh, 2004b); (3) employer and employee resistance to engaging in preparedness activities; (4) a need for professional training of workplace health and service providers in disaster mental health and service needs for disaster response and recovery (IOM, 2003a); (5) a common language to communicate the conceptual and practical implications of disaster mental health, preparedness and response (Holloway & Waldrep, 2004).

The first three barriers to preparedness deserve special attention (consult Table 1). Workplace professionals must address these to begin the process of equipping organizations and workers to deal with the psychological impact of terrorism.

Regarding the first barrier another way to view corporate continuity is through '3 R's': redundancy, reliability and resiliency (Ursano, Fullerton, & Vineburgh, 2004). Redundancy refers to a corporation's

TABLE 1. Organizational Barriers to Workplace Preparedness for Terrorism

1. Corporate focus on operational rather than human continuity.
2. Corporate silos that prevent the collaboration and coordination essential to facilitating employee preparedness.
3. Employer and employee resistance to engage in preparedness due to attitudes and/or emotions ranging from complacency, fear to denial.

© Copyright 2004 Center for the Study of Traumatic Stress, Uniformed Services University. All rights reserved.

physical back-up as in alternate sites and bench strength in terms of leadership roles. Reliability refers to a corporation's hardware as in its IT systems and operations. Resiliency represents the human capital of the organization–its people. It took 9/11 to demonstrate the first priority in the face of disaster is an organization's people who are also the most resilient element (Greenberg, 2002; Argenti, 2002; Coutu & Hyman, 2002).

The second major barrier to workplace preparedness is the effect of corporate silos that prevent important collaborations for employee preparedness. Corporate security is an excellent example of this silo effect. The traditional role of corporate security in the United States has been operational–guarding the perimeter. At a national Conference Board meeting (2003) of senior level security professionals, there was an expressed interest in expanding that role to prepare employees for terrorism. The security professionals present communicated their desire to play a more human role in protecting employees and were seeking creative ways to collaborate with the health and productivity functions within their organization. Partnering with their company's EAP program was of great interest.

The third organizational barrier to workplace preparedness is employer and employee attitudes about such activities that range from complacency, to fear, to lack of fitness! An interesting, newly reported phenomenon amongst employers who have tried to institute evacuation drills since 9/11 is employee resistance due to lack of fitness (Ursano & Vineburgh, 2003). A woman who experienced the burning of the Twin Towers and works in New York City remarked that her workplace subsequently engaged employees to practice evacuation from the 42nd floor. She commented that, "employees are not conditioned for terrorism, and most colleagues reported feeling the effects of this drill for an entire weekend" (L. Hall, personal communication, December 2003).

Not taking drills seriously or not wanting to participate because drills take too much time are attitudes that impede employee preparedness for terrorism. Several young attorneys in an urban law firm in a high-rise building reported that their boss told them not to participate in such drills, as they do not constitute billable hours! The attorneys said they would most likely participate if these drills were conducted in the context of an employee preparedness campaign that would educate them about the significance of disaster behaviors including evacuation, shelter-in-place and family communication plans. If such a campaign were to be national in scope, employees would feel part of a larger community in which everyone–employers, schools, community institutions–were joined in a united effort (Vineburgh, 2004).

Fear is a particular barrier to preparedness. A number of employee assistance and occupational health professionals of Fortune 500, multinational corporations interested in workplace preparedness expressed their primary concern as a question: how to raise awareness of this topic without raising undue anxiety in their workplace (Bender, 2003).

A Workplace Resiliency Model (consult Table 2) offers a framework around which to organize the workplace response to prepare, respond and recover from terrorist events and address these barriers to preparedness and response through integration and a focus on resiliency. This approach is both a strategy for moving organizations in the direction of terrorism planning, as well as a health promotion vehicle to educate leadership, management and employees about disaster preparedness. With an aim to establishing an integral and integrated role for the workplace health and productivity professional in this process and practice, this article advances a framework derived from a public health model that views terrorism as a threat to the health of an entire nation and its communities including workplace communities.

PREPARING AND RESPONDING THROUGH AN INTEGRATED WORKPLACE APPROACH TO TERRORISM PREPAREDNESS

Employers are important population health partners (IOM, 2003b) with resources and established relationships that can foster terrorism and disaster preparedness (IOM, 2003a). Workplace health and productivity professionals (employee assistance professionals, human resource professionals, corporate medical directors, and occupational health, wellness and work-life professionals) are ideally positioned for an important role in disaster preparedness, and must be at the table as corporations develop or expand their disaster plans to address 21st century issues around terrorism and bioterrorism.

The events of 9/11 dramatically raised the visibility of EAPs (Coutu & Hyman, 2002; Greenberg, 2002; Mankin & Perry, 2004). EAP providers (internal and external) of affected corporations were called upon to set up off-site family assistance centers, contract with grief counselors and provide direct counseling services throughout their corporations, in the immediate aftermath and overtime, including planning for workplace anniversaries of 9/11. Because EAPs deal on a day-to-day basis

TABLE 2. Integrated Workplace Resiliency Model: Role of Workplace Health and Productivity Professional

IMPLICATIONS		Behavioral	Psychological	Resiliency
EDUCATE	Event	☐ Senior management: Need for/assemble Integrated corporate Response model/ team ☐ Workforce: Disaster behaviors; i.e., evacuation, shelter-in-place, family communication plans	☐ Incorporate disaster health promotion into existing campaigns for depression, alcohol, anxiety	☐ Shared values ☐ Social cohesion
COMMUNICATE	Pre-Event	☐ Grief leadership ☐ Promote/partner/ stay on corporate risk communication message ☐ Integrate message into existing EAP resources (e.g., 800 numbers, Website, etc.)	☐ Provide psychological first aid to employees/ families ☐ Deploy resources off-site/family centers ☐ Promote personal care: Eat, sleep, exercise, resume schedule	☐ Corporate continuity ☐ Social capital/ human focus
EVALUATE	Post-Event	☐ Conduct health promotion of behavior risks: Increased smoking, alcohol, drugs, family violence	☐ Health promotion about normal distress; more serious reactions requiring evaluation ☐ Assess/evaluate over time problems requiring treatment ☐ Attention/out-reach vulnerable populations	☐ Expected outcome ☐ Need for human resources response to disaster fallout ☐ Opening of fault lines; race, ethnicity, perceived differences in medical treatment

© Copyright 2004 Center for the Study of Traumatic Stress, Uniformed Services University. All rights reserved.

with many of the psychological and behavioral risk issues that can result from disaster exposure, their involvement in disaster preparedness and behavioral and mental health response is logical, and can provide seamless resources and services.

Employee assistance programs and providers deal with a broad range of psychological and behavioral disorders. In the United States, workplace mental health programs began after WWII to address problem drinking in the workplace, expanding in the 1970s and 1980s to encompass the emotional health and distress of employees (Davidson & Herlihy, 1999). Most EAP programs were 'internal' featuring mental health counselors as employees working within the corporation. With the advent of managed care in the 1980s, behavioral health carve-outs (private companies that offer mental health benefits and services) began offering EAP services, and many corporations chose to outsource their mental health and substance abuse assessment and treatment to these large networks. Such programs are referred to as 'external EAP' programs. Some companies have both 'internal' and 'external EAPs' called a mixed model.

Although EAP programs vary, most conduct employee health promotion and education activities, mental health assessment and referral, and sometimes treatment including alcohol and drug or mental health counseling. Many EAPs conduct national mental health awareness programs like National Depression Screening Day and National Alcohol Screening Day, and offer confidential and interactive screening resources (800 numbers and online programs) that encourage self-identification and help-seeking for depression, anxiety, post-traumatic stress disorder, and a range of alcohol problems from risky drinking to alcohol dependence (Raskin & Williams, 2003). The majority of American employers offer EAP services (Roman & Blum, 2002), as do a growing number of employers worldwide (Masi, 2000; Reddy, 2003).

The events of 9/11 also gave rise to new roles and collaborations among many workplace health and productivity professionals that must be further developed and sustained to achieve organizational and employee preparedness. The role and relationship between employee assistance and human resources in response to terrorism provides an interesting example of new and needed collaborations and opportunities for integration of health and productivity with security functions to protect health and sustain the workforce.

To manage the human consequences of 9/11, EAPs worked hand-in-hand with human resource departments whose staff was present at off-site family assistance centers addressing the needs, immediate and long-term, of victims' families including benefits and services (Greenberg, 2002). Despite the leadership role of human resources during and after 9/11, and despite major workplace terrorist events (1993 World Trade Center attack and Oklahoma City bombing), no articles addressing employee consequences of terrorism were published in human resource journals between January 2001 and March 2003 (Mankin & Perry, 2004). Human resource departments are a logical locus for terrorism preparedness because most employee health and benefits activities reside in human resources, including EAP programs that provide direct psychological services.

Human resources and employee assistance can be formidable partners in equipping organizations and workers for the impact of terrorism. Because most EAP programs (internal and external) report to their corporation's human resources department, it is incumbent upon human resources to seek organizational buy-in for disaster preparedness planning, especially around terrorism; to advocate for the integration of a human continuity focus; and to include their organization's employee assistance and/or related occupational health, work-life and medical services in the process and planning. Presently, many human resource departments have been reluctant to collaborate with their employee assistance programs or bring the human focus of disaster response into alignment with operational planning. The reasons for this resistance remain unexplained.

The partnership between human resources and employee assistance can facilitate the creation of family communication plans, an essential aspect of preparedness for terrorism. The workplace is an excellent place to encourage families to have family/work and family communications plans, and to be knowledgeable about disaster policies and plans in settings where their children and loved ones reside when not at home such as schools, day care and elder care communities. On the morning of 9/11, the first concern amongst employees everywhere was for the safety and whereabouts of their families. EAPs joining with human resources can advance a new approach in population health: citizen preparedness through workplace preparedness.

A corporate trend to outsource critical incident planning and response to specialty firms or for a corporation's external provider to subcontract to such specialty providers runs the risk of undermining essential integration of internal health and productivity functions (human resources, occupational health, work-life, etc.) into corporate disaster planning. This trend also undermines the important work of employee preparedness that many specialty firms might not find profitable nor within their scope of work.

INTEGRATED WORKPLACE RESILIENCY MODEL: ADDRESSING AND OVERCOMING BARRIERS TO WORKPLACE PREPAREDNESS

A focus on integration and resiliency can reframe tasks and foster necessary collaborations for health and corporate operational continuity. Resiliency is a growing topic of interest in mental health and mental health promotion (American Psychological Association Help Center, 2004; Vineburgh, 2004). It is important to recognize that resiliency is the expected outcome in all studies of disaster (North, 2003; Ursano et al., 2003). Resiliency is also a growing topic of interest in the workplace as it bridges the health and continuity of the organization and its people (Coutu, 2002; Vineburgh, 2004). There is an interest amongst EAP programs such as Chevron/Texaco (Blair Consulting Group, 2003) and Dupont, as well as EAP professional associations (EASNA, 2004) to use resiliency as a health promotion vehicle and way to integrate mental health into other productivity functions and outcomes. A workplace strategy that reframes disaster preparedness as a means of fostering organizational and employee resiliency can be an effective way to communicate about and motivate preparedness.

The cornerstone of an Integrated Workplace Resiliency Model is its focus on resiliency as an outcome of preparedness planning, an approach that might be viewed as beneficial by organizations and workers rather than threatening. Resiliency has a positive connotation and can provide a positive framework for engaging reluctant corporations and employees to participate in terrorism preparedness. Resiliency is a meaningful disaster metaphor for workplace preparedness and response to disaster (Vineburgh et al., 2004; Vineburgh, 2004). Resiliency involves two perspectives that have workplace specific implications. From a clinical perspective, resiliency is the expected outcome of disaster and terrorism (North, 2003; Ursano, 2002), and aligns with workplace health and productivity. From an organizational perspective, resiliency is integral to corporate continuity, especially human capital continuity (see three R's).

PRE-EVENT PHASE: EDUCATE

In the pre-event phase, workplace health professionals must educate the workplace–senior management, management and employees–about the importance of preparedness including practical interventions. It is important to educate senior management in order to achieve executive level buy-in and participation. Educating senior management to integrate human continuity functions (employee assistance, medical, occupational health) within their business continuity planning is an essential first step to organizational preparedness for terrorism.

Workplace health providers must also educate employees about preparedness, both its psychological and behavioral implications. Working in collaboration with other functions like human resources or corporate security, EAPs can provide information on important disaster behaviors such as evacuation, shelter-in-place and the creation of family communication plans. Disaster behaviors can be taught in conjunction with corporate security that can facilitate the actual practicing of the drills. Existing health awareness events or a dedicated day on workplace preparedness can provide the vehicle for this activity (Vineburgh, 2004). Such a campaign on workplace resiliency incorporating terrorism preparedness could even be conducted as a global workplace initiative.

Make the Case

The 9/11 response of Morgan Stanley, a global corporation, is an excellent example of a collaborative approach involving operational and human continuity planning that greatly enhanced the resiliency of the business and its people. Soon after the 1993 WTC bombings, Morgan Stanley launched a preparedness program of serious evacuation drills directed by its corporate security department. On the morning of 9/11, one minute after the North Tower was struck, Rick Rescorla, security Vice President, instructed Morgan Stanley's employees to evacuate the South Tower immediately, to stay calm and follow their well-practiced drills. This resulted in a loss of only seven of its 2,700 employees. Tragically, Rescorla was among them, but this example represents the successful integration of security, facilities, human health and behavior and employee preparedness. Moreover, Morgan Stanley exhibited a trait attributable to corporations that are resilient: an ability to 'stare down reality' and plan for the worst having recognized after 1993, they could again be a target of terrorism (Coutu, 2002). This kind of planning amongst senior leadership, management and employees sends message of a strong and responsive organization, which creates social cohesion and shared values, two important components of organizational and individual resiliency.

EVENT PHASE: COMMUNICATE

In the event phase, the immediate, actual response to the terrorist event, workplace health professionals must *communicate* on behalf of and in sync with corporate leadership. It is essential to stay on the corporate message to reinforce information on employee safety, workplace resumption and schedules, and employee resources for information and help seeking. Employee assistance programs can integrate the corporate communication message into existing EAP 800 numbers and websites, and provide valuable support to human resources and corporate communications to alleviate anxiety by ongoing information as well as the important task of getting employees back to work around which there will be anxiety. An important role in this phase is provision of psychological first aid: promoting personal care, sleep, exercise and return to normal routine.

Make the Case

> Corporate leadership of affected corporations as a result of 9/11 recognized that second to and intertwined with a priority on employee well-being was the ability to communicate with clarity, compassion and an expectation of resiliency (Argenti, 2002; Greenberg, 2002). Strong, consistent communication fosters a sense of community and corporate continuity from which emerge resilient organizations and resilient employees (Argenti, 2002). Many corporations post 9/11 have brought together human resources, employee assistance, medical and corporate communications to mount integrated planning for phone trees, updating of employee contact information that is required on a frequent and regular basis. Another way in which communication has been stepped up is through corporate security reporting internally on PA systems and company intranet sites about any issues that might raise employee safety concerns. This kind of planning and this corporate security communication for human continuity builds and fosters a resilient workforce and business plan.

POST-EVENT PHASE: EVALUATE

In the post-event phase, workplace health and productivity professionals must evaluate the impact of the event and provide necessary resources to aid in the recovery. EAPs can provide health promotion materials on normal distress reactions of trauma and how to distinguish between normal distress and more serious psychiatric problems requiring evaluation and treatment. They can provide information on escalation of health risks such as increased smoking, alcohol, and even family violence. EAPs can promote use of existing, anonymous and interactive screening resources for case finding.

Human resource professionals must stay alert to the opening of fault lines from terrorist events. Terrorism opens the fault lines of a society revealing its vulnerabilities and divisive tendencies along racial, ethnic and religious lines (Ursano, 2002) that can result in scapegoating, discrimination against ethnicities perceived akin to the terrorist agent, as well as fallout around perceived inequities in treatment responses.

In the aftermath of the anthrax attacks of 2001, U.S. postal workers became disgruntled perceiving their medical treatment inferior to that given to employees on Capitol Hill despite the fact that theirs may have been a technically more effective protocol. This perception has historical roots around the fault lines of race and ethnicity in the United States. It resulted in serious and persistent mistrust that undermined the cohesion of the postal service workplace including legal ramifications (Steury et al., 2004; Holloway & Waldrep, 2004). These behavioral consequences of terrorism have important implications for the human capital and continuity of organizations about which human resource personnel must be knowledgeable.

Employee assistance programs and human resources departments must reach out to vulnerable populations. Specific groups may require special interventions. These include identified cultural groups whose perception of the disaster may be markedly different because of past experiences with disasters (i.e., refugees, individuals recently exposed to traumas, ethnic groups). The number of refugees worldwide is growing, and many are relocated in the United States, as well as in workplaces throughout the world. The unique characteristics of refugees groups, including cultural, ethnic and language considerations, torture or trauma experiences, multiple losses, minimal resources, and an uncertain future need to be considered in developing mental health services (Gerrity & Steinglass 2003).

Make the Case

> The events of 9/11 constituted a tipping point in which many corporations realized the importance of mental health issues, their link to employee health and productivity and the importance of functions that support this work–EAPs, occupational health, work-life– across a continuum from pre-event, event, post-event outreach (Mankin & Perry, 2004). While resiliency is the expected outcome of disaster, attention to the psychological and behavioral implications of trauma including vigilance and response to the opening of fault lines as described above can enhance the recovery and resiliency of organizations and workers (Ursano, 2002; Coutu & Hyman, 2002).

INTEGRATION AND RESILIENCY AS THE WORKPLACE PREPAREDNESS MODEL FOR TERRORISM IN THE 21ST CENTURY

The workplace is an important disaster preparedness setting for managing the organizational and human consequences of terrorism. Workplace health and productivity providers can play an important role in equipping organizations and employees to deal with the impact of such trauma. Because terrorism continues to be a global threat and one that frequently targets, disrupts and in some instances destroys the workplace, this role will be increasingly important worldwide.

Workplace preparedness for terrorism is an important dimension of and vehicle for population health in the 21st century. Employed individuals spend more than a third of their day at work (IOM, 2003b), and work is most often the source of one's health benefits. In addition, employees are avid health consumers for themselves and their families (Vineburgh, 2002). Interestingly enough, more than two times as many individuals experiencing persistent distress after 9/11 accessed information at work rather than from a medical practitioner, and over three times as many sought information and counseling at work rather than from a mental health provider assumedly in a community setting (Stein et al., 2003). There is increasing evidence that workplace health promotion activities and programs can change behavior and psychosocial risk factors for individual employees and the collective risk profile of the employee population (IOM, 2003b).

This is very encouraging for workplace health professionals seeking to play a proactive role in equipping organizations and workers to deal with the impact of terrorism. As corporations begin to develop and/or expand their capacity to respond to disaster and terrorism, outsourcing to firms that specialize in critical incident stress management may become a common practice. If so, workplace health professionals that reside *inside the workplace* must make an extra effort to make their voices heard that they can collaborate with operational functions like human resources, security and corporate communications to oversee employee preparedness education and activities.

Similarly, workplace health professionals affiliated with outsourced critical incident services should either provide human continuity information (evacuation, shelter-in-place, work/family communication plans) and/or recommend to employers or external employee assistance companies with whom they contract the importance of this human continuity aspect of disaster response and the importance of *its integration* with operational preparedness.

Workplace health and productivity professionals can provide the health promotion context and health promotion content to educate management, employees and even families on preparedness for terrorism. Organizational planning for terrorism must address and incorporate the human element of disasters in order to manage the human consequences. Because many corporations are multinational and/or engage in global trade, employee preparedness for terrorism must extend across organizations and geographical boundaries and encompass culturally sensitive and culturally relevant preparedness information and response interventions to terrorist events.

Language is an important element in motivating systems and attitudinal change organizing society, culture and organizations and certainly critical to preparing for, responding to and recovering from the effects of disastrous events (Holloway & Waldrep, 2004). The language of terrorism is frightening conjuring up images and events that provoke anxiety amongst large populations that can be a barrier to preparedness. Therefore the language used by health promotion professionals and public education campaigns aimed at preparedness for terrorism must strike a chord that engages organizations and individuals to take action in a way that does not provoke unnecessary anxiety.

New language (see Table 3) to communicate the significance of preparedness based on "positive affect messages" is needed to more effectively engage the public than traditional health communication strategies that have often used fear-based appeals or straightforward presentation of fact (Monahan, 1995; Vineburgh, 2004). In using language that engages the attention of our intended audience, in this case employers, management and employees, we join with them to respect and integrate their concerns, needs and objectives into a greater vision for the common good.

Employers and workplace health and productivity professionals can play a vital role in fostering the resiliency of their organization and its people in the face of terrorism and disaster. Such efforts will require co-operation among global workplace colleagues that can benefit the health of their communities and nation. Workplace preparedness for terrorism advances population health in the 21st century and highlights the valued role of employee health professionals in an integrated response to disaster consequence management and their contribution to homeland and global security.

TABLE 3. New Language to Promote Workplace Preparedness for Terrorism and Population Health–Partnerships for the 21st Century

---

☐ **Disaster Behaviors:** Human responses to disaster that can be reactive, chaotic and injurious such as mass panic and flight, or proactive and planned with the intention of preventing, mitigating and fostering recovery from its injurious consequences. Proactive disaster behaviors include evacuation, shelter-in-place and creation of family disaster communication plans.

☐ **Human Continuity:** That which applies to and maximizes the health, productivity, morale, social cohesion and shared values of a community.

☐ **Population Health:** A term that refers to 'the health of the population' or 'the population's health' for which public health and public health interventions are developed. Employers and employee health and productivity providers are important partners in population health who can provide disaster education to enhance the health of their workplace, their community and their nation.

☐ **Organizational Continuity:** That which applies to or ensures the continuance of a corporation's operations and its business.

☐ **Preparedness:** Education about disasters including terrorism and bioterrorism, as well as actions taken to prevent, mitigate and foster recovery from disaster. This includes knowledge of proper evacuation techniques; understanding and voluntary compliance with life-saving disaster behaviors including shelter-in-place, quarantine; the creation of family communication plans and disaster kits.

☐ **Resiliency:** In its most general sense, bouncing back from adversity. In the context of disaster mental health, resiliency is the expected, clinical outcome of disaster. In an organizational context, resiliency applies to the human element of the organization, in addition to its operational components (redundancy and reliability). The human element is the most resilient component of an organization.

© Copyright 2004 Center for the Study of Traumatic Stress, Uniformed Services University. All rights reserved.

REFERENCES

Aguirre, B.E., Wenger D., & Vigo, G. (1998). A test of the emergent norm theory of collective behavior. *Sociological Forum*, 13, 301-320.

American Psychological Association Help Center. (2004). *The road to resilience.* Retrieved July 20, 2004, *http://www.apahelpcenter.org/request/*

Argenti, P. (2002). Crisis communication: Lessons from 9/11. *Harvard Business Review*. Harvard Business School of Publishing Corporation.

Bender, E. (2003). Employers see value in raising workers' awareness of MH issues. *Psychiatric News*, 38(7).

Blair Consulting Group (2003). *Stress and Resilience Benchmarking Project for ChevronTexaco.*

Cavanagh, T.E. (2003). Corporate security management: Organization and spending since 9/11. *The Conference Board Executive Summary*

Cohen, D. (2002). HR implications of the attack on America: One year later. *Society for Human Resource Management.* Alexandria, VA.

ComPsych Survey (2004). *Employees feel sense of inertia around terror warnings.* Retrieved August 10, 2004, from *http://www.compsych.com/jsp/en_US/core/home/ pressReleasesList2004.jsp?cid=420*

Council for Excellence in Government (2004). *From the home front to the front lines: America speaks out about homeland security.* Hart-Teeter Research.

Coutu, D.L. (2002). How resilience works. *Harvard Business Review on Point.*

Coutu, D.L., & Hyman, S.E. (2002). Managing emotional fallout: Parting remarks from America's top psychiatrist. *Harvard Business Review.* Harvard Business School Publishing Corporation.

Davidson, B., & Herlihy, P. (1999). The EAP and work-family connection. In James Oher (ed.), *The Employee Assistance Handbook.* John Wiley and Sons, Inc.

EASNA 16th Annual Institute. (2004). Resiliency in the world of work. Ottawa, Canada.

Fullerton, C.S., Ursano, R.J., & Norwood A.E. (2003). Workplace interventions following trauma: A review of interventions to prevent or treat psychological and behavioral consequences of occupational or workplace exposure to mass traumatic events. *Final Report to NIOSH,* Bethesda, MD: Uniformed Services University of the Health Sciences.

Galea, S., Ahern, J., Resnick, H., Kilpatrick, D., Bucuvalas, M., Gold, J., & Vlahov, D. (2002). Psychological sequelae of the September 11 terrorist attacks in New York City. *New England Journal of Medicine,* 346, 982-987.

Gerrity, E.T., & Steinglass, P. (2003). Relocation stress following catastrophic events. In R.J. Ursano, C.S. Fullerton, A.E. Norwood (eds.), *Terrorism and Disaster: Individual and Community Mental Health Interventions,* pp. 259-286. Cambridge: Cambridge University Press.

Greenberg, J.W. (2002). September 11, 2001: A ceo's story. *Harvard Business Review.* Harvard Business School of Publishing.

Hall M.J., Norwood A.E., Ursano, R.J., & Fullerton, C.S. (2003). The psychological impacts of bioterrorism. *Biosecurity and Bioterrorism: Biodefense Strategy, Practice, & Science,* 1(2), 139-144.

Holloway, H.C., & Waldrep, D.A. (2004). Biopsychosocial factors in bioterrorism: Consequences for psychiatric care, society and public health. In R. Ursano, A. Norwood, & C. Fullerton (eds.), *Bioterrorism: Psychological and Public Health Interventions.* Cambridge: Cambridge University Press.

Holloway, H.C., Norwood, & A.E., Fullerton, C.S., Engel, C.C., & Ursano, R.J. (1997). The threat of biological weapons: Prophylaxis and mitigation of psychological and social consequences. *Journal of the American Medical Association,* 278, 425-427.

Institute of Medicine of the National Academies (IOM) (2003a). *Preparing for the Psychological Consequences of Terrorism: A Public Health Strategy.* Washington, D.C.: National Academies Press.

Institute of Medicine of the National Academies (IOM) (2003b). *The Future of the Public's Health in the 21st Century.* Washington, D.C.: The National Academies Press.

Mankin, L.D., & Perry, R.W. (2004). Terrorism challenges for human resource management. *Review of Public Personnel Administration,* 24(1), 3-17, Sage Publications.

Masi, D.A. (ed.). (2000). *International Employee Assistance Anthology, 2nd edition.* Washington, D.C.: Dallen Inc.

Monaghan, S. (2003). Developing an EAP Strategy. *Journal of Employee Assistance,* 2nd Quarter, 14-15.

Monahan, J.L. (1995). Thinking positively: Using positive affect when designing health messages. In Mailbach, E. & Parrott R.L. (eds.), *Designing Health Messages: Approaches from Communication Theory and Public Health Practice* (pp. 81-96). California: Sage Publications, Inc.

National Center for Disaster Preparedness (NCDP) (2003). *How Americans Feel About Terrorism and Security: Two Years After 9/11*, NCDP, Columbia University Mailman School of Public Health in collaboration with The Children's Health Fund, New York.

North, C.S. (2003). Psychiatric epidemiology of disaster responses. In R. Ursano & A. Norwood (eds.), *Trauma & Disaster: Responses & Management*, 37-62. Arlington, VA: American Psychiatric Publishing, Inc.

North, C.S., Nixon, S.J., Shariat, S., Malone, S., McMillen, J.C., Spitznagel, E.L., & Smith, E.M. (1999). Psychiatric disorders among survivors of the Oklahoma City bombing. *Journal of the American Medical Association,* 282, 755-762.

North, C.S., Tivis, L., McMillen, J.C., Pfefferbaum, B., Spitznagel, E.L., Cox, J., Nixon, S., Bunch, K.P., & Smith, E.M. (2002). Psychiatric disorders in rescue workers after the Oklahoma City bombing. *American Journal of Psychiatry,* 159, 857-859.

Pfefferbaum, B., & Doughty, D.E. (2001). Increased alcohol use in a treatment sample of Oklahoma City bombing victims. *Psychiatry,* 64, 296-303.

Raskin, E., & Williams, L. (2003). *Ensuring Solutions to Alcohol Problems*: Issue Brief 3; George Washington University Medical Center.

Reddy, M. (2003). A business strategy for workplace efficiency: Innovative global EAP application by increasing mental wellbeing at work. *The Third Annual Global Symposium on Business and Mental Energy at Work.* Geneva, Switzerland.

Roman, P.M., & Blum, T.C. (2002). The workplace and alcohol problem prevention. *Alcohol Research and Health,* 26(1), 49-57.

Schouten, R., Callahan, M.V., & Bryant, S. (2004). Community response to disaster: The role of the workplace. *Harvard Review of Psychiatry,* July/August, 229-237.

Silver, R.C., Holman, E.A., McIntosh, D.N., Poulin, M., & Gil-Rivas,, V. (2002). Nationwide longitudinal study of psychological responses to September 11. *JAMA,* 288(10), 1235-44.

Stein, B.D., Elliott, M.N., Jaycox, L.H., Collins, R., Berry, S., Klein, D.J., & Schuster, M.A. (2004). A national longitudinal study of the psychological consequences of the September 11, 2001 terrorist attacks: Reactions, impairment, and help-seeking. *Psychiatry,* 67(2), 105-117.

Steury, S., Spencer, S., & Parkinson, G.W. (2004). Commentary: The social context of recovery. Psychiatry, 67(2), 158-163.

The Conference Board (2003). Corporate security and crisis management conference: Emerging issues and strategic imperatives. New York City, NY.

Ursano, R.J. (2002). Terrorism and mental health: Public health and primary care. *Status Report: Meeting the Mental Health Needs of the Country in the Wake of Septem-*

ber 11, 2001. The Eighteenth Annual Rosalynn Carter Symposium on Mental Health Policy, The Carter Center.

Ursano, R.J., Fullerton, C.S., & Norwood, A.E. (eds.). (2003). *Terrorism and Disaster: Individual and Community Mental Health Interventions*. Cambridge: Cambridge University Press.

Ursano, R.J., & Norwood, A.E. (eds.). (2003). *Disaster: Responses and Management*. Washington, D.C.: American Psychiatric Publishing, Inc.

Ursano, R.J., & Vineburgh, N.T. (2003). Corporate preparedness for terrorism. *Screening for Mental Health Workplace Response Teleconference Series*. Wellesley, MA.

Ursano, R.J., Fullerton, C.S., Vineburgh, N.T., & Flynn, B. (2004a). Preparing for the psychological consequences of terrorism: Preparedness for mental health, behavioral change and distress related responses–neurobiology and public health. *Congressional Briefing*, Washington, D.C.

Ursano, R.J., Fullerton, C.S., & Vineburgh, N.T. (2004). Corporate health and preparedness: Bioterrorism preparedness: *The Imperative for a Public Private Partnership. Sam Nunn Bank of America Policy Forum*. Atlanta, GA

Ursano, R.J., & Vineburgh, N.T. (2004a). Fostering resiliency: New concepts in disaster preparedness and response. *EASNA 16th Annual Institute*. Ottawa, Canada.

Ursano, R.J., & Vineburgh, N.T. (2004b). Workplace resiliency in the face of terrorism: The role and integration of health promotion and natural debriefing. *EAP Consultation: U.S. House of Representatives, U.S. Senate, Library of Congress*: Washington, D.C.

Vineburgh, N.T. (2002). Fall teleconference series examines workplace impact of Sept. 11. *Mental Health Weekly*, 12(35).

Vineburgh, N.T. (2003). Threat of mental illness, stress, violence and terrorism. *The Third Annual Global Symposium on Business and Mental Energy at Work*. Geneva, Switzerland.

Vineburgh, N.T. (2004).The power of the pink ribbon: Raising awareness of the mental health implications of terrorism. *Psychiatry* 67(2), 137-146

Vineburgh, N.T., Ursano, R.J., & Fullerton, C.S. (2004) Workplace health promotion for disaster and terrorism: A resiliency paradigm. *American Public Health Association 132nd Annual Meeting*. Washington, D.C.

Vlahov, D., Galea, S., Resnick, H., Boscarino, J.A., Bucuvalas, M., Gold, J., & Kilpatrick, D. (2002). Increased use of cigarettes, alcohol, and marijuana among Manhattan, New York, residents after the September 11th terrorist attacks. *American Journal of Epidemiology*, 155, 988-996.

Weisaeth, L. (1989). The stressors and the post-traumatic stress syndrome after an industrial disaster. *Acta Psychiatrica Scandinavica*, 80 (Supplement 355), 25-37.

INTEGRATION BY AN EXTERNAL SERVICE PROVIDER

Chapter 10

Ceridian's Experience in the Integration of EAP, Work-Life and Wellness Programs

Brian Kelly
Jean Holbrook
Ronnie Bragen

SUMMARY. This article considers EAP services, work-life and wellness programs and the implications of integrating these services. The concept of how wellness programs enter into this equation is explored as well as how Web-based services have played a significant role. Ceridian's experience in providing these services is explored through a case study, anecdotal information, and other data. This article reviews why integrated EAP services, work-life and wellness programs offer more value when compared to pro-

---

[Haworth co-indexing entry note]: "Ceridian's Experience in the Integration of EAP, Work-Life and Wellness Programs." Kelly, Brian, Jean Holbrook, and Ronnie Bragen. Co-published simultaneously in *Journal of Workplace Behavioral Health* (The Haworth Press, Inc.) Vol. 20, No. 1/2, 2005, pp. 183-201; and: *The Integration of Employee Assistance, Work/Life, and Wellness Services* (ed: Mark Attridge, Patricia A. Herlihy, and R. Paul Maiden) The Haworth Press, Inc., 2005, pp. 183-201. Single or multiple copies of this article are available for a fee from The Haworth Document Delivery Service [1-800-HAWORTH, 9:00 a.m. - 5:00 p.m. (EST). E-mail address: docdelivery@haworthpress.com].

Available online at http://www.haworthpress.com/web/JWBH
© 2005 by The Haworth Press, Inc. All rights reserved.
doi:10.1300/J490v20n01_10

grams that contain individual components. It is concluded that wellness and the Internet continue to play a key role in programs becoming more integrated. It is also suggested that integration is now larger than traditional EAP, work-life, and wellness programs. Other human resource services are becoming more important components of integrated services. *[Article copies available for a fee from The Haworth Document Delivery Service: 1-800-HAWORTH. E-mail address: <docdelivery@haworthpress.com> Website: <http://www.HaworthPress.com> © 2005 by The Haworth Press, Inc. All rights reserved.]*

KEYWORDS. EAP, work-life, wellness, integration

INTRODUCTION

The concept that healthy employees are more productive employees probably is not going to make *CNN Headline News* these days. Companies have long recognized the benefits of helping employees lead healthier and more productive lives both on and off the job. The response has been to make EAP, work-life, and wellness programs a normal part of the workplace.

The *CNN*-worthy issue is a growing awareness of the need for a holistic approach to employee well-being. This approach recognizes the importance of addressing all aspects that contribute to employee well-being. It includes mental health, physical health, and a healthy balance between work and family life in a single solution rather than in separate silos. Equally important is the realization that providing multiple modes of access–telephone, Internet, and face-to-face services–into a seamless system for employee assistance improves efficacy and reach into the population by addressing multiple learning styles and needs.

To provide an overview as to how the concept of integration has evolved, a brief history of Ceridian's experience is provided. Results of an integrated model are presented through a case study as well as through research and Ceridian data. Future implications and new types of integrated services are also presented.

THE ROOTS OF INTEGRATED MODES OF ACCESS

Ceridian grew out of Control Data Corporation and the assets it acquired from IBM, two pioneering companies of the early Information

Age. Control Data acquired IBM's wholly owned independent subsidiary, the Services Bureau Corporation, in 1973 and thereby entered the human resources services arena. A year later, the company established a groundbreaking in-house employee assistance program to serve the 50,000 employees who then worked at Control Data. At that time, substance abuse and mental health issues were shown to interfere with the ability of many employees to effectively perform their jobs. The impact on Control Data's bottom line was significant, so the company designed the first EAP in the U.S. with access to master's-level consultants 24 hours a day, seven days a week. The new program was called Employee Advisory Resources (EAR). Initially EAR relied on face-to-face meetings between the employees and EAP counselors at the worksite. However, the on-site presence was found to discourage the use of the service. To address this issue Ceridian added another innovation–telephone access. With this addition, an EAP model with multiple modes of access was born. The results were impressive. Utilization immediately increased and positive results were realized.

FROM EAP TO EMPLOYEE EFFECTIVENESS

The 1980s was a time of continued growth for Control Data's human resources services business. The success of EAR led the company to begin offering EAR services externally in 1981. In 1992, Control Data Corporation split into two independent companies: Control Data Systems, Inc. and Ceridian Corporation. Ceridian built its business around a core of human resources services offerings, including EAR, later renamed Employee Assistance Program or EAP.

Ceridian then began a mission that continues to this day–being a single-source provider of integrated solutions covering the full range of employee effectiveness services. Recognizing that EAP was addressing only one segment of the productivity puzzle, Ceridian took another step along the road to integration and holistic service. In the second half of the 1990s, Ceridian made important acquisitions to expand its employee effectiveness offerings. In 1996 then again in 1998, Ceridian acquired two founders and leaders in the work-life industry–The Partnership Group and WFD (formerly Work/Family Directions). Additionally, Ceridian acquired EAA, an EAP and training firm. With the addition of in-house work-life capabilities, Ceridian pioneered the concept of an integrated EAP and work-life product. The notion was a single source to address the intersections between practical and emotional issues. Gradually, this model impacted the EAP industry, shifting perceptions of EAPs from providing resources for emotional, substance abuse and other crisis issues to providing broader support on a variety of issues to help individuals cope with and manage a range of work, life and family issues.

Integrated Programs Provide Solid Outcomes

A University of Maryland study evaluated the outcomes of Ceridian's integrated EAP and work-life program. In the first empirical study of its kind, results showed that after receiving services, individual stress levels decreased, attendance improved, work performance improved, and relationships with supervisors and co-workers improved (Masi and Jacobson, 2000).

This self-reported study conducted a random sample of individuals who had used Ceridian's integrated EAP and work-life program. Using a three-point Likert scale (1 = not at all helpful; 2 = somewhat helpful; and 3 = extremely helpful), individuals were asked how identified problems may have improved. A total of 201 participants agreed to be contacted via telephone in March 2000. After receiving services, mean scores for problem improvement including work stress, attendance, work performance, co-worker relationships, supervisor relationships, and personal stress all increased. For example, work-related stress improved 42 percent (mean = 1.72, standard deviation = .62 before services and mean = 2.44, standard deviation = .60 after services).

A WHOLE NEW WORLD

The 1990s brought another service innovation that would revolutionize HR benefit programs and every aspect of society–the birth of the World Wide Web. Recognizing the power of this medium and building on the experience of integrating telephonic access with face-to-face sessions, Ceridian introduced a Web-based offering that included EAP and work-life information and resources. In one Web site participants were then able to find an integrated solution online. These services provided immediate access to information and support. Resources such as articles, audios, and more interactive features like self-assessment tools and resource locators were available 24 hours a day, seven days a week. Major reasons why individuals accessed online services included the belief that going online would take less time, that their concern did not warrant a phone call or a face-to-face meeting, or that their issue was embarrassing (Masi and Back-Tamburo, 2001).

Although Web-based services are popular with many users, true integration provides an opportunity to also interact with consultants. A key to effective integration is to provide employees with multiple modes of service delivery. For example, upon completing a self-assessment (*e.g., Do You Have a Drinking Problem?*) participants can review results, access other related materials and have easy access to a counselor through e-mail capabilities online or by calling them through a phone number prominently listed in the results of an assessment. Although receiving results from a self-assessment may be sufficient for some individuals, contacting a counselor directly may be essential for others.

New technologies began to offer forums where online communities evolved. Features such as moderated chat and bulletin boards now encourage participants to share their experiences and learn from each other. Moderated chats allow participants to join a session on a particular issue and are moderated by trained counselors. They offer a forum for sharing ideas and experiences and the chats are moderated by trained counselors. Bulletin boards allow participants to post their thoughts and experiences on certain issues. Participants can add to previous messages, create new messages, or simply read existing messages. By having participants help each other, provide their viewpoints, and share experiences, this feature creates a sense of community.

HEALTH, THE NEXT PIECE OF THE PUZZLE

The increasing cost of health care, in addition to the aging work force, has contributed to health becoming a major concern for employers. Health insurance is the most expensive single employee benefit. By 2006, the average family health insurance premium is expected to exceed $14,500, an increase of $5,000 in just three years (National Coalition on Health Care, 2003).

Synergies between EAP and wellness programs have been studied by Healthy People 2010, a national initiative of the U.S. Dept. of Health and Human Services. It serves as a road map to improve the health of Americans over ten years. Healthy People 2010 set goals for improving the overall health of the American population and contains specific goals and objectives for worksite health. The overarching goals of this organization are to increase quality and years of healthy life and eliminate health disparities among different segments of the population.

Within that framework, Healthy People 2010 offers guidelines and objectives for worksites to promote and improve the health of its employees. Moreover, it defines best practices for worksite health promotion programs. According to Healthy People 2010, a comprehensive worksite health program has five elements:

1. *Health education*, which focuses on skill development and lifestyle behavior change along with information dissemination and awareness building, preferably tailored to employees' interests and needs.
2. *Supportive social and physical environments.* These include an organization's expectations regarding healthy behaviors, and implementation of policies that promote health and reduce risk of disease.
3. *Integration of the worksite program* into your organization's structure.
4. *Linkage to related programs* like employee assistance programs (EAPs) and programs to help employees balance work and family.
5. *Screening programs* ideally linked to medical care to ensure follow-up and appropriate treatment as necessary.

Why are the Healthy People 2010 elements of a comprehensive worksite health promotion important for this discussion? It is because they speak to the value and power of integration.

The first element, *health education*, focuses on core capabilities of EAP and work-life programs–skill development, lifestyle behavior change, information dissemination and awareness building. By leveraging the reach into employee populations enabled by seminar attendance and online education, EAPs and work-life programs are the perfect vehicle for disseminating health education and awareness. The second element refers to *supportive social environments*. EAPs have long sought to increase the supportiveness of the worksite by working directly with management to enhance understanding and awareness of, and responsiveness to, employee needs and motivations. The fourth element speaks directly to *linking to supportive programs* such as employee assistance programs (EAPs) and programs to help employees balance work and family. This speaks to the power of not just linking services but embedding them in an integrated whole.

Much of the value in integrating EAP, work-life and wellness programs is in the ability for employees to have one access point for assistance with issues that benefit from multiple kinds of solutions. Assessments become comprehensive mechanisms for not only exploring the presenting issue, but for uncovering issues not yet apparent to the caller. This approach facilitates early detection of life challenges and allows for solutions before the challenges present larger problems. For example, expectant parents who call for information on childcare issues are able to get pro-active assistance on a host of related issues. Assessments may uncover the need for pre-natal care, or questions about how to manage a pregnancy. Similarly, employees who are struggling with weight management and related emotional issues may get help developing a coordinated weight management plan that includes nutrition, fitness and emotional support.

MEASURED RESULTS

The true test of just how effective an integrated offering is in measuring results. As Figure 1 suggests, individuals who use integrated services

FIGURE 1

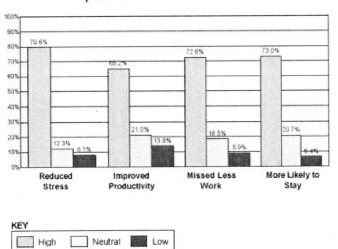

Impact on Work Performance

Source. Ceridian's self-reported user satisfaction questionnaire, January 1, 2004-August 31, 2004. Participants of an integrated program are asked to evaluate how strongly they would agree or disagree with the extent to which the service impacts various components of their work performance. Key: High = "Strongly Agree," "Agree"; Neutral = "Neither"; Low = "Disagree," "Strongly Disagree"

show a decreased level of stress and improved productivity. The data also suggests that participants are also less likely to miss work and more likely to stay with their organization.

A CASE STUDY:
A CREATIVE INTEGRATION OF EAP,
HEALTH PROMOTION, AND WORK-LIFE

Company

KPMG LLP is a U.S. audit, risk advisory and tax services firm with 17,700 partners and employees.

Need

KPMG continuously seeks ways to drive culture change, initiate a cost-effective wellness pilot program, help talented employees manage stress and long hours and enhance service to the organization's clients. This program was designed to increase the productivity of their employees.

EAP, work-life, and wellness programs each generate productivity gains by easing employees' emotional, physical and daily life stressors. Employers that provide wellness programs can reduce health care costs by 20-55 percent and reduce short-term sick leave by as much as 32 percent (Ceridian Proprietary ROI Tool, 2003). Organizations that embrace wellness programs see fast return on investment because illness prevention is a proactive strategy in today's world of rising health care costs.

Program Overview

The firm initiated a pilot wellness program in 2002 to determine where existing wellness challenges might be impacting the organization financially and to then provide targeted interventions and resources against those challenges. The goal was to create a healthy workforce and to empower KPMG's workforce to maximize functioning in all four domains of wellness: physical, spiritual, mental and emotional.

Solution

KPMG drew upon its longstanding relationship with Ceridian to create an appropriate health management plan. Ceridian already provided the firm with an integrated employee assistance program, work-life and health and wellness services. The program included services from Ceridian's partner WellCall, a provider of accessible and personalized health management services. These solutions made it possible for KPMG to analyze and evaluate the impact of wellness initiatives on productivity and other performance measures.

Barbara Wankoff, Director of Workplace Solutions for KPMG, said, "Wellness is a very individual journey. We took a lot of care in designing a pilot program that reflects the uniqueness of our partners and employees and encompasses various ways to combat the effects of business travel, working at client sites, and the other aspects of work that can lead to exhaustion and burnout. Ceridian and WellCall provided us with an innovative design that met the needs of our challenging work environment."

KPMG and Ceridian designed an approach for creating a workable wellness pilot program at two offices that involved its workforce in a positive cultural change and it tracked metrics to help shape an optimal strategy for change. The firm wanted to develop a profile of employee health and then use that data to provide support and resources targeted to the needs of its population. This would enable "corporate athletes" the ability to use the full range of their capacities to flourish in the most difficult circumstances, and to emerge from stressful periods stronger, healthier and eager for the next challenge.

KPMG wanted to focus on company locations where they could implement specific and detailed wellness interventions. True wellness is achieved by attending to all areas of life–physical, mental, spiritual, emotional, social, environmental, and occupational–to optimize performance, reduce the risk of illness, and improve communication and awareness.

The program was framed around the creation of a "Passport to Wellness." Similar to an actual passport, KPMG's Passport to Wellness included 20 to 30 activities in each of four crucial facets of life–physical, mental, spiritual and emotional well-being. "The program was run like a travel program that included mileage awards, and when participants completed a pre-determined number of activities, they won bonus points," Wankoff explained. KPMG's Passport to Wellness teams tallied points and kept score. Individuals achieved 'wellness athlete' status only after they logged activity across all four domains. Points earned premiums and prizes, including spa trips and airline tickets. "The program was a great incentive for many people to get involved in their own wellness," Wankoff added.

Results

For the first time, KPMG has data that profiles employee wellness at the office level. This enables the firm to target health management activity where it's most effective. "Through this pilot program we saw a rise in the number of employees and partners who sought needed and preventive care," said Barbara Wankoff. She stated, "Our hopes are that some of our employees with high risk factors for disease might have caught it in time. The Wellness Pilot was a worthwhile initiative as well as exciting and rewarding on many levels."

THE EMPLOYER'S GAINS

Employers are integrating EAP, work-life, and wellness programs in increasing numbers–with beneficial results. From the employer perspective, combining key employee effectiveness services results in, "the whole is greater than the sum of its parts." Combining these programs provides the employer with easier program administration, an increase in program awareness by employees, early detection and ultimately, a greater return on investment.

Ease of Administration

The integration of EAP, work-life, and wellness provides a number of advantages in addition to enhanced productivity. Working with a single provider for all three services, for example, creates efficiencies and reduces costs by simplifying implementation and management. This redundancy-reducing model simplifies administrative oversight as well, since a single vendor will offer one point of accountability.

Having one program for all services makes managing the program simpler. For example, employers need to manage the communication of access information for just one service (e.g., one username and password to a Web site), one communication program, and maintain access to just one online resource through a company intranet. With one access point that is fully integrated with other modes of access, avoiding redundancies helps employers reduce administrative costs. In addition, having one point of contact within a company for account management issues streamlines efforts and saves time. One integrated utilization report allows the employer to more quickly assess the value of their employee effectiveness programs and allows their program to more accurately determine the value of these programs.

Early Detection

An integrated model boosts the preventive potential of all three services. With all issues channeled through one service, early detection of problems is a far more likely scenario than when information is dispersed. Early detection is not only a boon to the employee in distress, but also to an employer who might have to otherwise bear the escalating costs of a more severe and lengthy treatment situation. Prevention and early detection is also critical to the decrease of absenteeism and turnover. A recent report conducted for the National Mental Health Association reports that the rate of absenteeism among depressed women is twice that of female employees overall (10.6 lost workdays per year compared to five) (National Mental Health Association, 2003). Ninety-four percent of women surveyed noticed improvements at work after seeking help for depression. Virtually all of the women surveyed agreed that they need more accessible help. An integrated program offers a highly accessible resource for problems that affect one's health and work situation.

Return on Investment

There is a direct correlation between the integration of services and a greater and a more rapid return on investment (ROI). Implementing an EAP can save companies $14 to $16 for every dollar invested. Returns of an integrated program are significantly higher. In fact, an integrated EAP and work-life program can save $20 to $29 for every dollar invested (Ceridian Proprietary ROI Tool, 2003).

THE EMPLOYEE'S ADVANTAGE

A combined offering of employee effectiveness programs provides a variety of benefits to employees. The differences in services encompassed in EAP vs. work-life vs. wellness programs are indistinguishable to employees who need help. An integrated approach can offer a more personalized, thorough solution and a simpler way to access services and take the burden off the employee to decide which service to call. In addition, there is often less stigma associated with contacting a service that is referred to as an integrated service vs. an EAP.

Personalization

Few problems are simple or one-dimensional. The help employees require often encompasses numerous interrelated areas. If an individual is diagnosed with prostate cancer, he is likely to need information and support on a variety of concerns and he will need it quickly. He might need to know how to find and interview physicians or perhaps he will need a referral to a therapist because he is distraught over his diagnosis. He may also need a legal referral because he has decided to draw up a will and may want to research the latest treatment options. If all of his employer's support programs were provided separately, he would have to take an arduous journey through a labyrinth of resources to acquire the information he needs. Moreover, he might have to repeat his tale, eventually growing weary of this process. If this frustration can be avoided, the employee is far more likely to persist in getting the information he needs, and getting it in a timely manner.

As another example, an employee who talks with a skilled counselor may determine that a principal cause of his depression is low self-esteem arising from a recent weight gain. It may also turn out that the employee's weight gain has led to marital problems. The consultant, in managing the case, links the caller with health educators who can offer coaching and behavior modification support on weight loss. The employee is also referred to a psychologist who will evaluate his depression and offer couples counseling.

Easier Access

Offering separate EAP, work-life, and wellness programs with unique objectives and different looks can be confusing to employees. Having one integrated program eliminates the need for multiple Web site addresses, usernames and passwords. The employee needs just one Web site and just one phone number. Typical participant comments on what they like best about services offered to them include responses like, "many resources available and accessible in one easily-accessed and navigated location." A common theme in customer feedback is that participants find it convenient and helpful to access one site that can help with their concerns. Rather than needing to access another service (with different access information) participants comment on the fact that they are able to find solutions to their concerns in one place.

CHALLENGES OF OFFERING AN INTEGRATED SOLUTION

Although offering an integrated solution provides a variety of advantages, it also presents unique challenges.

Communications

Having clear and consistent messages in communicating to participants presents a challenge. In today's era, it is difficult for many people to remember what commercials they saw on television last night, or the billboards they passed on the way to work. As a result, simple yet targeted messages have the greatest impact and are critical in maximizing program awareness and utilization. It also creates a challenge when one communication campaign must include messages that had been previously contained in as many as three unique campaigns (one for EAP, one for work-life, and another for wellness).

In 2002, Ceridian conducted a research project to capture the true voice of the customer through interviews and surveys. One key outcome was the need to build a brand wherever and whenever it was used. Another finding was the importance of creating differentiated communications. Only those message that are differentiated and relevant will command attention and generate action in today's cluttered workplace. Ceridian's research also suggested the importance of moving away from "one size fits all" campaigns. Developing different programs for different types of audiences is critical to maximize program awareness. Companies that have maximized awareness and utilization have used a variety of activities–from traditional methods like printed materials to initiatives like "Webinars," wellness campaigns, and links from company intranets.

Staying Current with Updated Content and Resources

It is critical to update content on a regular basis and introduce new resources. If content does not change and new features are not added, it is easy for individuals to lose interest. This is particularly important for services that have a Web-based component. A key trend is "the Amazon effect." Leading sites like Amazon continue to raise the bar. Users expect that the online experience will continue to improve. As a result, significant investments in technology and content are necessary to achieve this objective.

Web Site Design

A fully integrated program is also about offering resources that are easy to access and easy to navigate. Having two or three points of entry (one for each program) can create confusion for participants. The goal is to provide great ease of use, and a comprehensive Web-based resource that is intuitive and easy to navigate. A key attribute is to make sure it is clear that the site is not exclusively an EAP resource, a work-life resource, or a wellness resource–it is an integrated site that offers resources to address needs in all of these areas.

True integration is when the various modes of access are reciprocal and interactive. For example, providing easily accessible information on contacting a counselor maximizes program effectiveness. It is not enough that individuals can get access to self-help resources via the Web. Providing personalized assistance from a trained professional who can help the individual fully understand issues and options, and provide resources and support that enables the individual to change behavior towards improvement or resolution of the issue is critical.

A Brave New World

The Internet has emerged as the first new mass medium in a generation and arguably the fastest growing new technology in history. More and more people now have access to computers and the Internet than ever before. According to Internet World Stats, 69 percent of the U.S. population has access to the Internet. This has increased by 112 percent since 2000 (Internet World Stats, 2004). In today's fast-paced environment, the Internet gives users immediate gratification by providing information around-the-clock, accessible from the office, home, or on the road. People have become accustomed to immediate service from anywhere, at any time.

Ceridian's experience has mirrored this trend. User visits to Life-Works Online, Ceridian's Web-based offering, have increased by 23 percent in 2004 vs. 2003. As participants rely on Web-based services to a greater extent, its importance will continue to grow.

Health Information Online

Data from a Harris Poll, gathered in April 2001, indicates that almost 100 million adults go online to look for health care information. This amounts to 75 percent of all adult Internet users (Harris Poll, 2001). The limits of Health Maintenance Organizations (HMOs) and the limitlessness of the Internet have lately made self-help even more appealing. In 2002, Americans surfed more than 12,000 Web sites devoted to mental health (Psychology Today, 2001). An estimated 40 percent of all health-related Internet inquiries are on mental health topics and depression is the number-one most researched illness on the Web (Psychology Today, 2001). These statistics suggest the need for helpful and comprehensive Web-based resources.

NEW MODES OF ACCESS

Positive and promising future opportunities exist with online technology to deliver significant informational and referral services to participants (Masi and Jacobsen, 2002). Two promising technologies that integrate the experience to a greater extent include Voice over Internet Protocol (VoIP) and instant messaging (IM).

Voice Over Internet Protocol (VOIP)

Voice over Internet Protocol (often referred to as "voice over IP") offers the ability to transmit voice communications over the Internet. This usually requires a broadband connection, such as cable modem or DSL. According to Gartner, Inc. there were 150,000 VoIP subscribers in the U.S. at the end of 2003. Gartner predicts this number will reach 6 million by the end of 2005 (National Journal Tech Daily, 2004). Some experts predict that consumer use of VoIP could reach 40 percent of the market by 2009 (New Millennium Research Council, 2003). VoIP allows users to access an integrated EAP, work-life, and wellness service through one place–their PC.

The basic principal of this technology is in making phone calls via a PC. Upon making a phone call to a counselor a participant could then access materials online with the help of a counselor. Similarly, if a user starts by accessing Web-based resources, they could then make a call to a counselor, right from a PC. In these scenarios, one mode of access (the PC) would offer a more integrated approach. VoIP services do have drawbacks. Common issues include latency in the transmission and sounds being uneven.

In 2002, Ceridian conducted a pilot of Live Help, a form of VoIP. While online, this technology allowed users to speak directly with a counselor from any computer with a microphone or speakers or, if the user preferred, a separate phone line. At that time the counselor could provide additional assistance (e.g., guide them through materials or quickly forward articles). Utilization for this pilot program was very low. This was primarily due to many people not having this technology at their desktop, not being familiar with the new technology, and a low level of promotion. As with any emerging technology, it can take time to become accepted. This technology has more promise as it continues to evolve and become accepted to a greater extent.

Instant Messaging

Instant messaging allows users to communicate with another individual in real time over the Internet. Typically the user would receive an alert message when somebody is online. Then an online discussion can be initiated. A 2004 study from Pew Internet and American Life Project reported that 21 percent of individuals use IM at work. Although 90 percent of teens and young adults engage in instant messaging, 48 percent of those aged 55+ now use instant messaging (America Online, 2004). Many analysts expect that IM will soon overtake e-mail as the number one form of electronic communication.

Rob Kramer (from the Product Management Department at Ceridian) states that providing an option for IM allows providers to connect with people who may otherwise not use other modes of access (e.g., calling or sending an e-mail). Because participants need to present information about their concern in writing, they may take extra time to think about the information that they provide.

Security issues may be one reason that corporations have kept instant messaging from widespread adoption. However, as companies become more comfortable with the security of IM along with its benefits in improving productivity, its usage will increase. It also allows for a more integrated offering. By providing a new option, participants would have yet another mode of access and be able to connect in a more personal, yet confidential way.

BEYOND EAP, WORK-LIFE AND WELLNESS

In today's world, integration of HR services is taking a new meaning. Organizations are striving to capture even greater synergies by offering additional services in one integrated solution.

Human Resource Outsourcing

With greater emphasis on streamlining operations, it may become common for companies to provide services that are even more integrated–programs that include EAP, work-life, wellness programs as well as a variety of other human resource services.

Outsourcing has become an increasingly popular way to manage people and technology resources, enhance services, and reduce costs. It is clear that integration has evolved even further and that full suites of HR-related services will continue to evolve. Human resource outsourcing is a key industry trend and is dramatically changing the marketplace. With this model, organizations can streamline activities, lower costs, and increase service levels. Services offered through this model generally cover the entire employee life cycle including recruiting and hiring, human resources, payroll, benefits and pension administration, time and attendance and Web-based employee and manager self-service. Organizations that utilize this model benefit from a reduction in exposure to the effects of employee turnover, compliance-related risk, and the technology-related capital investment to support non-core administrative functions.

Absence and Presenteeism

Companies invest in their employees through EAP, work-life and health education and wellness programs because they enhance productivity by minimizing the life challenges and resulting distractions they face. This enables their employees to come to work and be engaged and "present" on their jobs. The next logical step in the continuum of these solutions will integrate programs to reduce the incidence and duration of absence, lower health care related expenses and identify and intervene to encourage employees to perform at optimal productivity levels.

A relentless increase in health care costs continues to be a top concern of employers. Healthy employees come to work more consistently and incur fewer health care costs. Absence and health care costs are eroding the bottom line of every employer. Although there are indications that health care costs may start moderating, average increases in 2003 were 14.7 percent (Hewitt, 2003). Furthermore, two articles in the *Journal of American Medical Association* last year reported that depression costs employers $35 billion a year in reduced performance at work and conditions such as arthritis, headaches, and back problems cost nearly $47 billion. Absences related to stress and personal needs rose to

33 percent in 2001 (as a percentage of the overall total) from 19 percent in 1995 (CCH Incorporated, 2002).

Forward thinking companies are addressing the next component of the productivity equation. Described as presenteeism, it is the dynamic loss of productivity that occurs when workers are on the job but not fully functioning or performing at their best. What is apparent today is that the causes of presenteeism often include an array of psychosocial issues addressed in EAP, work-life, and wellness programs today. Psychosocial issues, including stress-related issues, play a critical role in illness, injury and recovery. This confirms the rationale for companies to leverage capabilities to offer a set of absence management solutions. Whether it is personal problems, financial concerns, chronic illness or family care needs, these issues traditionally find their solutions using the core competencies of employee support programs. As a result, the next generation for EAP, work-life and wellness programs are likely to include targeted solutions aimed at improving absence and presenteeism.

REFERENCES

America Online, (2004). "America Online's Second Annual Instant Messaging Trends Survey."

CCH Incorporated, (2002). "Annual Employer Survey." http://hr.cch.com.

Evener, W., Hutchinson, W., & Richard, M.A. "A National Employee Assistance Program: The Ceridian Experience." *Employee Assistance Programs: Wellness/Enhancement Programming.* C.C. Thomas Publisher, LTD., 64-77.

Harris Poll, (2001). "Cyberchondriacs Update." http://www.harrisinteractive.com/harris_poll/index.asp?PID=229.

Herlihy, P., Attridge, M., & Turner, S., (2002). "The Integration of Employee Assistance and Work/Life Programs." *EAPA Exchange Magazine.*

Hewitt Associates, (2003). "Health Care Costs Continue Double-Digit Pace, But May Start Moderating in 2004."

Holbrook, J., (2004). "The Value of Integrated EAP, Work-life, and Wellness Integration." *EAP Digest.*

Internet World Stats, (2004). "Internet Usage Stats for the Americas." http://www.internetworldstats.com/stats2.htm.

Masi, D., & Back-Tamburo, M., (2001). "Motivation for the Use of an Online EAP and Work-Life Service."

Masi, D., & Jacobson, J., (2002). "Outcome Measurements of an Integrated Employee Assistance and Work-Life Program."

Murphy, Paul A., (2001). "Self-Help: Shattering the Myths." *Psychology Today.*

National Journal Tech Daily, April 13, 2004. "Internet Telephony Poses New Problems."

National Mental Health Association Report, November, 2003. "Depression Among Women in the Workplace."

New Millennium Research Council, December 16, 2003. "The Future of Internet Phone Calling: Regulatory Imperatives to Protect the Promise of VoIP for Industry and Consumers."

Pew Internet and American Life Project, June 2004. "VoIP Awareness in America." http://www.pewinternet.org/PPF/r/129/report_display.asp.

Simmons, H., & Goldberg, M., (2003). "Charting the Cost of Inaction." *National Coalition on Health Care.*

Stein, S., (2002). "Why Work/Life and EAP Should Be Integrated." *Behavioral Health Management.*

U.S. Department of Health and Human Services, (2000). *Healthy People 2010: With Understanding and Improving Health and Objectives for Improving Health.* 2nd ed. Washington, DC: U.S. Government Printing Office.

Walker, L., (2004). "Instant Messaging is Growing Up, Going to Work." *Washington Post.*

Chapter 11

Motorola Drives Strategic Initiatives Through Collaboration and Interdependence

Nancy K. Lesch

SUMMARY. This article describes an integrated approach to implementing a wellness program in a corporate setting. Motorola's wellness program is reviewed, including its history, rationale and strategic focus. Successful integration partners are identified, and strategies for integrated programs are outlined. Education, communication and prevention initiatives and program components are discussed, including recommendations and shared learnings for both small and large-scale wellness programs. *[Article copies available for a fee from The Haworth Document Delivery Service: 1-800-HAWORTH. E-mail address: <docdelivery@haworthpress.com> Website: <http://www.HaworthPress.com> © 2005 by The Haworth Press, Inc. All rights reserved.]*

[Haworth co-indexing entry note]: "Motorola Drives Strategic Initiatives through Collaboration and Interdependence." Lesch, Nancy K. Co-published simultaneously in *Journal of Workplace Behavioral Health* (The Haworth Press, Inc.) Vol. 20, No. 3/4, 2005, pp. 203-218; and: *The Integration of Employee Assistance, Work/Life, and Wellness Services* (ed: Mark Attridge, Patricia A. Herlihy, and R. Paul Maiden) The Haworth Press, Inc., 2005, pp. 203-218. Single or multiple copies of this article are available for a fee from The Haworth Document Delivery Service [1-800-HAWORTH, 9:00 a.m. - 5:00 p.m. (EST). E-mail address: docdelivery@haworthpress.com].

Available online at http://www.haworthpress.com/web/JWBH
© 2005 by The Haworth Press, Inc. All rights reserved.
doi:10.1300/J490v20n03_01

KEYWORDS. Motorola, wellness, integration, Club One, resilience

So many of our health problems can be avoided through diet, exercise and making sure we take care of ourselves. By promoting healthy lifestyles, we can improve the quality of life for all Americans, and reduce health care costs dramatically.

–Tommy G. Thompson, Secretary, Department of Health and Human Services, in an August 9, 2001, speech at the National Institutes of Health, "Diet, Exercise Delay Type 2 Diabetes"

CONCEPT OF INTEGRATION–MOTOROLA'S APPROACH

Motorola is a global leader in wireless, broadband, and automotive communications and technologies that help make life smarter, safer, simpler, synchronized, and fun. Sales were $27.1 billion in 2003. There are 88,000 employees worldwide. Motorola is focused on smart technologies, reducing cost and increasing efficiency and effectiveness in order to sell more products. A great deal of time and energy is spent creating streamlined, repeatable processes. There is a strong focus on the customers' specific needs and issues, but there is always an effort to re-use existing platforms in order to gain efficiency and speed. In finding new uses for existing technologies, working in silos would surely create failure. Instead, successful product teams work across boundaries to discover solutions. It's what the customer seeks; it's what the internal corporate culture demands.

Motorola's wellness program philosophy and approach is no different. The current corporate culture is one where integration, innovation and collaboration are expected. The clients for wellness services are Motorola employees; and just like external customers, they expect consistent solutions that are tailored to their specific needs and issues. An employee experiencing a particular life event may choose one of a number of 'points of entry' in seeking an answer to their questions. They may engage in discussion with their Human Resources Manager, their Benefits representative, a Wellness Center staff member, someone from the Employee Assistance program, or someone on the Work-life team. Employees may go to the intranet to search for a solution. Whatever their approach, all the "people" resources at Motorola seek to be aligned in providing consistent answers, tools and referrals. Human Resources,

Wellness, Work-life, EAP, Safety, Security, Occupational Health and others all seek to deliver information from one "standard platform"–a common knowledge base that reinforces key messages and points to key resources.

Some of the resources mentioned above are Motorola internal resources such as Human Resources and Occupational Health; some are outsourced, such as EAP. Whatever the case, each entity seeks to provide the right resource to the right person at the right time. Motorola's Wellness program has a history of collaboration, although there have been a variety of approaches over the years. Our journey has mirrored the many shifts within the culture. The focus shifts depending on leadership, business conditions and other factors. Many internal departments work together to focus on health, safety, retention, fitness, disease prevention, mental health and engagement, to name a few areas of focus. The most successful collaborative partnerships have come through building shared vision, common understanding of overall business goals, and a commitment to improving employee health. Although the journey has not always been smooth, the focus and intent has always been to eliminate "silos" and duplication of effort in order to work together across departmental lines to provide the best programs and resources for employees.

PROGRAM HISTORY, DESIGN AND DEFINITION

To best explain Motorola's approach to wellness, it's important to understand a little bit of the history and philosophy of the program. Why have wellness initiatives at all? In the early 1990s at the program's inception, employee retention in a booming economy was a key factor. In order to provide a workplace that was competitive, Motorola needed to address work-life balance issues. The wellness program was created not only to address employee needs, but also to integrate with business strategy. The program is based on a salutogenic model of wellness and health promotion–in other words, it's not about 'how did I get sick,' it is about how to stay well (Adams, 1997).

Focusing on current issues in health and wellness, while the corporate philosophy remains the same, the program design has changed somewhat to fit the times. The wellness team works closely with managers to make sure programs align with business goals and issues around 'people.' The health and well-being needs of all segments of the population are still considered, but a relatively new focus is grappling with the issue of rising health care costs. Goetzel found in 2001 that the 1998 median health and productivity management cost per employee was $9,992. This included health plan, turnover, absenteeism, disability and worker's compensation costs. Employers are burdened with rising costs, and there is a rising population of underinsured and uninsured. Who will be responsible in the future–employers or employees? Jeff Rubleski said it best in his WELCOA interview:

> When this cost shifting occurs on a large scale, health promotion and wellness will be uniquely poised to play a major role in a new type of system. I say this because, when more costs are shifted to employees, they'll start saying, "Wow, I'm really starting to feel these costs now. I'd better start taking my health a little more seriously. (Rubleski, 2004)

As companies like Motorola begin to seek ways to manage health care costs, it is inevitable that more of the responsibility will fall to the employee. Employees must become better consumers when it comes to decisions on spending health care dollars, as more of the dollars will come out of their own pocket or paycheck. Wellness programs must provide resources and information that aid employees in making wise health and wellness decisions. Physical health in terms of avoidance of illness is critical, but there are so many more factors that contribute to overall well-being. Motorola's program functions under a holistic wellness model–described by Jon Robison as one that doesn't just encompass biomedical risk factors, but also focuses on supportive factors for health, such as rest, pleasure and play, financial resources, laughter and humor, and movement/physical resilience (Robison, 2004).

Motorola's programs and resources address employees' ability to re-main resilient in challenging times, providing tools and tips on coping with stress, feeling connected and engaged, and making a productive contribution to the workplace. Through the utilization of population health management, employees are addressed at every stage along the continuum from illness to wellness. That is, in realizing that 85% of the population incurs 15% of health care costs and 15% of the population incurs 85% of the costs, Motorola's programs focus not only on the most costly events, but also on those that can prevent the "well" people from moving to the "ill" end of the continuum. David Anderson de-scribes population health management as a comprehensive strategy that cost-effectively improves the overall health of a defined population by segmenting the population based on health-related factors and targeting interventions to meet the needs of each segment (Anderson, 2003). Stated another way, when looking at causes of premature death, at least one-half of the mortality in the U.S. is attributable to behavior or lifestyle causes–modifiable risks such as smoking, elevated cholesterol, or obesity (McGinnis, 1993).

Motorola's wellness program, then, not only addresses health and disease management, but also the overall sense of well-being that can lead to heightened engagement and productivity. The Institute for Health and Productivity Management (www.ihpm.org) defines health and productivity management as "the integrated management of health and injury risks, chronic illness, and disability to reduce employees' total health-related costs including direct medical expenditures, unnecessary absence from work, and lost performance at work (i.e., presenteeism)." Health and productivity management bridges the medical, the behavioral, the psychological and the organizational aspects of wellness. The challenge is designing an infrastructure that seamlessly integrates all these areas, but still has elements of value and 'fun' for employees.

Health screening and health risk assessment data provides even greater opportunity to target efforts to populations who need them. Like most major companies, Motorola's screening results reveal that many employees would benefit from weight management information, self-care information, and information on fitness, nutrition and stress management. Goetzel (1998) found compelling evidence that the dollars that would be avoided if individuals did not need to seek treatment for these and other health issues could reach into the millions. Reducing the risk and severity of illness and injury is foremost in the minds of wellness professionals and companies alike. In 2002, Motorola won a C. Everett Koop award for wellness initiatives that realized a return on investment. The three-year baseline study focused on employees who regularly used the U.S. on-site Motorola Wellness Centers or used the reimbursement benefit for membership at external, non-Motorola fitness centers. The results were powerful–for every $1 Motorola invested in Wellness benefits, $3.93 was saved. For the U.S. in 2000, that meant a $6,479,673 savings. The study also showed that:

- Participating employees see a *nominal 2.5 percent increase* in annual aggregate health care costs compared with an 18 percent annual aggregate increase for non-participants
- Participating employees and Motorola enjoy an approximately *$6.5 million annual savings in medical expenses* for lifestyle-re-

lated diagnoses (e.g., obesity, hypertension, stress) compared with non-participants
- Motorola saves nearly *$10.5 million annually in disability expenses* compared with non-participants

WELLNESS PROGRAM DEVELOPMENT AND DELIVERY

Motorola's wellness charter states: "Design and deliver valuable healthy solutions to enhance employees' and their dependents quality of life. Respond to documented, high quality scientific research and health trend data to provide meaningful services/products that will attract, retain and engage employees." Based on research and benchmarking of best practices in corporate wellness, wellness initiatives are divided into three main areas: (1) prevention and screening, (2) fitness and recreation, and (3) education and awareness. With a large number of employees in the U.S., where most wellness initiatives are focused, program delivery is a challenge. As stated earlier, the ultimate goal is to get the right resource to the right person at the right time. An integrated, team-based approach is essential, and using project management methodology, staff and volunteers are aligned with the needs and interests of employees in the three focus areas.

PROGRAM EXAMPLES

In the area of *prevention and screening*, on-site health screenings and health risk assessments are offered that meet medical plan requirements and provide valuable data on each segment of the population. On-site flu immunizations occur each year. For *fitness and recreation*, Motorola contracts with Club One Professional Services, headquartered in Campbell, CA, to manage fourteen on-site Wellness Centers. These Centers offer a wide array of activities and programs including recreation leagues and tournaments, massage, exercise classes, specialty series and on-site physical therapy. Employees can take advantage of Wellness Reimbursement for the on-site centers, or they may choose to join an off-site center in their community and receive up to $240 (minus applicable taxes) in fee reimbursement. Having on-site centers managed by an external strategic partner has helped Motorola to achieve excellence in programming by tapping into Club One's expertise and resources. This shift in delivery from Motorola-run centers that occurred in 2003 has helped to contain costs and provide quality centers that focus on the customer while aligning with program goals. Current Center membership is at 53% of the eligible population, and participation averages approximately .6 visits per member per week.

For *education and awareness*, a variety of methods are utilized, both virtual and in person, so that employees may access information in the way that suits them best. From Web-based "tool kits" to on-site classes to posters and flyers focused on monthly health themes, programs are designed to address the population in convenient and accessible ways. Participation varies depending on the particular program; but evaluation and tracking includes Web hits, employee participation and satisfaction and other measures of quality and utilization. These programs are generally developed and delivered by internal staff, so the cost of implementation is minimal. Research would tend to support the preventive philosophy found in education and awareness efforts. In one study, medical-care cost and absenteeism savings ranged from $2.30 to $10.10 for every dollar invested in health promotion programs (Aldana, 2001).

Resilience Tools

One example of an education and awareness deliverable is our Resilience curriculum. Resilience is defined as "strength in the midst of change and stressful life events." Besides providing strength in the form of coping behaviors, resilient individuals also perceive change as a challenge rather than a threat. They perceive a higher level of supervisor support, co-worker cohesion and overall social support (Steinhardt, 1996). These perceptions can lead to significant health benefits. If a person can learn or enhance resilient behaviors, studies show that one's immune system function is enhanced, thereby creating not just psychological but physiological benefits as well (Segerstrom, 2004).

A Web-based Resilience Tool Kit was launched in the fall of 2004. The Kit contains self-assessments, Web links, tips and facts, and information on how to connect with all available on-site resilience resources. Additionally, there is a four-part resilience curriculum designed to be delivered in a classroom setting. Approximately 40 wellness, Occupational Health, HR and EAP staff have been trained to deliver the hour-long classes on-site at U.S. locations. The curriculum focuses on three areas where employees can work on behavior enhancement: "Taking Responsibility," "Reframing," and "Social Support." Along with a Resilience 101 overview, each component of the curriculum contains a business case for wellness and an overview of resilience. Data on how employees perceive these classes is being collected, and the hope is to be able to eventually link improvements in resilience to overall corporate employee engagement data. EAP and Occupational Health staff has found the materials valuable for one-on-one discussions with employees as well. Additionally, an interactive online resilience curriculum is being developed by an external resource, and should be available at no cost to employees by the end of this year.

Integration Partners

With such a robust collection of programs and services, it might sound like there is staff standing by 24 hours a day to deliver. The reality is that the wellness team faces the "do more with less" challenge just like everyone in the workplace. The work is accomplished through collaboration, integration and interdependence. The Wellness organization is run by a Practice Leadership Team (PLT). Other PLTs at Motorola include Work-life, Global Benefits and Health Care Strategy. These PLTs are simply the way work is organized in the Benefits organization. Within the Wellness PLT, there is a "Wellness Partners" team that consists of over 100 individuals including Club One staff, Occupational Health Nurses, Administrative Assistants, EAP staff, Benefits and HR managers and a couple of dedicated wellness resources who manage supplier contracts and project teams. Some resources such as the Wellness staff and Occupational Health Resources are internal Motorola employees, and others such as Club One and EAP are external suppliers; most volunteer their time for wellness initiatives on top of their "regular" jobs. These "partners" help deliver programs and services in their local areas by joining specific project teams and disseminating information and working through logistics of particular initiatives. Most of the teamwork is done via conference calls, and marketing tools and project information are housed on a shared intranet site.

Club One–A Key Strategic Partner

Club One provides experienced staff that leads many of our education and awareness initiatives, broadening their scope beyond traditional fitness/recreation roles and responsibilities. They not only manage Wellness Centers in a way that is consistent with Club One's overall business approach, but they provide leadership of other wellness initiatives as well. In this way, the Center operations are closely tied to the delivery of the overall wellness strategy, creating a synergy that makes for an easier time of planning, delivering and measuring programs. Wellness Center staff is able to use their fitness expertise to run state-of-the-art centers, and Motorola is able to utilize Club One Professional Services staff for delivery of strategic initiatives. Club One receives the benefit of rounding out their staff development and corporate wellness experience; Motorola receives the benefit of additional resources aligned to overall program goals. Recent program initiatives have included the development and delivery of both virtual and on-site tools for tobacco cessation, fitness and nutrition for parents and kids, self-care, weight management, low back pain/relief and resilience.

MORE ABOUT THE WELLNESS CENTERS

The current team-based, project-driven approach hasn't always been the case. Motorola's wellness efforts were decentralized up until a few years ago. In February of 2003, the transition was made to have all on-site Wellness Centers under Club One management. This allowed Motorola to share the risk reduction wellness efforts with Club One–a national fitness/wellness management company who has been in the industry for over 20 years. At the same time, wellness initiatives were also centralized as a corporate function, not as a function of each sector. Current Wellness Center locations are Arizona (4 in the Phoenix area), Pennsylvania (1 in Horsham), Illinois (4 in the Chicago area), Texas (3 in Austin, 1 in Ft. Worth) and Toronto, Canada.

The Centers are the kind of place a person would want to work out and spend time. Not only are the physical facility and equipment of the highest quality, but also the staff is as focused on employees as our employees are on their customers. This sets these Centers apart–because of the close integration with Motorola wellness staff and delivery of wellness initiatives, the Center staffs are committed to understanding the business environment and employee concerns in a way that many facilities just could not.

In making the transition to Club One-run wellness centers, Motorola's major objectives were to reduce costs associated with in-house management as well as effectively deliver consistency in programs and services across 14 Wellness Centers, in different regions of the country. This meant having an organizational structure that was designed to provide one staff person to every 300-400 members per center, regional managers to support the staff and operations for each center, as well as a corporate support center that could help manage the business, marketing, equipment, human resources and technology aspects of the center operations. Club One Pro Services has extensive expertise in managing on-site fitness centers and wellness programs for an array of corporate partners across the country and was able to meet these objectives. The "high touch-high tech" philosophy shared between Club One and Motorola has created powerfully aligned wellness integration.

The Centers have a diverse menu of offerings. In the program arena, group exercise classes are ongoing each week and include everything from SpinZen (combination of spinning and yoga) to a more traditional step aerobics class. Specialty classes, which typically run 6-8 weeks, include offerings such as Pilates, salsa dance and martial arts. Recreation events such as basketball, soccer, and softball leagues and tournaments are popular as well as trips to local professional athletic events and points of interest like a wildflower center or art museum.

PEDOMETER WALKING PROGRAM

Incentive programs, which can be facilitated online, reach not just the Wellness Center population but also the entire U.S. employee population. The recently offered "Spring in Your Step; 10,000 Steps to Your Health" centered on awareness of daily physical activity through the use of a pedometer and had 15% of the total U.S. and Canada population participating. This program was a direct result of the Secretary of Health's focus on weight management and preventable health risks. According to the "Prevention Makes Common Cents" report by the U.S. Department of Health and Human Services (2003), obesity-related health problems cost U.S. businesses an estimated $14 billion in 1994, including about $8 billion in health insurance costs, $2.4 billion for sick leave, $1.8 billion for life insurance and nearly $1 billion for disability. This initiative's success was due to all the wellness partners at large and small sites all over the country taking initiative to promote the program and coordinate the details. Conference calls were held to relay details of setting up the program; and pedometer orders exceeded expectations by about 25%. Site representatives posted ready-made flyers, distributed pedometers, and informed employees on how to track their progress online during the six-week initiative. Employees were "caught" taking the stairs, walking laps around cubicle areas, parking farther away from the building, all in an attempt to make sure they got their 10,000 steps in daily. During the course of the campaign, small blue pedometers became the accessory of choice for employees at every level of the company. People discovered how easy it was to incorporate physical activity into their daily routine. One employee shared that she wasn't wearing her pedometer at work, only on her walks at home. She was ecstatic to learn that all the steps taken in the Corporate Tower "counted" toward her overall fitness level!

WELLNESS CENTER PARTICIPATION

Over 50% of the total Motorola employee population residing at Wellness Center campus locations are members of their on-site center. Participation is measured by the number of visits per member per week. Current participation rates average sixty visits per member per week, with the goal of reaching 1.0 visit per member, per week. This is based solely on Wellness Center visits; however, participation is considerably higher when the attendance of non-members and retirees is factored in. Non-members, spouses and retirees regularly participate in wellness education and specialty classes, seminars, recreation events, incentive programs and massage. They may attend many classes and programs without becoming a member of a Center. Other program offerings include personal training and on-site physical therapy. The annual member survey conducted at the end of 2003 revealed that out of approximately 2,000 responses, 96% were satisfied (most of these were very satisfied) with the Wellness Center programs, services, staff and operations. Employee testimonials such as this one support that statistic: "Amy, you and your staff in the Activity Center have helped me a lot. You changed my life. My Vietnamese saying is 'Health is gold,' and all of you are giving me more than that treasure. A thousand words are never enough to say thank you. Please accept my great appreciation."

WELLNESS AND WORK-LIFE

Many corporate wellness programs also encompass work-life initiatives. At Motorola, a separate team focuses on work-life, but the wellness staff serves on that team. Wellness and work-life efforts are integrated in philosophy, brand identity and function. Issues of work-life flexibility have become significant business issues to be dealt with on a daily basis. Forty-six percent of employees either feel overworked, overwhelmed by the quantity of their work, or lack the time to step back and reflect on their work (Bond, 2002). According to the Radcliffe Public Policy Center (2000), sixty-one percent of adults say they would give up some of their pay for more time with their family. Motorola provides work-life tools including adoption assistance, dependent care, and long-term care, LifeCare resource/referral and discount services to help address pressures of everyday life. A Harvard Business Review article states that work-life efforts seek to create a culture where employees feel comfortable saying "judge me by the quality of my work, not by the amount of time I spend at the office" (Friedman, 1998). A recent example of collaboration was on a wellness initiative entitled "Healthy, Active Families." This initiative included team members from Club One, Occupational Health Resources, and Rewards (Benefits). The Healthy Active Families team consulted with the work-life team to create a Prenatal/Birth Checklist intended to provide an expectant parent with a guide to available benefits, programs and policies that may be of consideration in planning for the birth of a child. This provides a "one-stop shop" for employees, whether their point of entry is through work-life Web links or wellness Web links.

COMMUNICATION AND MARKETING

The challenge of disseminating information to a large diverse workforce is how to reach them with what they need, when they need it. Programs and tools are only as good as people's ability to access them. Therefore, communication and marketing is delivered in as many ways as possible. A large portion of news is delivered electronically, there is a wellness intranet Web site for still more information, and flyers, posters, table tents, closed circuit television, home mailings and information table outside the cafeteria are also utilized. There is close collaboration with the Employee Communications Department to ensure branding that is unique to the program, yet consistent with corporate brand standards.

Additionally, the Wellness Centers disseminate weekly or biweekly member e-news publications to a member distribution list. Some non-members also subscribe, as they have found this publication to be a valuable resource for classes and information. This Member News includes information regarding upcoming recreation events, specialty and group exercise programs, ongoing services such as personal training and massage, as well as a listing of community events from running races to musical and theatre events. Subscribers have let us know that this is unquestionably their preferred method for learning about what is offered by the Wellness Centers, Motorola wellness initiatives and their local community.

Another example of integration is the use of the concept of in the internal marketing of wellness messages. Every aspect of wellness education and awareness efforts contains messaging with a resilience component. For example, as messages, are delivered on weight management, self-care or even flu immunizations, the focus is on how employees can take responsibility for their health and well-being. Messages are positive, motivational, evidenced-based and holistic. For example, on the weight management home page, the language isn't about shame or blame. Instead, the text reads, "Frustrated by diets that don't work? Tired of bouncing back and forth between sizes? The key to successful weight loss is to develop daily eating habits that promote good health. Successful weight reduction programs include a satisfying and balanced diet, regular physical activity and a healthy overall attitude toward food."

Looking Ahead

Looking to the future involves examining and learning from the past. The most valuable lessons learned in Motorola's corporate wellness program center around collaboration and integration. The wellness team consists of many employees for whom wellness is an "add-on," not an integral part of their job function. However, in most cases, wellness team members have integrated wellness goals into their personal career development discussions. Wellness then becomes a larger part of the overall business plan. Just as products require "seamless mobility," so do health and wellness initiatives. The job simply cannot be done by one person, philosophy or department. The program must fit within the culture, and the current culture is one of cross-functional collaboration. Success occurs when the invitation to discussion comes *before* issues arise, rather than discussion only starting with the words, "I need . . ." In other words, relationships are critical and take time.

Looking to the future demands flexibility to respond to both industry trends and employee needs while still managing cost. An additional strategy employed in 2004 was to retain the services of an external wellness consultant whose role was to look at existing programs, determine how to position programs for future success, evaluate current trends from the literature and design a transition plan and metrics/evaluation plan. A big focus of future initiatives is how to demonstrate return on investment. Even during the redesign of the program and program metrics, accountability to the leadership of the company is maintained. This is accomplished by conducting semi-annual operations reviews where wellness teams and external vendors report on a standard set of metrics including participation, quality and attraction/retention. Wellness teams also meet monthly and deliver project updates to each other. Feedback from employees, team members and leaders helps to drive continuous improvement in program design, delivery and dissemination.

Another helpful benchmark by which to measure programs are the Healthy Workforce 2010 Elements of a Comprehensive Worksite Health Promotion Program. These elements would be a helpful starting point for anyone looking to create or enhance wellness at a company of any size (Appendix 1).

In closing, these suggestions are offered for implementing or enhancing a successful, integrated wellness program:

1. Do not become discouraged before you even start due to budget concerns or thoughts of how you will get things done. Many successful programs start with a committee and a shoestring budget. Set expectations high and have a clear vision.
2. Choose integration partners carefully and treat them well. The most effective partners will share your vision and seek to always make the relationship more effective, while looking to minimize cost.
3. Be patient when developing internal collaborative partners. Everyone has a full plate, but intentions are almost always good. Allow internal partners to participate as they can, and do not expect that everyone will share your goals or your enthusiasm initially. Offer to participate in the projects and meetings of your collaborative partners–it is a two-way street.
4. Seek support at every level of the company. Make sure senior leadership understands the value of your efforts by building a sound business case, including financials. Do not neglect the employee population, however. Conduct surveys and focus groups, formal and informal, to make sure that you are programming not just from your own expertise and data, but by listening to what employees are saying they want. Pilot large-scale programs with a smaller group and listen carefully to all feedback.
5. Communicate, communicate, communicate. Employees have a lot on their plate, and they are likely to miss the message the first

time. Persevere in your attempts to provide the right message to the right person at the right time.

6. Finally, have fun! If employee well-being is about feeling good, then you should feel good in every phase of planning, creation, implementation and evaluation.

REFERENCES

Adams, T., Bezner, J., & Steinhardt, M. (1997). The conceptualization and measurement of perceived wellness: Integrating balance across and within dimensions. *American Journal of Health Promotion*, Jan-Feb; 11(3): 208-18.

Aldana, S. (2001). Financial impact of health promotion programs: A comprehensive review of the literature. *American Journal of Health Promotion*, May/June: 15(5), 296-320.

Anderson, D. (2003). Building a first class workforce. *Absolute Advantage*, Wellness Councils of America, 2(5): 4-9.

Bond, J., Thompson, C., Galinsky, E., & Prottas, D. (2002). National Study of the changing workforce. Families and Work Institute, No. 3.

Chapman, L. (2003). Meta-evaluation of worksite health promotion economic return studies. *Art of Health Promotion Newsletter*, 6(6), January/February.

Friedman, S., Christensen, P., & DeGroot, J., (1998). Work and life: The end of the zero-sum game. *Harvard Business Review*, November-December.

Goetzel, R., Anderson, D., Whitmer, R., Ozminkowski, R., Dunn, R., & Wasserman, J. (1998). The relationship between modifiable health risks and health care expenditures: An analysis of the multi-employer HERO health risk and cost database. *Journal of Occupational and Environmental Medicine*, 40(10): 843-854, The Health Enhancement Research Organization (HERO) Research Committee.

McGinnis, J., & Foege W. (1993). Actual causes of death in the United States. *JAMA*, 270: 2207-2212.

Rubleski, J. (2004). Beating healthcare costs: Is it really possible? Wellness Councils of America Interview, 2004, *www.welcoa.org/freeresources*

Segerstrom, S., & Miller, G. (2004). Psychological stress and the human immune system: A meta-analytic study of 30 years of inquiry, *Psychological Bulletin*, 130(4): 601-630.

Steinhardt, M., from unpublished research study conducted by The University of Texas at Austin.

APPENDIX 1

Healthy Workforce 2010 Elements of a Comprehensive Worksite Health Promotion Program

1. Health education focused on skill development, lifestyle change, awareness building and tailored to meet employee needs and interest.
2. Supportive social and physical environments that mirror an organization's expectations regarding healthy behaviors, using policies that promote health and reduce disease.
3. Integrate the program into the organization's structure.
4. Linkages to related programs like EAP and programs that help employees balance work and family.
5. Screening programs ideally linked to medical care to ensure follow-up and appropriate treatment as necessary.
6. Process for supporting individual behaviors change with follow-up interventions.
7. An evaluation and improvement process to help enhance the program's effectiveness and efficiency.

    (*http://www.prevent.org/publications/Healthy_Workforce_2010.pdf*)

Chapter 12

Wells Fargo's Employee Assistance Consulting Model: How to Be an Invited Guest at Every Table

Rick Bidgood
Arne Boudewyn
Betsy Fasbinder

SUMMARY. Wells Fargo and Company's Employee Assistance Consulting (EAC) is an established and successful internal corporate-based EAP that delivers organizationally congruent services to a diversified financial services company with 80+ businesses and over 146,000 team members. While some elements of traditional EAPs are evident in the services provided by this entity, EAC also provides highly specialized and customized consultations to its corporate partners, business group customers and employees. Using a highly integrated service model that aligns closely with the specific strategy and operations of each Wells Fargo business, EAC is an invited guest at many of the company's most influential tables. EAC collaboratively partners with senior and line management, Human Resources, the Employment Law Department, Disability Management (called WorkAbility at Wells Fargo) and Risk Management, Corporate Benefits, Corporate Security, Learning and Development, and others to provide leadership and organizational influence on such wide ranging issues as threat assessment and management, business incident management, workplace trauma, health and productivity, and organizational

[Haworth co-indexing entry note]: "Wells Fargo's Employee Assistance Consulting Model: How to Be an Invited Guest at Every Table." Bidgood, Rick, Arne Boudewyn, and Betsy Fasbinder. Co-published simultaneously in *Journal of Workplace Behavioral Health* (The Haworth Press, Inc.) Vol. 20, No. 3/4, 2005, pp. 219-242; and: *The Integration of Employee Assistance, Work/Life, and Wellness Services* (ed: Mark Attridge, Patricia A. Herlihy, and R. Paul Maiden) The Haworth Press, Inc., 2005, pp. 219-242. Single or multiple copies of this article are available for a fee from The Haworth Document Delivery Service [1-800-HAWORTH, 9:00 a.m. - 5:00 p.m. (EST). E-mail address: docdelivery@haworthpress.com].

Available online at http://www.haworthpress.com/web/JWBH
© 2005 by The Haworth Press, Inc. All rights reserved.
doi:10.1300/J490v20n03_02

and employee effectiveness. This article describes proven methods and strategies for maximizing organizational influence and positioning EAP consultants as effective business partners. *[Article copies available for a fee from The Haworth Document Delivery Service: 1-800-HAWORTH. E-mail address: <docdelivery@haworthpress.com> Website: <http://www.HaworthPress.com> © 2005 by The Haworth Press, Inc. All rights reserved.]*

KEYWORDS. Consultation, integration, organizational congruence, strategic change

INTRODUCTION

Unlike traditional "bricks and mortar" banks, Wells Fargo and Company is now a diversified financial services organization compromised of 80+ distinct businesses–covering services from mortgage to insurance, phone banks, "in store" supermarket branches and traditional branches to Internet services, brokerage to small business lending–with over 146,000 employees, working in all 50 states and several international locations. As Wells Fargo has evolved, so has its internal EAP. Even its name–Employee Assistance Consulting (EAC)–intentionally reflects a strategy of continuous integration with the company, its values, and its core business strategies. A traditional EAP model simply cannot serve this dynamic and evolving company (Sciegaj et al., 2001). To promote individual and organizational effectiveness EAC shifted to focus equally on its traditional assessment/short-term problem solving/referral services and its business consultative practice.

As the Wells Fargo brand expanded–through planned growth and a series of high profile mergers and acquisitions in the 1990s and 65 smaller acquisitions since 1998–from a California-only bank to a national financial services company, it became clear that traditional assessment, short-term problem solving and referral, cookie-cutter consultations and a one-flavor-fits-all approach to EAP services no longer met the complex needs of the company. Had EAC remained only a traditional broad-brush EAP, the company might well have chosen to outsource this function as so many of its competitors have because a traditional model is usually delivered more efficiently from a vendor. While other companies outsourced their EAP services, EAC has become one of the largest internal EAPs in the United States (while maintaining a very competitive expense control on a per FTE basis) and an influential partner at the highest levels of the organization. Why has EAC remained an invited guest at some of the most important decision-making tables at Wells Fargo?

STRATEGY

It's so beautifully arranged on the plate, you know someone's fingers have been all over it.

–Julia Child

Employee Assistance Consulting: A Mix of Three Recipes

EAC's development has paralleled that of Wells Fargo that focuses on gaining greater market share of an existing customer base by deepening relationships and achieving cross-sell of services and products (Van Den Bergh, 2000). The current EAC model and philosophy grew out of the combination of the best ingredients from three separate programs brought together through corporate mergers: Wells Fargo's Employee Assistance Services (EAS); First Interstate Bancorp's Employee Assistance Program (EAP); and Norwest's Employee Assistance Resource (NEAR) program. The new Wells Fargo is a dynamic organization in which EAC is a fully integrated contributor.

Prior to 1992, Wells Fargo was a San Francisco-based, California-only bank with approximately 30,000 employees that served customers. EAS, which had been in existence since 1979, operated out of San Francisco and had only recently added a second office location in Los Angeles. EAS consultants were primarily generalists answering calls from employees and managers that came in through a centralized number. EAS services were offered telephonically to fit the organizational culture and were available during regular business hours, Monday through Friday, with limited overnight and weekend support for calls picked up by an outside answering service. One of the higher profile services provided by EAS during this time was a robbery response protocol that often included onsite Critical Incident Stress Debriefing (CISD) services provided by EAS and forged relationships with branch managers and security partners within the company. EAS leadership was also strongly aligned with corporate human resources leadership prior to the merger.

These relationships proved vital throughout the changes that were to come.

The 1996 merger of Wells Fargo with First Interstate Bankcorp expanded not only the employee population–bringing it to over 60,000 in number–it also made Wells Fargo a multi-state bank for the first time in its history and a company with 24/7/365 services to customers. The merger of differing EAP cultures and similar program services necessitated a radical change to the EAS design. The change was not simply adding a new ingredient to a favorite old dish. First Interstate's program had been complementary in scope, focus, and services to the EAS program. However, the way services were delivered had differed considerably. After the merger, the task and challenge was to understand the customer experience and needs outside of California, understand needs by business groups, and decide on how best to provide uniform services across 13 states. Staff from both Wells Fargo and First Interstate programs were retained and the merged team worked together to design a customized approach to EAP services to fit the culture and organizational needs of the new Wells Fargo. For example, EAS recognized the importance of a physical presence in other key market areas and opened an office in Phoenix, Arizona (and later another in Portland, Oregon). An evening/weekend EAS team organized to respond to the company's new round-the-clock culture and the inevitable increase in calls coming after regular business hours. EAS was also structured to deliver services virtually where possible and leveraged vendor relationships to allow immediate onsite services when required.

With the merger, EAS also gained an increased appreciation for the value of strategic business partnerships as a way of integrating services and collaborating with line human resources within Wells Fargo. This alignment resulted in gaining HR partners as champions for the value and quality of the internal EAP. The EAS team reorganized so that each consultant (while still a generalist) was assigned to collaborate with HR partners in specific business groups. Consultants were responsible to learn the business needs of the groups they supported and provided tailored programs and services to meet the needs of their *Human Resources customers*. This was the beginning of EAS's recognition that a customized service was required for each business culture, size and style. EAS learned that it could not offer the same menu to every customer or assume that everyone has the same tastes or appetites.

In 1998 Wells Fargo and Company and Norwest Corporation merged. Prior to the merger (Wall Street Journal, 1998), Norwest Employee Assistance Resources (NEAR) provided internal EAP services for Norwest, based in Minneapolis, Minnesota. The NEAR program and that of Wells Fargo differed greatly in terms of culture, service model and philosophy. Whereas Wells Fargo's EAS had begun to be more "business-focused" services, NEAR offered a more traditional approach to EAP, providing face-to-face sessions for employees and a limited relationship to the lines of business. Business consultation was seen by this organization as a function of the Human Resources staff, while EAP services were designated to traditional mental health and substance abuse arenas. The EAP was well regarded but organized under the umbrella of health and wellness programs offered to employees rather than positioned as a centralized corporate function.

While its EAP structure was traditional, the philosophy of Norwest's leadership was revolutionary. Norwest understood that financial service products are duplicable across competitors, but held that a company's employees are its differentiator. "People as a Competitive Advantage" (PACA) was a stated core value shared by the Norwest CEO, Dick Kovacevich (who became CEO of the new, larger Wells Fargo) and his team. The PACA philosophy is that to be successful as a company, ". . . we must attract, develop, retain, and motivate a diverse team of the most talented people who care and who work together as partners across business units and functions," says Dick Kovacevich. PACA philosophy was applied in many ways throughout the Norwest business.

With the merger of Wells Fargo and Norwest (and their respective EAP programs) came a collision of cultures, strategies and business structures. Wells Fargo was seen as the technology leader that lacked personal touch. Norwest, known for personal touch as demonstrated by its PACA philosophy, appreciated Wells Fargo's strong brand recognition and aggressive business practices. With a new organization of approximately 120,000 team members in fifty states, the company embarked on a strategy that would eventually create a new culture and business structure that embraced each company's strengths. The job of the yet to be named EAP was to select the best practices from each source company's program and to redesign its business to serve the newly formed company.

Having learned about the complexity of cultural integration from the speed of the First Interstate merger, company leaders elected to adopt a "slow cook" model when approaching culture shift, business practice redesign and staffing decisions. The combined EAP groups, following the lead of the larger organization, elected to allow time to elapse as part of their strategy for redesign. The group took this time to read the company's direction, to assimilate the EAS and NEAR cultures, and to form a single team. The new team elected to retain the traditional and high touch elements of the NEAR program while adopting the business focus of EAS. The ideals and beliefs of PACA were core to the design of the new team yet all the while keeping one step ahead of the larger organization to ensure their ability to provide stable support and consultation to a company undergoing substantial reorganization. The new team elected to retain a high-touch approach and many of the traditional elements of the NEAR program while adopting the business focus of EAS. The ideals and beliefs of PACA were core to the design of the new team.

The new group was purposefully renamed Employee Assistance *Consulting* (EAC) to reflect its highly consultative approach and emphasis on collaboration and integration with the larger company. This was a departure from the traditional EAP mental health/treatment model. Broadening the business liaison function reflected in the old Wells Fargo group, EAC forged partnerships with line HR staff in the new company as well as with Employee Relations, Corporate Security, Corporate Benefits, Employment Law Department and Disability (called WorkAbility at Wells Fargo), and Risk Management. To reflect its services across business lines, EAC was located as a distinct entity under the umbrella of Corporate Human Resources. So situated, EAC is seen as a core and central organizational function and strategic partner packaged alongside other corporate functions that support individual employee and business performance such as compensation and recruitment rather than simply an adjunct service needed only in times of crisis (Sciegaj et al., 2001; Van Den Bergh, 2000). In this way corporate HR services are resources that are linked to business success and brand the employment experience at Wells Fargo. Rather than being segmented in separate departments, these offerings are available through multiple channels to make them more accessible to employees. Within Corporate HR the emphasis on "cross-selling" these benefits to team members is strong. This is reflective of Wells Fargo culture and business strategy.

Another core element of EAC's business strategy was taken from the company motto "run it like you own it." This was a philosophy of the pre-merger Wells Fargo that carried over into the post-merger company. The spirit of entrepreneurship captured in this frequently articulated philosophy dates back to the early stagecoach days and encouraged EAC to be innovative in the design and delivery of products and services that were "cutting edge." At both the macro and micro levels EAC was afforded great latitude in determining how it would meet its mission to the organization.

Essentially what Wells Fargo looked for from EAC was support for the success and well-being of its team members. At its core, Wells Fargo is a sales and service organization. Success in these two arenas is largely defined by behaviors. Behaviors that lead to success in sales and service can be greatly affected, positively and negatively, by a team member's state of mind. Anxiety and mood can sway the success of a team member who is focused on selling the right Wells Fargo products to make a customer financially successful or a team member who is trying to provide to a Wells Fargo customer a "surprise and delight" service experience. Behavioral health then takes on more significance in this type of business context. EAC focused on how to leverage its behavioral health expertise to promote individual and organizational effectiveness.

STRUCTURE

Appetite comes with eating.

–French Proverb

Wells Fargo's EAC Business Model: A Custom Menu

Through a commitment to high touch customer service and responsive, customized products EAC has whetted the appetites of its enterprise customers and continues to be a sought out partner in an ever-increasing number of arenas. This appetite is reflected in increased utilization year after year, growing sophistication of management consultations requested, greater EAC brand recognition at every level of the organization and an assumption that EAC expertise should be included in strategic initiative design and implementation.

The current EAC business model is built around the premise that customers are best served by an EAP structure that is reflective of the organization. Like many of the business groups that it supports, EAC operates in a virtual team environment with a staff of 40 plus consultants located in three time zones and four cities (Los Angeles, Minneapolis, Phoenix, and San Francisco). Team members (the term Wells Fargo uses for employees) and their family members calling a centralized toll-free number located at a dedicated call center are provided with seamless telephonic service irrespective of geography, business line, time of call or presenting concern. Callers may not even be aware of where their EAC consultant is located. This is reflective of Wells Fargo's business call center structure and its "on demand" service approach.

Whether team members call for individual assessment/referral needs or a manager seeks consultation around a troubled team member or critical incident, a single point of access through an internal call center will ensure *immediate* routing to the next available consultant. The promise of instant access to professional consultants is at the core of the EAC model. With extended call-center hours and 24/7 consultant availability, EAC has branded "immediate service" as an anytime, anywhere commitment to the organization.

In addition to an immediate service function, EAC has formalized its business liaison services. A dedicated staff of consultants, EAC Business Consultants (or BCs), are assigned to partner with line Human Resources consultants and key leaders within each of Wells Fargo's eight major business divisions, comprising 80+ sub-businesses. Formerly business consultants were assigned to several business lines. Through experience has come the learning that it is best to assign business consultants, as a team, to a single line of business to allow them to drill deeper into organizational understanding and to form more concentrated partnerships in their respective groups, and to develop customized EAC products that have specific business value. Business consultants often bring the flavors of their business groups back to the entire EAC team so that staff can provide consultation that is congruent with the organizational culture to all callers.

In the same way that EAC has dedicated consultant staff to support individual business lines, there have been advantages to devoting a regular group of consultants to staff the immediate service function at EAC. Called Immediate Service Consultants (or ISCs), this group fields the bulk of calls that come in on the toll-free EAC line. Their consultations with individual team members as well as their management consultations are informed by information derived from the Business Consultants who have more direct contact with the business groups themselves. Conversely, Business Consultants (or BCs) are informed about trends, volume, and presenting concerns in their business groups by what Immediate Service Consultants gather on the phones. This mutual feedback loop is successful because regardless of role, all EAC consultants, though from diverse disciplines, are selected for their clinical and consultative acumen as well as their ability to grasp nuances of the organizational culture. This approach has a strong parallel to EAC's relationship with the larger organization. For example, Wells Fargo branches (or "stores") routinely collaborate with the Wells Fargo mortgage business, and vice versa, to provide for customers' financial needs. In the same way, business line partners have an option to reach a specific Business Consultant at their direct number or to utilize the toll-free number for immediate service.

Organizational congruence does not begin or end with EAC's consultants. EAC dedicates similar attention to the customer experience at the first point of contact with EAC. Call center staff are selected, trained and supported so that they are able to provide a high-touch experience right from the beginning of their EAC experience. EAC call center staff provides extended hours so that callers experience a live receptionist from 5am to 11pm Central time on weekdays. Even overnight and weekend callers experience a maximum delay of about 15 minutes in reaching on-call consultants to help meet their needs.

EAC fosters a successful virtual team environment across four offices (and in the home offices of consultants who are dedicated to night and weekend services) through shared project work, regular staff and team meetings and a "culture of internal consultation" around complex cases. Through its active, virtual connections, EAC has created a regular information flow conduit through which consultants are regularly updating one another on organizational trends and priorities.

Another core component of the EAC model is dedicated consultant teams (called service groups) that function as research and development groups around EAC products. These teams focus on:

- Workplace safety and work trauma services.
- Threat assessment and threat management, including partnerships with Corporate Security.
- Vendor management, including relationships with CISD responders and mental health/substance abuse treatment providers available through a carve-out, wrap-around benefit design.
- Quality assurance in regard to EAC standards and practices.
- Training and online products specific to business groups and/or the Wells Fargo enterprise across businesses, including through the EAC Website.
- EAC staff development, including continuing education licensure requirements and staff recruitment.

Service groups originate EAC initiatives and often coordinate with EAC business partners in project development and implementation.

SERVICES

Never eat more than you can lift.

–Miss Piggy

EAC Services Marketing: Setting an Attractive Table

Within Wells Fargo, EAC has created for itself a wonderful problem. Because of the business support model, an "anytime anywhere" response and an organizationally congruent consultation practice, EAC has become included in a wide range of business and strategic decision-making processes (Van Den Bergh, 2000). The entity must forever balance being well integrated with managing volume of demand. Remembering that EAC is not a revenue-generating entity, nor a provider of mental health treatment, there is a continual focus on demonstrating value to the company and its directives (Sciegaj et al., 2001). EAC is regularly included as a collaborative partner in many key initiatives and programs (Van Den Bergh, 2000).

> The consultant who assumes a collaborative role enters the relationship with the notion that management issues can be dealt with effectively only by joining his or her specialized knowledge with the manager's knowledge of the organization. Problem solving becomes a joint undertaking, with equal attention to both the technical issues and the human interactions involved in dealing with technical issues.
>
> –Peter Block (2000)

Threat Management and Security Consultation

EAC has found a natural partnership with Corporate Security, which deepened during a number of high profile/high risk domestic violence cases that emerged in 2000. Long relationships between EAC and Corporate Security that had initially formed in robbery response now evolved to include the complexity of workplace threat management. EAC consultants bring behavioral health expertise in the workplace to collaborations with Corporate Security partners. In 2003 threat management teams responded to more than 2500 security incidents for Wells

Fargo and more than 1400 security incidents in just the first six months of 2004.

For the past three years EAC has partnered with Corporate Security in a company-wide education initiative called Violence Free Workplace Training (VFWT). The initiative began in response to an escalating number of consultations posing a high safety risk to Wells Fargo. Analysis indicated that many of these situations were not identified by management soon enough to prevent the risks from escalating. Enterprise-wide education of management and HR was determined to be part of the remedy. Results after two years of VFWT delivered to thousands of HR staff, managers and team members showed that while consultations about workplace safety continued to increase, the severity of risks posed decreased significantly. The organization's decision to promote this training is both an effort to promote a safe workplace for all team members and an acknowledgement that domestic violence disproportionately impacts women in the workplace. Since Wells Fargo's workforce is more than two-thirds female, domestic abuse is prevalent in the team member population. The VFWT initiative aims to address situations where domestic abuse may affect workplace safety and shows consideration for issues affecting many women at Wells Fargo, another expression of PACA values.

Another value of being housed internally is that EAC utilization is cost neutral on a per usage basis to the business lines. This is particularly advantageous when it comes to threat management. Managers do not have to consider cost in deciding which workplace safety issues require consultation with EAC or Corporate Security. Instead, they are able to bring any threat concerns–big or small–to EAC and Corporate Security for evaluation. The end result is that EAC conducts frequent and early threat assessments and designs threat management plans which in many cases allow for prevention or early intervention of risks to the workplace.

Corporate Benefits and Work-Life Programs

EAC has shared in decision-making regarding the provision of mental health and substance abuse benefits (MH/SA). Early on EAC and the Corporate Benefits department recognized the need for parity of MH/SA benefits with medical health benefits. A combination of a carve-out and a wrap-around MH/SA benefit was negotiated with all Wells Fargo medical plans so that team members could enjoy a single point of access with one behavioral health vendor regardless of specific health plan enrollment. Making access simple and easing restrictions to care did not result in extraordinary expense increases. Therefore, additional MH/SA benefit changes were made to allow more robust behavioral health treatment services without the traditional limits to the number of treatment sessions. Access to care was seen as more valuable to helping people stay healthy and productive than micro managing the utilization of care. Despite its potential expense, this was seen by senior managers as another demonstration of PACA values, i.e., a method to keep an organization and its individual team members healthy and productive (Levy et al., 2003). Ironically, these benefit changes have had minimal cost impact.

The MH/SA benefit is a tool that allows EAC to better serve both team members' and Wells Fargo's interests. Although team members have multiple options for contact points for accessing MH/SA benefits, EAC has assumed a position as primary contact and maintained an "assess and refer" role in order to facilitate the initial connection between team members and treatment providers. This allows EAC to screen for any workplace issues, especially about workplace safety, that might get overlooked if the team member accessed treatment directly with the MH/SA vendor. At the same time, EAC expedites referrals into treatment and monitors team member feedback about the quality of their experience with MH/SA providers and facilities (Harris et al., 2002). Where appropriate, and always preserving confidentiality, this information is looped back to the MH/SA vendor and corporate benefits. Benefits design decisions are influenced by this feedback. Additionally, EAC learns about Wells Fargo business trends from MH/SA utilization that enriches its ability to consult effectively with its business partners.

EAC collaboration with Wells Fargo's MH/SA vendor focuses on providing the least restrictive care appropriate to functionality. EAC has found that by promoting immediate and convenient access to treatment and the appropriate use of outpatient benefits, the need for use of inpatient benefits by those with chronic or catastrophic conditions is reduced. Overall, EAC's model of an internal EAP combined with a self-insured MH/SA carve-out is extremely effective in improving access to MH/SA benefits while maintaining cost of claims for the self-insured plan. The success of EAC's gatekeeper function and its independent oversight of the MH/SA vendor can be correlated with the resulting MH/SA utilization rates (Levy et al., 2003).

Complex Case Management

EAC works off of the Corporate Human Resources platform within Wells Fargo and has established, trusted relationships with HR, Employee Relations (ER), the Employment Law Department, Disability (called WorkAbility at Wells Fargo) and Risk Management and Corporate Security partners. EAC regularly participates in or facilitates management of complex consultations involving some or all of these partners. Frequently, these are situations involving behavioral risk management, potential fitness-for-duty assessment for a troubled team member, performance issues impacted by behavioral health concerns, or complex threat management cases with potential risk for the workplace. Connecting leaders from each of the above disciplines in an integrated partnership improves decision-making on behalf of both the employee and the company (Chima, 2001).

Critical Incident Response and Emergency Preparedness

EAC's role in robbery response–a core and central service found in all of the pre-merger EAPs discussed here–continues to be an opportunity to demonstrate an added value to the Wells Fargo enterprise and more than 6000 banking stores in twenty-three states. In 2003, EAC consultants responded to more than 400 bank robberies (averaging more than one per day), providing rapid behavioral risk assessment and managing triage of appropriate behavioral health resources for employees most affected in these events. EAC responded to 230 bank robberies in the first six months of 2004 alone, suggesting that its collaborative role in managing these incidents will continue to be needed. EAC's partnerships with Corporate Security, Human Resources, and Risk Management in responding to robberies have provided an excellent platform for highlighting added value to the organization and to the Wells Fargo employee population.

Building upon the reputation EAC has gained through high touch, compassionate and timely response for robbery victims, EAC is now included in an organizational strategy for responding to critical incidents of all kinds. These include employee deaths, bomb threats, biohazard threats (particularly after 9/11), natural disasters and other high profile events. Recognizing inherent limitations in an ability to get to remote locations quickly when onsite services are indicated, EAC has become the vendor manager for two external CISD provider networks. Here EAC partners with vendors to ensure that onsite services are delivered in accordance with EAC standards and Wells Fargo culture and policies. EAC also established and administers a "work trauma fund" that provides company-paid individual, in-person trauma counseling for any Wells Fargo team member affected by a robbery, or other traumatic event at work. This fund aims to provide quick access to specialized care that can help restore individual functionality while at the same time demonstrating that Wells Fargo cares about its team members.

While all critical incidents require sensitive management, certain situations stand out as particularly troublesome or have potential for wide-ranging or serious impact to the company and its employees. To respond to these special concerns, Wells Fargo formed the Enterprise Incident Management Team (or EIMT). The EIMT is comprised of representatives from Corporate Communications, Corporate Security, Corporate Business Continuity & Site Emergency Plans, HR, business line leaders and EAC representatives. EAC's participation in the EIMT ensures both that "people issues" are highlighted in coordinating any incident response and that EAC can bridge its business customers to situations involving their team members. Additionally, vital information about the critical incidents is routed back to EAC staff to prepare them for potential calls and increased call volume surrounding an event.

Wells Fargo Corporate Initiatives

EAC consultants are also Wells Fargo employees and are intimately aware of the company's initiatives and directives. Therefore, EAC is well positioned to support these initiatives in both design and implementation. The company's diversity initiative offers a compelling example. At the highest levels of the organization, there is commitment to valuing diversity, identifying strengths and areas for improvement in this area, and incorporating recommendations into business practices, recruitment and retention. EAC representatives participate as members in the Wells Fargo Corporate HR Diversity Council and contribute to diversity support through the regular inclusion of core diversity messages (e.g., respect for differences, creating an inclusive work environment) in training programs and product design.

Recognizing the impact of depression in the workplace, EAC has partnered with Corporate Benefits and Wells Fargo WorkAbility in the planning and implementation of a company-wide depression awareness and screening initiative. This initiative seeks to reduce the impact of depression on workplace productivity, absenteeism and workplace behavior (Chima, 2001). For preventing and managing depression, an equally important goal is to inspire team members to take full advantage of the many educational and healthcare resources available to them at Wells Fargo. While handling depression as a presenting issue from callers represents the daily bread of any internal or external EAP, EAC is uniquely positioned to fully leverage all of Wells Fargo's resources, staff and energies to address depression in a strategic and comprehensive manner rather than using a one-case-at-a-time approach.

Collaboration between EAC and corporate partners results in products that reflect the language, culture and style of the organization and include strong behavioral health elements. EAC's collaborations with corporate partners and business lines deepen its integration into the company's culture. Initiatives such as leadership training, employee retention, interpersonal communications, work/life balance resiliency development and change management provide other opportunities for EAC and its collaborative partnerships to flourish.

Communications and Support Materials

Wells Fargo is a communication hungry organization. *Teamworks*, Wells Fargo's intranet Website, is a widely used source of information, updates and company resources as are special Team News e-mail updates used to quickly deploy important information on critical issues or topics. Both centralized hard copy publications such as *Connections* and business specific publications are regularly distributed to convey timely information, to recognize outstanding accomplishments and to communicate the company's message and values. EAC has become a frequent contributor in the form of articles, resources and tip sheets for managers and team members in both online and hardcopy publications. EAC often collaborates with benefits and ER partners to draft protocols and procedural materials that involve a behavioral health component. Understanding Wells Fargo culture, language and style is invaluable to EAC in producing materials that are culturally compatible with an organization.

EAC offers a wide array of informational and educational materials on a dedicated Website that is available to Wells Fargo team members, accessible both at work and at home. In addition, the EAC intranet Website hosts "online communities" to foster more connection and support among team members at Wells Fargo. Preceding the first anniversary of the 9/11 tragedy, EAC invited team members to share their thoughts and feelings of remembrance and actively promoted the "EAC Online Community" feature via the Wells Fargo Teamworks intranet site, EAC articles and company-wide e-mail announcements. This on-line event proved especially valuable to team members judging by participation numbers and members posted.

Summary of Services

> If the purpose of the business is not customer focused, the business will eventually atrophy and fail.

> –E. Michael Shay (1993)

Wells Fargo's core business strategy of aligning with its customers provides both the model for EAC and creates receptivity to EAC's integration into the planning and implementation of major corporate initiatives. This is readily apparent even to front line team members who see EAC mentioned throughout the Wells Fargo Team Member Handbook, on its Teamworks intranet site, and in multiple publications. EAC has grown and changed with its company, Wells Fargo. Providing organizationally congruent consultation in a customer-focused way is a large part of why EAC is an invited guest at so many of Wells Fargo's tables. While EAC has gained its knowledge of Wells Fargo by being part of its culture, outside EAP providers can benefit from the lessons EAC has learned about serving its customers.

Standards of Style

> Success to me is having 10 honeydew melons and eating only the top half of each one.

> – Barbra Streisand

While Ms. Streisand enjoys the luxury of picking and choosing the choicest of fruit, EAC's success does not quite afford the entity this luxury when it comes to picking the work done for customers. The integration EAC has achieved within the organization has resulted in its being utilized in more significant ways–less of an appetizer, more of a main course. Bread and butter calls (marital difficulties, difficulty with a co-worker, stress and depression) still represent a significant portion of EAC's utilization. However, all EAC consultants (Immediate Service Consultants and Business Consultants) also handle management consultations, threat assessment and complex consultations that cross their phone lines. Neither type of call, either clinical assessment or management consultation is viewed as the bottom half of the melon. Opportunities for the practice of organizationally congruent consultation are found in all aspects of EAC consultation services.

It is important to be specific about what organizational congruence really means in everyday practice. At EAC it begins with a nuanced understanding of the whole business as well as the individual business lines EAC supports. This involves more than just understanding the business function (although that is important). It is more about understanding the contextual factors that will allow EAC to gain credibility, buy-in and trust from those it serves (Van Den Bergh, 2000). Here are some practical examples of how this group of behavioral health experts has adapted to serve their corporate client:

- *EAC, not EAP.* The 1998 Norwest-Wells Fargo merger forced Wells Fargo's EAS and Norwest's NEAR program to critically examine their services and positions in the organization and to choose a fresh model that would fit in the new Wells Fargo. A pivotal decision to rename the EAP business "Employee Assistance Consulting" reflected both the intention and strategy of the new group to move from a service-provider role to a consultative role and to differentiate itself from traditional EAPs in the process. Like the parent organizations from which they originated, the best practices of NEAR and EAS were culled and incorporated into the redesign. The reverberations of this decision have continued to positively impact EAC's reputation and position within the enterprise.
- *Formal qualifications, informal presentation.* While all EAC consultants are qualified clinicians, staff steers clear of touting their formal credentials. EAC's partners know and trust that EAC consultants are licensed professionals; it is not EAC policy to remind them. Wells Fargo's CEO, Dick Kovacevich, is known to most employees by his first name so EAC follows suit. Consultants leave their titles, and sometimes their clinical egos at the door.
- *Customers not clients.* Wells Fargo is in the business of selling financial products. It is not a community mental health setting. Therefore, EAC conforms to the Wells Fargo company culture by referring to callers as "customers." Conforming to this culture does not prevent EAC consultants from retaining their clinical expertise. "Customers" are treated with clinical respect, adherence to

clinical standards of confidentiality and professionalism while also receiving high touch, high quality customer service.

- *Brand conformity.* A big part of Wells Fargo's success is its brand recognition. The company has put great thought and expense into designing conventions that convey its image in print. EAC understands the power of this brand and leverages it by adhering in all of its written communications to branding conventions and company-adopted style guidelines. This is another way of subtly communicating to the company that EAC supports who they are. EAC uniquely brands its products to ensure a high profile and consistent "look and feel" which is believed to build EAC's reputation and trust. Consistency of communication is key to communicating a strong brand (Cucka, 2003). This is no less true for employee assistance providers than it is for the companies they support.

- *High touch with high tech.* Wells Fargo is a technology-forward company. E-mail, voicemail, teleconferences set up in minutes not hours, pagers, cell phones and PDAs are a part of the company culture and the staples of communication and connection. Clinicians typically value face-to-face contact. At EAC, consultants have learned to use technology to bridge connection rather than viewing it as a hindrance to relationship management and good assessment. Learning which mode of communication each of its key customers prefers, becoming facile with ever changing technologies and working in a virtual environment while still building and maintaining the relationships that sustain EAC's business is key to its success. Wells Fargo's team members conduct much of their business and many of their internal relationships in a virtual environment. Their comfort in virtual media lends itself to effective telephonic consultation by EAC.

- *Talking the talk.* Through established partnerships consultants at EAC are able to learn and use a common language that is reflective of the Wells Fargo business culture. For example, employees at Wells Fargo are "team members," time off is "PTO" (Paid Time Off) and it is not uncommon to hear segments of company initiatives uttered as common phrases: "walking the talk," "run it like you own it" and "doing the right thing for the customer"–these phrases have genuine meaning to EAC's business groups and team member customers and contribute to a shared culture in EAC's communications.

- *It is a business.* In EAC's consultations, written materials and trainings, it is imperative to keep in mind that Wells Fargo's main objective is to run a successful business. Taking team members and managers away from business tasks is sometimes necessary and even valuable but should always be measured against the health of the business and ultimately the organization. Clinicians who persist in viewing the business goals as completely competitive with their consultation objectives miss out on the opportunity to partner with the company that employs them or contracts for their services (Sciegaj et al., 2001). A successful EAP provider understands that individual health and organizational health are not incompatible. Consultants can maintain their personal styles while upholding company identity through a delicate balancing act (Cucka, 2003).
- *Preserving company trust.* EAC consultations are subject to the most stringent confidentiality standards. Unrestricted by the DOT regulations that some EAP colleagues face in other organizations, EAC services are voluntary, with the exception of outreach after robberies and workplace traumas when EAC consultants initiate calls to team members. At the beginning of every call customers are assured of confidentiality and informed of confidentiality limits (concerning safety to self and others and reporting requirements as required by law). Folding together the delicate ingredients of confidentiality into EAC's consultation model requires the subtle finesse of gently educating collaborative partners about EAC's role, professional ethical standards and a promise to the organization. As a non-revenue-generating "business," EAC staff continuously review their business practices to ensure expense control and to fine tune operational efficiencies.

Quality Assurances

EAC holds itself to an exceptional quality standard that mirrors the company's expectations of the service. EAC staff strive to deliver a "surprise and delight" experience in every customer transaction. Wells Fargo is a diversified, fast moving, highly successful financial services company and tasks its employees at every level with high performance demands. EAC is no exception. EAC needs to continually demonstrate value to the enterprise and is subject to evaluation and review each year as well as in an ongoing way.

How EAC Stays at the Table

Even with great food and spectacular service, the best restaurants depend on good word-of-mouth and positive reviews to keep people coming to their tables. Though challenging to quantify and gather, EAC actively solicits feedback on every level of consultation and service it provides. Callers to EAC's toll-free line are offered an opportunity to give feedback immediately after they call via a touch-tone Interactive Voice Response (IVR) survey. Data from these surveys are collected for each consultant for the purpose of performance evaluation and aggregate data is used for group feedback about service standards. IVR data are supplemented by Key Customer Surveys (given to corporate partners and key customers of EAC) and training evaluations to give a fuller sense of customers' experience. These satisfaction data combined with unsolicited positive or negative feedback inform a continual redesign for the purpose of meeting and exceeding customers' expectations. Utilization data of EAC services are also important evidence of EAC's perceived value to the organization. Data are one kind of evidence; testimonial is another. EAC has benefited from enthusiastic support by highly placed organizational champions of its programs and services.

Consultant Support

To ensure that EAC provides callers (whether they require individual assessment and referral or high profile management consultation) with a consistent consultation product, the entity has established an internal collaboration and coaching process for all of EAC consultants. Senior consultants very familiar with the company, its resources and EAC's standards and practices provide immediate 24/7 availability of peer consultation and support to EAC consultants. This function is called "Coach on Call." It is neither a clinical supervision role nor a managerial function. Using Coach on Call allows a place for both new and seasoned consultants to:

- Talk through their thinking on a case
- Brainstorm about possible resources
- Double check protocols, practices and procedures
- Debrief volatile or upsetting cases
- Obtain support around complex or challenging cases

The consultant in a Coach on Call role also serves as a second set of eyes and ears, highly tuned to both clinical and organizational risk. The Coach on Call function encourages and reflects EAC's highly collaborative approach to consultation and desire to provide a standard of service to its customers. Consultants from the beginning of their work at EAC are discouraged from working in silos. Synergistic thinking, tapping into shared expertise and simply feeling supported helps EAC to deliver quality consultation reflecting values of integration and collaboration.

An active learning environment is encouraged in a number of ways beyond the Coach on Call function. Rapidly convened internal case conferences on topics of threat, fitness for duty and other complex cases are frequent. These are supplemented by a regular program of internally offered continuing education opportunities in which consultants are encouraged to take part. This is an extremely efficient way of helping professional staff obtain their needed CEUs for licensure and certification as well as a way of developing a shared understanding of complex or relevant topics.

Staff Recruitment and Training

The selection and fit of new EAC consultants with an established internal culture as well as the culture of the Wells Fargo enterprise is the highest priority in the staff recruitment process. Prerequisites to employment at EAC include prior EAP or management consultation experience, a strong clinical background and credentials, a keen sense of customer service and business savvy, and demonstrated commitment to or experience with cultural diversity. The entire consultant and operations teams participate in the highly structured orientation and training program for new staff.

STRUGGLES

Fame is a fickle food Upon a shifting plate.

–Emily Dickinson

Success comes with a cost. While EAC enjoys the benefits of being an integrated partner within Wells Fargo, managing the utilization that results from this partnership is a constant challenge. Like many EAPs, a typical day at EAC is far from being routine. Calls through EAC's toll-free line bring a bounty of new demands and opportunities to contribute in new ways. Finding ways to say "yes" to the many requests EAC fields while still balancing capacity and volume is the ongoing challenge. The challenge of offering consistent "high touch" customer service is that it becomes the expectation of the organization. What was once viewed as "stellar" is now an expected standard of service. While EAC consultants enjoy the professional challenge that comes with the variety and intensity of the cases EAC handles, there is an ongoing struggle with issues of pace and volume.

The expense of maintaining an internal EAP that is available "anytime, anywhere" means constant attention to managing a limited budget and staff resources while also meeting company demands and demonstrating value across numerous domains (Swihart & Thompson, 2001). EAC continuously evaluates what is core to its business and what is peripheral in deciding what and how much it can offer.

Like many EAPs, utilization data only goes so far in telling the story of the value added to the company. In the end when Wells Fargo does well it reflects well on EAC. When employee retention is strong, job satisfaction is high, work productivity is up, threats are safely managed, critical incidents are ably handled and employees and managers feel that EAC is a tangible expression of PACA, then EAC has done its job (Harris et al., 2002). This success increases demand for EAC's presence at many tables, creating both new opportunities and new challenges (Van Den Bergh, 2000).

EAC must remain ever mindful of the quality contributions of its corporate and line partners. Constant vigilance must be used to respect boundaries around subject expertise and function. For example, Wells Fargo maintains an established Learning and Development function that is staffed by qualified educational professionals. While EAC does conduct numerous trainings, EAC consultants are careful not to delve into content areas that would create the impression of competition with Learning and Development partners.

The shape of the Wells Fargo enterprise is highly responsive to the changing direction of market forces, customer demand and technological advances. This company changes as it needs to, reorganizing businesses to keep them nimble and competitive, integrating newly acquired companies to expand or deepen market share and simply doing what makes good sense. EAC has remained successful by responding rapidly to these organizational changes and structuring the business in a manner that closely matches the larger organization. From rural to urban, across gender, generation, race, ethnicity, business cultures and products, from entry level to senior executive–Wells Fargo embraces its exponential diversity and holds it as a value. So, too, must EAC. Providing services to this exponentially diverse population is at once a professional opportunity, an ongoing challenge, and a recipe for viability.

The pull between providing general EAP services and specialized consultative support inevitably arises in servicing a diverse organization like Wells Fargo, but is germane to both internal and external EAPs of all shapes and sizes. To remain vital and viable, EAPs must balance the generalist versus specialist roles, making sure not to stray too far from the services customers expect while also looking ahead in a proactive manner to anticipate specialized services that may be needed down the road. "Common where possible, customized when necessary" is another common Wells Fargo expression that is embodied everyday at EAC. Strategy cannot be kept in a straightjacket; creativity is the key to keeping it alive and functional (Shays, 2003). Moreover, strategy and creativity are worthless unless well executed. Above all, EAC places a high premium on meticulous delivery of its services.

CONCLUSION

Wells Fargo Employee Assistance Consulting offers a compelling example of the shift from traditional EAP services to more nuanced, organizationally congruent, and consultative approaches to supporting individual effectiveness and both organizational health and wellness. Colleagues in both internal and external programs can take advantage of EAC's experiences to build strong and effective partnerships with the organizations they serve. Helping customers to be successful, understanding their environments and unique pressures and offering new ways to assist and support their management and line employees is EAC's definition of stellar customer service. Aligning with the cultures of the companies they service can help many EAPs move from being a clinical side dish to a nourishing consultative main course offered and appreciated at not only company picnics and employee cafeterias, but in the executive dining room.

REFERENCES

Block, M. (2000). *Flawless Consulting: A Guide to Getting Your Expertise Used. Second Edition*. Jossey-Bass/Pfeiffer, San Francisco, CA.

Chima, F.O. (2001). Employee Assistance and Human Resource Collaboration for Improving Employment and Disabilities Status. *Employee Assistance Quarterly*, 17(3), 79-94.

Cucka, M. (1993). To Brand the Consultancy or to Brand Its Consultants. *Consulting to Management*, 14(2), 23-25.

Harris, S.M., Adams, M., and Hill, L. (2002). Beyond Customer Satisfaction: A Randomized EAP Outcome Study. *Employee Assistance Quarterly*, 17(4), 53-61.

Levy Merrick, E., Horgan, C.M., and Garnick, D.W. (2003). The EAP/Behavioral Health Carve-Out Connection. *Employee Assistance Quarterly*, 18(3), 1-13.

Sciegaj, M., Garnick, D.W., and Horgan, C.M. (2001). Employee Assistance Programs Among Fortune 500 Firms. *Employee Assistance Quarterly*, 16(3), 25-35.

Shays, E.M. (1993). Helping Clients to Control Their Future. *Consulting to Management*, 14(2), 48-54

Van Den Bergh, N. (2000). Where Have We Been? . . . Where Are We Going?: Employee Assistance Practice in the 21st Century. *Employee Assistance Quarterly*, 16(1/2), 1-13.

Wall Street Journal (1998). Norwest, Wells Fargo Agree to Form Banking Giant in $31.4 Billion Pact. *Wall Street Journal*, 6/9/98.

Chapter 13

Ernst & Young's Assist:
How Internal and External Service
Integration Created a 'Single Source Solution'

Sandra Turner
Michael Weiner
Kate Keegan

SUMMARY. EAP and work-life services have distinct, rich histories of developing and delivering workplace-based programs for employees

Author note: Writing this article brought forth memories of Rosemarie Meschi, who worked tirelessly on issues and policies relating directly to the advancement of women and minorities. In her 22 years with the firm, she had a strong impact on Ernst & Young's culture, laying the foundation for the firm's current goal to be the employer of choice among professional services firms.

[Haworth co-indexing entry note]: "Ernst & Young's Assist: How Internal and External Service Integration Created a 'Single Source Solution.'" Turner, Sandra, Michael Weiner, and Kate Keegan. Co-published simultaneously in *Journal of Workplace Behavioral Health* (The Haworth Press, Inc.) Vol. 20, No. 3/4, 2005, pp. 243-262; and: *The Integration of Employee Assistance, Work/Life, and Wellness Services* (ed: Mark Attridge, Patricia A. Herlihy, and R. Paul Maiden) The Haworth Press, Inc., 2005, pp. 243-262. Single or multiple copies of this article are available for a fee from The Haworth Document Delivery Service [1-800-HAWORTH, 9:00 a.m. - 5:00 p.m. (EST). E-mail address: docdelivery@haworthpress.com].

Available online at http://www.haworthpress.com/web/JWBH
© 2005 by The Haworth Press, Inc. All rights reserved.
doi:10.1300/J490v20n03_03

and their dependents. They have different professional staff, technologies, scope of service, operations and methods of program evaluation. However, they reach out to the same clients (organization, individuals and families) with problem-solving skills and solutions, resulting in a positive impact on workplace productivity, recruitment and retention. These two services have the potential for great compatibility and synergy, if directed by a host employer to pursue common goals in an integrated fashion. There are various ways for an employer to provide integrated EAP and work-life resource and referral services for its employees. This case study argues for contracting with two specialized vendors, EAP and work-life, and shows how the employer collaborates with them to create a multi-faceted program that has a single point of access and seamless, integrated service. This article provides the rationale for such a model of integration, a graphic depiction of this model, and an analysis of the successes and challenges of the close working relationship required by this model. Speculation about the how the model will adopt future innovations is suggested as well. *[Article copies available for a fee from The Haworth Document Delivery Service: 1-800-HAWORTH. E-mail address: <docdelivery@haworthpress.com> Website: <http://www.HaworthPress. com> © 2005 by The Haworth Press, Inc. All rights reserved.]*

KEYWORDS. EAP, work-life, integration, technology transfer, quality of work life, work and family, organizational change, teamwork

INTRODUCTION

This article is written jointly by Ernst & Young's EY/Assist program, with vendors Managed Health Network (MHN) and LifeCare. Ernst & Young contracted with MHN and LifeCare in 1999 to provide EY/Assist services to partners, staff and family members. This article describes the genesis of that integrated program model. It offers the strengths, limitations, and compromises required by such a model over time. This portrayal of EY/Assist allows other employers to consider this model for their workplaces, and to enhance the implementation and maintenance of such a service. This article is both a theoretical and practical analysis of this program.

BACKGROUND

Ernst & Young is a global leader in professional services with 100,000 people in 140 countries around the globe. Within the United States, the firm has approximately 23,000 partners and staff in 95 locations. These individuals have a multitude of skills required to provide clients with solutions based on financial, transactional, and risk-management knowledge in Ernst & Young's core services of audit, tax, and transaction advisory services. The firm is organized as a partnership, with partners constituting about ten percent of the total headcount.

Ernst & Young's ability to improve the businesses of clients rests upon the integrity, quality, and professionalism of its people. Their teamwork, continuous learning, skills, and customer focus are paramount to the success of the firm. At Ernst & Young, people are the reason for the firm's leadership in the profession. Clients contract for these professionals' time. Their intellectual capital and passion for the work distinguish Ernst & Young from other public accounting firms. By providing work life/assistance services to all its people, the firm intends to contribute to the success of people's careers, and the profitability of the firm.

The recent scrutiny of U.S. corporations for ethics violations, and the ensuing governmental regulation of accounting firm practices and standards have stimulated changes in the cultural context of this workplace. There is stress and work-life imbalance as the firm adjusts to the new business environment. The consequences of these external pressures have been acknowledged, and are being addressed directly through the firm's goals related to people, quality and growth or 'balanced scorecard' priorities. 'People First' is the firm's commitment to collaborate with its employees to create great careers, foster an inclusive, innovative and flexible work environment, offer intellectual stimulation from co-workers, provide competitive rewards and compensation, and work with great clients.

RATIONALE

According to Keith Hammonds of We, Incorporated in *Fast Company*, "Organizations are not just places where people have jobs. Rather, they are our neighborhoods, our communities, our world. They are where we join with other people to make a difference for others and ourselves. If we think of them only as the places where we have jobs, we not only lose the opportunity for meaning, but we endanger the planet."

History of EAP and Work-Life Services at Ernst & Young

The firm has had an internal/external employee assistance program since 1975 at both predecessors (Ernst & Whinney and Arthur Young), and an external work-life resource and referral service at the merged Ernst & Young since 1994. Prior to all three implementations, there was a workplace condition that augured for an organizational intervention, and internal champion who successfully made the business case that recruitment, retention, enhanced productivity and brand loyalty would be enhanced by that service addition. In the case of EAP at each predecessor firm, alcoholism was the stimulus; the work-life resource and referral service in the combined firm was prompted by the objective of retaining women in the workplace. Thereafter, these programs were sustained by virtue of their high quality and professionalism, confidentiality, and the satisfaction of clients and referents in all job classifications at the firm. Immediate access to expert clinicians or work-life specialists suited the high standards of customer service demanded by the firm for its business clients and for its people.

These EAP and work-life services were managed in different departments within Human Resources, now called Americas People Team (APT) at the firm. EAP was managed by a Certified Employee Assistance Professional (CEAP) in National Benefits. Privacy and confidentiality were strongly associated with EAP because it dealt with private health information. Work-life was part of a gender diversity initiative to recruit and retain women at the firm. The work-life services focused on home responsibilities, which were more often the domain of women than men at that time. That gender strategy and initiatives program was also in Human Resources (APT). Stigma was the reason for the separation between the programs. The model is diagrammed in Figure 1.

Impetus for Integration

As each program grew in recognition, stature and utilization at the firm, operational redundancies and conflict between the two programs became more evident: competition between the program managers, duplicate internal program promotion, advocacy, and evaluation; growing confusion among partners and staff about when to use which program;

FIGURE 1. Distinct EAP and Work-Life Resource and Referral Programs at the Firm

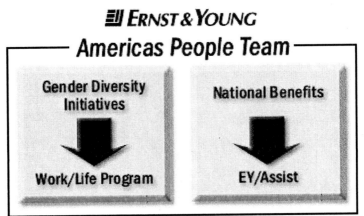

lack of coordination of vision and goals with the firm's mission; failure to coordinate the assets of the two vendors. While these deficits were acknowledged by the managers of both programs, the differing missions of the programs stated above was the stronger cultural force for maintaining the status quo.

That inertia changed with new leadership in Human Resources. The newly appointed Vice Chairman for Human Resources asked the obvious question in 1998. "Why do we have two services with separate access telephone numbers that focus on resolving personal matters? How do people know where to call for help?" That question became the impetus for integration. As well, the coming expiration of the work-life contract with the current vendor provided impetus to act quickly. Finally, the anticipated combining of Ernst & Young with another professional services firm motivated the managers of these two programs to develop a prototype for joining together work-life with EAP services that could be expanded to the combined firm. Culturally, the firm strove to improve the work experience of its employees. Therefore, this search for a better model was in keeping with that cultural value.

So an internal team comprised of National Benefits, EAP, work-life, and actuarial services met to challenge the status quo, and quickly found that it could not justify its continuance. In addition to the reasons for integrating stated above, the stigma associated with chemical dependency and mental health issues had lessened because of efforts in the broader public community to address that stigma. Treatment was readily available and utilized, so there were examples of successful outcomes that gave the general public more hope and greater empathy for these behavioral health conditions. This awareness led to greater tolerance for addressing these matters through the workplace.

Reaching Consensus on a New Program Model, Design, and Organizational Position

Early, guarded discussions gave way to enthusiastic debate and brainstorming about the opportunity to create a better way to serve Ernst & Young people. Interviews with leading edge family friendly employers produced a wealth of information and ideas. The internal team was then able to formulate the right questions. What were the needs of our people given their demographics? What were the current models and future trends in service delivery in the marketplace? What internal support was necessary for success? Who would be the internal champion(s)? How would success be determined? The group emerged from these discussions with a new program design and model of service delivery.

The first decision made was that one internal director should manage both programs. This would be a mental health professional knowledgeable about both EAP and work-life programming. Perhaps the cost savings from eliminating redundant internal program(s) administration could result in additional services for our people. Another decision was that providing these services would continue to require contracting with vendors. Internal staffing was not realistic to serve 23,000 people in 95 locations. Vendors had national staff and affiliates already in place. The internal group easily agreed that the 'best in class' services would be secured for Ernst & Young people. There was an expectation that more than one vendor would likely be needed to provide 'best in class' EAP and work-life resource and referral services.

Contracting with more than one vendor did not pose a problem. The firm contracts with many vendors who collaborate on special projects and service delivery mechanisms. As a professional services firm itself, Ernst & Young provides expert tax and advisory business services by contract to its clients. It believes in getting expert consultation for its people. Vendor management is also a strength of the firm. National Benefits is responsible for contracting with various vendors for medical and dental, life insurance, 401K and retirement benefits, and a host of other benefits.

The EAP was already part of National Benefits, and the Director of Benefits was a champion of the program. A Director of Women's Initiatives had been recently hired at the firm. That department focused on strategy, policy, and organizational development. The delivery of work-life resource and referral services did not fit within its mission. Therefore, National Benefits was the preferred site for the new integrated program. The new model is shown in Figure 2.

Ernst & Young is bounded by the dark color. The dotted line between National Benefits and EY/Assist reflects the confidentiality of the program within National Benefits. Further, there is confidentiality of personal health information between the internal EY/Assist and the outside vendors.

The services included in EAP and in work-life would be determined by the responses of the selected vendor(s). Collaboration between the vendors accounts for the permeable boundary between the EAP and work-life vendors.

The organizational position of an integrated program should be determined by the program's champion(s) within an organization. Optional departments housing these services may be benefits, medical, human resources, organizational effectiveness, diversity, safety, operational management, etc. Each employer or union is unique in its organi-

FIGURE 2. Integrated EAP and Work-Life Resource and Referral Services: EY/Assist

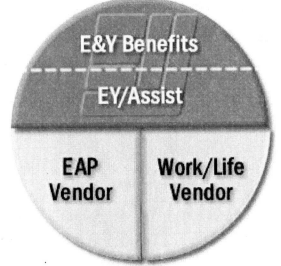

zational structure and culture, and have different champions for the program.

Table 1 shows the personal services that the internal team decided on including in the new integrated program.

This list was created from answers to the questions posed by the internal team as discussed above when it was crafting the new design of the integrated program. All of the desired services were simply listed together. Internally, there was no longer an EAP realm and a work-life realm with distinct services. These were all just personal services to enhance career and personal life. Externally, however, the marketplace was still divided into EAP and work-life realms.

Vendor Identification and Selection

A Request for Information (RFI) was developed and distributed to vendors with the greatest likelihood of matching the firm's national distribution of office locations. This list was culled from Monica Oss's *Open Minds'* compilation of national EAP providers–1998. All existing national work-life service providers received the RFI as well. In that document, respondents were invited to partner with other vendors in completing their proposal to the firm. Proposals needed to address all

TABLE 1. Personal Services Selected for Inclusion in EY/Assist

Addiction disorders	Adoption	Career assessment and planning
Child care	Parenting	Education selection and financial management
Elder care	Consumer affairs	Emotional/mental health
Critical incident stress debriefing	Fitness-for-duty evaluations	Marriage/family relationship consultation
Stress management	Financial matters such as budgeting and financial planning	Federal tax controversy assistance
Domestic violence	Health and wellness	Pre-retirement lifestyle planning
Legal issues	Personal adjustment	Convenience services such as pet care, home repair, chore services, and event planning
Job performance referrals	Management consultation	

aspects of the integrated service model. The internal selection team wanted the respondents to select a partner with whom they could collaborate to deliver this integrated product. Most responses posed a partnership between an EAP vendor and a work-life vendor. One vendor proposed that both services were integrated within its organization. From among the respondents to the RFI, four were selected to receive a Request for Proposal (RFP). They represented seven vendors: three partnered teams, and one with integrated service delivery.

Decision Guide and Contracting

The selection of vendors was reached by consensus of the internal team. Eligibility and selection criteria were established with a numeric scoring guide. The ideal vendor(s) would serve four primary groups: partners and staff and their families, the firm's internal integrated EAP and work-life resource and referral program, Human Resources (APT), and the firm itself (the partnership). The respondents were rated in their perceived ability to deliver to these internal audiences.

Each respondent was evaluated on the following service elements: call triage and transfer, EAP services, work-life resource and referral services, additional services, electronic delivery of services, account management/senior management, interface with the firm's internal program, customization, outcomes research, reporting, and program promotion.

This grid portrays the internal teams: expectations of service from the vendors, perception of the vendors' ability to provide that service, and perception of the value they could provide to the firm (Table 2).

The written responses to the RFP, oral presentations by each vendor, references, and site visits to each vendor by the internal team comprised the selection process. The Decision Guide captured the outcome of the

TABLE 2. Decision Guide

Service Above	Elements	Listed	Vendor A	Vendor B	Vendor C	Vendor D
Internal value	team's	perceived				
Cost of program						
Return on Investment (ROI)			%	%	%	%

search in an executive summary that represented the consensus of the internal selection team.

Since Ernst & Young is a professional services firm, an actuary was key to the internal group. He assisted with quantifying the experience of reviewing the competing vendors. His Decision Guide and one-page Executive Summary posed the findings of the internal group in a business format with language that was familiar and acceptable to the firm. Other employers might want to weight their selection team and process with representatives from their business, e.g., a designer from a graphics firm, an engineer from a manufacturing company, or a chemist from a pharmaceutical company.

The result of the search process was the selection of EAP provider Managed Health Network (MHN), and work-life service provider LifeCare. The contract for services with each vendor established performance guarantees for access, case disposition, response time, staff/affiliate retention, user satisfaction, appeals, utilization, reports, security/confidentiality, and program promotion. This explained to the selected vendors what was valued by the firm. More importantly, however, was the establishment of expectations that the success of this integration experiment was the joint responsibility of all parties: Ernst & Young, MHN, and LifeCare.

While each of these vendors offers a host of services, not all of them were requested by Ernst & Young. The list in Table 3 represents the vendors' noted areas of expertise for the array of services requested by the firm.

The work-life vendor LifeCare was selected to deliver a customized Website for Ernst & Young of work-life and EAP-related content. Articles, links to other Websites, access to specialists, an 'Ask the Expert' section, and live, online seminars were features considered desirable by the firm's people. MHN would contribute to the development of the EAP-related content of that work-life Website. This is an example of leveraging the best capabilities of vendors and charging them to innovate together.

Vendor Perspectives on the Selection Process

MHN and LifeCare strive for close relationships with all of their vendor partners for the good of the client customer. Based on prior experiences servicing accounts together, and current discussions about LifeCare managing a Website for MHN, these two vendors determined that their combined strengths would most effectively meet the needs of the

TABLE 3. Vendor Designated Areas of Expertise

MHN	LifeCare
Addiction Disorders	Adoption
Emotional/Mental Health	Career Assessment and Planning
Critical Incident Stress Debriefing	Child Care
Fitness-for-Duty Evaluations	Education Selection and Financial Management
Marriage/Family/Relationship Consultation	Elder Care
Stress Management	Consumer Affairs
Financial Matters Such as Budgeting and Financial Planning	Health and Wellness
Federal Tax Controversy Assistance	Convenience Services, Such as Pet Care, Home Repair, Chore Services, and Event Planning
Pre-Retirement Lifestyle Planning	Parenting Education
Legal Issues	Management Consultation
Personal Adjustment	
Domestic Violence	
Management Consultation	
Job Performance Referrals	

Ernst & Young proposal. LifeCare also partnered with another EAP vendor in response to Ernst & Young's RFP. There were more EAP than work-life firms at the time. It was expected that a work-life vendor would partner with more than one EAP in response to this RFP.

MHN and LifeCare continuously evaluate each client organization's goals and objectives to determine whether an integrated partnership model would be most beneficial and effective. Both MHN and LifeCare are always encouraged by proposals requiring partnering between an EAP and work-life vendor. This demonstrates an understanding of the value that can be achieved by combining the expertise of leading vendors. Typically these services reside in different internal departments at companies, or when they are managed within the same internal department, there may be a lack of integration for a variety of reasons. Both MHN and LifeCare believe that there is more value for the "benefit dollar" when there is a high degree of partnership between EAP and work-life vendors.

With an understanding of Ernst & Young's unique needs, MHN and LifeCare proposed a customized model that would leverage the strengths of each vendor organization. This model requires continuous open communication between the vendors. As a result, the vendors have a deeper understanding of one another's respective services and processes for serving clients. While some vendors offer an "integrated model," there are few situations where a client organization would have the benefit of two account managers sharing their vendors' strengths to result in a powerful alignment of EAP and work-life services.

Program Implementation–Setting the Basis for Collaboration

Providing an orientation to the firm for MHN and LifeCare was important to establish their familiarity with the firm's culture and expectations for service delivery to partners and staff. Vendor account management staff participated in a two-day orientation alongside new hires to the firm at its U.S. headquarters location. These vendor account management staff learned about the history, operations, business strategy, benefits, and human resources policies of the firm, met key leaders, and came to know a little about the profile of a newly hired person at the firm.

Operations staff at each vendor location was oriented to the nuances of the firm via videotapes and oral presentations by the internal Ernst & Young selection team. Written information about benefits and contact persons at Ernst & Young were updated periodically to enable vendor intake staff to respond to questions from callers about Ernst & Young benefits. Gifts with Ernst & Young logos were presented to each staff member on the vendor's Ernst & Young service team to engage them and establish brand loyalty. Future phone contacts between the EY/Assist director and vendor staff would be easier, because of establishing a level of personal familiarity.

There was a reciprocal orientation to MHN and LifeCare conducted for the internal Ernst & Young selection team at each of these vendors' key locations. Discussions about program philosophy, structure, operations, quality initiatives, staffing criteria, and future goals were more in-depth than the cursory view provided during the selection process. Alignment with firm values and human resources practices was highlighted, when appropriate, in order to reinforce the basis of collaboration, which is a common vision and shared set of values.

This relationship among the parties has evolved over the years. There was less account management integration at the beginning. Over time, the roles, tasks, and responsibilities of participants evolved among Ernst & Young, MHN, and LifeCare. For others adopting this model, it would be valuable for vendors to have a clear understanding of the company's vision of integration, and define the roles of each participant. This is necessary in order to make it easier for the client company to ensure that its expectations will be met, and to hold the vendor(s) accountable. This role delineation can be imposed by the client company or strategized between the vendors.

The type of orientation provided by Ernst & Young for LifeCare and MHN staff is considered a "best practice." The extensive original orientation, as well as the ongoing updates is not necessarily industry standard procedures, but they contributed to the success of the integrated model. This approach allows the LifeCare and MHN staff to feel more knowledgeable and invested in the outcome of cases. The encouragement of a "partner" approach vs. a "vendor/client" approach yields more collaboration and innovation, ultimately resulting in more successful service to the firm.

Vendor Observations About the Strengths and Liabilities of This Integration Model

The LifeCare and MHN account mangers refer to themselves as Co-Account Managers. They strengthen each other's knowledge of the other's services. There is competition and challenge from each to the other to satisfy Ernst & Young. The problem-solving results for Ernst & Young and its people are enriched by the different perspectives and resources of two vendors. This model leverages the best practices in both areas.

For the firm's people, access is easier, stigma is reduced for those seeking help with mental health and chemical dependency issues, and utilization increases due to the ease of accessing the service for a wide range of issues and concerns. Clear communications direct people to a single source for assistance with any personal matter. More job performance referrals result because referents no longer stigmatize a troubled employee by a referral to EAP. Rather, they are referring to EY/Assist. The impact on the firm's utilization of the program resulting from this integrated program is significant. The EAP had a utilization of 8%. The work-life service had a utilization of 12%. Together, they have achieved an annual utilization of 25%.

A significant advantage of this model involves program promotion. Ernst & Young dedicated considerable time to developing the unified brand for the program, EY/Assist, as well as positioning and packaging the program. In addition, imagery, typeface, and messaging were carefully considered in a very collaborative way among Ernst & Young, LifeCare, and MHN. LifeCare's creative team was engaged to offer illustration designs and editorial expertise. Through the involvement of all parties, Ernst & Young was able to produce marketing collateral for the program that was balanced, stigma-free and that resonated with all partners and staff. Careful thought was put into the description of services to be sure that, for example, work-life concerns were not tacked on as a single bullet at the end of a list of emotional health and substance abuse services, or vice versa. The end result was a truly integrated service listing without demarcations between work-life and EAP, under a company brand that is well recognized as a positive support tool within the firm.

Another strength of the integration of vendors was that certain individual cases were successfully managed and resolved by discussing them in a collaborative format. Outcomes have sometimes been favorably altered. In short, partnering with another vendor enables additional perspectives that open up more opportunities for successful case resolution.

One disadvantage of this model is that more people and time are required to build consensus on issues among Ernst & Young, LifeCare, and MHN than would be required if one vendor provided both services. The involvement among Ernst & Young, LifeCare and MHN is substantial. This model requires an internal manager at the employer who has technical expertise and experience in EAP and work-life programs, who stays apprised of current professional trends, and who can interact with the vendors on a weekly if not daily basis to collaborate on matters related to service delivery. A quarterly review of program operations by an internal manager and the vendors would never be sufficient in this model. A significant allocation of resources by the employer through an internal work-life and EAP experienced professional is required in this model.

As vendor systems and products change, a disadvantage of the integrated model is the need for the account managers to update and apprise each other of program modifications or enhancements. Additional time is needed to analyze combined data and prepare common reports. However, the data is more meaningful when capturing and combining information from both programs.

Program Growth and Enhancement Through 'Partnership'

The recent hurricanes in Florida wreaked havoc on Ernst & Young's people and offices. At the direction of the firm, LifeCare and MHN developed materials for the people in Ernst & Young's Florida offices. These informational flyers were distributed electronically to all employees in the area. A teleconference call was scheduled for people in the area to gain support and practical assistance. Then a counselor came onsite the first day that people returned to work to provide information about EAP and work-life program services. EY/Assist, including LifeCare and MHN, participated with area operations people on the crisis leadership conference calls that were held daily during the hurricanes.

Recently Ernst & Young, LifeCare and MHN have developed a quality assurance survey questionnaire for all EY/Assist intakes. With clients' permission, a survey is e-mailed to them at two months after intake. The clients provide the e-mail addresses to which the surveys are sent. MHN poses this request during intake and collects the e-mail addresses. The LifeCare and MHN account mangers analyze the data and submit an integrated report to Ernst & Young.

Ernst & Young identified a need to assess EY/Assist's ability to positively impact stress-related issues at the firm. While MHN and LifeCare reported this information previously, Ernst and Young challenged the two vendors to develop a unified survey geared to Ernst & Young's specific needs. Research and survey experts from both vendors collaborated to develop the survey.

Program Maintenance

Quarterly meetings are held in person at alternating locations at Ernst & Young and the vendors. Newly hired vendor staffs are given an orientation to Ernst & Young as they are assigned to this account. Vendor staffs share their observations about Ernst & Young callers and recommend program adjustments to better assist Ernst & Young people. Weekly conference calls are held between Ernst & Young and the vendors to discuss a variety of operational matters.

Integration, but Not Assimilation

The close working relationship required by this model should not diminish the fact that services are being provided to the client organization via contract with the vendors. The vendors are to be held accountable by the client for meeting performance standards. On the part of the vendors, they must allocate their time among all of their various clients, not just one client with whom they work in especially close collaboration. Confronting service failures may result in a fix by only one of the parties, which failed to perform to expectations. Finally, upon renewal of the existing contract(s), the contracting employer should defer to its purchasing agent for assistance in defining the RFP, re-assessing the marketplace, establishing selection criteria, and recommending the successful vendor(s). The close working relationship depicted by EY/Assist can result in great camaraderie among the parties that should not influence business decisions regarding renewal.

Future Expansion of the Model

There will be opportunities to expand the scope of EY/Assist services. Depending upon the nature of that service, a decision will be made whether to add that vendor to the 'partnership' or include the new service under the existing EAP or work-life service cluster. For example, a lactation program at each Ernst & Young location would be included in the array of work-life services. The launch of a wellness program, however, would likely require an expansion of the existing 'partnership' among the firm, LifeCare and MHN. That wellness vendor represents a category of distinct, specialized services that should be incorporated into the primary team of Ernst & Young, MHN, and LifeCare. Accordingly, the integration model can adapt to handle such an addition of services.

The above commentary is from the internal EY/Assist Director. The vendors MHN and LifeCare have a different perspective. Adding another 'partner' to the model contributes expertise and creativity; however, it expands the time and communication required to make the integration succeed.

Therefore, a dialogue among the EY/Assist collaborators needs to occur to reach consensus and synergy. Imposing a firm decision on vendors does not inspire commitment. Even when the client is paying, enthusiasm for the model is necessary from all parties. The dialogue that will occur may explore alternatives, one of which may be better suited to this circumstance.

CONCLUSIONS

Using two separate vendors to create an integrated EAP and work-life offering can result in a powerful, world-class program–as it has at Ernst & Young. Indeed, the experience of many organizations has shown that constructing a true best-in-class program actually requires the integration of two distinct vendors, i.e., no single vendor provides EAP and work-life services of truly superior standards. However, creating such a program requires a significant investment of resources and the sustained personal commitment of key individuals at every level of the participating organizations. Clearly, this is not feasible or even desirable for some employers.

For those who wish to build a high quality, integrated program, the ultimate goal is always the same: a single point of access for users, the seamless delivery of services, and service offerings that genuinely address the needs of employees and their dependents. Therefore, the planning phase is crucial. This experience has shown that it is best to begin with several key questions in mind:

- What are the specific needs of the individuals the program will serve, given their demographics, corporate culture, past requests to Human Resources or senior management, etc.?
- What are the current models and future trends in service delivery in the marketplace?
- What internal support will be necessary for the program's success?
- Who will champion the program?
- Who will champion the program at a senior level?
- How will success be measured and determined?

Vendor identification and selection are the next critical items. Vendors should be evaluated on any/all of the following service elements: call triage and transfer, EAP services, work-life resource and referral services, additional services, electronic delivery of services, account management, senior management, interface with the company's integrated program design, ability to customize, outcomes research, reporting, program promotion, anticipated ROI, and cost.

Once vendors have been chosen, it must be clearly established that the success of the integrated program will be the joint responsibility of all three entities. This 'partner' approach yields more collaboration and innovation while the program is being built and implemented.

As previously noted in this article, one disadvantage of a multiple-vendor model is that more people and resources are required to build, manage, and monitor it. The commitment from all three 'partners' is substantial. Communication–among the 'partners' and to the users of the service–also requires greater effort and demands consistency of message at all times. There are, frankly, plenty of opportunities for communication and promotional efforts to go awry. By establishing and adhering to specific rules of collaboration, all three parties can work together quite effectively. In fact, the quality and creativity of the communications can be enhanced through these joint efforts.

While a multiple-vendor integrated program may be beyond the reach of some organizations, it is Ernst & Young's conclusion that such a program is well worth the effort, so long as this effort is sustained. In terms of quality and employee satisfaction, Ernst & Young's integrated program has lived up to or exceeded expectations. This is the unmistakable result of the ongoing dedication of all three 'partners.'

The Director of EY/Assist, and the staff of MHN and LifeCare who are dedicated to this account want to be successful together on behalf of Ernst & Young people. Each keeps the others motivated and directed toward that goal in order to help Ernst & Young people reach their potential in this world.

REFERENCES

Burud, S., & Tumolo, M. (2004). *Leveraging the New Human Capital: Adaptive Strategies, Results Achieved and Stories of Transformation* (First ed.). Palo Alto: Davies Black Publishing.

Cappelli, P. (1999). *The New Deal at Work: Managing the Market-Driven Workforce.* Boston: Harvard Business School Press.

Chambers, E. G., Foulon, M., Handfield-Jones, H., Hankin, S. M., & Michaels, E. G. I. (1998). The War for Talent. *McKinsey Quarterly*, 3, 44-57.

Davenport, D. O. (1999*). Human Capital: What It Is and Why People Invest It.* San Francisco: Jossey-Bass.

Herlihy, P. (2000). EAPs and Work/Family Programs: Different Paths, Same Purposes. *EAPA Exchange*, 30(5), 24-26.

Kaplan, R. S., & Norton, D. P. (1996). *The Balanced Scorecard: Translating Strategy Into Action*. Boston: Harvard Business School Press.

Oss, M. E., & Clary, J. (1998). Industry Analysis: EAPs Are Evolving to Meet Changing Employer Needs. *Open Minds*, January.

The Independent. (1998). Get the Biggest Perk of All: A Life. Vol. July 9, Features, p. 16. Newspaper Publishing PLC.

Tulgan, B. (2000). *Managing Generation X: How to Bring Out the Best in Young Talent*. New York: Norton.

Turner, S., & Davis S. (2000). EAPs and Work-life Programs: Solutions to the Whole Puzzle. *EAPA Exchange*, 30(5), 21-23.

Work and Family Connection. (2000). Evaluation of Work-Life Efforts. www.workfamily.com.

APPENDIX

EY/Assist
1-800-333-4119

ERNST & YOUNG
Quality In Everything We Do

EY/Assist   Can   Help   You   Cope   With   Hurricanes
and Prepare for Emergency Situations!

We understand that many Ernst and Young personnel and their family members have been affected by the recent hurricanes and tropical storms in Florida and other parts of the country. We'd like to take this opportunity to remind you about EY/Assist -- an Ernst and Young-paid benefit that offers education and referrals to help you and your family prepare for and cope with hurricanes and other emergencies. Contact EY/Assist for assistance with the following issues:

- Local Emergency Contacts (United Way; Red Cross; FEMA; Emergency Resource Centers, etc.)

- Emergency Shelters and Hospitals

- Food and Clothing Assistance

- Public Insurance Adjuster Associations

- Alternate Housing

- Child Safety

- Adult Safety

- Temporary Care for Children

- Caring for Pets During a Disaster

- Outreach Programs

- Post Traumatic Stress Disorder

- And More!

You can also log on to www.eyassist.com to:

- Read helpful articles on coping with hurricanes, keeping food safe during an emergency, preparing for disasters, caring for pets during a disaster, preparing for emergencies, and other topical safety issues.

- Download helpful guides on coping with hurricanes, emergency preparedness, helping children cope with a disaster, and other emergency resources.

- Download a wallet-sized *Emergency Family Plan Card* so your entire family knows what to do in an emergency.

- Access resources that can help you clean up and get your life back to normal -- including cleaning services, home repair contractors, relocation services and more.

To access this valuable benefit, simply log on to www.eyassist.com. New users will need to register for the site by clicking the "New User? Click here to Register" link and entering company code: eyassist. For assistance logging on to the web site, contact the Help Desk at 888-604-9565.

And don't forget, if you need information or referrals for local emergency resources, or if you are seeking assistance with health and wellness, child care, adult care, pet care, or schools, you can call a LifeCare specialist at 800-333-4119 — 24 hours a day (or 800-873-1322 if you are deaf or hard of hearing).

© 2004 LifeCare®, Inc., P.O. Box 2783, Westport, CT 06880

Chapter 14

Fairview Alive–An Integrated Strategy for Enhancing the Health and Well-Being of Employees

Barbara D. Eischen
Jessica Grossmeier
Daniel B. Gold

SUMMARY. This article describes the successful integration between EAP and wellness programs at Fairview Health Services–a program called *Fairview Alive*. A brief history of integration between EAP and wellness at Fairview is provided including the shared mission these two programs serve at Fairview. Next, this article outlines the Population Health Model on which *Fairview Alive* was built, and the specific programs and services provided under each segment of this model. This article then focuses on how Fairview addresses depression–one of their

---

The authors would like to acknowledge their colleagues for their contributions to much of the work reported here: Kate Roth, Manager, EAP; Linda Brink and Lisa Lair, Co-Managers, Fairview Alive; Ellen Eichten, Director, Employee Occupational Health; Chuck Felion, Benefits Manager; Cindy Fruitrail and Natalie Nowytski, Corporate Communications; Margaret Knutson, Data Analyst, Fairview Alive; and the rest of the devoted staff of Fairview Alive; Lesley Lesch and Brandy Reinke of StayWell Health Management; and Bruce Kelley and Ron Bonnell of Watson Wyatt Worldwide. The authors also gratefully acknowledge the executive leadership at Fairview Health Services for their ongoing support and guidance.

[Haworth co-indexing entry note]: "Fairview Alive–An Integrated Strategy for Enhancing the Health and Well-Being of Employees." Eischen, Barbara D., Jessica Grossmeier, and Daniel B. Gold. Co-published simultaneously in *Journal of Workplace Behavioral Health* (The Haworth Press, Inc.) Vol. 20, No. 3/4, 2005, pp. 263-279; and: *The Integration of Employee Assistance, Work/Life, and Wellness Services* (ed: Mark Attridge, Patricia A. Herlihy, and R. Paul Maiden) The Haworth Press, Inc., 2005, pp. 263-279. Single or multiple copies of this article are available for a fee from The Haworth Document Delivery Service [1-800-HAWORTH, 9:00 a.m. - 5:00 p.m. (EST). E-mail address: docdelivery@haworthpress.com].

Available online at http://www.haworthpress.com/web/JWBH
© 2005 by The Haworth Press, Inc. All rights reserved.
doi:10.1300/J490v20n03_04

largest cost drivers–in a coordinated effort. Finally, preliminary outcomes from a comprehensive program evaluation, including the impact on medical costs, workers compensation costs and absenteeism costs, are discussed. *[Article copies available for a fee from The Haworth Document Delivery Service: 1-800-HAWORTH. E-mail address: <docdelivery@haworthpress. com> Website: <http://www.HaworthPress.com> © 2005 by The Haworth Press, Inc. All rights reserved.]*

KEYWORDS. Integration, population health management, health promotion, wellness, EAP

INTRODUCTION

In the summer of 1992, Erfurt, Foote and Heirich published a prophetic discussion on the benefits of integrating employee assistance and wellness programs in a model they coined "mega brush." Erfurt and colleagues predicted four important gains would result from these two programs working closely together in a coordinated effort. First, due to the popularity and broader population reach of wellness programs, wellness programs would enhance early detection/prevention of substance abuse and mental health problems. Second, the coordination of wellness and employee assistance programs would encourage cross referrals of employees with specific health or behavioral problems. Third, because employees are more easily engaged in wellness than employee assistance due to the lack of stigma associated with their programs, employees who are initially engaged by the wellness programs would be more easily transferred to EAP services, when applicable. And finally, integrated programs would lead to greater cost-containment and employee well-being due to the formation of a comprehensive risk reduction and health improvement system.

Unfortunately, in the 12 years since the publication of this landmark piece, the authors' vision of the mega brush approach has not been fully realized in the majority of organizations. Wellness programs and EAP have continued to work towards the same goal of improving the health and well-being of employees, with few successful examples of integration available in the published literature.

This article describes the successful integration between EAP and wellness programs at Fairview Health Services (Fairview). In this article we will review a brief history of integration between EAP and wellness and the shared mission they serve at Fairview. Next we will outline the model on which this program was built, and the specific programs and services provided under each segment of this model. We will then focus on how Fairview addresses depression–one of their largest cost drivers–in a coordinated effort. Finally, we will share some of the preliminary outcomes from a comprehensive program evaluation, including the impact on medical costs, workers compensation costs and absenteeism costs.

FAIRVIEW ALIVE–AN INTEGRATED STRATEGY

Fairview Health Services is a community-based health care system that serves Minnesota's Twin Cities of Minneapolis and St. Paul and surrounding communities. Fairview employs 13,000 benefit-eligible employees that are geographically located in over 100 care locations. Eighty-five percent of the benefit eligible workforce is female and the average age is 42.

Throughout Minnesota, in hospitals, community centers, homes and long-term care centers, the mission of Fairview Health Services is to improve the health of the communities they serve by providing the finest in health care. Fairview does this by addressing the physical, emotional and spiritual needs of individuals and their families. Fairview believes that their employees are the organization's most valuable assets, and that Fairview's future lies in its ability to attract and retain highly engaged and high-performing employees.

To help contribute to the organization's employee engagement, financial and operational performance strategies, a total health management initiative was created, called *Fairview Alive*. The mission of *Fairview Alive* is to enhance the overall health and productivity of employees and their families. Fairview believes there is a shared responsibility between the employee and the organization. Fairview's success will be achieved by offering the environment, the tools and the opportunities to assist employees with managing their own health.

HISTORY OF INTEGRATION

A key focus of *Fairview Alive* has been the integration of health and benefit-related departments. This includes the functional and operational integration of Employee Assistance, Wellness (a.k.a., Health Promotion, or in broader terms Health Management), Employee Occupational

Health and Employee Benefits. Together these departments provide products and services to Fairview employees and their family members in an integrated manner.

As is the case with many employers, these programs were not always integrated. The EAP was established in 1983 as an arm of outpatient counseling. Prior to 1996, the EAP, Benefits, and a decentralized Occupational Health department each existed in their own silos. During this time EAP was linked to Human Resources as an internal customer. In 1996, the EAP began reporting to Benefits directly, but was not formally integrated. That same year, a pilot of the Health Promotion Program was introduced and was linked to Benefits. In 1997, Occupational Health converted to a centralized disability management strategy. In 1999, EAP discontinued using staff from the outpatient counseling service to provide its EAP services and began using fully dedicated staff to serve employees. In 2001, the same year the Health Promotion Program was launched corporate-wide, EAP, the Health Promotion Program, Employee Occupational Health Services (EOHS), and Benefits formally combined efforts and became fully integrated under the Director of Health and Benefits. Today in 2004, all four of these areas (EAP, Health Promotion, Occupational Health and Benefits) report through the Director of Health and Benefits up to the Vice President of Human Resources of Fairview Health Services.

Broad program direction and oversight for the program is provided by the Director of Health and Benefits, along with the *Fairview Alive* leadership team, which consists of managers from each of the four programming areas. Dedicated corporate communications and data management staff support the initiative, and a Medical Director provides consultation from a preventive and occupational medicine perspective with regard to program products and services.

FAIRVIEW ALIVE STAFF TEAM

The *Fairview Alive* team hails from a variety of backgrounds, including health education, behavioral health, dietetics, nursing, sports medicine, occupational and physical therapy, occupational health nursing, benefits administration and quality improvement, psychology, and employee assistance. *Fairview Alive* staff consists of a combined total of 56.5 full-time equivalents (FTEs) and is separated into the following four working teams:

The Fairview Alive Health Management Team. This team is dedicated to the wellness, risk management and demand management areas of Fairview employees. The corporate team oversees the onsite staff, program planning, product development, system communication, program data tracking and evaluation. The *Fairview Alive* onsite team is responsible for onsite implementation, promotion and evaluation.

The Employee Assistance Program Team. This team is dedicated to promoting and maintaining the well-being of employees both in the workplace and in their personal lives. The team is made up of a manager and counselors that provide one-on-one counseling services to employees and their family members. They also provide support to the organization in creating a healthy work environment through education, team support and critical incident stress management services.

The Employee Occupational Health Team. This team is dedicated to providing onsite support for employees' health and how it relates to their work at Fairview. This team is made up of registered nurse specialists, generalists and physical therapists. The nurse specialists oversee regulatory and mandatory requirements like respiratory fit testing and immunizations and perform return-to-work case management. Nurse generalists are responsible for the implementation and day-to-day delivery of occupational health services. Injury prevention specialists deliver musculoskeletal health services.

The Employee Benefits Team. This corporate team includes a call center, data analyst, manager and other expert and transactional staff. It oversees the planning and implementation of the health and welfare benefit plans. The onsite team is made up of benefits representatives that specialize in the day-to-day operation of employees' health/dental/life/disability insurance, spending accounts and leave of absence administration.

Vendor Partners. In addition, *Fairview Alive* has partnered with several "best of class" vendors to provide programs and services to influence their outcome goals of improved health and productivity. Integration across vendors is demonstrated by development of an integrated data warehouse. National vendors provide resources dedicated to health management, disease management, disability management, nurse advice line services, self-care resource materials, health plan administration, and data integration.

Significant ongoing work takes place to further integrate the vendors and the internal *Fairview Alive* departments. The goal of the work is to ensure that employees and their family members receive integrated and appropriate resources customized to their health needs. This has helped to eliminate gaps and overlaps of the services provided. Fairview and the vendors aim to provide transparent, integrated access and services to employees and family members. Towards that end, they conduct face-to-face meetings twice a year and conduct monthly teleconference calls to continue to work on identified strategic objectives.

BUILT ON THE PRINCIPLES
OF POPULATION HEALTH MANAGEMENT

Fairview Alive was developed within the framework of a Population Health Management model (Breslow, 1999). Anderson (2003) describes Population Health Management *as a comprehensive strategy that cost-effectively improves the overall health of a defined population by segmenting the population based on health-related factors and targeting interventions to meet the needs of each segment.* For Fairview, this means providing resources and services to employees along the entire continuum of health, with multiple delivery channels and formats (see Figure 1). From health and low risk, to moderate and high risk, to acute and chronic conditions, to serious or life-threatening disabilities, Population Health Management integrates cost-effective interventions that encompass Wellness Management, Health Risk Management, Demand Management, Disease Management, and Disability Management. The goal of Population Health Management is to lower the risk of higher-risk individuals while maintaining the risk status of low-risk individuals.

INTEGRATED PROGRAM OFFERINGS

The Fairview Alive Program is comprised of an integrated group of activities.

Health Risk Assessment. The foundation of the *Fairview Alive* program is the Health Risk Assessment (HRA) offered online or on paper annually, free of charge to all benefit-eligible employees. The HRA provides the gateway to lifestyle and some disease management health coach programs. HRA and disability data are assessed to identify the most prevalent population health risks and to plan programming to address these risks.

New Employee Health Kits. Fairview Alive provides employee health kits to all new employees. The kit contains several items that support

FIGURE 1. Fairview Alive Program Framework: An Integrated Strategy Across the Health Continuum

Health →		Continuum →		Illness →
Wellness Management • Information • Motivation • Preventive Screening	**Risk Management** • Targeted Intervention • Targeted Screening • Behavior Change	**Demand Management** • Self-Care • Nurse Advice Line	**Disease Management** • Compliance • Risk Management	**Disability Management** • Case Management • Decision Support
Optimal Health Health & Well-Being Low Risk	**At Risk** Inactivity, Obesity, Stress Nutrition	**Minor Illness/Injury** Doctor Visits ER Visits	**Chronic Disease** Diabetes Heart Disease	**Disability** Traumatic Injury Cancer
FAIRVIEW ALIVE • Awareness classes, promote preventive exams, referrals to community programs, encourage work with providers BENEFITS Preventive care coverage design WELLNESS VENDOR Health Risk Assessment EOHS Flu shots, safe lifting, ergonomics, respiratory protection, communicable disease exposure treatment	FAIRVIEW ALIVE • Behavior Change Onsite classes WELLNESS VENDOR • Print and phone-based personal health coaching, health education campaigns BENEFITS Health plan coverage EAP Short term counseling, stress management critical incident, conflict management, healthy work relationship, counseling	FAIRVIEW ALIVE • Self-Care book NURSELINE VENDOR • NurseLine, Website, Audio Library WELLNESS VENDOR • High risk and health care consumerism BENEFITS Health plan coverage EAP Assessment, referral and treatment	DM VENDORS • Disease Management WELLNESS VENDOR Disease Management PBM Condition/drug care management BENEFITS Health plan coverage	TPA Large Case Management DISABILITY CARRIER Short-term disability, long-term disability EOHS LOA Case Management RTW/Transitional Duty WORK FORCE DEVEL. Placement Services BENEFITS Health and disability plan coverage

employees in maintaining and achieving optimal health, including an HRA, self-care book, phone line resource flyer with all *Fairview Alive* resources listed and incentive program brochure.

Onsite Health Education Activities and Onsite Classes. A variety of single-session onsite classes including self-care, lifestyle and disease management initiatives are offered to Fairview employees at all care systems in partnership with internal and external resources.

Community Classes. Employees are encouraged to participate in community classes on a variety of health education topics. The employee can complete a community class form, have the instructor sign it and return it to *Fairview Alive* for credit toward the incentive program.

Fairview Alive Newsletter. Fairview Alive collaborates with internal departments to promote Fairview system programs and services in a variety of health and productivity topics through the *Fairview Alive* newsletter. This bi-monthly newsletter is mailed to the homes of all benefit-eligible employees.

Fairview Alive Intranet. The intranet site contains health information and a schedule of *Fairview Alive* activities and classes. The intranet site easily links employees to other Fairview health and benefits-related departments.

Fairview Alive Phone Line. An integrated phone line provides access to all employee health-related programs and services, including *Fairview Alive* Onsite Staff, HelpLine, NurseLine, Employee Assistance Program (EAP), Employee Occupational Health Services (EOHS) and the Benefits Service Center.

Work-Related Illness and Injury Prevention. A variety of programs are delivered by EOHS to protect employees against work environment potential exposures and prevent illness and injury. Other services include: flu shots, ergonomic assessments, occupational injury prevention programs and numerous health information services.

Lifestyle Management Programs. Fairview Alive partners with an outside vendor to deliver phone-based health coach programs based on risk in one of eight health risk areas indicated on the HRA.

Integrated Demand Management. Demand management programming takes place in a variety of ways described previously. Briefly they include: self-care book, health care provider engagement, nurse advice line, health care consumerism program, and integrated employee assistance program offerings.

Fairview Alive NurseLine, Audio Library and Health Forums Web Site. Fairview Alive partners with an outside vendor to deliver three health information services to employees and their families. These services provide 24-hour access to health information via a telephonic nurse advice line, an audio library and a Web site. The health audio library has information on over 1300 health topics.

Employee Assistance Program. EAP provides short-term counseling, referrals and support to individuals. EAP offers educational and support services to employee groups, consultations services to managers and supervisors, and collaborates with other employee service departments. Short-term counseling consists of six-session episodes of care per employee and family member. Ongoing tracking indicates that 84% of clients receive services within five business days. Same-day call back services are provided to people in crisis or with immediate needs.

In addition, EAP manages the Critical Incident Stress Management Program (CISM). A critical incident is any event outside the normal realm of human experience that is distressing and overwhelms the person's normal coping skills. EAP triages requests for services and facilitates and arranges CISM sessions for work teams.

The EAP leads multidisciplinary healthy work environment intervention teams, which include members from Spiritual Health Services, EOHS, Safety, and other employee services support departments to deliver CISM and initiatives to prevent workplace violence.

Throughout the year, EAP works collaboratively with multiple internal departments to provide ongoing educational sessions. Some of the topics include stress (e.g., *Stress Management, Managing Holiday Stress, Critical Incident Stress Management*), mental health (e.g., *Maintaining Your Mental Health, Banishing the Winter Blues, Depression),* resiliency (e.g., *Resilience in the Workplace*) and how to work with others (e.g., *Building Healthy Work Relationships, Respectful Workplace, Conflict Resolution, When Women Work With Women*).

INTEGRATION PROCESS

Integration opportunities are purposefully sought out through a joint planning process leadership team, which meets annually, with quarterly updates. This process is designed to proactively identify opportunities for joint product development, delivery of service, marketing and communications, and leadership and physician employee engagement. The goal is to most effectively leverage the best resource and talent for the initiative at hand. Quarterly, joint performance measurement is reported showing results organized by the organization's strategic focus areas of clinical excellence, customer service and responsiveness, financial and operational performance, and employee and physician engagement.

DRIVING PARTICIPATION IN FAIRVIEW ALIVE

In addition to offering resources and services along the entire continuum of health, driving appropriate program participation is key to the success of any program. Key factors for building program participation include appropriate incentives, significant management support, and a comprehensive communications plan (Serxner et al., 2004).

Incentives. Fairview has found that incentives are a key driver of participation. *Fairview Alive* offers an annual incentive program based on a Population Health Management model. Because lifestyle choices are the single biggest factor affecting employee health, the certificate-based incentive program rewards employee participation in health and lifestyle activities. Employees are invited to participate in a comprehensive menu of activities each year for which they can earn up to $75 in Work Perks (company store) certificates. The program is voluntary and confidential. To earn a $25 certificate, employees must complete a health risk assessment. This is offered each fall in conjunction with open enrollment to all benefit-eligible employees. To earn an additional $50 certificate, employees must participate in two different personal health management activities such as campaigns, targeted interventions, onsite classes; be up to date on preventive exams; or work with their health care provider to manage a chronic health condition. These activities are designed to help employees learn more about a health area, set goals and take steps to manage their health.

Management Support. All managers and supervisors must participate in 40 hours of leadership development classes each year. To assist with this, *Fairview Alive* developed and implemented a course called "Life Balance for Leaders." The focus of the course is to encourage Fairview leaders to understand the relationship between balancing work and family and how that affects their health. Making healthy choices also influences the employees who work for them. *Fairview Alive* continues to work collaboratively to develop additional courses in partnership with the Fairview Leadership Development Center. Fairview also hosts a Quality Leadership Conference each year. *Fairview Alive* has offered products and services at the conference and has sponsored speakers for the employee sessions. The focus of leadership engagement is to integrate health and well-being as a priority in leadership development. In

2003, 69% of Fairview managers and supervisors participated in some aspect of the *Fairview Alive* initiative.

Communication. Integrating four separate programs has allowed Fairview Health Services to combine resources and hire dedicated communications staff to oversee communications efforts across all functional areas. Under the old model, EAP and Health Promotion were in charge of their own communications. Due to small staff sizes, large caseloads, and minimal communications training, program communication was oftentimes not given the priority it deserved. In an integrated model, dedicated communications staff–specifically trained to effectively communicate at the population level–oversee these efforts. The communications staff coordinates all initiatives, both within and across disciplines, and cross promotes using multiple delivery channels (e.g., newsletter, intranet, internet, integrated benefits package). An integrated communications plan decreases costs due to economies of scale, at the same time increasing effectiveness due to increased message exposure and synergistic communication opportunities.

A FOCUS ON DEPRESSION

One of the greatest benefits of integrating EAP and wellness is in the ability to address a major costs driver in a coordinated effort. As Erfurt and colleagues suggest, integrated programs more effectively promote awareness, which leads to early detection and prevention. Increased awareness also engages a larger portion of a population, which increases referrals to appropriate services.

At Fairview, depression is one of the top two diagnostic categories in terms of preventable medical and pharmaceutical costs. To better manage the financial and human risks related to depression, Fairview developed an integrated strategic initiative that functions across the depression continuum.

For low-risk individuals, the strategy focuses on awareness and prevention. This includes awareness materials, campaigns and workshops that are co-developed and delivered by the wellness program and EAP. For moderate risk individuals, the goal is primary prevention. For this segment, EAP provides screening, short-term counseling, referrals and educational materials. The program focus for high-risk individuals is secondary intervention. Any Fairview employee or dependent that incurs a claim related to depression is eligible to participate in a Disease Management program, where depression is treated as a co-morbidity.

Additionally, collaborative relationships and linkages are being established across Fairview metro clinics, Behavioral Healthcare Providers (a carved-out behavioral provider network and utilization manager), and Fairview Counseling Centers to provide more integrated care.

Fairview's three-year plan for the Depression Initiative focuses on:

1. Employee Engagement–increasing understanding and utilization of resources for managing depression among employees;
2. Leadership Engagement–increasing understanding and utilization of resources for managing depression among organizational leaders;
3. Internal Process Improvement–improving employee referrals to appropriate resources across internal and external partners; establishing a defined EAP standard protocol to treat employees and dependents for mild to moderate depression; and identifying gaps or duplication of depression resources;
4. Establishing clinical disease management programs managing depression as a co-morbidity; and
5. Developing collaborative relationships.

Soul Journey–A Well-Being Campaign. One of the first self-paced campaigns jointly developed by EAP and the wellness team was the *Soul Journey* Campaign. Soul Journey is a five-week campaign allowing participants to explore possibilities for self-discovery and emotional well-being, as well as enhancing personal growth and development. Participants are encouraged to choose a path that meets their needs and interests. The paths include: *Understanding Your Mood, Finding Your Passion,* and *Connecting with Others.* Participants are encouraged to track an action item during the campaign by checking off days they worked on their action item. Examples of action items include: increasing daily physical activity, completing meditation exercises, journaling, and exploring what activities energize the participant. In 2004, over 2200 employees registered for the program. Of those that registered, 55% were at-risk for stress and 32% were at-risk for mental health. A stress management campaign will be launched in 2005.

PROGRAM EVALUATION

While the clinical and cost-effectiveness of worksite health promotion programs is well established (see reviews by Aldana, 2000; Heaney and Goetzel, 1998; Pelletier, 1991, 1993, 1996, 1999, 2001; Riedel et al., 2000), little evidence exists to describe the impact of integrated programs such as *Fairview Alive*.

Recognizing the need to document outcomes for the overall *Fairview Alive* program, Fairview commissioned a comprehensive evaluation of the program, which includes a prospective, quasi-experimental study of the program's impact on total medical costs, absence, and workers' compensation costs. Utilizing 18 months of baseline data and 30 months of follow-up data (to date), self-selected program participants are compared with program non-participants to determine program impact.

Data Sources. As part of the evaluation, a third-party data integrator developed and maintains an integrated data warehouse. The data integrator receives data files from five sources to populate the data warehouse, including eligibility data, absence records, workers' compensation claims, medical and retail pharmacy claims, NurseLine utilization data and integrated program participation and program costs data.

Data are collected monthly and quarterly from the various data sources. The data warehouse is updated on a semi-annual basis, and a person-centric study database is created semi-annually and provided to a third party for analysis. All unique identifiers are removed from the data before it is transferred to protect the confidentiality of Fairview employees.

Participation. Overall, *Fairview Alive* has been successful in building awareness, engaging employees and improving employee health. Participation in all aspects of *Fairview Alive* has increased significantly since the program's launch in 2001. Participation rates grew from 54% (after only 6 months of programming in 2001) to 82% by the end of 2003. Of the 82% of employees who have participated to date, 62% chose to participate in all major components of the *Fairview Alive* program.

Employee Engagement. Key indicators of employee engagement include:

- *Employee Assistance Program Utilization.* One of Fairview's goals around the employee assistance program was to encourage employee utilization of program and services. Since Fairview's EAP began using fully dedicated internal staff, utilization has increased from 4.3% to 5.9%. Client satisfaction of EAP services increased from 94% to 98% during the same time period.

- *NurseLine Utilization.* NurseLine services were first offered in 2002 and utilization since then has varied. By the end of 2003, approximately 11.3% of employees were using the NurseLine.
- *Health Risk Assessment Participation.* The HRA is offered to all benefit-eligible employees annually, in conjunction with open enrollment. Each major launch has yielded participation rates of almost 60%, with a cumulative participation rate of 82%.
- *Targeted Lifestyle and Disease Management Programs.* Employees who are at high risk for developing health problems in a specific area are targeted for participation in Lifestyle or Disease Management Programs. Of those invited, about a third of them choose to participate. This is consistent with research that suggests only a third of those eligible are ready to make significant lifestyle behavior changes at a given time.
- *Fairview Alive Service Center Utilization. Fairview Alive* offers four different service centers or phone lines to help employees access the health care resources and services most appropriate for them. A total of approximately 5,500 calls are made to the four service centers every quarter.

OUTCOMES

One of the leading indicators of improved health status is decreased number of health risks in a population. Since program launch, *Fairview Alive* HRA participants report a 22% decrease in average number of health risks, from 4.1 risks in 2001 to 3.2 risks in 2003. More importantly, the *Fairview Alive* program evaluation research has demonstrated beneficial impacts on reduced total medical costs, workers' compensation costs, and absence days lost (see Attridge and Gold, 2004).

Medical Costs. Total medical and pharmaceutical claims paid are adjusted for changes in health plan design and for inflation (based on national medical CPI as reported by US Bureau of Labor Statistics). Cohort analyses compared change in total medical costs between participants and non-participants over time. Since program launch in 2001, the program has yielded a cost savings of over $340 per employee.

Workers' Compensation Costs. Includes total medical, rehabilitation, indemnity and wage replacement costs attributed to workers' compensation claims, not including settlement and legal fees. Using methods similar to those used to measure impact on medical costs, cohort analyses revealed a cumulative savings of about $188 per employee since 2001.

Absence Days Lost. Total unscheduled time off, not including non-occupational medical leave, FMLA, or other scheduled time off (vacation/holidays). Monetary value of days lost was calculated using employee authorized work hours and mean hourly wage. Cohort analyses yielded an estimated cumulative savings of approximately $230 per employee.

DISCUSSION

Though Erfurt and colleagues first coined the idea of a mega brush model to co-join EAP and wellness services over ten years ago, the literature provides few successful models with demonstrated impacts on employee health and well-being. The *Fairview Alive* program provides one of the first published case studies that meet this vision of mega brush. During the concluding remarks in their 1992 article, the authors cautioned that these programs work best when they are,

> . . . structurally separate . . . but organizationally linked, functionally coordinated, and effectively working together. EAPs should be staffed by employee assistance professionals, and wellness programs should be staffed by wellness professionals, both trained and certified in their respective fields. (Erfurt et al., 1992, page 27)

The Fairview model has successfully captured the spirit of this original charge by fully integrating the planning, implementation, communication, and measurement of EAP and health management program offerings, while maintaining the unique identity of each functional area. Program leadership and staff recognize the value of the service offerings provided by each program, and the synergy that comes from working together in parallel towards a common goal.

Fairview as an organization has also benefited by increasing its standing as an employer of choice in a field where attraction and retention of experienced staff is critical to the organization's success. In the past two years, Fairview Health Services has been the recipient of two prestigious awards. In 2003 Fairview received the C. Everett Koop National Health Award, and was awarded the Corporate Health Achievement Award by the Institute for Health and Productivity Management the following year. Both awards recognize programs that demonstrate leadership and measurable results in promoting employee health and well-being.

While recognizing the niceties of such recognition, Fairview refuses to rest on such laurels. As this article is being written, *Fairview Alive* staff are pouring over the data from the previous year and carefully plotting their stretch goals for the next year. They recognize that consistent measurement and reporting are essential for documenting the value of the *Fairview Alive* initiative. However, if you asked them, they would surely tell you that it is the individual success stories and testimonials that fuel the passion they bring to their work each day. Each person on *Fairview Alive*'s staff can tell you how their individual work contributes to the success of their department, and also to the organization's broader strategic goals of Clinical Excellence, Customer Service and Responsiveness, Financial and Operational Performance, Employee Engagement, Physician Engagement, and Overall Growth, Integration and Performance. In this way each person is a walking testimony of the *Fairview Alive* vision.

REFERENCES

Aldana, S.G. (2001). Financial impact of health promotion programs: A comprehensive review of the literature. *American Journal of Health Promotion*, 15(5):296-320.

Anderson, D.R. (2003). Building a first class workforce: The sky's the limit with population health management. *Absolute Advantage*, 2(5):4-9.

Attridge, M. & Gold, D.B. (2004, October). *Improving Employee Performance by Improving Health: Secrets of Successful Health and Productivity Management Programs*. Presented at the Fourth Annual International Conference of the Institute for Health and Productivity Management. Phoenix, AZ.

Breslow, L. (1999). From disease prevention to health. *JAMA* 281:1030-1033.

Erfurt, J.C., Foote, A., & Heirich, M.A. (1992). Integrating employee assistance and wellness: Current and future core technologies of a mega brush program. *Journal of Employee Assistance Research*, 1(1):1-31.

Heaney, C.A. & Goetzel, R.Z. (1997). A review of health-related outcomes of multicomponent worksite health promotion programs. *American Journal of Health Promotion*, 11:290-298.

Pelletier, K.R. (1991). A review and analysis of the health and cost-effective outcome studies of comprehensive health promotion and disease prevention programs. *American Journal of Health Promotion*, 5:311-313.

Pelletier, K.R. (1993). A review and analysis of the health and cost-effective outcome studies of comprehensive health promotion and disease prevention programs at the worksite: 1991-1993 update. *American Journal of Health Promotion*, 8:50-62.

Pelletier, K.R. (1996). A review and analysis of the health and cost-effective outcome studies of comprehensive health promotion and disease prevention programs at the worksite: 1993-1995 update. *American Journal of Health Promotion*, 10:380-388.

Pelletier, K.R. (1999). A review and analysis of the clinical and cost-effectiveness studies of comprehensive health promotion and disease management programs at the worksite: 1995-1998 update (IV). *American Journal of Health Promotion*, 13:333-345.

Pelletier, K.R. (2001). A review and analysis of the clinical- and cost-effectiveness studies of comprehensive health promotion and disease management programs at the worksite: 1998-2000 update. *American Journal of Health Promotion*, 16(2): 107-116.

Riedel, J.E., Lynch, W., Baase, C., Hymel, P., & Peterson, K.W. (2001). The effect of disease prevention and health promotion on workplace productivity: A literature review. *American Journal of Health Promotion*, 15(3):167-191.

Serxner, S.A., Anderson, D.R., & Gold, D.B. (2004). Building program participation: Strategies for recruitment and retention in worksite health promotion programs. *The Art of Health Promotion*, March/April:1-9.

Chapter 15

An Integrated EAP–
Defining One's Place in the Organization:
A Perspective from the Internal
EAP Side of the Fence

Bernard E. Beidel

SUMMARY. With the continuing evolution of employee assistance services over the past few decades, terminology in the field has become increasingly confusing, resulting in a number of misconceptions about the employee assistance service and its "integration" into the company, labor union or organization. In this article, the author argues for a more traditional concept of "organizational integration"–focusing on the actual process of an employee assistance service becoming part of the fabric of its host or sponsoring organization with a corresponding ability to

[Haworth co-indexing entry note]: "An Integrated EAP–Defining One's Place in the Organization: A Perspective from the Internal EAP Side of the Fence." Beidel, Bernard E. Co-published simultaneously in *Journal of Workplace Behavioral Health* (The Haworth Press, Inc.) Vol. 20, No. 3/4, 2005, pp. 281-306; and: *The Integration of Employee Assistance, Work/Life, and Wellness Services* (ed: Mark Attridge, Patricia A. Herlihy, and R. Paul Maiden) The Haworth Press, Inc., 2005, pp. 281-306. Single or multiple copies of this article are available for a fee from The Haworth Document Delivery Service [1-800- HAWORTH, 9:00 a.m. - 5:00 p.m. (EST). E-mail address: docdelivery@haworthpress.com].

Available online at http://www.haworthpress.com/web/JWBH
© 2005 by The Haworth Press, Inc. All rights reserved.
doi:10.1300/J490v20n03_05

recognize, understand and even change the very organizational culture of which it has become a part. In today's conceptual framework, the critical challenges and opportunities presented to an employee assistance service during this critical integration process are often overlooked and even lost with a premature rush to integrate other service components that can cloud the true value of the core employee assistance functions and services to the organization as a whole. Thus, the critical question becomes whether "integration" reflects the merging of EA with other behavioral and work/life services or, as the author argues, the merging of the EA with other organizational operations and systems and its ultimate desegregation in terms of how it is viewed by other strategic and operational elements of the organization. The author's experience in initiating, implementing and integrating internal EAPs in two very distinct organizations over the past twenty-four years provides evidence that many of the service enhancements sought in today's employee assistance service "integration" marketplace are only viable and certainly enhanced if the EAP has achieved true organizational "integration" at the front end. *[Article copies available for a fee from The Haworth Document Delivery Service: 1-800-HAWORTH. E-mail address: <docdelivery@haworthpress.com> Website: <http://www.HaworthPress.com> © 2005 by The Haworth Press, Inc. All rights reserved.]*

KEYWORDS. Employee assistance services, organization, integration, EAP

INTRODUCTION

As evident throughout this publication, the concept of "integration" takes on multiple and divergent meanings when applied to today's employee assistance field. Over the years the concept has come to primarily reflect the coming together and partnering of varied workplace services with the more traditional employee assistance efforts and core functions. In order to ultimately enhance the performance of the individual and the organization, however, it is critical that the employee assistance field not overlook the most critical aspect of integration–the actual process by which an employee assistance service weaves itself into the fabric of the company, labor union or organization that it serves. As with the articles included in this journal, Oher's (1999) edited compilation of programmatic examples provides very strong evidence of the successful integration of core employee assistance functions with managed behavioral healthcare, work/life, disability management, risk management, workplace safety, critical incident stress, wellness and health promotion, and other related activities. This author maintains that all of these strategies are contingent on a fundamental "integration" of the EAP into and with the larger organization that it serves—an integration that is not limited to the human service and/or health dimensions of the organization, but one that injects employee assistance services into the very "business" core of the organization. An EAP can only be considered fully integrated when it interfaces with the strategic and operational heart of the company, labor union or organization at both a service delivery and organizational effectiveness decision-making level.

While the integration of employee assistance services with these related behavioral and human service components in an organization is important, it is critical that EAP not stop there. The true potential value of an employee assistance service extends beyond the traditional human service and performance/productivity enhancement dimensions of an organization. An EAP's real value emerges as it realizes its ultimate potential of actually impacting the organization's operational mission and strategic vision. While the employee assistance service logically impacts the people or human capital dimension of the organization, an EAP that is truly integrated into the organization finds itself capable of opening other doors of opportunity and sitting at other tables of influence in the organization. Such "integration" results in a value added proposition beyond the traditional parameters of many EAPs. Thus, the successful "integration" of an employee assistance service is reflected in that service's reach into the organization's other operational and strategic domains. For far too long these strategic and operational venues in the organization have been perceived as the non-traditional playing fields for the EA professional. The ability of the employee assistance professional to interface with the organization and its decision makers at levels other than the human resource, medical, safety, work-life and wellness dimensions offers a glimpse into the largely untapped arena of organizational "integration." A number of excellent discussions, however, have begun to map some exciting and promising ventures of employee assistance services into these often-uncharted waters of larger organizational change and influence (Dickens, 1999; Ginsburg, Kilburg & Gomes, 1999; Zimmerman & Oher, 1999). In Dickens' summation of the need for EAPs to create strategic business alliances and partnerships to advance and maximize EAP efforts, she writes:

> The integrated approach to EAP planning has great potential power in planning and delivering services that impact overall or-

ganizational health. As companies recognize the need to compete in a global market, the stress associated with continuous improvement and change never abates. Transitions are a way of life that, even when welcomed, impact the health and well-being of individuals throughout the organization. Productivity and profitability are directly related to the care and maintenance of human capital as well as of machines and technology. The EAP is a critical partner in developing approaches and handling stress associated with organizational change. (Dickens, 1999)

The critical partnership of the employee assistance service and the organization indeed extends far beyond helping the business manage stress at the back end of an event or significant change initiative. A truly integrated EAP has the potential to mitigate the stress of such activities through its effective engagement with the organization's planning efforts and decision makers at the front end.

A FRAMEWORK FOR UNDERSTANDING THE CONCEPT OF INTEGRATION

In their landmark study of the implementation of policies to deal with employees of the federal government with alcoholism problems following the 1970 passage by the U.S. Congress of the Hughes Act (P.L. 91-616), Beyer and Trice (1978) developed a model of social change. This model can be used to retrospectively study a significant change undertaking in an organization as it moves through what they describe as seven distinct stages. These stages include:

1. Sensing of unsatisfied demands on the system
2. Search for possible responses
3. Evaluation of alternatives
4. Decision to adopt a course of action
5. Initiation of action within the system
6. Implementation of the change
7. Institutionalization of the change

Table 1 provides a more detailed enumeration of the stages and the corresponding innovation, policy development, planning and decision-making activities at work within each stage.

TABLE 1. Necessary Stages in a Completed Change Process Within a Purposive System

STAGE	EXPLANATION
1. Sensing of Unsatisfied Demands on the System	Some part of the system receives information indicating a problem or potential problem with organizational functioning. For example, some part of the system becomes internally imbalanced, subsystem relations become imbalanced, new demands are made on the system, or the relation between inputs and outputs is unfavorable.
2. Search for Possible Responses	Elements in the system consciously or unconsciously set about finding alternative ways of dealing with the issues sensed in the previous step. Alternatives can involve programs that are preexisting, are readily available, are located with difficulty, or must be invented.
3. Evaluation of Alternatives	A comparison is made between desired outcomes, probable outcomes of alternatives located, and costs. Probabilities are derived for alternative actions (means) leading to desired outcomes (goals). The values of outcomes are more or less explicitly assessed relative to systems of values. Cost of means are also assessed relative to systems of values.
4. Decision to Adopt Course of Action	An alternative is chosen from among those evaluated. Goals, operative goals, and means are more or less specified, i.e., a strategy for dealing with the demands is adopted.
5. Initiation of Action Within the System	A policy or other directive for implementing the change is formulated. This involves a choice of tactics based on the strategy already chosen. The initial diffusion of information about the changes takes place within the system. This information is more or less explicit about the policy or directives that have been developed, the demands that have made the change desirable, the connection between desired outcomes or goals and the means prescribed, and the general rationale behind the strategies and tactics chosen to implement the change.
6. Implementation of the Change	Further information is diffused to all involved members. Resources are allocated toward implementation efforts, e.g., training, hiring, new equipment, reallocation of time. Attitudinal reactions occur relative to prescribed means, including changes in role expectations and definitions. Role behaviors change as specified, i.e., compliance with prescribed means occurs.
7. Institutionalization of the Change	Attitudinal reactions toward goals occur relative to values held. Values are modified to accept goals. Goals are internalized into modified value system.

Reprinted with the permission of The Free Press, a Division of Simon & Schuster Adult Publishing Group, from IMPLEMENTING CHANGE: Alcoholism Policies in Work Organizations by Janice M. Beyer and Harrison M. Trice. Copyright © 1978 by The Free Press. All rights reserved.

The researchers contend that the critical outcomes at the implementation stage and at the institutionalization stages are largely reflective of the degree to which the social change has been integrated into the organization. This is accomplished when the "attitudinal reactions toward" the "goals" of the change "occur relative to" the "values held" by the organization. They further assert that the values of an organization or business are actually frequently modified to accept these new goals, with the goals becoming internalized into the organization's modified value system (Beyer & Trice, 1978).

In a ten-year longitudinal study of the implementation and integration of the EAP into a state law enforcement agency (New Jersey State Police), Reichman and Beidel (1994) used the work of Beyer and Trice as a framework to study the EAP as it moved through the diffusion, receptivity and utilization or use stages of program development and implementation. This unique partnership between the EAP, the organization and an outside researcher tracked the movement and progression of the New Jersey State Police EAP as the program evolved through these seven distinct stages of organizational change during its initial ten years of operation. From the organization's perspective, the critical processes were program diffusion, organizational receptivity and ultimately use by individuals and the organization as a whole. During the diffusion stage, the program became known within the organization through a myriad of traditional promotional, education and training-related activities. At the receptivity stage, members of the organization learned, became more familiar with and began to accept the principles, values, goals and procedures of the program. The utilization stage ultimately occurred when individuals became willing to use that program, actually used it, and reported satisfaction with its use (Reichman & Beidel, 1994, p. 22). As the program moved through these critical implementation stages, the "integration" of the EAP into the organization necessitated and drove a number of significant value and attitudinal changes at the heart of the organization. As assessed through a series of attitudinal and knowledge surveys of the organization's personnel over the ten years of research, several key attitudinal shifts were targeted and measured, including the perception of the organization and its law enforcement personnel toward fellow officers in recovery from alcoholism, the organization's trust in the ongoing capabilities of recovering officers to meet the demands of a law enforcement career, and the willingness of their fellow officers to serve as patrol partners in the future.

An interesting phenomenon occurred in the organization during the course of the ten-year evaluation effort. The attitudinal and knowledge surveys undertaken to assess the diffusion, receptivity and use stages of implementation actually became a catalyst for furthering some of the very attitude and knowledge changes necessitated to fully integrate the EAP into the organization. As employees became more and more familiar with this routine survey process and as reflected in their sustained exceptionally high response rates of 49-79% (Reichman & Beidel, 1994), the EAP and organization benefited from this indirect, but effective, informational and educational vehicle itself.

A Personal Perspective. This initial conceptual framework and the actual program implementation experience gained from the author's over twenty-four years of internal EAP management will serve as a backdrop to the balance of this discussion. The successful "integration" of an employee assistance service into the larger company, labor union or organization is contingent as much on the employee assistance service's ability to influence and even change the organization, as it is on the organization's influence over and the parameters established for the service's operations. Experience from the "internal side of the EAP fence" supports a belief that the EAP is often an untapped source of influence within the organization. Influence that can be more effectively leveraged and value that is more often realized when the employee assistance service crosses the threshold from its more traditional realms of interface and ventures into the heart of the organization's initiatives, activities, discussions and dilemmas.

THE TRADITIONS BEHIND INTEGRATION

This concept of the employee assistance service integrating itself into the organization is not a new one. As is evident in the Beyer and Trice (1978) study of the United States government's early alcoholism policy implementation efforts, the mark of a successful program implementation is solely dependent on how well the concepts and goals behind the effort are integrated into the values and operational systems of the organization, particularly when the organization is "introducing an emotionally charged innovation" (Trice, Beyer & Hunt, 1978). One need only look at some of the most comprehensive discussions of employee assistance program development, implementation and evaluation to see evidence of the view that an EAP's true success is measured to the degree that the program or service is integrated sufficiently into the organization. This integration is measured by how effectively the EAP is viewed as a vital player not only in the enhancement of the employees and manager's day-to-day performance and productivity, but ultimately on the long-term effectiveness of the organization (Masi, 1984; Presnall, 1981; Shain & Groeneveld, 1980; Wrich, 1980).

This author's experience within the unique environment of a legislative institution (the U.S. House of Representatives) exemplifies this evolution toward full integration within an organization. With the initial thrust of the EAP focused solely on alcoholism and drug addiction issues in the workplace, an immediate challenge existed to expand the services beyond this limited perspective. In a microcosmic replication of the experience of the larger employee assistance field, the EAP's initial programmatic experience similarly realized the added implementation bonus of more effectively managing performance difficulties in the workplace by expanding the focus of the program to the broader universe of behavioral, mental health, workplace and work/life management issues. The rationale for such expansion was pitched to the organization as an essential step to position the EAP to provide a broader value to the organization. This was of particular interest to the organization since few resources existed within the institution to serve the needs of managers and employees dealing with the complexities of performance difficulties, in and of themselves. To have the EAP involved at the grassroots of manager development and training activities helped the organization identify and respond to a critical need. As a result of this initial program expansion beyond traditional EAP supervisory training and consultation, the EAP actually became the lead organizational resource and strategy for dealing with performance issues and providing consultative services to managers and supervisors; often well beyond the traditional employee assistance performance identification and employee referral framework.

As the program became more and more adept at responding to the unique needs of managers and supervisors in the workplace, opportunities for expanding the employee assistance service presented themselves. The program's initial supervisory training program became the basis for other training efforts within the institution. Many of the trainings involved the EAP itself and addressed the needs identified through the EAP's formal and ongoing assessment of the training interests of managers and employees.

With this initial expansion of the EAP's services, it became evident that the program was in a position to influence the organization on a number of levels. The integration process was underway on multiple levels. While the initial thrust was a programmatic integration of adding other workplace services to the employee assistance continuum of services, it was also an integration of the service further into the essential business and operational needs of the organization. The EAP and its employee assistance professionals were being viewed as larger contributors to the health, well-being and vitality of the organization, not just to the employees and managers who used its assessment and referral services. As the EAP interacted with and demonstrated its ability to serve the organization on dimensions other than those at the foundation of its initiation within the organization, it found itself on the receiving end of invitations to be part of a myriad of other organizational initiatives and activities, including a performance management design team, a rewards and recognition development team, and the organization's strategic planning team, to name a few. These invitations were pursued with earnest, resulting in the further leveraging of the service and its richer integration into the organization. Table 2 provides a listing of other organizational task forces, working groups, projects and initiatives in which EAP personnel have been involved and that have provided additional "integration opportunities" for the EAP.

THE CHALLENGES PRESENTED DURING INTEGRATION

It would be misleading to leave one with the impression that this road to integration is without its bumps and detours. With each opportunity for further integration, challenges and risks also emerge. Through the author's experiences with these two internal program planning, development, implementation and integration efforts, with two very distinct and different organizations, a number of challenges have become evident along the way.

Every EAP is challenged with the complexity of blending its service to the unique culture of its host or sponsoring organization (Herlihy, 1997; Dickens, 1999). Particularly when implementing a program within a "closed" organization (i.e., law enforcement, legislative agency), the culture of the organization often plays a critical role in the EA professional's ability to fully integrate the EAP into the organization. While understanding the culture of an organization is certainly a challenge, whether for an internal EAP or an external provider of EA services, it also presents opportunities for the EAP to capitalize on that very culture (Herlihy, 2000).

For instance, something as simple as the name that the EAP or employee assistance service goes by can imply a subtle or even more profound message throughout the organization. While many EA professionals have grown up using the "EAP" name and the concept of employee assistance as a "program," the reality in many organizations is

TABLE 2. Integration Opportunities

ORGANIZATIONAL TASK FORCES/ WORKING GROUPS	ORGANIZATION-WIDE PROJECTS/ INITIATIVES
Human Resources' Task Force	Organization's Employee Health & Wellness Fair–Project Lead
Personnel Policies Task Force	Literacy & GED Program–Project Lead
Performance Evaluation Process Improvement & System Development Team	New Employee Orientation Project–Team Participant and Facilitator
Rewards and Recognition Enhancement Team	Staff Recognition Project–Team Lead
Drug-free Workplace Development Task Force	Drug-free Workplace Training–Project Lead
Workplace Safety Task Force	Violence in the Workplace Response Initiative–Team Participant
Learning & Development Working Group	Organizational Training Consolidation Initiative–Team Participant
Competency-based Training Development and Facilitation Team	Training Evaluation Enhancement Project–Team Participant
Law Enforcement Leadership Development Team	Stress Management for Senior Police Executives Training Initiative–Project Lead and Training Facilitator
Human Resource/Payroll System Replacement Steering Committee	Organizational Web System Enablement Initiative–Team Participant and Human Resource Lead
Human Resource Business Process Improvement Team	Annual "State of the Organization" Presentation to Work Force–Development & Presentation Team Participant
Organizational Customer and Staff Satisfaction Survey Development & Implementation Teams	Human Resource Survey Response Implementation Initiative–Team Lead and Participant
Organizational Proposal Review & Contract Selection Teams	Emergency Response Support Initiative– Project Participant
Financial System Replacement Team	Business Unit Budget Development & Execution Initiative–Team Participant
Continuity of Business Development Team	Organization-wide Emergency Response Communications Activities–Team Lead
Emergency Preparedness & Response Team	Emergency Escape Hood Training Initiative–Training Facilitator
Critical Incident Response Development and Management Team	Critical Incident Response Policy Initiative– Team Lead
Organizational Transition Team	Career Transition & Outplacement Project–Team Lead
Strategic Planning, Development and Implementation Teams	Strategic and Operational Implementation Activities–Team Participant
Organizational Leadership Team	Leadership Team Development and Teambuilding–Team Facilitator

that "programs" are temporary entities within the organization with a set and often limited lifespan. Clearly, the concept of program may not always be in the best interest of further integrating the program into the organization. A better approach may be to align the employee assistance service in name with other valued and permanent operational and strategic entities within the organization. Specifically, if the organization and its personnel are used to dealing with "departments" or "sections," does the employee assistance service make a subtle case for inclusion and integration by using a similar moniker in its title. The author contends that "Office of Employee Assistance" implies an equal playing field within an organization that refers to all operational and strategic entities as the "Office of. . . ." Further validation is found from a colleague who has achieved a level of program integration within a law enforcement agency by not only better aligning the EAP within the vernacular of the organization chart, but by expanding the conceptual framework of the program's name to reflect its value-added role within the organization– "Office of Employee and Organization Development."

As indicated above, however, a name change alone does not assure a successful integration within the larger organization. An "EAP" that is viewed as a resource for individual employees and managers dealing with job performance issues does not transform itself into a dynamic organizational player contributing on multiple performance, operational and strategic dimensions through a mere change of its designation on the table of organization or within the company literature. A number of questions need to be asked. Does the name change reflect the service capabilities within the grasp of the EAP or the actual delivery of an expanded array of organizationally valued services? Does the name change place the EAP on the larger organizational or corporate playing field, providing a venue for demonstrating value beyond its current experience? Often the answers to these questions can only be ascertained through the evaluation of the integration process itself. The long-term longitudinal study that the author participated in with the New Jersey State Police EAP implementation and integration effort provides an excellent example of such an evaluation (Reichman & Beidel, 1989, 1994).

EVALUATING THE INTEGRATION PROCESS

The integration process is no doubt a complex one. There are a myriad of contributing factors to its success, many of which may in fact be outside the domain and control of the employee assistance service, but which nevertheless wield a heavy influence on the degree and extent to which the service is truly integrated into the organization. An employee assistance service looking strictly at utilization data as a measure of its effectiveness in the organization may in reality have overlooked some early programmatic and operational steps. Utilization rates do not reflect the service's real value to or reach within the organization. It was this realization that resulted in the author's initiation of and involvement in a longitudinal study of the "EAP implementation and integration process" within a state law enforcement agency.

The EAP had the benefit of a ten-year evaluation effort conducted initially by an outside EAP consulting firm, and later through a university graduate school program in organizational/industrial psychology. The diffusion, receptivity and utilization stages from the Beyer and Trice model were used as the conceptual framework to assess the service's movement from initiation to full integration into the organization (Beyer & Trice, 1978; Trice, Beyer & Hunt, 1978). The evaluation effort examined the implementation process from several dimensions:

1. the actual program promotional and service delivery activities being undertaken by the EAP to make inroads into the culture of the organization, to influence the attitudes of employees and managers on dimensions of relevance to support the EAP initiative, and to align the values of the organization with those of the EAP (Reichman & Beidel, 1989);
2. the specific role of the EAP's supervisory training process in overcoming barriers to supervisors making referrals to the EAP by changing managerial attitudes and behaviors (Googins & Kurtz, 1980; Hartog, Hickey, Reichman, & Gracin, 1993) and laying the groundwork for an examination of the potential influence of these changes beyond the interests of the EAP–assessing the impact of supervisory behavior on the larger performance of the organization, not just in managing the troubled employee or poor performer; and
3. the actual results and influence of the evaluation project itself in introducing a unique partnership of the EAP, the researcher, the police organization, and the bargaining unit, and assessing the role of this critical "collaboration on bringing innovative programs and procedures to a law enforcement organization" (Reichman & Beidel, 1994).

A critical part of this project was the initiation of an Advisory Committee to the EAP. Comprised of representatives of labor and management as well as the EAP and research team, the committee "was always the first group to receive the reports on the evaluation data and the researcher's recommendations for program modifications and initiatives" (Reichman & Beidel, 1994). The committee functioned on two distinct levels; first by providing critical input to the EAP on operational and administrative dynamics throughout the organization, and second by also serving as a conduit to the organization and its bargaining units on issues of critical importance to the EAP's implementation, integration and ultimate success. Much of this was due to the relevance of the research project design and its inclusion of issues of general importance to the organization, not simply the issues related to the EAP. The other critical factor was the ability of the research team to assimilate itself into the organization and, by proxy, to demonstrate the added value of the EAP beyond purely being viewed as a performance enhancement resource in the workplace. This latter issue illustrated in the following summation of this critical transition.

The relationship between the researcher and the EAP Advisory Committee evolved over the 10 years of the research project. Early on, the researcher and his assistants were viewed as outside consultants reporting to the committee on the results of their study of the EAP and the related issues to the organization. Over the course of the evaluations, the committee members came to view the researcher as a senior adviser to the committee, the EAP, and the organization itself. By the 6th and 7th years of the research project, the researcher had earned acceptance as an active and participating member of the committee. This evolution and transformation process was possible not only because of the longevity of the project but, more important, because of the researcher's ability to report his findings in a practical and empirical fashion rather than a judgmental one (Reichman & Beidel, 1994).

The EAP's alignment with a credible outside evaluation and eventual consultative resource enabled the program to demonstrate its ability to provide information and specific recommendations to the organization beyond "employee assistance" self-interest. For instance, the critical support for the law enforcement agency's development in the early 1980s of its inaugural critical incident stress response program (CISM) came about as a result of data gathered during the evaluation project's attitude and knowledge surveys. Although this author had formally proposed the initiation of the critical incident response program three years prior to its actual adoption, the recommendations made through the research project convinced the organization to implement the program. The resulting CISM policy and procedures also brought about significant changes to the investigative, operational and administrative procedures within the organization, ultimately changing the agency's fundamental response and management of personnel involved in critical incidents. Clearly, the EAP's initial proposal for the critical incident response program did not include or even anticipate some of the sweeping organizational changes that ultimately came about as a result of the effectiveness of the EAP evaluation project and its ability to uncover the critical expectations of the organization's personnel in this potential program development area.

FINDING OPPORTUNITIES FOR INTEGRATION

The opportunities for integration sometimes present themselves without much opportunity for dedicated planning and implementation development. At other times, the EAP needs to devise a specific plan and strategy for influencing the organization, whether in the traditional health, wellness and work/life related areas, or in the more traditional business and operational domains of the workplace. Historically, EAPs have been responsive to these types of situations and proactive in seizing such opportunities. The emergence of the employee assistance field itself and the integration of many of the initial internal programs in industry and labor came about as a result of a recognized need in the workplace to deal with alcoholic employees (Steele, 1989; Steele & Trice, 1995; Trice & Roman, 1978; Trice & Schronbrunn, 1981). Indeed, many of the field's pioneers took this opportunity to advance a rather straightforward process of supervisory constructive confrontation and job performance accountability to identify employees with problems, and to generate employee referrals to the EAP for assistance (Googins & Kurtz, 1980).

So, where do the opportunities exist today for this level of organizational integration? It can be argued that the traditional approach to integration has been to explore the EAP's interaction with human resources, wellness, health management, critical incident stress response, work/life, and safety and risk management. There are great illustrations in Part Two of Oher's *The Employee Assistance Handbook* (Oher, 1999) of how specific EAPs have blended effectively within these areas. Yet, it is this author's view that the greatest opportunity today is to look beyond these traditional partners and search for other avenues for further integration that potentially places the EAP at the decision-making and/or strategy tables in the organization. As Korman and Associates (1994) recount in their review of human dilemmas in the workplace, many of the situations present a myriad of opportunities for the EAP to serve as a critical change agent in and for the organization. This capability can only be realized and sustained by positioning the EAP as a part of the organization's guiding coalition in the fulfillment of its operational mission and as an equal partner with other organizational entities in driving toward the organization's strategic vision.

The key to identifying these opportunities is seeking out and aligning with other critical entities and partners within the organization. While it would be valuable to provide a checklist to serve as a guide in identifying the right opportunities and partners within the organization, the reality is that those determinations are specific to the organization and the EAP. They are contingent on the organization's business, its operational and developmental cycle, the organizational culture, the program model followed by the EAP, the existing relationship between the organization and its employee assistance service, to name a few. With that as a caveat, Table 3 provides a more detailed listing of possible organizational partners and functions that can provide the very opportunities for a more complete integration into the organization.

THE IMPACT OF 9/11

The experiences throughout the world's business community following the events of September 11, 2001, bear witness to the enhanced value that many organizations began to place on their EAPs. Certainly no organization or EAP anticipated the horrific events of that day and the resulting needs of their work forces and their organizations in the aftermath, but the reality was that many EAPs responded to the situation quickly and effectively. In the process, many EAPs re-positioned themselves in the eyes of the organizations they served. For some employee assistance services, their response to the events of 9/11 has placed them at the heart of the organization's continuity of business operations discussions and ongoing planning efforts. For others, it has elevated the EAP to being a valued discussant with leaders at the most senior levels of the organization as employers and employees alike prepare for the possibility of future events and their short- and long-term human capital, operational and strategic implications.

TABLE 3. Prospective Organizational Partners (Adapted in Part from "Organizational Entities or Functions for Partnership Consideration")

TRADITIONAL AND NON-TRADITIONAL PARTNERS AND FUNCTIONS	
Benefits	Labor Relations
Compensation/Payroll Administration	Marketing
Conflict Resolution/Mediation/Alternate Dispute Resolution	Medical/Occupational Health
Continuity of Business Operations	Operations
Corporate Change Management	Organizational Measures/Outcomes
Corporate Communications	Organizational/Workplace Diversity
Corporate Ethics Office	Outplacement
Corporate Ombuds Office	Professional/Career Development
Corporate Planning (Strategic)	Public/Media Relations
Drug-free Workplace/Drug Testing	Quality Control/Quality Assurance/Process Improvement
Equal Employment Opportunity/Affirmative Action/Compliance	Recruiting/Hiring/Selection
Emergency Preparedness/Response	Relocation/Expatriate Services
Employee Relations	Research and Development
Environmental Health/Safety	Retirement Planning
Family/Work-Life Programs	Risk Management
Finance/Comptroller	Security
Fitness-for-Duty	Training/Development
Human Resources	Wellness (Employee and Organization)
Legal/Corporate Counsel	Worker's Compensation/Disability Management

(Beidel, 1999, p. 109)

CONSULTATION SKILLS

Finding the right opportunities and the right partners necessitates that the EA professional possess and hone one of the essential core competencies of our profession–excellent consultative skills. The very skill that so many professionals use daily in their work with managers and employees around individual job performance issues translates to the larger organization as well, because no matter how one approaches the consultative process, it largely comes down to a one-on-one exchange, whether with the line supervisor or the chief executive officer. For the EA professional lacking these consultative skills, volunteering to participate in organizational working groups provides a rich environment to observe others within the organization who exhibit the very consultation skills desired. Similarly, seeking out a mentoring relationship with a more seasoned EA professional can provide the specific coaching one needs in this critical employee assistance competency.

KNOWLEDGE OF THE ORGANIZATION

In addition, the EA professional needs a solid and practical working knowledge of the organization he or she serves. For the internal EAP, there are several vehicles critical in gaining that knowledge and in serving as catalysts to open the doors of organizational integration. These can include: serving on task forces and initiative teams that are outside the routine domain of the EAP; participating as part of a larger organizational effort; participating in an executive coaching or mentoring program within the organization (Swihart & Thompson, 2002). These activities present opportunities for the EAP and EA professional to be viewed in a different, value-added light by other members of the organization. Both Tables 2 and 3 provide examples of these opportunities for integration that are also rich resources for information and knowledge about the organization.

TRAINING

It can be particularly helpful to position any training done by the EAP in the larger context of the organization's training effort. For instance, every training conducted by the EAP with the state law enforcement agency, mentioned earlier, was done through the auspices of the organization's training academy. Over a ten-year period, the EAP training moved from a separate "employee assistance supervisory training" session to a block of instruction in every training program taught at the academy. These trainings ranged from a line supervision course, through mid-level management training, to a senior leadership seminar on effective management and administration of a law enforcement agency. Similarly, within the legislative agency, the employee assistance training function is positioned as part of the larger training function in the organization, with many of the EA professionals regularly engaged in teaching a variety of courses beyond those traditionally conducted by an EAP. In many situations, the EA professional co-teaches the course with a professional from another operational entity in the organization, helping the EAP further integrate with other operations and exposing the EA professionals to other key organizational personnel, and vice versa.

ORGANIZATION CONTACTS AND GUIDES

As indicated above, the key to better integration of the EAP within the organization may be held by the entity or individual with whom the EAP partners in the organization. The EA professional who looks beyond human resources or the other logical partners to seek out advocates and fellow "integrators" can often gain a valuable perspective on the organization. Sometimes the most critical understandings of the organization can be gained by developing relationships with the organization's strategic planner, the director of organizational measurement, and the director of communications. These individuals can offer a perspective that strikes at the heart of where the organization is going, how it is doing along the way, and how it translates that message to its employees, customers and stake/stockholders. For an EAP interested in playing a larger part in the core business operations and functions of the organization, these three perspectives are very important.

In the author's experience, these kinds of partnerships have resulted in greater participation in many areas of the larger organization. For example, the EAP has found itself sitting at the strategic planning table on an annual basis and helping to determine the organization's strategic plan and vision. On another level, the EAP has participated in the design, implementation and analysis of the organization's fundamental operational measures, customer and staff satisfaction surveys, and the link of both to the organization's corporate scorecard and the individual employee's performance and productivity on the job. While still at another time, the EAP served as a major contributor to an organization-wide communication effort during a series of traumatic events that impacted the work force and the workplace over several months. One result from these kinds of integration efforts is that key aspects of EAP service delivery can be better aligned with other organizational functions. The follow-up process with employees, managers and the organization at large, and the internal marketing or promotion of the employee assistance service (Beidel, 1999, 1992) is two prime examples.

SOME TIPS FOR ORGANIZATIONAL INTEGRATION

While a checklist does not exist for making these determinations, some guidelines can be helpful. Partnerships struck today can quickly dissolve as personnel in key positions transition in and out of an organization. Having worked with a fairly stable work force in a law enforcement agency, and also a highly transitional legislative agency, the author has become keenly aware of the need to not limit one's time to cultivating exclusive relationships with the primary leads in those operations. Rather one needs to also identify potential secondary support personnel, back-ups or other interested parties. Interestingly, the latter can actually turn out to be the informal or hidden change agents in the organization. They may in a very indirect way have more success in driving organizational change or promoting and implementing initiatives within the organization. They are also frequently the individuals with their finger on the real pulse of the organization. So, an initial guideline is to identify the organization's change agents, both formal and informal, and study their respective approaches.

Another guideline is to look at the placement of the EAP within the organization. Frequently the EAP is housed within the human resources, medical or benefits department. As is evident in some of the current literature (Herlihy, Attridge & Turner, 2002), the work-life, wellness or managed behavioral healthcare partnerships may find the EAP positioned within those domains as well. Wherever the position, the EAP needs to look at whether it is the best alignment considering its goal of optimizing its integration in the organization. Again, this decision needs too be based on the individual organization and EAP. As human capital issues move more to center stage in some organizations, so to has the stock of the human resource department. So, for some EAPs that find themselves part of the human resource structure, this opportunity to be an integral part of the organization's discussions along with human resources may in fact offer the best and most dynamic placement for the service. For others, a closer alignment with the highest levels of the organization may be the most desirable location if the EAP is looking to be viewed as a critical player and strategic partner in guiding the organization and interfacing with the other critical organizational entities and operations. Often, however, the EAP is not in a position to advocate for such placement realignment unless it has already made critical integration inroads and demonstrated its value beyond the traditional assessment, referral, problem resolution and job performance consultation competencies. The question of where is the best alignment or organizational placement for the EAP can neither be answered in haste nor in a vacuum. This author's experience has found two very different organizational placements–both of which have contributed to significant integration within their respective organizations. As a direct administrative operation on an equal level with medical, personnel, planning and training in a law enforcement agency, and as an office under the Office of Human Resources within a legislative body, the EAP has found both integration opportunities and partnerships. The key guideline is that this ideal placement may only be determined over time, may result from the perspectives brought by other significant partners in the organization, and may not be a stagnant placement. In other words, as the organization changes over time, so too may the need for the organizational positioning of the EAP.

WITH OPPORTUNITY COMES RISK

As with most opportunities, potential risks are not far away. As important as the EA professional's consultative skills are, so too is the EA professional's business acumen and organizational savvy. The pursuit of the wrong initiative, at the wrong time, with the wrong partners can bring disastrous results for the EAP's organizational integration initiative. A critical part of any program integration effort, whether looking at the blending of the EAP with another workplace service or the fuller integration of the EAP as a strategic business or organizational partner, must be the EAP's capability to accurately assess and navigate the internal politics of the organization. And yes, every organization, no matter how large or small, is "political" to some extent. Some partnerships are best left undeveloped if the alignment calls into question the integrity, confidentiality and independence of the employee assistance service or any of the professionals employed therein. Similarly, involvement in an initiative that has all the appearances and perceptions within the organization as the managerial "flavor of the month" or the organizational issue "du jour" should probably give the EA professional pause to assess the potential risks along the way. The complexity of such assessments is that many of the most innovative changes in organizations are indeed perceived with some degree of skepticism and even resistance at the onset. Again, the lessons of our rich history of EAP development and implementation over the past fifty years attest to this reality; one need only read some of the accounts of those early days of the field's most legendary internal EAPs to find accounts of the barriers, resistance and erroneous perceptions of those early programmatic efforts (Steele, 1989; Steele & Trice, 1995; Trice & Roman, 1978; Trice & Schronbrunn, 1981). As indicated earlier, the experiences over the ten years of the New Jersey State Police EAP evaluation project bear specific witness to the receptivity barriers rooted in the attitudes, behaviors and perceptions of personnel in the organization (Reichman & Beidel, 1989; Hartog, Hickey, Reichman & Gracin, 1993; Reichman & Beidel, 1994). A solid risk assessment framework and risk management capability are critical necessities for the EAP to effectively manage through this decision process.

Additionally, the EAP must contend with several issues at the heart of its service delivery model and operational capabilities. Does the pursuit of integration initiatives dilute the EAP's delivery of core technology services? Additionally, in pursuing other initiatives or getting involved in organizational operations and strategic undertakings, does the EAP begin to take on appearances of "being all things to all people"? Each EAP must wrestle with these fundamental questions. While some in our field would argue that any pursuit of activities beyond the delivery of the EAP core technology (Roman & Blum, 1985) places the EAP at risk of losing its unique, value-based identity in the organization, others would postulate that the very expansion beyond the parameters of the core technology is essential to fully integrate the EAP into the organization and to seize those hidden opportunities to demonstrate value in a different light and through an expanded role. Whatever viewpoint one takes, the EAP is continually challenged with balancing the centrality of the EAP core technology with its true potential within the organization. Clearly, there is value in providing those core employee assistance functions (Attridge & Amaral, 2002). The challenge is maintaining their integrity in the pursuit of those other value-added and often larger organizational activities.

A current experience from the author's organization exemplifies this tension. With the EAP's involvement over the past few years in a number of the strategic planning efforts within the legislative organization, members of the EAP staff have been invited to sit on several leadership teams within the organization. These teams are responsible for both the strategic, operational, human capital and budgetary direction of the organization. The invitation reflects the regard with which the individuals and the EAP itself are viewed within the organization. The EAP, however, must balance this potential new level of engagement in the organization with a number of other issues germane to these challenges:

1. Does this new role cloud the EAP's function in the organization? In other words, will it be difficult for employees, managers and the organization's leadership to understand "what hat the EAP is wearing today"?
2. Does the new role present potential ethical issues, conflicts of interest and other additional complexities for the EAP in managing this emerging role at the highest decision-making level of the organization, when some of those decisions may, in fact, be grist for pursuit of assistance through the EAP by employees and managers in the organization? The EAP literature is limited in terms of guidance through the ethical minefield that these multiple roles may create, but clearly every EAP is well served if it adopts and follows a specific ethical framework for making such decisions. While almost any business ethics publication can provide such a framework, every EA professional would be well served to follow the ethical decision-making models presented by the Employee Assistance Professionals Association (Houston EAPA, 1996).
3. Are the skills of the EA professional staff adequately matched to the expanded role of the EAP? As evident in one discussion of the EAP and work/life interface (Davidson & Herlihy, 1999), this question cuts to the heart of any EAP's potential for fuller integration into an organization. Again, whether the EAP is integrating its services with those of a related workplace service or in pursuit of a fuller integration into the larger context of the organization, EA professionals must be assured that they are prepared with the requisite skills and competencies to take on the expanded role to which they aspire or to pursue the integrated tasks to which they ascend. To be anything less is a sure prescription for disaster.

THE MEASURE OF SUCCESS

The real measure of whether the EAP achieves its goal of full organizational integration must be assessed along multiple dimensions. Clearly the EAP's perspective and interests will vary from those of the organization as a whole. Many years ago, Walter Reichman, a personal and professional mentor and a true pioneer in employee assistance evaluation, taught this author two critical lessons that laid a philosophical foundation for an ongoing approach to employee assistance organizational integration. Lesson 1, when doing research or conducting an evaluation, never ask a question that you really do not want to know the answer to. And Lesson 2, even with the most effective EAP that may be reaching upwards of 8 or 10% utilization through its traditional assessment and referral services, is it not fair for the organization's leadership to ask, "what are you doing for the other 90 to 92% of the work force?" Both of these lessons continue to resonate with this author's continued drive for full EAP "organizational integration." While they have served as the unifying thread throughout this discussion of integration, they are lessons that are at the root of the author's professional efforts to blend the administration and evaluation of the EAP into a critical partnership, capable of further driving the EAP's integration into the organization.

While this volume offers other more qualified discussions of the measurement and evaluative dimensions of program integration, the EAP's ability to fully integrate itself into its host or sponsoring organization has implications on both of the above dimensions. The critical questions along this larger integration dynamic are whether the business or labor union actually sees the EAP as a potential critical strategic and operational partner; and whether the positioning of the EAP along these additional dimensions or in these expanded roles provides the opportunities for the EAP to demonstrate its value-added proposition by influencing the organization in a way that extends the reach of the service into those operational, strategic and human capital segments that our traditional utilization rates never reflect. These dynamics have the potential to change the entire spectrum of EAP evaluation and measurement efforts, while presenting another opportunity for the employee assistance field and the individual EAP to better align and integrate its very measurement processes with those of the business community (Amaral & Attridge, 2004; Attridge, Amaral, & Hyde, 2003; Attridge, Hyde & Amaral, 2003).

CONCLUSIONS

In the end, the critical question remains for each EAP and EA professional to define its own concept of program integration. As reflected throughout this discussion, this author's years within the internal EAP arena, initially within a state law enforcement organization and now a legislative agency, have resulted in a perspective in which integration means only one thing–how well positioned and integrated is the EAP into the fabric and culture of the organization. The essential role of the EAP is to manage itself to a position of influence and change within the organization. While many EAPs get off the ground by responding to the needs of the organization and the work force, the truly integrated EAP eventually gets to a position where it can actually change or mitigate some of those needs by influencing the organization at a more strategic and operational level. While this discussion does not offer a road map for realizing a successful organizational integration, it is my hope that the view offered from my internal side of the fence will provide encouragement and a bit of guidance for those with a similar "integration" mindset.

REFERENCES

Amaral, T. & Attridge, M. (2004, November). Communicating EAP business value: Successful strategies for measurement, reporting, and presentations. *Presented at Employee Assistance Professionals Association Annual Conference*, San Francisco, CA.

Attridge, M. & Amaral, T. (2002, October). Making the business case for EAPs with the core technology. *Presented at the Employee Assistance Professionals Association Annual Conference*, Boston, MA.

Attridge, M., Amaral, T.M., & Hyde, M. (2003). Completing the Business Case for EAPs. *Journal of Employee Assistance*, 33 (3), 23-25.

Attridge, M., Hyde, M., & Amaral, T. (2003, April). Making the business case for organizational assistance. *Presented at Employee Assistance Society of North America Annual Institute*, San Antonio, TX.

Beidel, B.E. (1992). Employee Assistance Programs: The Function of Follow-up. In L.J. Katz (Ed.), *Psychiatric Rehabilitation: A Handbook for Practitioners* (pp. 330-369). St. Louis: Warren H. Green, Inc.

Beidel, B.E. (1999). Internal Marketing Strategies to Maximize EAP Visibility and Effectiveness. In J.M. Oher (Ed.), *The Employee Assistance Handbook* (pp. 91-115). New York: John Wiley & Sons, Inc.

Beyer, J.M. & Trice, H.M. (1978). *Implementing Change: Alcoholism Policies in Work Organizations*. New York: Free Press.

Davidson, B.N. & Herlihy, P.A. (1999). The EAP and the Work-Life Connection. In J.M. Oher (Ed.), *The Employee Assistance Handbook* (pp. 405-419). New York: John Wiley & Sons, Inc.

Dickens, R.S. (1999). The Alignment of EAP and Business Unit Goals. In J.M. Oher (Ed.), *The Employee Assistance Handbook* (pp. 421-438). New York: John Wiley & Sons, Inc.

Ginsberg, M.R., Kilburg, R.R., & Gomes, P.G. (1999). Organizational Counseling and the Delivery of Integrated Human Services in the Workplace: An Evolving Model for Employee Assistance Theory and Practice. In J.M. Oher (Ed.), *The Employee Assistance Handbook* (pp. 439-456). New York: John Wiley & Sons, Inc.

Googins, B. & Kurtz, N. (1980). Factors Inhibiting Supervisory Referral to Occupational Alcoholism Intervention Programs. *Journal of Studies on Alcohol*, 41, 1196-1208.

Hartog, S.B., Hickey, D., Reichman, W., & Gracin, L. (1993). EAP Referral and the Supervisor: An Examination of Perceptions of Situational Constraints and Organizational Barriers. *Journal of Employee Assistance Research*, 2 (1), 47-63.

Herlihy, P. (1997). Employee Assistance Programs and Work/Family Programs: Obstacles and Opportunities for Organizational Integration. *Compensation and Benefits Management*, Spring 22-30.

Herlihy, P., Attridge, M., & Turner, S. (2002). The Integration of EAP and Work/Life Programs. *EAP Exchange*, 32 (1), 10-12.

Herlihy, P. & Davidson, B. (2000). Work/Life and Employee Assistance Programs: Collaboration or Consolidation. In Karol, R. *Work/Life Effectiveness*. CT: Kubu Communications.

Houston EAPA Chapter. (1996). *Ethical Dilemmas in Workplace Counseling: A Casebook*. Houston, TX: Employee Assistance Professionals Association.

Korman, A.K. & Associates (Eds.) (1994). *Human Dilemmas in Work Organizations: Strategies for Resolution*. New York: Guilford Press.

Masi, D. (1984). *Designing Employee Assistance Programs*. New York: American Management Associations.

Oher, J.M. (Ed.) (1999). *The Employee Assistance Handbook*. New York: John Wiley & Sons, Inc.

Presnall, L.F. (1981). *Occupational Counseling and Referral Systems*. Salt Lake City: Utah Alcoholism Foundation.

Reichman, W. & Beidel, B.E. (1989). Implementation of a State Police EAP. *Journal of Drug Issues*, 19 (3), 369-383.

Reichman, W. & Beidel, B.E. (1994).The Evaluation of an Employee Assistance Program as an Agent for Organizational Change. In A. K. Korman & Associates (Eds.), *Human Dilemmas in Work Organizations: Strategies for Resolution* (pp. 13-36). New York: Guilford Press.

Roman, P.M. & Blum, T.C. (1985). The Core Technology of Employee Assistance Programs. *ALMACAN*, March, 8-9, 16, 18-19.

Shain, M. & Groeneveld, J. (1980). *Employee-Assistance Programs: Philosophy, Theory, and Practice*. Lexington, MA: D.C. Heath and Company.

Steele, P. (1989). A History of Job-Based Alcoholism Programs–1955-1972. *Journal of Drug Issues*, Fall, 511-533.

Steele, P. & Trice, H. (1995). A History of Job-Based Alcoholism Programs: 1972-1980. *Journal of Drug Issues*, Spring, 397-417.

Swihart, D. & Thompson, D. (2002). Successful Program Integration: An Analysis of the Challenges and Opportunities Facing an EAP that Integrated with Other Programs Reveals the Keys to Successfully Servicing the Systemic Needs of Employees and Work Organizations. *EAPA Exchange*, Sept./Oct., 10-12.

Trice, H. & Roman, P. (1978). *Spirits and Demons at Work: Alcohol and Other Drugs on the Job* (Second Edition). Ithaca, NY: ILR Press.

Trice, H. & Schronbrunn, M. (1981). A History of Job-Based Alcoholism Programs: 1900-1955. *Journal of Drug Issues,* Spring, 171-198.

Trice, H.M., Beyer, J.M., & Hunt, R.E. (1978). Evaluating Implementation of a Job-Based Alcoholism Policy. *Journal of Studies on Alcohol,* 39 (3), 448-465.

Wrich, J.T. (1980). *The Employee Assistance Program–A Primer.* Troy, MI: Performance Resource Press, Inc.

Zimmerman, J.K. & Oher, J.M. (1999). From Management Consultation to Management Development. In J.M. Oher (Ed.), *The Employee Assistance Handbook* (pp. 457-477). New York: John Wiley & Sons, Inc.

Chapter 16

Integration of Occupational Health Services in the Federal Sector

Diane Stephenson
Mark Delowery

SUMMARY. Federal Occupational Health (FOH) is a federal sector model of the integration and collaboration of occupational health (OH) programs that includes on-site health clinics, and environmental health as well as EAP, work-life, and wellness/fitness programs. This article reviews several aspects of integration at various levels of this public health organization.

The broad objectives of occupational health programs are to promote, support, and provide a healthy and productive, highly functioning workforce to the employer. FOH staff has special expertise and knowledge related to federal procedures, regulations and agency culture, as well as the OH disciplines. With its mission to provide occupational health services to federal agencies and federal employees, FOH has the unique opportunity to provide integrated OH services, thereby providing a more comprehensive approach to the occupational health care of the individual employee, as well as a more comprehensive approach to the health and productivity efforts of the federal agencies.

Although we have made strides and engage in continuing efforts to promote integrated programs and care, a number of additional program enhancements are in discussion and/or in process. FOH is a unique entity

[Haworth co-indexing entry note]: "Integration of Occupational Health Services in the Federal Sector." Stephenson, Diane, and Mark Delowery. Co-published simultaneously in *Journal of Workplace Behavioral Health* (The Haworth Press, Inc.) Vol. 20, No. 3/4, 2005, pp. 307-323; and: *The Integration of Employee Assistance, Work/Life, and Wellness Services* (ed: Mark Attridge, Patricia A. Herlihy, and R. Paul Maiden) The Haworth Press, Inc., 2005, pp. 307-323. Single or multiple copies of this article are available for a fee from The Haworth Document Delivery Service [1-800-HAWORTH, 9:00 a.m. - 5:00 p.m. (EST). E-mail address: docdelivery@haworthpress.com].

Available online at http://www.haworthpress.com/web/JWBH
© 2005 by The Haworth Press, Inc. All rights reserved.
doi:10.1300/J490v20n03_06

and the largest provider of comprehensive OH services within the federal government. It has achieved some notable success with the integration of its services across various levels of the organization with different federal organizations. Efforts have been particularly successful in bringing a coordinated response to various crises and emergency situations. With increasing knowledge and data on the benefits of integration, FOH is working to reduce both internal and external organizational barriers to bring integration of services to their maximum potential. *[Article copies available for a fee from The Haworth Document Delivery Service: 1-800-HAWORTH. E-mail address: <docdelivery@haworthpress.com> Website: <http://www.HaworthPress.com> © 2005 by The Haworth Press, Inc. All rights reserved.]*

KEYWORDS. Occupational health, federal occupational health, health and productivity, integrated occupational health program

INTRODUCTION

Over the past few years, employee assistance program (EAP) and work-life researchers, program evaluators, and practitioners have published a number of articles and studies focusing on the integration of EAP and work-life programs, as well as EAP and wellness/health promotion programs (Herlihy, Attridge, Turner, 2002; Mulvihill, 2003; Erfurt, Foote, Heirich, 1992; Herlihy, 2002; Derr, Lindsay, 1999). Looking at the broader scope of occupational health (OH) programs that includes on-site health clinics, and environmental health as well as EAP, work-life, and wellness/fitness programs, provides an opportunity to analyze other models of integration. This article focuses on such a model in the federal sector, and reviews several aspects of integration at various levels of this public health organization.

The broad objectives of occupational health programs are to promote, support, and provide a healthy and productive, highly functioning workforce to the employer. Many employers offer a variety of occupational health programs, as well as employee benefits, in order to support that effort. Although it has been common practice to offer these programs for several decades, such programs may not be integrated either in evaluation of cost-benefit to the employer, in integration of care of the employee, or in administration of the occupational health programs within the organization. Offering integrated programs increases both the viability and the visibility of the individual programs and provides a more comprehensive approach to health and productivity management for the employer.

There has been a recent explosion of research addressing the quantification of employer costs for employees' mental and physical problems and risks. The *Journal of Occupational and Environmental Medicine* recently devoted a supplemental issue to the effects of disease on workplace activity. The research moves us significantly forward in our scientific understanding of the monetary impact of health issues in the workplace. Health and productivity management (HPM) literature and research over the past several years provides a structure that allows for the cost benefit analysis of intervention programs that could address any of the occupational health arenas, or a combination of occupational health programs. Offering an integrated OH program gives employers a unique opportunity to implement the workplace-based components of HPM to improve employee quality of life while promoting the organization's business objectives.

FEDERAL OCCUPATIONAL HEALTH MODEL– AN ORGANIZATION OFFERING A FULL RANGE OF OCCUPATIONAL HEALTH SERVICES

The U.S. Department of Health and Human Services (DHHS) has been charged with promoting the health and wellness of U.S. citizens and is engaged in two special initiatives, the HealthierUS presidential initiative and Steps to a Healthier US. A component of DHHS, the National Institute for Occupational Safety and Health (NIOSH), is the federal agency responsible for conducting research and making recommendations for the prevention of work-related injury and illness, and has unveiled the Steps to a Healthier US Workforce initiative to encourage workplace safety and health programs throughout all U.S. businesses. FOH Service, a unit within DHHS' Program Support Center and a component of the U.S. Public Health Service, is the DHHS agency responsible for encouraging and supplying workplace health and wellness programs within federal agencies for federal employees. FOH's mission is to work in partnership with its customers, that is, other federal agencies, to deliver comprehensive occupational health solutions that improve the health, safety, and productivity of the federal workforce. FOH's catalogue includes a broad array of clinical, wellness/fitness, employee assistance program (EAP), work/life, and environmental health (EH) services.

FOH is a unique entity within the federal government in that it is a fully reimbursable entity and receives no appropriations from Congress. This means that FOH essentially must cover its operating costs solely through its revenues, and must act like an entrepreneurial business within the government. Other federal agencies "contract" with FOH through interagency agreements to provide occupational health services and consultations. Agencies pay FOH as they would any other public or private organization. FOH must compete with the private sector for this government business and has nearly sixty years of experience providing these services exclusively to federal agencies. FOH is the largest provider of occupational health and safety services to the federal government, serving 377 federal departments and agencies, reaching more than 1.5 million federal employees, and generating over $150M in revenue in fiscal year 2004. FOH provides these services in major cities and towns all across the country as well as in some of the most remote corners of the United States and territories in the South Pacific. In addition, the organization's EAP and work-life services are available to federal employees and their families stationed in more than 100 countries overseas. The support and services FOH provides enable agencies to promote health, wellness, and safe work environments for their employees as well as maintain compliance with Occupational Safety and Health Administration (OSHA) and other federally mandated standards.

Organizationally, FOH has three primary lines of service or divisions: clinical services, employee assistance (e.g., workplace behavioral health), and environmental health. A brief summary of the functions and services of each can be found in Appendix A.

Integration at the Organizational Level

Prior to 1996, like many federal agencies, FOH was organized regionally, providing occupational health services through teams consisting of employee assistance, environmental health, clinical and wellness/fitness professionals. Although this model promoted integration of the different occupational health services for federal agencies within the regions, generally consisting of three to six states, it was not conducive to implementing, managing, and evaluating programs for federal agencies on a nationwide scale. To meet growing customer demand for nationwide program consistency and administration, FOH restructured and organized by product line and service, resulting in the current divisions: employee assistance, environmental health, and clinical services. This structure has enabled FOH to deliver standardized services at standardized prices across the country and was a key factor in its growth. Today, over two-thirds of its revenues are generated through national agreements with its customer agencies, with the remaining revenue derived through agreements with local, regional, or other agency components.

While organizing by product or service has had enormous benefits to FOH and its customers, avoiding the creation of silos between these units has been and continues to be a challenge. In order to address this, FOH has taken steps at several levels to reduce isolation and promote communication among lines of service. These include: formation of a standing advisory committee made up of representatives of each of the divisions to develop strategic planning, recommend policy changes, and review cross-service line issues; creation of a time-limited task force consisting of a large number of management and line staff from all segments of the agency to make recommendations on future organizational changes, focusing on integration and promotion of services; and interdisciplinary work groups designed to address specific needs, problems or issues. These interdisciplinary work groups have worked on such topics as HIPAA compliance, blood borne pathogen policy, guidelines for nurses on handling the inebriated employee, and an assessment tool for wellness/fitness coordinators to assist them in making appropriate referrals of clients to the EAP counselor. The decision to develop an integrated FOH-wide service tracking software system, enabling systematic tracking of accounts covering all lines of service, gives staff a concrete vehicle for the promotion of integrated agreements and care for our serviced agencies.

Also, FOH has maintained staff from each of the service lines in major regional cities. At these area offices, the employee assistance consultants, the nurse administrators, the environmental health managers, the wellness/fitness managers, and other FOH employees meet together regularly for staff meetings, hear updates about each other's projects, address local issues, and share ideas about how to further integrate programs to the benefit of the customer agency and its employees. This close physical proximity increases the frequency of both formal and informal "curbside consults," e.g., an EAP specialist consulting with a physician and a wellness/fitness specialist on an obesity management program. Staff from throughout FOH, from environmental health specialists and scientists, to physicians, nurses, psychologists, and social workers, are all available as resources on complex situations and on new program development and enhancement, both internally to each other as well as externally to our agency customers, providing enormous depth and breadth to the program, unique to organizations both inside and outside the government.

Spectrum of Agencies Served

FOH provides services to an unusually wide spectrum of federal agencies and their respective employees. Each is unique and differs in culture, structure, mission, occupations, and locations, and include the Department of Defense, Homeland Security, Housing and Urban Development, the U.S. Postal Service, the Bureau of Prisons, Defense Commissary Agency, Internal Revenue Service and the Bureau of Engraving and Printing–to name but a few. Employees served by one or more of FOH's occupational health programs include scientific researchers, mail carriers, animal and plant inspectors, law enforcement and security officers, nuclear waste transporters, administrative and management personnel, commissary staff, internal revenue agents, military personnel, and many, many more job titles. This list shows that the agencies FOH serves and their employees have specialized needs with unique health risks, ranging from constant lifting of heavy objects, to the stresses of law enforcement and security work, to working in isolated locations, to employment in traditional office settings.

Integration for Customer Agencies: Barriers and Benefits

Like most other entities in the public and private sectors, the majority of FOH's federal agency customers do not have all OH-related services neatly bundled in one seamless department. Different people and/or different organizational entities often manage employee health, workers' compensation, safety, EAP, work/life, fitness, and environmental health, depending on the size of the company or agency. Such services are commonly divided among health and safety, human resources, employee benefits or medical departments, and usually have separate funding. The decentralized nature of oversight for these programs within many agencies may severely inhibit efforts to completely integrate many services. Maneuvering through bureaucratic entanglements of procurement and program authority within the public sector may be a bigger barrier than in the private sector, where there is significantly more flexibility and autonomy by companies to organize in ways that achieve maximum efficiency. However, administration and management of occupational health programs is often spread among different departments in the private sector as well.

Of the 377 federal agencies that contract with FOH for OH services, 46% purchase services from more than one product line, even though the same person may not manage them. The breakdown of percentage of customers by product area is as follows:

Clinical Only	160	(42%)
EAP Only	39	(10%)
EH Only	6	(2%)
Clinical and EAP	85	(23%)
Clinical and EH	35	(9%)
EH and EAP	3	(1%)
Clinical, EH and EAP	49	(13%)

With such a broad menu of services available to them, agencies have options to mix and match in an almost infinite variety of combinations. FOH has anecdotal confirmation from customers of the benefits to employers of having OH services provided by the same entity, including: centralized promotion, easier cross referrals between services, better handling of emergency situations, economies of scale resulting from reduced administrative efforts and improved contract efficiency, as well as increased employee health and productivity through coordinated, integrated health interventions.

Integration at the Point of Service– Clinical and EAP Services

With over 265 occupational health clinics, 35 wellness/fitness centers and 215 on-site counselors, there are many models and opportunities for integration. In some cases, nurses, employee assistance counselors, wellness/fitness coordinators, and other occupational health staff may be dedicated to and located at the same site within one agency. At some locations, FOH OH staff may serve employees from multiple agencies. However, because agencies may choose only one of FOH's offerings from our catalog of occupational health services, the EAP counselor may provide services to a different or overlapping set of clients than the occupational health nurse. Therefore, some models/sites are more conducive to integration of services than others.

We identified 16 sites where the occupational health nurse and the EAP counselor are co-located in the same office suite and took a closer look at their interaction. Discussions with occupational health nurses, EAP counselors, and managers indicate that there are several perceived benefits to both employees and managers when the counselors and nurses share the same office suite. The most commonly cited was the added convenience and improved sense of confidentiality for employees seeking services, noting there may be less of a stigma associated with being seen going to a health unit where a counselor may be located vs. going to a designated EAP office. There also was a sense of better coordination of care and earlier detection of co-morbidities, such as stress and hypertension, smoking cessation and substance abuse, and chronic illness and depression, which theoretically would lead to better outcomes. However, there is no data yet to support these observations. Additionally, staff believed there were increased referrals and increased utilization of services, but again further collection and analysis of data would be necessary to confirm this.

Interestingly, feedback from staff was not uniformly positive from sites where counselors and health unit staff share space. Some noted specific negatives. For example, although an EAP client may feel less conspicuous going into a workplace health clinic, it could also be more likely that the client would be seen there by other employees who have come to an appointment with the nurse. Also, although a good relationship between the EAP counselor and the occupational health nurse can result in optimizing coordination of care, conversely, a poor working relationship due to space issues, misunderstandings about roles and responsibilities, or personality clashes could result in dissention that could be evident to clients, employees, and even agency management. Clearly, these can be significant challenges to achieving the full benefits of integration.

EVALUATION OF SERVICES

Customer Satisfaction

As a reimbursable agency that must compete for its business, FOH has become a customer-driven organization, measuring customer satisfaction for several years. Among several methods FOH employs to evaluate client satisfaction are surveys conducted at two levels: at the agency level from agency managers who purchase the services and at the end-user level from employees who actually receive counseling or health services. The agency manager satisfaction surveys are coordinated across divisions at the national level to eliminate redundant questionnaires among common customers and improve data collection and comparison by utilizing the same questions. The end user level surveys, however, are conducted within the respective program area (e.g., EAP, clinical, environmental), tailoring questions unique to their services.

The clinical services end-user surveys measure satisfaction on a five-point scale on ten variables such as promptness, flexibility, professionalism, privacy and thoroughness and are offered to each client at the end of each encounter (e.g., walk-in care, examinations, immunizations, etc.). Data are collected in a central location and reported monthly to senior managers. Results have consistently indicated high levels of satisfaction on these variables for seven years, with average overall satisfaction rated 98% (4.9 out of 5) for the last three years. In a separate analysis of the most recent year's data, there were no significant differences on individual variables or on overall satisfaction of services with those sites where clinical and EAP staffs are co-located compared with the averages of all sites combined (Table 1).

EMPLOYEE ASSISTANCE PROGRAM CUSTOMER SATISFACTION SURVEY RESULTS

EAP end-user client satisfaction is obtained through several means, including a client satisfaction survey given to every user of EAP coun-

TABLE 1. Clinical Customer Satisfaction Survey Results: All Sites vs. Those Co-Located with EAP Services, 10/1/03-9/13/04

The following average scores are based on a 5-point scale, with 5 indicating the highest score.

Variable	All Sites n = 9628	Co-Located n = 895
Flexibility in scheduling	4.80	4.79
Prompt attention upon arrival	4.88	4.87
Courteousness of staff	4.93	4.94
Explanation of procedure	4.86	4.85
Thoroughness of service	4.90	4.88
Privacy/confidentiality of environment	4.81	4.81
Explanation of results/answer questions	4.88	4.84
Clarity on follow-up actions to take	4.86	4.88
Helpfulness of education/information	4.80	4.85
Overall helpfulness of our services	4.90	4.90

seling services. Questions cover many of the same criteria as the clinical survey: timeliness and accessibility of service, the provider's courtesy, knowledge and responsiveness, perceived benefits of the counseling, and overall satisfaction with the service received. Satisfaction ratings are historically in the 97% to 99% range. We have not yet had the opportunity to evaluate EAP client customer (end-user) satisfaction by co-location with health clinic. This would be useful data to compare against the health clinic end-user satisfaction data cited above.

SELECTED CLIENT OUTCOMES

Employee Assistance Program

Although we do not yet have client outcome data for all of our lines of service, over a period of three years, FOH staff collected and analyzed data from nearly 60,000 EAP clients who utilized their EAP services (Selvik, Stephenson, Plaza, Sugden, 2004).

FOH obtained information that measured six areas of functioning: (1) Productivity affected by mental health; (2) Productivity affected by physical health; (3) Work and social relationships; (4) General health status; (5) Absenteeism from work or tardiness; and (6) Global Assessment of Functioning (GAF). Both clients and their counselors contributed information about functioning and level of activity. EAP clients were asked to complete questionnaires before utilizing EAP services and upon completion of EAP counseling services, while counselors used the GAF scale, a diagnostic measure of psychosocial functioning. Based on the pre- and post-EAP questionnaires, FOH found that clients who used the EAP experienced significant improvements in all six areas of functioning.

The key findings of the study show that use of the EAP had the following effects, which strongly support the health and productivity benefits of the FOH EAP:

- Unplanned absences and tardiness from work decreased by an average of 1.5 days per EAP client.
- Counselors' clinical assessment of the clients' general psychosocial functioning (based on the GAF) rose an average of 10 percent.
- People reporting a great amount of difficulty accomplishing their daily work due to emotional problems (e.g., presenteeism) before

using the FOH EAP counseling services showed a 73% improvement in productivity after counseling.

- Persons reporting that their perception of their health status was fair or poor before using FOH EAP counseling services showed a 31% improvement in health perception after counseling.

Conducting a comparable end-user pre/post service survey is less meaningful in the health unit setting, since employees often use the health clinic for discrete services such as a blood pressure check. Such health and productivity data is better obtained through organization-wide health and productivity questionnaires.

Smoking Cessation

Although soon to be eclipsed by obesity, smoking is still the leading cause of preventable death and disability in the United States. It is estimated that annual U.S. deaths from tobacco-related causes exceeds 430,000 and costs to employers for medical treatment, early death and disability, lost work time, and decreased productivity are staggering.

In 2002, FOH inaugurated a smoking cessation (SC) program that provided participants an intake interview, a personalized, written quit plan, a four-week supply of nicotine replacement therapy (NRT) of patches, gum or lozenges and follow-up counseling, support, and problem-solving assistance. The programs are fully funded by the employing agency and the participant has no out-of-pocket expenses to enroll. Participants must simply agree to an intake interview and work with the interviewer to formulate a written quit plan. The intake interview covers smoking history and past quit attempts. Following the interview, the participant selects which NRT to use. Support from FOH after the interview varies by availability and interest on the part of the interviewer and the participant. There is no predetermined number of contacts the participant must make with FOH staff. Approximately 95% of participants enrolled in the SC program are served by face-to-face contact with an FOH nurse; the remainder are served by phone contact only.

Since its inception, FOH has enrolled approximately 6,000 employees and has helped over 1,000 federal employees stop smoking. Throughout this time, smoking cessation rates have remained steady between 17-18%, more than double the national average of 5-10% estimated by the Centers for Disease Control and Prevention (CDC) for unassisted individual cessation efforts. There is no significant difference found in the cessation rates for the two contact methods (e.g., face-to-face or telephonic).

Stop smoking statistics are collected through phone calls and are self-reported. No biological testing to verify status is performed. To be qualified as a cessation, the participant must not be smoking cigarettes at all at 6 or more months from the initial start of the cessation effort. FOH attempts to contact all participants, but in excess of 20% of participants are lost to contact because they are seasonal or temporary employees. Failure to reach a participant is counted as an "unsuccessful" attempt. Although we gather statistics on those who reduce cigarette consumption, this group is also counted as "unsuccessful" for cessation statistics.

SPECIFIC EXAMPLES OF INTEGRATION EFFORTS

Smoking Cessation and EAP

In training interviewers for the SC program, FOH suggests that at least 50% of participants should be referred for voluntary EAP support to address co-morbidity factors such as alcohol abuse, poor stress coping skills, other substance abuse issues and various unaddressed mental health components identified during the interview process.

Because the majority of participants in the SC program work at locations where an EAP counselor is available onsite during the workweek, FOH has a good mechanism for feedback from these EAP counselors related to the numbers of voluntary referrals that actually contact EAP for follow-up. Unfortunately, over the past 3 years we have found that such self-referral simply does not happen. Of hundreds of suggested EAP referrals only a few have reported follow-up.

To better integrate EAP with smoking cessation, FOH is planning to pilot a proactive phone contact from an EAP counselor when the participant consents to such contact at the time of their intake interview. The rationale for this approach is that long-term success at smoking cessation is expected to be enhanced if co-morbid factors are appropriately addressed. Even if cessation rates are not affected, there are still potential significant benefits these individuals and their employers can reap from positive behavior changes related to these co-morbidities. Such EAP use also enhances EAP utilization, and increases the value-added benefit of the EAP to both the employee and employer.

Integration During Response to Crises

There have been many outstanding examples of coordination and integration of services in FOH across product lines in response to crises in recent years. The bombing of the Murrah Federal Building in Oklahoma City in 1995 and the attacks and collapse of the World Trade Center Towers on September 11, 2001, provided FOH an unfortunate opportunity to mobilize its substantial resources to meet the complex needs of the many federal agencies who were impacted by these disasters and/or involved in the subsequent clean-up efforts. In both cases, FOH provided health care, counseling and respiratory protection to employees of federal agencies that were responsible for emergency response and investigation, such as Federal Emergency Management Administration (FEMA), Federal Bureau of Investigation (FBI), and Alcohol, Tobacco and Firearms (ATF)–utilizing skills and expertise of each area of FOH. Medical monitoring and follow-up counseling are still being conducted today with many of these federal employees.

Similarly, during the anthrax exposures at the Capitol and U.S. Postal facilities later in 2001, FOH provided critical assistance in exposure assessment, testing, antibiotic prophylaxis, management consultation, and counseling to thousands of postal and other federal workers who risked severe illness and death. During the evolution of the crisis, FOH developed and distributed to federal agencies a series of timely fact sheets that integrated medical information on the disease, appropriate safety precautions to take within the mail handling systems, guidance to agency leaders on managing during a time of crisis, and ways to manage employees' stress and emotional reactions during and after the crisis.

NEXT STEPS–PROGRAM ENHANCEMENTS

FOH staff has special expertise and knowledge related to federal procedures, regulations and agency culture, as well as the OH disciplines. With its mission to provide occupational health services to federal agencies and federal employees, FOH has the unique opportunity to provide integrated OH services, thereby providing a more comprehensive approach to the occupational health care of the individual employee, as well as a more comprehensive approach to the health and productivity efforts of the federal agencies. Although we have made strides and engage in continuing efforts to promote integrated programs and care, a number of additional program enhancements are in discussion and/or in process, including:

- Creating broader cross-product knowledge within FOH staff
- Gathering additional data to assess care and program integration, such as:
  - cross-referrals between lines of service, e.g., clinical and EAP, clinical and EH, wellness/fitness and EAP;
  - outcomes and satisfaction related to co-location of direct service
- Increasing integrated programs: smoking cessation and EAP (facilitated referrals); Lighten Up (weight management)
- Offering integrated health and productivity management consultation and program services
- Developing consistent sets of client satisfaction and outcomes measures usable across lines of service
- Continue refinement of formal, integrated plans and methods of response to emergencies and disasters, such as hurricanes, floods and terrorist attacks.

CONCLUSIONS

FOH is a unique entity and the largest provider of comprehensive OH services within the federal government. It has achieved some notable success with the integration of its services across various levels of the organization with different federal organizations. Efforts have been particularly successful in bringing a coordinated response to various crises and emergency situations. With increasing knowledge and data on the benefits of integration, FOH is working to reduce both internal and external organizational barriers to bring integration of services to their maximum potential.

REFERENCES

Derr, W.D. and Lindsay, G.M. (1999) EAP and wellness collaboration. In J.M. Oher, (Ed). *The Employee Assistance Handbook*, New York: John Wiley & Sons, 305-319.

Erfurt, J.C., Foote, A., and Heirich, M.A. (1992). Integrating employee assistance and wellness: Current and future core technologies of a mega-brush program. *Journal of Employee Assistance Research*, *1*, 1.

Herlihy, P.A. (Sept./Oct., 2000). EAPs and work/life programs: Different path, same purpose? *EAPA Exchange*, 24-26.

Herlihy, P.A., Attridge, M., and Turner, S.P. (Jan./Feb., 2002). The integration of employee assistance and work/life programs. *EAPA Exchange*, 10-12.

Mayne, T.J., Howard, K., and Brandt-Rauf, P.W. (June, 2004) Measuring and evaluating the effects of disease on workplace productivity. *Journal of Occupational and Environmental Medicine*, 46, 6 supplement, S1-S2.

Mulvihill, M. (4th Quarter, 2003). The definition and core practices of wellness. *Journal of Employee Assistance*, 13-15.

Selvik, R., Stephenson, D., Plaza, C., and Sugden, B. (2nd Quarter, 2004). EAP impact on work, relationship, and health outcomes. *Journal of Employee Assistance Research Report*, 18-22.

APPENDIX A
Federal Occupational Health Lines of Service

Organizationally, FOH has three primary lines of service: the clinical services, the employee assistance program services (i.e., workplace behavioral health), and the environmental health services.

Clinical Services

Basic Occupational Health Center Services are provided through FOH's 265 Health Centers located in or near federal buildings throughout the United States. Services include but are not limited to:

- Emergency response/walk-in care and first aid
- Physician-prescribed services such as blood pressure and glucose monitoring, and allergy shots
- Immunizations
- Health and wellness seminars and programs on topics such as stress reduction; good nutrition and weight management; reducing cholesterol levels; breast, prostate, colorectal and skin cancer awareness, etc.
- On-line health risk appraisals
- Health screening for: High blood pressure, diabetes, vision, tuberculosis, hearing, glaucoma
- Individual health counseling
- Outreach programs

Wellness/Fitness Services including:

- Design and development of customized wellness and fitness programs
- Fitness assessments and pre-participation screenings
- Design and presentation of wellness/fitness seminars on such topics as weight management, nutrition, and stress management
- Promotion of wellness/fitness programs

Additional offerings include:

- smoking cessation
- automated external defibrillator (AED) programs
- workplace drug deterrence programs and MRO services
- injury prevention and disability management services
- a wide variety of exams including periodic health, medical surveillance, pre-placement, return-to-work and fitness for duty
- Development and review of medical standards for law enforcement agencies

Employee Assistance Program Services (Workplace Behavioral Health)

EAP services are generally provided on a per-capita basis. Face-to-face counseling services are provided by licensed, professional counselors located in more than 200 counseling offices in federal buildings across the country as well as through a vast network of affiliate counselors in approximately 14,000 locations across the country and overseas.

The employee assistance program offers a comprehensive work-life program for federal employees. The program provides services both online and telephonically by trained work-life counselors.

EAP services include:

- 24/7 service center
- EAP Website
- Employee and supervisor orientations
- Critical Incident Stress Management (CISM) Services
- Consultation to supervisor and managers
- Financial and legal services
- Educational/health and wellness seminars

The EAP has also developed a set of specialized programs including:

- Organizational Development (OD) Programs to help organizations and their employees develop business, organizational and behavioral strategies to adapt to the rapidly changing workplace.
- Law Enforcement Assistance Program to provide specialized services to members of the federal law enforcement community.
- Alternative Dispute Resolution (ADR) Services

Environmental Health Services

FOH's nationwide network of environmental health and industrial hygiene specialists provides environmental, health and safety consultations and services to help federal managers establish and maintain safe, healthy and productive work environments and to comply with OSHA and Environmental Protection Agency (EPA) regulatory compliance mandates. Services provided within this Division include but are not limited to:

- Indoor air and water quality assessments to investigate and evaluate situations where building occupants experience health problems that may be linked to air or water quality
- Hazard assessments to identify physical, chemical, radiological and biological stressors
- Asbestos detection, monitoring and abatement services
- Ergonomics–related to routine office settings (e.g., chairs, computer placement) as well as to a full scope of workplace activities (e.g., lifting, climbing)

Chapter 17

Integrating Employee Assistance Services with Organization Development and Health Risk Management: The State Government of Minnesota

Stephen P. Birkland
Adib S. Birkland

SUMMARY. This article outlines a case in which the employee assistance program of a large, public-sector employer has worked with other service areas within the organization to minimize health care costs, reduce counterproductive behaviors, and increase organizational effectiveness. A model is presented that illustrates the rationale for the steps taken in the integration process. This is followed by a more detailed description of the action-research process experienced in the organization. *[Article copies available for a fee from The Haworth Document Delivery Service: 1-800- HAWORTH. E-mail address: <docdelivery@haworthpress.com> Website: <http://www.HaworthPress.com> © 2005 by The Haworth Press, Inc. All rights reserved.]*

KEYWORDS. EAP, integration, organizational, health care costs, productivity

---

[Haworth co-indexing entry note]: "Integrating Employee Assistance Services with Organization Development and Health Risk Management: The State Government of Minnesota." Birkland, Stephen P., and Adib S. Birkland. Co-published simultaneously in *Journal of Workplace Behavioral Health* (The Haworth Press, Inc.) Vol. 20, No. 3/4, 2005, pp. 325-350; and: *The Integration of Employee Assistance, Work/Life, and Wellness Services* (ed: Mark Attridge, Patricia A. Herlihy, R. and Paul Maiden) The Haworth Press, Inc., 2005, pp. 325-350. Single or multiple copies of this article are available for a fee from The Haworth Document Delivery Service [1-800-HAWORTH, 9:00 a.m. - 5:00 p.m. (EST). E-mail address: docdelivery@ haworthpress.com].

Available online at http://www.haworthpress.com/web/JWBH
© 2005 by The Haworth Press, Inc. All rights reserved.
doi:10.1300/J490v20n03_07

INTRODUCTION

Organizations of all sorts are struggling to cut costs, eliminate wastes, and create more productive work environments. In response, many Employee Assistance Programs (EAP) have emerged as integral, and even pivotal, to initiatives designed to integrate the various staff functions and external resources contributing to the achievement of these objectives. This article attempts to describe the action-research process of one organization in which the EAP is playing a central role in this integration of services. The organization is a large, public-sector employer (a state government with 52,000 employees). This integration process is part of several larger, ongoing initiatives aimed at improving productivity and efficiency and mitigating the costs associated with health problems and counterproductive behaviors.

After a brief description of this organization and the EAP, a model is presented that is being used to conceptualize possibilities for integration and to determine priorities for the process. The model delineates three primary areas for integration: Health care costs, counterproductive behaviors, and organizational effectiveness. Each of the three sections that follow the model attempts to report the rationale for and the steps taken in the integration, as well as lessons learned and current thinking about the process. The final portion of the article delineates future directions in this integration process such as the refinement of utility measurement efforts and the reduction of the range of counterproductive work behaviors.

HISTORY OF THE ORGANIZATION

Over the past three decades, in response to the goals of a series of "administrations" (management teams formed by a chief elected official), programs and practices were created by professionals in the fields of employee assistance, benefits, human resource management, health care, disability, training and development, and organization development to address the performance of the organization and mitigate the rising costs of employee health problems and counterproductive behavior. Additionally, continual attempts have been initiated to increase job satisfaction, organizational citizenship, and retention through team-building, training, workforce and succession planning and more. Before describing in detail the most recent steps in the evolution of the EAP, a brief history of this evolution may be useful.

This organization's EAP began, like many others in the United States in the mid-1970s, as a part of a federal government initiative to establish Occupational Alcoholism Programs with peer counselors and experts in substance abuse and addictions. By the late 1970s, a more broad-based EAP had evolved with an expanding staff including an occupational health nurse. By the late 1980s, the EAP began adding more formal organizational-effectiveness services to its ranges of professional technologies. Serving a widely dispersed employee population necessitated that the EAP, early on, add to its "internal" staff by contracting with "external" clinicians and clinics around the state. Further structural steps included the creation of formal position classifications for the counseling staff, the elimination of the nurse position and the increased collaboration with the newly established state Wellness Program.

During its first few decades of existence, the EAP developed wide support among politicians, administrators, and particularly the labor unions. Its benefit to the organization was rarely questioned and there was little or no demand for formally proving its utility. The internal staff and contracted external provider network were both expanded during the 1990s. In response to an internal drive to improve the quality of services, the EAP began collecting feedback on client satisfaction from a random sample each quarter and used the responses as a valuable element in annual strategic planning meetings. With the advent of personal computers, the EAP created and launched a comprehensive database. Since 1997 it has had the ability to generate more elaborate reports for state departments and agencies that benefit from EAP services and the ability to conduct more sophisticated analyses of its services and its impact. Still, like many other EAPs, success was measured by the number of clients (utilization/penetration rates) and anecdotal reports of client satisfaction from both managers and employees.

Additional developmental stages saw the intensification of organization development (OD) services in collaboration with other internal OD functions and a newly established state workplace mediation project. EAP staff also received initial Critical Incident Stress Management (CISM) training in 1990 and this led to the formation of several formal CISM teams in state departments whose employees had the highest risk of trauma in their work.

By 2000, the EAP began trying to measure the extent of the impact of assessed problems on each client's job performance and attendance. As this evolved, there were attempts to combine the results of the ongoing client satisfaction survey with responses to questions about impact on work.

In 2003, the EAP began to look for ways to better manage the network of contracted EAP clinical service providers around the state and decided to contract with one external EAP provider for all clinical services outside the metropolitan area where nearly half of the employees worked and resided. At the same time, the effects of a government budget crisis and subsequent downsizing efforts reached internal EAP staff and set in motion the departure of most internal EA professionals. This, in turn, prompted the parent department to contract with one external provider for EAP clinical services for all employees and their dependents–both inside and outside the metropolitan area.

The remaining internal EAP then consisted of two EA professionals who managed the relationship with the external provider and continued to provide EAP organizational services.

A DESCRIPTION OF THE MODEL

A model normally associated with studies of utility is used as a framework for describing the stages of development for this EAP. By elaborating on this model and overlaying it with a range of staff functions and programs presently in place to mitigate losses and increase productivity, it is believed that the reader will better understand the current directions and see the potential for even more integration and collaboration in the future.

Theoretical Orientation

The preliminary approach to the productivity of the workforce of the state government was based on the work of Huselid (1995), who provided evidence that High Performance Work Practices (including, for example, job design, high levels of employee training, information sharing, etc.) were related to the organization's performance. In addition to this, the approach was influenced by a number of studies indicating how employee assistance programs reduced withdrawal behaviors (e.g., Attridge, 1999, 2001) and the number of employees whose productivity was handicapped by chronic health issues (e.g., Stern, 1990). The distribution of productivity among this workforce was envisioned to graphically approximate a bell curve where about half of the employees were above average performers and half of them below (see Figure 1). The ideal distribution (or goal) was thought of as more negatively skewed with an increase in the mean level of productivity and fewer "poor" performers (see Figure 2). The integration of EAP services with other staff functions was expected to lead to this more desirable distribution through both an increase in High Performance Work Practices (Huselid, 1995) and a reduction in the proportion of the workforce impeded by untreated or improperly treated chronic health problems.

Construction of the Model

There are many ways to define utility (see Boudreau & Ramstad, 2003; Roth, Bobko, & Mabon, 2001), but here it was envisioned as illustrated in Figures 3 and 4. The productivity of a workforce is modeled as a curvilinear function. While utility is often thought of as linear (Guion, 1997; i.e., higher performers are more productive), this model assumes that this pattern does not hold consistent for the extreme ends of the function. For example, extremely low performers might be engaging in counterproductive work behaviors and actually cost the organization much more than they are producing. Conversely, extremely high performers are capable of producing far more than is invested in them. Thus, extremely low performers have highly negative net productivity (the cost to the organization of an employee beyond what he or

FIGURE 1. Current distribution of employee productivity.

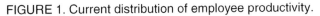

FIGURE 2. Ideal distribution of employee productivity.

FIGURE 3. Current average cost of employee assistance interventions and employee productivity.

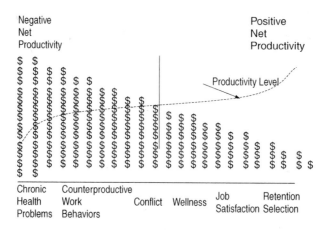

FIGURE 4. Goal average cost of employee assistance interventions and employee productivity.

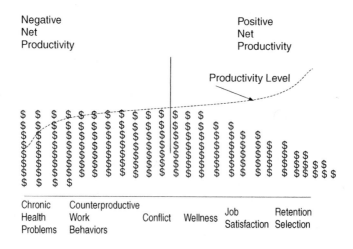

she contributes) while very high performers have highly positive net productivity (the benefit they bring to the organization beyond what is invested in them).

Next, this productivity function was superimposed onto a graph of costs related to services, behaviors, and interventions in this organization (the relative costs are demonstrated by the dollar signs). Those on the left side of Figure 3 are the most costly but possibly most preventable and easily measurable, while those toward the right may be less costly and related to interventions that increase positive performance behaviors. This figure demonstrates how the medical costs of chronic health problems, as well as the loss in productivity that is often associated with an afflicted worker, combine to result in a highly negative net productivity for that employee. A similar pattern can be observed for those workers engaging in counterproductive work behaviors and conflicts within the organization. However, as employees are healthier, satisfied, and performing better, their benefit to the organization increases to a point where the cost they bring to the organization (e.g., compensation, HR interventions) is recouped and their net productivity increases.

Figure 4 illustrates the goal for the net productivity of this workforce. It was assumed that a realistic aim was not to eliminate all chronic health problems among employees, but to effectively manage them and reduce their toll on the organization and its employees. This goal also applied to counterproductive work behaviors and conflict. Through effective management and collaboration between various staff functions, the influence that chronic health problems, counterproductivity, and conflict have on the lower ends of the productivity function can be mitigated and the above-described performance curve will become more negatively skewed (see Figure 2) as individuals are enabled to perform better.

With this brief description of the conceptual model, the reader can understand the current priorities for this EAP. First, especially in light of the increasingly limited resources, the evolution of the EAP is being driven by the current administration's overriding concern about the costs of healthcare and the least healthy employees. The second priority has been to focus attention on refining EAP services that help mitigate the negative impact of a range of counterproductive behaviors in the workplace. The third priority is to focus the unique skills and technologies of EA professionals on efforts to increase the effectiveness of managers and supervisors and help them create more productive and satisfying work environments. The integration initiatives and progress of each of these priorities or "fronts" will now be discussed along with expanded rationale for each priority.

Health Care Costs

The intensity of efforts to integrate EAP with services rendered by the health care providers is a consequence of the crisis resulting from the rising costs of health care. The reader is no doubt aware of numerous articles and studies documenting this crisis (e.g., Ferman, 2003; Kennedy, 1992; Simmons, 1998). The organization in this case study reported that medical claims for employees and their dependents reached $400 million in 2003. As its Risk Management Division examined these rising costs closer they found the following:

- Approximately 20% of members (employees and their dependents) incur 80% of medical claims. This is typically called the Pareto Group.
- Average age of employees is 47 years. Older members (51+) cost nearly twice as much as younger members (21-50).
- Members with one or more high-cost disease states accounted for 69% of total annual health care claims in 2001, 70% in year 2002, and 71% in year 2003. These disease states included asthma, diabetes, hypertension, cholesterol, malignancies, cancer, severe heart conditions, and psychosocial conditions.
- Thirty-one point four percent of members had one or more high cost disease states in year 2001, 33.2% in year 2002, and 34.7% in year 2003.
- Psychosocial disease states were second only to hypertension and cholesterol as the highest cost disease states. The psychosocial conditions included depression, anxiety disorders, substance abuse and/or dependence, and psychosis.
- Regarding co-morbidity, members diagnosed as obese have 3 times the average cost.
- Members diagnosed with tobacco abuse have 2.7 times the average cost.
- Members with behavioral health diagnoses cost more than twice as much as an average member.
- Nearly 40% of people with a behavioral health diagnosis have no record of behavioral health service.
- The number of members who received a diagnosis of depression, but who had no record of treatment or filling of a prescription for antidepressant medication reached nearly 6,000 in 2003.
- The costs of general medical services for members who also have a behavioral health diagnosis increased 21% from 2002 to 2003.
- Antidepressants continue to be the top prescription drug group and cost the employer over $8.3 million in 2003.

Organizational Response to Costs

After observing this troubling pattern, this organization created the Health Risk Management program for the purpose of analyzing the risks that are impacting the costs of health care, workers' compensation and absenteeism for the state government and developing effective interventions to minimize those risks and gain improvements in employee health and productivity. The EAP formally became part of this program and the two internal EA professionals became part of the Health Risk Management team.

Initial steps included contracting for the services of a consultant who first helped analyze health claims data and the current model for delivery of health care and then promoted new integrated models with specific measurements for success. Next, a project manager was hired and initiated a series of activities to implement the recommendations of the consultant. These recommendations were to determine current processes, explore points of potential integration, develop an integrated model, and develop criteria for measuring success.

Goals

The immediate goals of this behavioral/medical integration project were to:

1. reduce health claims costs
2. eliminate duplication of services between benefit service areas
3. streamline processes
4. improve health outcomes and return to work potential of employees, and
5. strengthen EAP services and value

Challenges

The challenges were enormous due to the complexity of the issue and the existing structure and culture. Chief among the immediate obstacles and challenges were (1) limited staff and resources, (2) HIPAA (federal privacy regulations), (3) health plan structures–separate arms for medical and behavioral health, (4) programs serving employees operated in "silos," (5) multiple forms and different processes for programs serving same employees, and (6) employer reluctance to address "mental health" issues.

The initial steps taken by the EAP included the documentation of a process map showing the decisions the EAP would make from the first contact with an employee to the closure of a case (see Appendix A). Other staff functions, including workers compensation, disability, occupational health and safety, as well as each of the services (case and disease management and short- and long-term disability) of the health plan providers, documented a similar process map for their work. The maps were "overlaid" (see Figure 5; Attridge, 2003) and the project manager highlighted all the possible points of collaboration. Through a series of joint meetings all the protagonists agreed on the most critical points of collaboration and the legal work related to data privacy began. Concurrent with this process, workshops on case management and common "triggers" for referral were conducted to familiarize all the protagonists from the various professional fields with concepts and processes of managing the most costly disease states and making sure that these employees received the most appropriate, timely health services.

Data

Metrics and measurement are increasingly important elements of the health risk management integration process and, since the year 2000, the health plan providers for this organization have deposited health claims data and records into a central data warehouse managed by

FIGURE 5. Overlay of Attridge Model of the EAP Value Triad

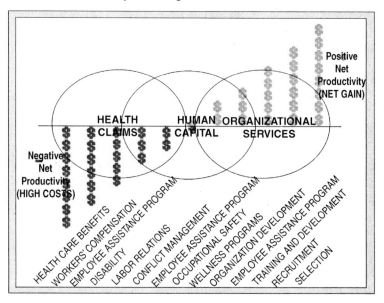

Deloitte. This data warehouse has made it possible to generate reports about patterns and trends related to the most costly disease states. Since 1997 the EAP has been depositing client data into a separate database designed to report utilization and the extent of the impact of personal problems of all types on work performance and attendance. Finally, the organization has a third database for all other employee information including their use of leave. This organization continues to distinguish between leave used for health and medical reasons and all other leave.

The task then has become how to integrate the data from all three databases for analyses and the action-research process. Without a "unique identifier" for each employee shared by all three databases it would be very costly to maintain the standards of confidentiality and combine information for reports. An agreement, in principle, was reached about a safe method of merging data and this set in motion the steps to obtain approval from the respective legal advisors and initiate the use of a unique identifier.

The primary challenges for the EAP was how to maintain the integrity of the initial assessment process–building a relationship with a client–while obtaining the unique identifier such as their health insurance provider number or employee I.D. number. This organization's EAP has not historically required such identifying information. Today, this data point is collected from all clients who are employees.

Specific EAP Response-Depression Awareness

Because of the documented costs of certain disease states, the EAP initiated a depression awareness project in 2001 to 2002 with the objective of screening more employees, referring more employees to the EAP, and educating supervisors and managers about how depression can manifest itself in the workplace. Briefly, hundreds of employees participated in training workshops delivered by EA professionals and/ or used the telephone and Web-based self-screening instruments. EAP utilization increased by 10% during this project. Follow-up and other measurements were not part of this project.

The EAP is planning the second phase of this project to be launched in the beginning of 2005. An important feature of this next phase of the EAPs Depression Awareness Project is the action-research approach and the use of target departments as pilots to try to more accurately measure the impact of this initiative on "sick leave." Another special feature is the increased collaboration with the health insurance providers and the State Department of Health.

Counterproductive Behavior and Withdrawal Costs

The second priority of this EAP is to refine its approach to helping the organization reduce and mitigate the impact of absenteeism and counterproductive behaviors. Currently the EAP is looking to academic research to refine its understanding of counterproductive behaviors and "withdrawal" or absenteeism. This section will briefly explore some of its findings and describe the ideas and constructs that have influenced the evolution of the EAP.

Performance

In order to explore a withdrawal from performance, it is important to have a clear idea of what this construct actually describes. One of the interesting processes that occur as a field develops is that constructs that everyone assumed were universally understood are better defined. Sometimes, the assumption of universal understanding results in a lack of research and subsequent confusion. This was the case with the construct of job performance (Campbell, Gasser, & Oswald, 1996). Though many people have a clear idea of what they believe job performance refers to, the constructs could relate to a host of behaviors. The last fifteen years have seen significant advances in the refinement of the definition of job performance (e.g., Borman & Motowidlo, 1993; Campbell et al., 1996; Organ, 1990).

Some of the more prominent efforts to behaviorally define job performance include Campbell, McCloy, Oppler, and Sager's eight factors (1993; as cited in Campbell et al., 1996), Borman and Motowidlo's task and contextual performance (1993), Organ's organizational citizenship behavior (1988), and counterproductive work behaviors (Sackett, 2002). According to the model used by this EAP, certain types of workplace behavior play a part in increasing an employee's net productivity through improving organizational effectiveness (e.g., job performance, task performance, and organizational citizenship behavior). Conversely, other types of performance contribute to more negative net productivity (e.g., counterproductive workplace behaviors). While improved clinical, organization, and health care services can all improve the first category of performance definitions, this section focuses on the latter–those definitions of performance that relate to behaviors that contribute to the additional cost of an employee–and means for their reduction. These costly types of performance are discussed in more detail below.

Counterproductive Work Behavior

Very broadly, counterproductive work behavior (CWB) is a term used to describe intentional actions on the part of an employee that oppose the intention of the organization (Sackett & DeVore, 2002). This could include anything from intentionally working slow to theft, from being absent for an unreasonable purpose to attacking coworkers and customers. CWB can be an aggressive, unprovoked attack on the organization or a reaction to some kind of perceived injustice or unpleasantness (Cullen & Sackett, 2003). While an unprovoked attack on the organization or other individuals is very costly, this type of behavior is not very common. Somewhat more common are counterproductive withdrawal behaviors, misuse of organizational resources, intentionally poor work quality, inappropriate verbal actions, and substance abuse.

Work Withdrawal

In general, withdrawal behaviors refer to "behaviors dissatisfied individuals enact to avoid the work situation" (Hanisch & Hulin, 1990). These include lateness (when an employee arrives "after the scheduled starting time"; Adler & Golan, 1981), absenteeism ("the failure to report for scheduled work"; Johns, 2001) and turnover ("permanent removal, voluntary or involuntary, of an employee from the organization"; Koslowsky, Sagie, Krausz, & Singer, 1997). Even though not all types of withdrawal behavior would be considered avoidable or counterproductive by the above definition (i.e., they might not be an intentional act meant to oppose the organization), the primary concern here is with those that are. For example, a worker who is ill might engage in unavoidable absenteeism, but one whose absence is due to being upset, distracted, or living the previous day like it was the last night on Earth would be engaging in avoidable and/or counterproductive absenteeism (Dalton & Mesch, 1991).

These avoidable, counterproductive forms of withdrawal are quite costly to the organization. The results of a 2002 survey estimated that 15% of payrolls were spent on absenteeism alone (Gale, 2003). For even a medium-sized organization these costs could easily reach well into the millions of dollars per year. In one recent report from this state government, the EAP found that roughly 3% of the employees used 15% of the total sick leave for the year. This cost is only compounded by the loss of productivity and morale that accompanies not only one's own absenteeism, but the absence of a co-worker.

EVOLUTION OF EAP EFFORTS TO MITIGATE COUNTERPRODUCTIVE BEHAVIOR

From the very beginning of this EAP there was significant focus on helping managers and work units to better mitigate and manage counterproductive behavior. Each of the EA professionals on staff possessed well-developed capabilities to consult with managers and union representatives about dealing with the most troublesome and disruptive employees. Certain elements and perspectives came to be central to the success of these consultation services. They included (1) Viewing counterproductive behavior situations as systemic, (2) Framing troublesome attitudes and behaviors in job performance terms consistent with the labor contracts and the position descriptions, and (3) Understanding behavioral psychology and simple theories of motivation.

Another vital perspective that became part of this EAPs vision statement was the view that EAP consultation services must be viewed as successful only if they help build organizational capacity. Frequently managers looked to EA professional to simply solve the problems for them and EA professionals, all of whom came from helping professions, had to become skilled at avoiding this tempting, but dangerous invitation.

Not infrequently, the most troublesome counterproductive behavior situations involved formal disciplinary action and the involvement of the labor unions and the Labor Relations professionals. Through experience and close collaboration with these other entities, the EAP developed an informal policy that the involvement of EAP staff would be circumspect, and even quite restricted, during open investigations or an ongoing grievance process.

Efforts to Address Hostility in the Workplace

Since the early years of this EAP the organization has turned to it for help dealing with hostility and violence. The EAP services that evolved included initial assessments of dangerousness, referrals for "fitness for duty" evaluations, and even mediation as several EA professional on staff had received formal training in win/win mediation techniques. Two significant developments contributed to the evolution of these services. First, the State Legislature passed a bill that called for implementation and enforcement of a "zero tolerance" for violence policy in all state agencies. Second, the state government created a workplace mediation project with staff and trained mediators in many of the state agencies.

The role of the EAP then evolved to one of support of and referrals to the mediation project rather than providing direct mediation services. In addition the EAP provided regular training sessions for managers on the zero-tolerance policy and recommendations for making the work environments "low-risk for violence." These recommendations have led to the development, by the EAP, of formal workshops on civility and respect in the workplace. (Crisis invention services will be discussed in the next section.)

These consultation and training services, focused on managing the impact of counterproductive behaviors, no doubt contributed significantly to the positive reputation of this EAP during its first decades of existence.

Attempts to Measure Utility

The EAP has, for four years, asked employee-clients to share their perception of the whether or not their presenting problems has had a negative impact on their work performance and attendance. Data show that only 12% report no impact. However, for the 88% who answered affirmatively, they were then asked to rated the extent of the impact from "minimal" to "extreme." Recent data shows the following range of results to this negative workplace impact item:

    19% Extreme
    24% Heavy
    24% Moderate
    33% Minimum

EAP clients were also asked how their performance was impacted and offered a choice of four areas of their work: (1) attendance, (2) concentration, (3) work relationships, and (4) productivity. Quarterly and annual reports would then cross tabulate the level of impact for these self-report measurements with various assessed problems and other contributing factors–such as depressed mood, career and work environment problems and conflicts with one's supervisor. An example of these reports, from 2003, is presented in Table 1. As can be seen in Table 1, across these three problem areas, work attendance was negatively affected in about 30% of cases, concentration was impacted in over

60% of cases, work relationships were impacted in 30% to 55% of cases, and productivity was affected in about 40% of cases.

The EAP initially used client-satisfaction reports to demonstrate generally that EAP services were perceived by the users to be helpful in improving performance and attendance. Regularly, 94% to 100% of the respondents reported that EAP was helpful. However, there was no method by which specific clients (or the employer) could demonstrate the specific effectiveness of EAP services and there was no systematic follow-up to determine evidence of improvement over time.

After consultation with the current provider of EAP clinical services an approach has been initiated by which each client is asked to assess the impact of their personal issues on just attendance and productivity by completing a brief series of questions (see Appendix B). While no results have been compiled yet, the plan calls for EAP staff to conduct a three-month telephone follow-up to obtain a self-report assessment of the client's attendance and productivity. The collection of this data will allow the EAP to generate reports from its database and correlate these with reports from the employer's database containing attendance data. Finally, the EAP has also begun consultation about the possibility of a Web-based follow-up assessment and a telephone recording follow-up assessment instrument.

The internal organizational services of the EAP focus nearly 60% of its resources on providing consultation for supervisors and managers and most of this consultation focuses on performance management and management of counterproductive behaviors. The EAP has initiated a

TABLE 1. Percent of EAP clients at initial assessment with self-rated negative impact on workplace performance by problem type.

Area of Workplace Performance	Problem Type		
	Depressed Mood	Career and Work Environment Problems	Conflicts with One's Supervisor
Attendance	36%	30%	30%
Concentration	66%	58%	60%
Productivity	49%	42%	44%
Work Relationships	41%	55%	30%

N = 2,100.

pilot study to try to measure the cost savings of these services. In the current study, EA professionals first try to determine the number of hours per week supervisors spend managing each of the most troublesome employees. This is then compared with the number of hours of EAP consultation and the time required by the supervisors by the same issue after the intervention.

ORGANIZATIONAL COSTS AND PRODUCTIVITY

Utility of These Interventions

A third priority for this EAP is the continual development of organizational services. While it is comparatively simple to measure the value of interventions related to healthcare integration or some organizational services, researchers have struggled for decades to find a way to measure the utility of other organizational services and clinical interventions (Roth et al., 2001). These are the interventions illustrated on the right side of Figures 3 and 4–those that aim to increase more positive performance behaviors (e.g., wellness, retention, and selection programs). This organization has defined the utility of these to be their marginal productivity–the difference between their cost and the productivity of individuals after the intervention. However, this raises the questions of how an economic value can be assigned to the productivity of workers and what it should be. In some jobs (e.g., production line worker) it might be possible to count a specific number of units produced and use this as a proxy for productivity, but in this organization a large proportion of workers are in jobs with less tangible output. Researchers have attempted to develop means for measuring productivity in these types of jobs too, but they all have drawbacks and there is still not a universally accepted technique (Roth et al., 2001). Currently, because of an inability to adequately measure productivity, this organization has turned to other indicators of the benefit of these interventions, as well as improving managerial reactions to them. For example, wellness, retention, and selection interventions may very well improve productivity, but it is easy to observe how they also improve job commitment, job and organization fit, and stress levels. All of these outcomes, in turn, reduce conflict, withdrawal, and even some health problems, which clearly demonstrate the utility of such interventions. Thus, it is possible to establish the effect they have on the organization's bottom line without providing evidence for their direct influence on productivity.

Another way that the value of an intervention might be shown (considering the absence of a universally agreed upon technique) is through managerial reactions. Some recent research has suggested that managerial reactions to interventions can be more important than mathematic demonstrations of utility (Latham & Whyte, 1994). In other words, it might not be important to clearly demonstrate increased productivity as long as managers perceive an improvement.

Evolution of EAP Organizational Services

This EAP's organizational services evolved out of the traditional EAP training for managers and supervisors and expanded as the EA professionals became increasingly involved with work units, initially facilitating meetings, consulting with management teams, mediating interpersonal conflicts, and offering training on broader topics related to wellness and success in the workplace. With a few EA professionals particularly interested and skilled in organization development (OD) the EAP took on more and more projects and developed a weekly staff meeting just to reflect on the OD efforts and refine the interventions.

After three or four years experience offering OD services, the EAP limited itself to interventions related to interpersonal conflict and managing change efforts, while a separate Management Analysis Division was established to focus on issues related to strategic planning, organizational design, and restructuring. During the past 12 years there has been accidental overlap with other internal staff functions including this Management Analysis Division. The relationships have been strained and distant at times and efforts to integrate services and build collaboration have often been fruitless. Progress in this integration process has been due mainly to the persistence of certain EA professionals who nurtured relationships with specific OD professionals and to the unique human behavior knowledge that EA professionals could bring to complex and dysfunctional work units.

The current budget crisis and subsequent layoffs have led to extraordinarily high levels of the stress among an employee population accustomed a greater sense of job security. The stress has also been exacerbated by new initiatives of the current administration to improve the organization's efficiency and change the culture from traditional "government bureaucracy" to a more flexible, innovative and responsive orientation.

In response, the internal EA professionals have been conducting regular workshops and presentations on the subject of change and transition. The workshops, often conducted in collaboration with human resource management teams, highlight the need to understand the impact of continual, and often dramatic, change on the employees. The training also includes recommendations for both the work groups and individual employees to help them build resilience and sturdiness.

This emphasis on resilience and sturdiness often includes discussions of "employability" and career development. This EAP has offered career counseling services since first becoming a "broad-brush" program, but this emphasis on feeling satisfied and successful in one's career has intensified in recent years probably due to many workplace changes and new (often younger and more diverse) employees with different values and ethics about work. Opportunities to collaborate with the workforce planning efforts by this organization are just beginning to appear.

As a state government whose chief executive officer (governor) changes regularly, the leadership of the various departments and agencies are also often in transition. In light of these politics and the constant changes due to state and federal legislation, the challenges to department heads, at any given time, can be extraordinary. The EAP has come to be regarded as an excellent internal, but objective, resource for many of these executive managers. Initially, the EAP was viewed simply as a coach, confidant, and consultant, but more recently the internal EA professionals have developed, in collaboration with departmental OD and training programs, specific leadership training for these managers and their respective teams. Some of these initiatives are described below.

Management Evaluation

One particularly successful initiative has been the development of a 270-degree self-evaluation for management teams. It is designed to help the members of a management team examine and refine their functioning based on ten capabilities of high-functioning management teams. This initiative has led to an expansion of the EAP's coaching services for managers.

Grief and Loss

As was noted above, this EAP had been involved in crisis intervention for workplace trauma and loss. The EAP had developed an extensive set of training materials on grief and loss along with the capacity to help work units where a loss had occurred. Special services were available to managers to help them restore the productivity following a traumatic loss.

Critical Incident Stress Management

When the first training for Critical Incident Stress Management (CISM) became available in the United States the entire staff of this EAP participated and became skilled at conducting debriefings. The EAP then worked closely with several state agencies where trauma and violence were greater risks in the workplace like correctional facilities, natural resources enforcement, and treatment centers. Formal debriefing teams consisting of peer "debriefers" and EA professionals were formed and this set in motion 14 years of ongoing development of crisis intervention services for these employee populations.

Training and Development

This EAP has collaborated, since its birth, with the training and development functions of state government. One notable collaboration has been the contributions that EA professionals have made to the development and delivery of modules of the "core training" required for all new supervisors and managers. This collaboration has recently became even closer when a completely new core-training program for managers was developed. The internal EA professionals developed and conduct nearly a third of the training sessions over four days.

Collaboration with internal and external OD consultants continues to be strengthened and it has become particularly valuable to the organization when OD efforts are challenged or even become stalled by dysfunctional interpersonal conflict and counterproductive behaviors.

Metrics currently being used to measure the contributions of this EAPs organizational services include the self-report client satisfaction surveys and the documentation of the number of hours that EA professionals spend on coaching, consultation, and training that is compared to the cost of contracting with external consultants for the same services.

LESSONS LEARNED AND FUTURE DIRECTIONS

The following is a summary of some of the lessons learned during the last few years of this ongoing integration process.

This EAP has benefited from EA professionals and managers who valued and nurtured an open system in which influences from multiple fields and functions (both within and outside the organization) could be incorporated into the discourse at each stage of the program's evolution. EA professionals were always eager to pursue new technologies and training opportunities and this pursuit became part of the EAP culture.

Progress in this integration process has also been largely due to the persistence of certain EA professionals who nurtured relationships with specific internal human resource management professionals. Additionally, the unique knowledge of human behavior that EA professionals brought to complex and dysfunctional work units served to ensure the advancement of the integration.

The evolution of integration efforts accelerated as more and more staff functions (workers' compensation, health plans, case and disease managers, disability insurance carriers, unions, training and development, disability, etc.) began to take responsibility for the effort. Several factors helped bring about this "ownership" by staff functions including the unambiguous support by the leadership of the organization, a skilled project manager, and a lengthy, but necessary, joint discourse.

The importance of good data about the specific employee population became more and more obvious as the discourse developed. As more data was collected and analyzed, the points of collaboration among the staff functions became clearer and the planning-action-evaluation process was enhanced.

More progress in the integration initiative was also observed when each protagonist had specific goals and expectations for their contribution (including deadlines). The project manager scheduled regular follow-up meetings with each of the staff functions to clarify expectations, encourage them, and monitor their progress. It must also be noted that the protagonists assigned more value to in-person consultation than to electronic correspondence.

Negotiating with health plans and providers requires clinical expertise and this integration effort benefited enormously from the knowledge and stature of the physician who served as consultant to the project.

With the exception of the consultant fees and costs of the complex data reports generated by Deloitte, this organization discovered that much of the integration process is "low cost." There is an expectation that the cost of time and staff resources initially required to execute the process would prove, in the long run, to be insignificant.

While the consent-approval process is very complex and seemed daunting at the beginning of the initiative, the superordinate goal of integration and better service for employees opened possibilities for solutions that were not initially considered.

The participation and support of information technology professionals, labor relations professionals, and labor union officials has been essential for the level of collaboration and integration be pursued in this organization.

Finally, it should be noted that the use of the term "action-research" in this case study might imply, for the reader, a more methodical and systematic approach than was actually experienced. The evolution of this EAP has been actually characterized by a more "far-from-equilibrium" state with unpredictable forces regularly causing course corrections and even driving decisions and priorities. An annual internal EAP review and discussion of "stakeholders" combined with regular staff reflection on the current strategies throughout each year has been vital to the continued evolution of the program.

Future Plans

The action-research approach ensures that there will be continual refinement and change as this EAP and its parent organization reflect on these efforts and attempts to measure their impact. The most immediate challenges involve defining metrics for a variety of staff functions and EAP services and strengthening the attitude of learning and the appreciation for the value of collaboration.

Integration with health care functions has clearly been a priority of this EAP due to the accessibility of health care metrics. Integration with other staff functions will no doubt accelerate, as measurement efforts are refined.

Workforce planning remains a frontier for collaboration. EAPs, as they become more sophisticated at gathering and analyzing data about the various employee populations, can contribute significantly to the efforts of organizations to plan for the future workforce. EAP data and experience may also become particularly valuable to those involved in recruitment and selection, functions that, based on this experience, help skew the curve toward positive net productivity.

REFERENCES

Adler, S., & Golan, J. (1981). Lateness as a withdrawal behavior. *Journal of Applied Psychology, 66*, 544-554.

Attridge, M. (1999, November). *Worksite trainings: A nationwide study of hot topics, evaluation and outcomes.* Paper presented at the annual conference of the Employee Assistance Professionals Association, Orlando, FL.

Attridge, M. (2001, August). *Personal and work outcomes of employee assistance services*. Paper presented at the meeting of the American Psychological Association, San Francisco, CA.

Attridge, M. (2003, November). *Making the business case for employee assistance programs: Annotated bibliography of key research studies*. Paper presented at the annual conference of the Employee Assistance Professionals Association, New Orleans, LA.

Borman, W. C., & Motowidlo, S. J. (1993). Task performance and contextual performance. In N. Schmitt & W. C. Borman (Eds.), *Personnel selection in organizations*. San Francisco: Jossey-Bass.

Boudreau, J. W., & Ramstad, P. M. (2003). Strategic industrial and organizational psychology and the role of utility analysis models. In I. B. Weiner (Series Ed.) & W. C. Borman, D. R. Ilgen, & R. J. Klimoski (Vol. Eds.), *Handbook of psychology: Vol. 12. Industrial and organizational psychology* (pp. 193-221). New York: Wiley.

Campbell, J. P., Gasser, M. B., & Oswald, F. L. (1996). The substantive nature of job performance variability. In K. R. Murphy (Ed.), *Individual differences and behavior in organizations*. San Francisco: Jossey-Bass.

Cullen, M. J., & Sackett, P. R. (2003). Personality and counterproductive workplace behavior. In. M. R. Barrick & A. M. Ryan (Eds.), *Personality and work: Reconsidering the role of personality in organizations*. San Francisco: Jossey-Bass.

Dealton, D., & Mesch, D. (1991). On the extent and reduction of avoidable absenteeism: An assessment of absence policy provisions. *Journal of Applied Psychology, 76*, 810-817.

Ferman, J. H. (2003). The rising cost of healthcare. *Healthcare Executive, 18* (2), 70-71.

Gale, S. F. (2003). Sickened by the cost of absenteeism, companies look for solutions. *Workforce Management, 82* (9), 72-73.

Guion, R. M. (1997). *Assessment, measurement, and prediction for personnel decisions*. Mahwah, New Jersey: Lawrence Erlbaum Associates.

Hanisch, K. A., & Hulin, C. L. (1990). Job attitudes and organizational withdrawal: An examination of retirement and other voluntary withdrawal behaviors. *Journal of Vocational Behavior, 37*, 60-78.

Huselid, M. A. (1995). The impact of human resource management practices on turnover, productivity, and corporate financial performance. *Academy of Management Journal, 38* (3), 635-672.

Johns, G. (2001). The psychology of lateness, absenteeism, and turnover. In N. Anderson, D. Ones, H. Sinangil, & C. Viswesvaran (Eds.), *Handbook of industrial, work, and organizational psychology* (Vol. 2, pp. 233-252). London: Sage.

Kennedy, B. J. (1992). Sick system demands commonsense remedies. *Management Review, 81* (7), 63.

Koslowsky, M., Sagie, A., Krausz, M., & Singer, A. (1997). Correlates of employee lateness: Some theoretical considerations. *Journal of Applied Psychology, 82*, 79-88.

Latham, G. P., & Whyte, G. (1994). The futility of utility analysis. *Personnel Psychology, 47*, 31-46.

Organ, D. W. (1988). *Organizational citizenship behavior: The good soldier syndrome*. Lexington, MA: Lexington Books.

Organ, D. W. (1990). The motivational basis of organizational citizenship behavior. *Research in Organizational Behavior, 12*, 43-72.

Roth, P. L., Bobko, P., & Mabon, H. (2001). Utility analysis: A review and analysis at the turn of the century. In N. Anderson, D. S. Ones, H. K. Sinangil, & C. Viswesvaran (Eds.), *Handbook of industrial, work and organizational psychology* (pp. 363-384). London: Sage.

Sackett, P. R. (2002). The structure of counterproductive work behaviors: Dimensionality and relationships with facets of job performance. *International Journal of Selection and Assessment, 10* (1/2), 5-11.

Sackett, P. R., & DeVore, C. J. (2002). Counterproductive behaviors at work. In N. Anderson, & D. S. Ones (Eds.), *Handbook of industrial, work and organizational psychology, Volume 1: Personnel psychology*. London: Sage.

Simmons, H. E. (1998). Lessons from the failed healthcare debate. *Healthcare Forum Journal, 41*(1), 46-51.

Stern, L. (1990). Why EAPs are worth the investment. *Business and Health*, May, 14-19.

APPENDIX A

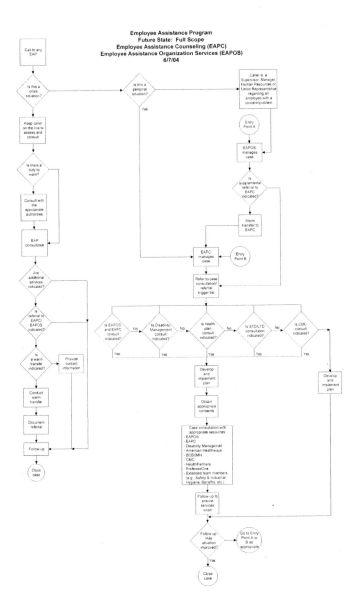

APPENDIX B

1. Do you think this situation has caused you to miss work?

    Yes/No

    How much sick leave, annual leave, or leave without pay do you estimate you miss per pay period (directly or indirectly related to this situation)? (Average since this situation developed)

    0---80 hours

2. Do you think this situation has affected your productivity (concentration, relationship with others, quantity)?

    Yes/No

    On a scale from 0 to 100, 100 being a very productive day for you, how would you estimate you current (average) productivity?

    0---100

Copyright 2004 by Stephen Birkland

INTERNATIONAL PERSPECTIVES OF INTEGRATION

Chapter 18

Australian Perspectives on the Organizational Integration of Employee Assistance Services

Andrea K. Kirk
David F. Brown

SUMMARY. This article considers the commonalities and differences between Australian EAPs and their counterparts in the United Kingdom and the U.S.A. The unique characteristics of Australian EAPs are examined, including an account of the approach taken to the integration of EAP services and other employee services such as work-life and wellness. Three case studies illustrate the forms of integration presently being explored in Australia. It is concluded that efforts to engage in the type of

[Haworth co-indexing entry note]: "Australian Perspectives on the Organizational Integration of Employee Assistance Services." Kirk, Andrea K., and David F. Brown. Co-published simultaneously in *Journal of Workplace Behavioral Health* (The Haworth Press, Inc.) Vol. 20, No. 3/4, 2005, pp. 351-366; and: *The Integration of Employee Assistance, Work/Life, and Wellness Services* (ed: Mark Attridge, Patricia A. Herlihy, and R. Paul Maiden) The Haworth Press, Inc., 2005, pp. 351-366. Single or multiple copies of this article are available for a fee from The Haworth Document Delivery Service [1-800-HAWORTH, 9:00 a.m. - 5:00 p.m. (EST). E-mail address: docdelivery@haworthpress.com].

Available online at http://www.haworthpress.com/web/JWBH
© 2005 by The Haworth Press, Inc. All rights reserved.
doi:10.1300/J490v20n03_08

351

"big picture" thinking characteristic of integration are apparent, even though there is little evidence of the type and degree of collaboration seen to be emerging in the U.S.A. *[Article copies available for a fee from The Haworth Document Delivery Service: 1-800-HAWORTH. E-mail address: <docdelivery@haworthpress.com> Website: <http://www.HaworthPress.com>* © 2005 by The Haworth Press, Inc. All rights reserved.]

KEYWORDS. Australian, EAP, work-life, wellness, integration

INTRODUCTION

Australian Employee Assistance Programs (EAPs) have certain commonalities with their counterparts in the United States and the United Kingdom. However, there are also marked differences in the way that Australian EAPs have evolved due to particular industrial and social influences. In order to provide an understanding of these influences a brief review of the history of Australian EAPs is presented. This includes an overview of the social and industrial trends that provide the context for the development in Australia of innovative HR practices such as EAPs, work-life, and wellness programs. While the focus is on Australian EAPs the arguments presented embrace the broader debate on the nature of organizational integration of EAPs with other employee services. Australian views on the organizational integration of EAPs are provided from both theoretical and empirical perspectives. The approach taken to the integration of EAPs with other employee services in Australia is illustrated using case studies. Conclusions are presented relating current practices and future trends in Australian EAPs to other employee services such as work-life and wellness programs.

INDUSTRIAL CLIMATE SURROUNDING THE DEVELOPMENT OF EAPs IN AUSTRALIA

The development of EAP provision in Australia has occurred within an industrial climate characterised by shifting demographic trends and by the efforts of both government and business bodies to address these issues. In a similar manner to other developed nations there have been considerable changes in the demographics of the Australian workforce over the past 30 years, with the current situation characterised by an increase in labour force participation by women, by dual earner families with dependent children, and by single parents, along with an increase in the number of hours worked by Australian employees (Bardoel et al., 2000; Australian Bureau of Statistics, 2000). These changes coupled with other demographic factors such as the aging population (Australian Bureau of Statistics, 2000) has meant that there are increased pressures on Australian workers to manage the demands of different life domains. Australian organizations have become increasingly aware of the need to develop and implement practices to facilitate the management of work-life issues by Australian employees and their families (Bardoel et al., 1999; Kramar, 1997; Spearritt and Edgar, 1994).

Early attempts by the Australian Government to address the issues arising from these demographic changes included the introduction of anti-discrimination legislation in 1975. Although this initiative was aimed specifically at issues facing women employees it was, at the time, the foundation of a number of more widely ranging legislative proposals addressing the needs of all employees facing the demands of balancing home and work (Strachan and Burgess, 1998; Spearritt and Edgar, 1994). A key body pushing for change in work practices in order to acknowledge these shifting demographics has been the Australian Council of Trade Unions, who in 1991 developed strategies aimed specifically at workers with family responsibilities (Strachan and Burgess, 1998). The Australian government's ratification of the ILO Convention 156 on Workers with Family Responsibilities in 1990 has ensured that employers cannot deny or terminate employment on the grounds of family responsibility (Spearritt and Edgar, 1994). There is now widespread agreement across all sectors of Australian industry that matters such as the management of life-cycle issues requires serious attention, although the uptake of practices specifically designed to address these issues has been modest within the private sector (Bardoel et al., 1999; Bagwell, 1997).

EVOLUTION OF EMPLOYEE ASSISTANCE PROGRAMS IN AUSTRALIA

Historically, Australian EAPs have not been linked to health benefit structures as they have been in the U.S. Neither does Australia have the strong history of industrial welfare experienced in the UK. This has meant that Australian EAPs have developed a somewhat unique service-delivery model, grounded in local legislative and industrial influences. The evaluation of contextually embedded trends in HRM must take into consideration the impact of local workplace conditions (Zanko, 2003). Consequently, both general trends and factors specific to the Australian experience need to be addressed when considering the development of EAP practices.

The first EAP services in Australia were funded by the Australian government in 1977 and were designed specifically to target drug and alcohol abuse (Nankervis, Compton and McCarthy, 1996). The Australian Foundation on Alcohol and Drug Dependence funded industrial program coordinators to deliver these services in each of the states and territories (Roman, 1983). A distinguishing feature of Australian EAPs was the tripartite representation of Government, trade union movement, and peak employer organizations on Boards of Management of the funded providers (Keys-Young, 1993). An additional distinguishing feature was the early emphasis on self-referral as the main route of entry to EAP services. Throughout the 1980s EAP service providers expanded their service delivery models in order to cope with a wider range of personal and social problems faced by employees and their families (Buon and Compton, 1990). However, the early EAP services in Australia were not without their critics. An officer of the ACTU, for example, noted that EAPs "have gone from bible bashing fanatics warning against alcohol, to policy flashing executives offering in-depth programs for personal problems often in revolting work environments" (cited in Nankervis, Compton and McCarthy, 1996, p. 361). Government funding through drug and alcohol grants to EAP providers was withdrawn in 1993 as drug and alcohol issues were accounting for only a small number of referrals (Peters, 1997).

The 1990s witnessed the growth of EAPs in Australia as a significant vehicle for the provision of psychological services at both the individual and at the organizational level. Just prior to and during the 1990s private providers had entered the market in increasing numbers leading to the establishment of the Employee Assistance Professionals Association (EAPA) in 1987 and the Employee Assistance Professionals Association of Australia (EAPAA) in 1991. These are the two major professional bodies representing EAP providers and practitioners throughout Australia, although at the time of writing the two associations are reviewing options for consolidation. Although little research has been conducted on the current profile of EAPs in Australia, the data available suggests that individual level counselling represents the core activity for both internal and external programs (Kirk and Brown, 1999; Kirk and Brown, 2001).

AUSTRALIAN PERSPECTIVES ON THE ORGANIZATIONAL INTEGRATION OF EAP SERVICES

EAP researchers and practitioners have progressed from these early days and have frequently argued for the need for EAP counsellors to adopt an organizational orientation, and not to simply duplicate the services provided in mental health settings (Carroll, 1997; Cooper and Cartwright, 1994). In the U.S. it is argued that workplace changes, such as the aging of the workforce and globalisation, are driving a general movement toward the integration of related employee services including EAPs, work-life and wellness programs (Herlihy, 2000). Australia is encountering similar demographic, social and industrial changes, albeit within a different industrial context.

Many Australian EAP providers do view EAPs within a broader human resource context and have traditionally offered organization level interventions such as wellness programs as part of their package of services. This is understandable as to a great extent Australian EAPs have evolved from within the type of organizational counselling perspective described by Ginsberg, Kilburg and Gomes (1999) where the broader needs of organizational development are considered alongside the counselling requirements of individual employees. While EAP providers offer, to some extent, integrated services Australian organizations are still grappling with how to incorporate the strategic use of these services.

Conceptually integration may be viewed as occurring either across program providers, which requires appropriate mechanisms for managing inter-program roles and responsibilities, or within program provision whereby the EAP provider offers a more holistic package of services (Herlihy, 1997; Herlihy, Attridge and Turner, 2002; Swihart and Thompson, 2002). The defining feature of effective integration has been argued to be more than a matter of offering different services–these services should be characterised by administrative or other linkages (Lewis, 1991). It is about "big picture" thinking and appropriate links between specialized initiatives.

The two forms of integration most commonly referred to in the EAP literature (Herlihy et al., 2002; Swihart and Thompson, 2002) are evident in the Australian EAP experience. The first form, which comprises a range of employee services offered by the one EAP provider, is more commonly seen in medium-sized organizations, but is also historically the preferred form of service delivery by Australian providers. The second form, which consists of different program providers collaborating to deliver more integrated services, has been less evident, but has been seen predominantly in larger organizations and in the public sector. Part of the reason why EAPs have evolved as providers of integrated services is that Australia has a smaller number of organizations large enough to be able to resource internal programs such as wellness or work-life services. There has therefore been less evidence of the stand alone or 'silo' programs more commonly experienced in the U.S. Indeed the preponderance of SMEs within the Australian industry profile has been argued to have limited the uptake of strategic HR initiatives such as work-life programs in general, as such initiatives are less evident within this sector (Michelson and Kramar, 2003). These authors note that "Small organizations are less likely to use HRM than large organizations so it is not surprising that, in an economy like Australia's which is characterised by a large number of small firms and a smaller number of large firms, HRM is not consistently adopted" (p. 144). Thus, in the absence of dedicated HRM departments in SMEs the opportunity arises for the provision of integrated EAPs by external providers.

The degree of movement towards integration across providers of related employee services seen in the U.S. has not, however, been a prominent feature of the Australian EAP experience. Nonetheless, examples of diverse forms of integration can be found where Australian EAPs are facing similar challenges to those faced by their counterparts elsewhere. These changes include the transformation of HR division functioning and the expansion of related employee services such as work-life and wellness (Ginsberg et al., 1999). The following case studies are used to illustrate the forms of integration presently being explored in Australia.

AUSTRALIAN EXPERIENCES OF ORGANIZATIONAL INTEGRATION OF EAP SERVICES

The following three case studies provide examples of the forms integration has taken in the Australian context from the perspective of both EAP providers and client organizations. The first case is an example of the way that one particular EAP provider has extended and integrated its services with a client organization. The second case considers an organization that has developed a model of integration between the wellness programs offered by its human resource department and the services offered by its external EAP provider. The final case is an example of integration between health programs offered by external specialist providers and managed by the occupational health and safety department of the organization, and services offered by its external EAP provider. It has been noted that the practice of integration does not necessarily entail the various stakeholders offering different services, but that the range of services offered are characterised by administrative or other linkages between the organization, the EAP and other external specialist service providers (Lewis, 1991).

A CASE STUDY OF INTEGRATION DRIVEN BY AN EXTERNAL EAP PROVIDER

BSS Corporate Psychology Services is a well-established external EAP provider organization that has a large proportion of its work concentrated in the resources sector, including large mining corporations. This is a fairly conservative industry sector where moves to introduce practices such as employee assistance have largely been driven by safety and productivity-related concerns with industrial accidents being a precursor in some instances.

Bronwyn Simpson, Director of BSS, believes that the key to integration is moving an organization's thinking from purely reactive responses to current issues into more proactive forms of intervention. An example of this is BSS "Fitness for Work" program. In addition to its EAP the Fitness for Work program is provided by BSS to client organizations within a proactive-reactive continuum that addresses employee needs from a range of perspectives. Fitness for Work involves providing a three-stage package of services tailored to the organization's needs, commencing at the proactive level of assistance in policy development for the management of issues such as drug and alcohol use, shiftwork and fatigue. Following the first stage of policy development organizations are then offered the second stage of education and training programs to assist employees to self-manage potential problem development. These programs may involve stress management, drug and alcohol use, management of depression, or training for supervisors to identify emerging issues in the workplace. If it becomes apparent that the employee is not going to be able to 'self-manage' their particular issue (i.e., the employee's problem is impacting directly on their work performance) then a third stage case management process is implemented that involves the employee, their supervisor, the HR or OH&S manager, and the EAP provider. This process begins with an individual assessment and management plan, followed by recommendations for treatment and workplace management strategies.

BSS have accepted the challenge of increasing the awareness of organizations within the resource sector of the need to consider employee needs more broadly. That is, BSS is providing to client organizations proactive wellness programs in addition to its traditional focus on workplace counselling. Bronwyn considers that the resource sector in Australia is only just beginning to address wellness and work-life issues from a proactive position and sees the Fitness for Work program as a vehicle for promoting this awareness. BSS have witnessed within their client organizations a range of responsiveness to integrated service packages. This diversity in the recognition of the value of integrated services tends to reflect the reactive or proactive cultures of organizations in the resource sector. Bronwyn notes that work-life initiatives are still predominantly at the reactive level for many organization's, but that there is an emerging trend for organizations that BSS deal with to consider wellness and work-life initiatives as potentially value-added activities.

In this example integration is occurring through the external EAP provider designing their service delivery package in such a way that client organizations can take advantage of additional proactive services at the policy development and self-management stages of intervention. It is likely that additional wellness and work-life services will be added to the package over time. This example does not involve integration across program providers as the EAP has developed its integrated package of services to meet the specific industry sector requirements. However, this case does illustrate the way that one major provider in Australia is providing proactive programs in addition to its traditional EAP counselling roles that integrate with the organization's needs and add value to the employee. This case is an illustration of the way that an external service is providing and managing an external program delivered to a client organization. The following case, by comparison, is an example of how an external service provider works with the client organization that internally manages and delivers the program.

A CASE STUDY OF EAP INTEGRATION WITH A PRIVATE SECTOR HUMAN RESOURCE DEPARTMENT'S WELLNESS PROGRAM

The Flight Centre is Australia's largest retail travel group, with over 1,000 outlets and 6,500 employees in seven different countries. The company originated with the purchase by two Australians in the 1970s of an aging bus in the UK, which they used to offer budget double-decker bus trips across Africa and Asia. In 2003 the company reported pre-tax profits of AUS \$102 million. The company has twice won Hewitt Associates "Best Employer" award.

Michael Murphy, Future National Leader within the human resource PeopleWorks division reports that the introduction of their EAP just over two years ago was carefully managed in order to present the program as a proactive service aimed at improving employee well-being. In this context, the externally provided EAP is integrated as a part of their internally managed overall corporate health program. The Flight Centre has developed within its 'Healthwise' program a range of employee services managed from within their PeopleWorks division. The externally provided EAP was branded internally as the 'Guidance and Coaching Centre' to distinguish it from the other services provided such as dietary advice, quit smoking assistance, discount low-fat food and exercise equipment, massage, personal training, physiotherapy and injury management. The Flight Centre has gone to some lengths to ensure that employees do not perceive that the sole purpose of the EAP is to provide assistance with existing personal or work-related problems. Michael points out the Flight Centre has integrated the EAP service so that it interfaces with the Healthwise program and proactively supports the prevention and escalation of problems that employees may develop, particularly those related to stress. The company is presently expanding their Healthwise program to include work-life initiatives such as child-care assistance.

In this case service integration is occurring in the form of a package of employee services being managed through the company's human resource division. The externally provided EAP is promoted as an equally proactive and developmental opportunity for employees to seek assistance alongside the internally managed Healthwise program. According to Michael Murphy there are no specific mechanisms for linking the different services offered. Although program integration is the company strategy, Michael explains that the Flight Centre acknowledges the need to ensure a clear independence of the EAP counselling services from other Flight Centre wellness programs. The Flight Centre emphasises the importance of this independence in order to maintain employee perceptions, and the reality, of the confidentiality of the counselling service.

In this case a range of external providers are contracted by the company to provide wellness programs which operate alongside the externally provided EAP. A human resource division (PeopleWorks) of the company is responsible for managing the integration processes for delivering these services to employees. It is this division's responsibility to promote the services package as proactive and developmental. Integration is therefore most evident at the policy and management levels, with the company cautious about introducing linkages across providers due to concerns regarding confidentiality. This approach assumes several of the features of integration identified by Lewis (1991) who suggested that integration begins with the development of a common philosophy, theme and identity for the various programs offered and then progresses to various stages of implementation.

A CASE STUDY OF EAP INTEGRATION WITH HEALTH SERVICES ADMINISTERED BY THE OCCUPATIONAL HEALTH AND SAFETY OFFICER IN THE PUBLIC SECTOR

The two previous cases have illustrated different approaches to the integration of a range of wellness programs with an externally provided EAP. The first case was an example of the external provider of the EAP integrating wellness programs into its service package offered to the organization. The second example illustrated how a large organization integrated its externally provided EAP and a wellness program promoted and managed by its human resource division. The final case, when compared to the previous two, involves a much greater degree of integration between the external EAP and an internally managed wellness program.

Redlands Shire Council in South-East Queensland manages the public resources and utilities for a population of over 125,000 permanent residents spread across 539 square kilometres. The Council has just over 1,000 employees. Ross Aberfield is the Senior Occupational Health and Safety rehabilitation officer for the Council. Ross has a passion for promoting the health of employees and has arranged for a wide range of external services to be made available in the workplace or during work time for staff, either free of charge or at a minimal cost. These include a smoking cessation program, cardiovascular health tests, yoga classes, physiotherapy, bowel scan kits and influenza immunisations. These programs are well received by staff, with 600 taking advantage of the cardiovascular check and over 700 having skin cancer scans over the past year.

The EAP is viewed as an integral part of the wellness program. The monthly EAP reports received from the provider are used to track any organizational issues that may need attention. Carefully managed promotion of the EAP in conjunction with the other wellness initiatives is viewed by Ross as the key to achieving service integration. "At first" said Ross, "we aggressively promoted the EAP to employees, which resulted in them backing away. We now know that you have to ensure that employees have very easy access to promotional materials about the EAP, and that this occurs in conjunction with the other wellness programs." Staff in the occupational and safety department have worked with the EAP provider to design promotional materials that will appeal to the Council employees, and have regular briefing sessions with the different providers to discuss usage of the services. Ross pointed out that it is, of course, much easier to track the use of physiotherapy sessions that are booked through the occupational and safety department than those booked through the EAP. This again draws attention to the difficulty with managing integrated wellness services where one specialist counselling service such as the EAP requires and relies on complete confidentiality. There is, however, anecdotal evidence from employees that the wellness and EAP services are being successfully integrated. Ross described a recent case of one employee seeking physiotherapy for muscular strain who was then referred to the EAP counsellor who in turn was able to address the emotional stress underlying the physical condition. In this way, both the physical and psychological parameters of the condition could be successfully managed to the advantage of the employee.

In this case administrative linkages across different services are being managed internally by the organization, and are being driven by key personnel such as the occupational health and safety officer. The entire wellness program has been so successful that the Council are facing the necessity of providing additional resources to manage the program in order to cope with the increasing demands on the time of the occupational health and safety staff. Although of the three cases illustrated, this case demonstrates the greatest degree of integration between the organization's internal wellness program and the externally provided EAP, Ross was keen to point out that the need for complete confidentiality of the EAP would always put limits on the extent to which the EAP and other employee services could be integrated.

CONCLUSIONS FROM THE AUSTRALIAN EXPERIENCES OF ORGANIZATIONAL INTEGRATION OF EAP SERVICES

Each of the three examples contains elements of integration that appear to be providing the basis for more effective use of different employee service initiatives. Efforts to engage in "big picture" thinking (Lewis, 1991) are apparent, even though there is little evidence of the type and degree of collaboration among program such as EAPs and work/family seen to be emerging recently in the U.S. (Herlihy, 2000). It is interesting to note the caution expressed by both providers and client organizations over the potential of integration across programs to compromise the EAP's confidentiality. Having assurances of complete confidentiality is regarded by Australian human resource representatives as one of the key advantages of having an EAP (Kirk-Brown, 2003).

EAPs have become a firmly established part of the Australian industrial and organizational landscape, with the growth of EAP service provision expected to continue mirroring trends of increased usage in the UK and in the U.S. (Kirk and Brown, 2003; Sciegaj et al., 2001). The advantages of providing an integrated service package have been pointed out by a number of authors, and include the possibility that an integrated service may provide a less threatening entry point for employees who may be reluctant to admit to a mental health issue (Greenwald, 2004). However, a past president of EAPAA, Paul Flannagan, has expressed a concern shared within the profession that there is a danger of EAP providers overselling themselves by offering interventions well outside their areas of expertise (personal communication). Noting that the individual should never be lost sight of within the EAP program, Paul observed that EAPs could manage the needs of both the organization and the individual by engaging in organizational level interventions such as wellness programs and organizational change management. Clearly defining the dimensions of EAP expertise seems to be at the core of the EAP provider problem.

EAPs are now frequently included as an employee benefit in Australian enterprise bargaining agreements and increasingly regarded as evidence of duty of care by employing organizations. Despite the positive perception of EAP services and high levels of satisfaction reported by employees and client organizations (Keys-Young, 1993; Kirk and Brown, 2003) there remains among the human resource community a widespread lack of understanding of the role of EAPs, and of their strategic integration within a firm's human resource practices. A recent study of over forty Australian organizations revealed that one of the main reasons organizations gave for initially contracting an EAP provider was to deal with unusual or exceptions circumstances that were beyond the organization's usual coping mechanisms (Kirk-Brown, 2003). Such circumstances included employee deaths, industrial accidents, and in one case an employee's gender reassignment. When human resource representatives from organizations that contracted an external EAP were asked why they continued to use the service, as opposed to why they initially adopted it, their responses shifted to reflect an awareness of the strategic and humanistic value of EAPs. For organizations using an EAP there was an awareness of the value of the type of holistic service provision offered by the majority of EAP providers, although the uptake of these services varied depending upon factors such as cost and perceived priority of employee needs. Not surprisingly there was greater evidence of employee service integration in public sector organizations, as the public sector is regarded as a key driver of work-life initiatives (Ingram and Simons, 1995).

Paul Senior, current president of Employee Assistance Professionals Association of Australia (EAPAA) (personal communication) notes that the self-referral, broad-brush model adopted early in the history of Australian EAPs meant that EAPs were attuned to the need for identification and referral to appropriate community services in addition to being well placed to offer organization level interventions such as training and wellness programs. Australian EAPs have therefore offered integrated services supplemented with referral to community services, although Paul states that the current industry climate is seeing EAPs consider the provision of an even broader range of services such as child care or elder care, particularly with the recent emergence of global players in the EAP market. Paul cautions that the market isn't ready for one vendor offering a full range of services, as Australian organizations are used to shopping around for their service provision. The future for Australian EAPs, according to Paul, will mean the brush having to become broader, and that this is likely to be achieved through working on the development of linkages with other service providers. Paul's main concern here is that this will mean having to become clear about trust levels within a competitive business environment. "We have to work together to build each others' businesses, rather than see it as competition for the same business."

FUTURE TRENDS IN EAP PROVIDER AND INTEGRATED SERVICES IN AUSTRALIA

In Australia, as is the case elsewhere, the functional relationships between EAPs and other human resource divisions have yet to be clearly delineated. Such integration is clearly linked to the need for a model of workplace counselling that provides EAP staff with guidance in formulating their roles and responsibilities, and their relationships with other human resource service providers. In 1997 Carroll pointed to the lack of a theoretical basis to understanding counselling in organizational settings, and this observation appears to hold true today. The development of integration between EAPs and other employee services therefore requires both the development of a theoretically based model of workplace counselling in addition to the resolution of issues such as levels of trust across different vendors. In Australia it seems unlikely that we will see the emergence of fully integrated service provision in the near future, either within the programs offered by individual EAP providers or across different employee services. The two main reasons for this are the current lack of market demand, and the caution expressed by organizational representatives that integration has the potential to compromise the confidentiality of the EAP. However, as the three cases presented in this article illustrate, both EAP providers and client organizations are engaged in developing linkages between different services and fostering an approach to service provision that is meeting the broader needs of Australian employees.

REFERENCES

Australian Bureau of Statistics. (2000). *Labour Force Status and Other Characteristics of Families, Australia* (Vol. Catalogue 6224.0). Canberra, ACT: Australian Government Printing Service.

Bagwell, S. (1997), "Family friendly policies have yet to be sold." *The Australian Financial Review*.

Bardoel, E.A., Moss, S., Smyrnios, K., & Tharenou, P. (1999). Employee characteristics associated with the provision of work-family policies and programs. *International Journal of Manpower*, 20 (8), 563-573.

Bardoel, E.A., Tharenou, P., & Ristov, D. (2000). The changing composition of the Australian workforce relevant to work-family issues. *International Human Resource Issues*, 1 (1), 58-80.

Buon, T. & Compton, B. (1990). Alcohol and other drug programs in the Australian workplace. *Business Insights*, 6, 24-29.

Carroll, M. (1997). Counselling in organizations: An overview. In M. Carroll & M. Walton (Eds.) *Handbook of Counselling in Organizations* (pp. 8-28), London: Sage.

Cooper, C.L. & Cartwright, S. (1994). Healthy mind; healthy organization–a proactive approach to occupational stress. *Human Relations*, 47, 455-471.

Ginsberg, M., Kilburg, R., & Gomes, P. (1999). Organizational counselling and the delivery of integrated human services in the workplace: An evolving model for employee assistance theory and practice. In J.M. Oher (Ed.) *The Employee Assistance Handbook* (pp. 439-456), Toronto: John Wiley & Sons.

Greenwald, J. (2004). Joint EAP, work/life programs cut costs. *Business Insurance*, 38 (13), 3-6.

Herlihy, P. (2000). EAPs and work/family programs–Different paths, same purpose? *EAPA Exchange*, 30 (5), 24-26.

Herlihy, P. (1997). Employee assistance programs and work/family programs: Obstacles and opportunities for organizational integration. *Compensation & Benefits Management*, 13 (2), 22-31.

Herlihy, P., Attridge, M., & Turner, S. (2002). The integration of employee assistance and work/life programs. *EAPA Exchange*, 32 (1), 10-12.

Ingram, P. & Simons, T. (1995). Institutional and resource dependence determinants of responsiveness to work-family issues. *Academy of Management Journal*, 38 (5), 1466-1483.

Keys-Young (1993). *National review of employee assistance programs.* Canberra: Commonwealth Department of Health, Housing, Local Government and Community Services (Drugs of Dependence Branch).

Kirk, A. & Brown, D.F. (1999). Practices of external employee assistance programmes in Australia. *The Journal of Occupational Health and Safety*, 15 (3), 1-18.

Kirk, A. & Brown, D.F. (2001). A comparison of internal and external providers of employee assistance programmes in Australia. *Journal of Occupational Health and Safety*, 17 (6), 579-585.

Kirk, A. & Brown, D.F. (2003). Employee assistance programmes: A review of the management of stress and wellbeing through workplace counselling and consulting, *Australian Psychologist*, Special edition on Occupational Stress and Wellbeing, 38 (2), 138-143.

Kirk-Brown, A. (2003). An analysis of attitudes towards the adoption and utilisation of Australian employee assistance programmes. *11th National Employee Assistance Professionals Association of Australia Conference*, Melbourne, October, 2003.

Kramar, R. (1997). Developing and implementing work and family policies: The implications for human resource policies. *Asia Pacific Journal of Human Resources*, 35 (3), 1-18.

Lewis, D. (1991). The new trend in life cycle benefits. *Risk Management*, 38 (12), 30-37.

Michelson, G. & Kramar, R. (2003). The state of HRM in Australia: Progress and prospects. *Asia Pacific Journal of Human Resources*, 41 (2), 133-148.

Nankervis, A. Compton, R.L., & McCarthy, T.E. (1996). *Strategic Human Resource Management*. South Melbourne: Thomas Nelson.

Peters, R. (1997). *Employee assistance programs in Australia*. Unpublished report by R.F. Peters and Associates, Newcastle, Australia.

Roman, P.M. (1983). Employee assistance programs in Australia and the United States. *The Journal of Applied Behavioral Science*, 19 (3), 367-380.

Sciegaj, M., Garnick, D.W., Hogan, C.M., Merrick, E.L., Goldin, D., Urato, M., & Hodgkin, D. (2001). Employee assistance programs among fortune 500 firms. *Employee Assistance Quarterly*, 16 (3), 24-35.

Spearritt, K. & Edgar, D. (1994). *The Family Friendly Front: A Review of Australian and International Work and Family Research*. National Key Centre in Industrial Relations, Monash University, Melbourne.

Strachan, G. & Burgess, J. (1998). The "family friendly" workplace–origins, meaning and application at Australian workplaces. *International Journal of Manpower*, 19 (4), 250-265.

Swihart, D.L. & Thompson, D.A. (2002). Successful program integration: An analysis of the challenges and opportunities facing an EAP that integrated with other programs reveals the keys to successfully serving the systemic needs of employees and work organizations. *EAP Association Exchange*, 32 (5), 10-13.

Zanko, M. (2003). Change and diversity: HRM issues and trends in the Asia-Pacific region. *Asia Pacific Journal of Human Resources*, 41 (1), 75-87.

Chapter 19

Work-Life and EAPs in the United Kingdom and Europe: A Qualitative Study of Integration

Linda Hoskinson
Stephanie Beer

SUMMARY. This article describes the development and current degree of integration of the Employee Assistance Programme (EAP) and Work-life (WL) professions in the United Kingdom (UK) and Europe. It is based on a qualitative survey of leading providers and industry consultants conducted by the authors specifically for this publication. The study results suggest that the process of integrating the two industries in the UK and Europe has not been the issue it has in North America to date. While they can be distinct services to employers, in the UK and Europe WL and EAP have grown together and there has been little competition between the two professions. Instead, they are generally seen as synergistic and are usually offered to employers as a combined product, with a seamless delivery to employees. Despite this already high level of integration, there are significant future challenges for both professions. *[Article copies available for a fee from The Haworth Document Delivery Service: 1-800-HAWORTH. E-mail address: <docdelivery@haworthpress.com>*

The authors thank those study participants from the EAP and WL industries, both internal and external in the UK and mainland Europe, for supplying information on which this chapter is based.

[Haworth co-indexing entry note]: "Work-Life and EAPs in the United Kingdom and Europe: A Qualitative Study of Integration." Hoskinson, Linda, and Stephanie Beer. Co-published simultaneously in *Journal of Workplace Behavioral Health* (The Haworth Press, Inc.) Vol. 20, No. 3/4, 2005, pp. 367-379; and: *The Integration of Employee Assistance, Work/Life, and Wellness Services* (ed: Mark Attridge, Patricia A. Herlihy, and R. Paul Maiden) The Haworth Press, Inc., 2005, pp. 367-379. Single or multiple copies of this article are available for a fee from The Haworth Document Delivery Service [1-800-HAWORTH, 9:00 a.m. - 5:00 p.m. (EST). E-mail address: docdelivery@haworthpress.com].

Available online at http://www.haworthpress.com/web/JWBH
© 2005 by The Haworth Press, Inc. All rights reserved.
doi:10.1300/J490v20n03_09

Website: <http://www.HaworthPress.com> © 2005 by The Haworth Press, Inc. All rights reserved.]

KEYWORDS. Work-life, employee assistance, integration, United Kingdom, Europe

A BRIEF HISTORY OF THE UK MARKET

Employee Assistance Programmes (EAP) and Work-life (WL) services grew in the UK largely together and later than in the USA/North America. They began to emerge in the late 1970s. However, before this period, employees in the UK were, and continue to be, supported, and still are in many organisations, by a range of excellent services including internal welfare, human resources and occupational health services. These other services have provided a valuable mixture of EAP-type interventions, including proactive support and coaching for line managers, along with practical assistance for the full range of WL issues.

Many large government departments, for example, have been slow to contract out such services to the external vendors because they see their internal services that have evolved over decades, as comprehensive and tailored to their particular workforce. In response to this, some external vendors now have a marketing strategy that targets one particular sector where they will dedicate a team of specialists–such as those with experience of the health service sector, government or education.

There are few EAP/WL vendors in the UK who developed from the Work-life profession. Most were vendors first of EAP and then later embraced the need for WL. However, there are at least two vendors who were WL first, mainly offering child and eldercare/family care in their earlier days, and these have embraced and now offer the wider EAP services. This history of UK vendors has given the buying employers some interesting variations to consider when tendering for work. Employers can choose from those in the WL industry who demonstrate impressively extensive information services and a respect for the callers' presenting issues, and those from the EAP origins with their ability to assess the full mental health picture before offering assistance.

Variable Government Support

The UK government has been quick to encourage employers to consider work-life balance issues for employees increasingly under pressure with busy lives. This has assisted the WL component of the industry. Only recently the Chancellor confirmed his reputation as the "childcare champion" (according to the Day-care Trust–the national childcare charity), with his commitment to create 120,000 new childcare slots by 2008 and to allocate an extra £100 million to create 2,500 children's centres by 2008 (Day-care Trust, 2004).

In spite of this progress, unions continue to voice their impatience for a greater range of integrated EAP and WL services. A recent survey by the Trades Union Congress (TUC) and the charity Working Families concludes that long working hours remains a serious issue for families. While there has been a decline in hours worked in the UK since the Working Time Directive was implemented in 1998, both the incidence and the absolute number of hours worked are still greater than it was in 1992. It is also estimated by the TUC that at least 1 million employees have been pressured to work long hours in ways that are currently illegal (Working Families, 2004).

The UK is not alone, as the pressure to prolong working hours has increased in a number of European countries as well. German companies, for example, are arranging with their staff in exchange for an increase in working time. Following on developments among the Finnish employers association, some Belgian enterprises have been calling for an extension of the normal working week (EFILWC, 2004).

However, governments in the UK have been slower to acknowledge the contribution of EAPs to the well-being and mental health of employees. In contrast, the value of more traditional remedial counselling, while more limited in its availability, is becoming better understood.

This development, on the one hand has given employers and vendors time to try different EAP models and services, but it has also confounded the meaning of the term EAP and allows for wide a range of isolated components, such as a solo mental health counsellor, who claim they are delivering EAPs.

The challenge for EAPs in the UK market is to clearly communicate its strategic role for the organization and that its primary mission is on individual employee assessments and interventions that are proactive, holistic and work-productivity focused. Too few today in the general UK business landscape fully appreciate that EAPs are designed to reach people who can benefit from assistance earlier than they would receive from other more reactive counselling services. EAPs also can engage with and coach line managers who are shown how to refer people successfully, and join with the employer to predict forthcoming people issues. EAPs create more cost savings and greater well-being for more people when compared with remedial, largely self-referred counselling services with which EAPs are often confused (Roman & Blum, 1995; Attridge & Gornick, 2003).

A recent university research report, on behalf of the British Association for Counselling and Psychotherapy (BACP), has finally put an end to uncertainty about the value of counselling in relation to the workplace by bringing together over 80 evaluations. Even though many of the positive outcomes were from EAP services globally, particularly from the USA, the report has anchored the benefits of counselling, and has usefully confirmed their applicability to the UK (McLeod, 2004). The UK government's Health & Safety Executive (HSE) stress management standards are to be published during the Autumn/Fall of 2004 (see HSE Website in the Appendix). These will make it difficult for employers to ignore their duty of care, including the need to conduct a stress risk assessment. Also in 2004, the UK House of Lords ruled in the Barber v. Somerset County Council case to extend the employers' liability. It is no longer sufficient to have an EAP or a counselling service–it has to be promoted proactively.

This brief review has shown that the EAP and WL fields in the UK and in Europe have tended to emerge together, with some integration of services occurring naturally along the way. Various trends in the workforce indicate a need for EAP and WL services. There is also slow but growing recognition of the effectiveness and value of counselling in general and of EAP specifically to a lesser extent. It is also evident that the role of government has helped to create a business need for such services and that this role is increasing in the future.

The rest of this paper presents the findings from an original study of leading providers in the UK and Europe on several issues key to the integration of EAP and Work-life services.

METHODOLOGY

While the authors are specialists in the EAP/WL profession in the UK and Europe, for the purpose of this article they conducted a survey among significant and important practitioners in the EAP/WL industry in order to ensure an up-to-date overview.

Interviews were conducted in 2004 with representatives of major registered providers of EAP and WL services. The sample included representatives of the large multinational and the smaller specialist organisations, as well as those with external, internal and combination models. A list of questions was asked of all participants. The respondents were promised confidentiality in return for market sensitive information. It was also expressed that no supplier would be given inappropriate exposure compared with others in the report, hence some sources of information, while available, are not presented in this article.

RESULTS

Integration

The first theme concerned the level of service integration. Most of the larger, external vendors of EAPs offer both traditional EAP services and WL. They offer the customer choices to create tailored services, perhaps an EAP with full WL or with just a legal helpline, or childcare only, eldercare perhaps–or whatever the employer needs to create the overall package that builds upon their existing services to employees.

WL in the UK covers a broad range of life services with very few limits as to what an employee can call to discuss. Some providers position the services as anything which is 'serious enough' to affect the well-being of the staff member, and therefore their potential performance at work, such as the financial situation around a difficult divorce; while others invite any issues or concern which could help employees with busy lifestyles, such as how to plan a wedding.

Concierge services are considered to be more of a luxury for busy staff and usually offer support such as collecting the employee's dry cleaning, being in their home to receive the gas repair technician or picking up a video to watch at home in the evening. These services are less offered by the EAP/WL industry and more often offered by stand-alone vendors. Some concierge services are paid for by employers that acknowledge the impact on their staff of the demands of the job, while other concierge services are available for employees to purchase for themselves. One supplier mentioned recently covering 22,000 individual subscribers.

While all of the larger EAP vendors offer WL services, the range of assistance provided varies. Some smaller EAP providers make a virtue of focusing only on EAP interventions, and counselling in particular; they refer on all WL matters, sometimes to another specialist at their own expense and sometimes to 'free' services within the community.

Some stand-alone WL vendors sell direct to their own customer organisations. However, many of these are also supplying the medium-sized external EAPs that might not have their own in-house WL services. They may also supply the internal EAP and welfare services that would not find it cost-effective to develop extensive services of their own.

There has been no resistance in the UK from EAP providers about the role of WL specialists. WL has been welcomed by the counselling profession as an essential part of assisting an employee holistically, and as a way of protecting the counsellor from practicalities best dealt with outside of 'the counselling session.'

In addition, the trades unions have always supported employees and have introduced their own help lines. These have often been more WL focused, with a large emphasis on legal and financial services.

Service Delivery

The methods of providing the service were also examined. EAP interpersonal interventions remain mainly delivered by telephone and face to face, but increasingly e-mail or online support is offered by some vendors and is being cautiously extended in certain situations as more is learned about the benefits and risks. Online services proliferate and help to supply particularly the WL components of any service more widely and cost-effectively.

The larger vendors have been able to build up extensive suites of WL specialists able to tackle almost any employee request for assistance. These providers are demonstrating the economies of scale to large employers who might have previously attempted this internally. As a result, some purchasers may have an internal EAP with an external WL service.

There are endless variations emerging, of course. This is the challenge for the UK market in that vendors need to split their services into smaller units to allow the employer, say with a legal helpline already with which it is satisfied and has no reason to change, to purchase the larger package of WL without duplication.

Range of Services

WL services in the UK cover a wide range of topics. The basic services of legal, financial and general information are provided as part of the EAP package by all the major EAPs. This would include help with issues such as those raised by relationship breakdown, separation, and housing and debt problems. The level of service provided ranges from basic information sheets on these topics to more extensive help with the details of arranging court hearings, new housing and researching and organising childcare.

The provision of financial advice for those with multiple debt problems is an important part of the UK service. This can include negotiating with creditors as well as collection and distribution of payments. Many companies outsource this to one of a number of specialist debt services but several EAPs continue to provide this in-house as they believe it is easier to case manage these difficult situations when everything remains under one roof.

There is also a wide provision of child and eldercare services. These range from sending out simple fact sheets and telephone helpline numbers to assistance with the interviewing and choice of nannies and child-minders. Some services also provide access to emergency childcare by previous reservation of some day nursery places or by employing a qualified childcare specialist who can be sent to a parent's home when a child or their carer is sick. This service is also provided through online extranets by a number of providers.

Service Utilisation

It is possible to see how vendors position their services, and their history, by looking at service utilisation. Some vendors are clearly EAP driven with only around 30 to 40% of all contacts being for work-life issues. For others, the WL component is dominant and may be nearer to 80 to 85%. The average utilisation mix for the UK is approximately 55 to 60% for WL.

Market Penetration

Overall market penetration would appear to be around 15 to 20% of the employed population in the UK, as estimated reasonably consistently by those involved in the related professions. However, analysing the figures in more detail raises difficulties around who is counting what–internal/external/combinations/EAP/Help lines only/WL and so on. The higher figure is appropriate when the Childcare Services provided within the National Health Service are included. All NHS Trusts are required to provide their staff with access to childcare information. The National Health Service is the one of the largest employers in Europe.

Coverage is greater in larger employers such as FTSE 500 companies but much less for the smaller or medium-sized employers. There is also more penetration in the service industries such as banking and insurance with a lower level in the shop floor industries such as retail and food. There is still work to be done in persuading employers that providing this type of service to lower paid staff gives sufficient return on investment with improved productivity.

As of June 2003, tighter UK independent statistics exist for market penetration of joint external EAP/WL services. It is estimated that 1,343 customer organisations are employing external vendors. This is equivalent to 2.7 million employee lives covered, and with a market value of approximately £25.5 million (McLeod, 2004).

Trends

Some EAPs have seen a change in the type of WL services accessed by employees in recent years as staff becomes increasingly aware of their legal rights. In the past, there was little provision of information on employment or grievance procedures but many EAPs now find this is a major part of their WL service.

The explanation of grievance procedures and provision of mediation or investigation services are increasingly accessed by all parties. As the cost of these employment disagreements and disputes rise, this is one area where it is not difficult to prove to an employer the cost benefits of earlier and skilled intervention. The government has introduced new legislation that took effect in October 2004 requiring all organisations to have clear grievance procedures and all employees to make proper use of them before taking a case to tribunal.

One of the growing services is the provision of career or life coaching. Employers in the UK are increasingly asking their employees to adapt to changing work environments and new challenges. This can be provided as part of the EAP or bought by the employer on an "as required" basis. Career advice is provided either by telephone or face to face and varies from simple help with preparing a CV to executive coaching to enable managers to cope with needs of relocation and change of direction. There is strong competition for this share of the market from stand-alone providers that have been in the aggressive outplacement and career business for decades and which are seen by many as the next area of competition for the EAP market.

There are likely to be changes in utilisation during the next 12 months in the UK as managing stress at work becomes a higher priority for both employers and employees in the light of the new Health and Safety Executive guidelines. These are likely to lead more employees and employers seeking information and guidance from their EAP providers about possible action and obligations.

Some vendors have noted that more WL calls are about eldercare as more employees become 'the sandwich generation' with both child and eldercare responsibility. While women largely used to call about childcare, more men, often now up to 50% call about eldercare. For whatever reason, the rise in the use of such services by men is viewed positively.

Challenges

The main challenge is to emphasise the proactivity of an EAP, compared with remedial counselling. This affects everything, as it does in the USA/North America. If this differentiation is not held, if the true value of an EAP/WL service is misunderstood, it is hard to remain providers of quality services as the price is forced down by employers putting contracts out to tender.

The competition is fierce for these contracts even though they are demanding more and more services to be included within the EAP for a lower price. There is also a growing emphasis on well-being and assistance with healthy lifestyles. Both of these pressures may lead to problems for the smaller EAPs who do not have sufficient volume to provide this at a suitable price.

The EAP profession has set standards clearly for EAP/clinical services. However, the WL field has a greater range of services on offer, each with their own professional bodies' governing standards, such as in law, financial advice and childcare. It has been difficult to coordinate these bodies and to ensure consistency, and progress is slow.

The new sub-committee for EAPA in the UK, currently tasked with revising standards, is committed to taking this challenge forward. It remains the hallmark of the better providers of EAP/WL services that the quality of the first 'intake assessment call or face-to-face session' with an employee dictates the quality of all subsequent EAP/WL services coordinated for the client.

Healthcare costs in the UK must be addressed. The EAP/WL professions have not done well here, in spite of lessons from the United States. Integration between EAPs and the healthcare insurance world could be better in the UK but efforts have been hampered by the complexity of working with the National Health Service. Private healthcare insurers are paying more than necessary for mental healthcare through the private health system, using often inappropriately qualified psychologists and inflexible medical treatment models for mental illness, when sometimes the EAP profession and counselling can be part of a coordinated, integrated solution at greatly reduced cost. Some independent consultants are working with employers, healthcare insurers and EAP/WL providers to address this, but engaging the NHS remains a major challenge.

A new public/private partnership (Work-life Partnerships Ltd) has been put in place to bring together NHS and private resources. It has been given the focus of targeting assistance for people who wish to remain in the workforce in spite of psychosocial risk situations, including mental ill health. This should provide a sound basis for more integrated approaches in the UK that are long overdue.

Europe

Another challenge is the prospect of providing services more widely across Europe. Many EAP/WL contracts now ask for services in a number of different countries as employers seek to provide the same spectrum of HR conditions to all their employees. With the expansion of the European community this year to 25 countries and the opening up of Eastern Europe, the need for services, which are culturally and linguistically appropriate, becomes more challenging and difficult to supply. The size of the challenge is reinforced by the fact that, were Europe to be a country, with its 453 million people it would be the third largest in the world after India and China, with the United States fourth.

In addition to the language issues, each country has a different historical context to their welfare and health services so the view of what would be considered "normal" or appropriate requirements of an EAP or WL service varies greatly from place to place. The percentage of WL cases to EAP cases varies from country to country with Spain, France and Germany being most like the UK at 50-60%, with Scandinavia using WL services less.

Many employers have needed to ensure employees travelling globally have sufficient support for themselves and their families and as a result, services for expatriates have developed, both internally and externally. However, services required by expatriates will differ from those required by local nationals as the culture and language needs are significantly different.

"Taking EAP or WL services separately to Europe is a challenge, without trying to integrate them!" said one experienced provider. A small and entrepreneurial number have sought to deal with this in a variety of ways. Some have opened offices staffed by local nationals–an expensive option and not open to all providers–others have collaborated with local psychological or WL companies to provide a suitable service to both local and expatriate employees.

Richard Ennals is Chair of the Club of Geneva and Professor of Working Life at the Centre for Working Life Research at the Business School of Kingston University in the UK. At the July 2004 Global Symposium, he noted that we need more research and working models to change the world of work. He summarised a number of key projects in Europe, including the following examples:

1. Health impacts of international outsourcing. This project brings together the Global Network for Research in Mental and Neurological Health, the Club of Geneva, the World Bank, and a growing consortium of sponsors and partners to address how the outsourcing of work affects health.
2. *World Wide Guidelines for EAPs* was introduced in Geneva in 2004.
3. Other organizations that are addressing health and workplace issues include: the European Network for Workplace Health Promotion, the Institution of Occupational Safety and Health (IOSH) and the International Commission on Occupational Health (ICOH).
4. The Healthy Working Centres project. This effort in South East England addresses new forms of organisations aimed at meeting the needs of mobile workers. It is supported by the European Social Fund and the South East England Development Agency.
5. "MOSAIC." This project is focused on mobile work environments and mobile technologies. It is supported by the European Commission Sixth Framework Programme, as part of an initiative on "Ambient Intelligence at Work," with an emphasis on "well-being at work."

Together, these projects represent examples of how different organizations are conducting research and analysis of important aspects of work and health. The reader is directed to the Appendix for a list of Website addresses for these organizations and related reference resources.

CONCLUSIONS

The overall picture is of a strong WL push in the UK and Europe supported by academic research and government, and a less supported EAP industry making its own progress but with well-developed EAP standards for delivery. They work together well providing seamless services to clients.

The challenge for the WL industry is to define its full range of services to help buyers understand what is available and purchase units only as required, building on existing facilities already in place for their staff. For example, a purchaser would not need legal information or childcare twice as part of two different packages. The WL industry also needs standards to be uniform across all of its services, a daunting task requiring many distinct professions to work together, such as legal, financial and dependent care.

The challenge for the EAP industry remains that it must differentiate itself from remedial counselling alone. The value of the proactivity of an EAP, working with line managers on workplace as well as domestic issues, has not been fully appreciated, hopefully a temporary situation. Government wants more people 'in work'; including those managing a range of mental health issues, and it has not yet been helped to appreciate the benefit of an active EAP.

If the WL and EAP industries are to succeed in the UK and Europe then they must protect the services from being reduced to simple commodities, which minimise their benefit and encourage the current undermining of fees.

New ways are being found to integrate the excellent National Health Service mental health facilities in seamless delivery with those available in the private sector. This is taking time, although the outcomes are being evaluated and are encouraging. The key will be the consolidation of a sufficiently large professional army of those skilled in 'case management' in the holistic delivery of all mental health and rehabilitation services.

It appears to the authors, having spoken with key people that the value of the European EAP and WL industries is that they are active and working together where appropriate and are growing in line with customer requirements. The complexity of Europe will mean that those parts of the industry that succeed in addressing local needs accurately and in a culturally sensitive manner will have the blueprint for global success.

REFERENCES

Attridge, M., & Gornick, M.E. (2003, November). Making the business case for EAPs and work-life: Research review and workshop. Presented at *Employee Assistance Professionals Association Annual Conference*, New Orleans, LA.

Blum, T.C., & Roman, P.M. (1995). *Cost-Effectiveness and Preventive Implications of Employee Assistance Programs*. Rockville, MD: U.S. Department of Health and Human Services.

McLeod, J. (2004). "Counselling in the workplace: The facts." ISBN 0 946 181 81 1. Special report by Professor John McLeod, Chair of Counselling, Tayside Institute of Health Studies, School of Social and Health Sciences, University of Abertay, Dundee, Scotland. 128 pages. Available from: Book Orders Dept. of the British Association for Counselling and Psychotherapy.

APPENDIX

Resources on EAP and Work-Life in the UK and Europe

Day-care Trust, 2004. For report see Website: *http://www.daycaretrust.org.uk/article.php?sid=227*. Day-care Trust, 21 St George's Road, London, England. SE1 6ES.

Working Families, 2004. *http://www.workingfamilies.org.uk/asp/main_downloads/Families%20Need%20Time%20Report.doc*. Address: Working Families, 1-3 Berry Street, London EC1V 0AA1.

EFILWC, 2004. European Foundation for the Improvement of Living and Working Conditions. See Website report at *http://www.eiro.eurofound.eu.int/2004/08/inbrief/be0408301n.html*.

HSE. Health and Safety Executive. Draft Stress Management Standards for the UK, HSE. See *www.hse.gov.uk/stress/revdraftstandards.pdf*.

PARN. Independently audited EAP provider research conducted by the Professional Associations Research Network (PARN) on behalf of the UK Employee Assistance Professional Association (UK EAPA). Dr Mary Phillips, PARN, University of Bristol, 43 Woodland Road, Clifton, Bristol BS8. E-mail = *Mary.Phillips@bristol.ac.uk*.

BACP. British Association for Counselling and Psychotherapy. Address: 1 Regent Place, Rugby, CV21 2PJ. *www.bacp.co.uk*.

The Healthy Working Centres research initiative can be accessed at *www.hwc.uk.net*.

MOSIAC. The MOSAIC mobile work environments and technologies research initiative can be accessed at *www.mosaic-network.org*.

The Centre for Working Life Research at the Business School, Kingston University in the UK can be accessed at *www.kingston.ac.uk*.

The Institution of Occupational Safety and Health (IOSH) can be accessed at *www.iosh.co.uk*

The International Commission on Occupational Health (ICOH) can be accessed at *www.icoh.org.sg*.

The Club of Geneva can be accessed at *www.wspartners.com*.

Chapter 20

A Social Partnership Approach
to Work-Life Balance in the European Union–
The Irish Experience

Maurice Quinlan

SUMMARY. Over the past number of years there has been considerable focus on the integration of employee assistance and work-life
programmes in the United States. A national survey conducted by
EAPA, EASNA, and AWLP found there is a trend towards the integration of employee assistance and work-life. Many US providers and multinational companies will seek to extend their EAPs and work-life
programmes globally. It is sometimes assumed that the EAPs and
work-life models that operate in the US will transfer but this is often not
the case. There is a cultural dimension to EAPs and work-life programmes
that is often overlooked. The European Union (EU) is involved in the
greatest example of integration in recent history and an understanding of
the EU and its legal system will assist those providing their services. In
the EU, EAPs did not follow the same growth pattern as in the US. Professionals in European countries working with business such as psychologists, social workers, and counsellors did not recognise the need for
EAPs as, in their view, programmes to deal with personal problems in
the workplace already existed. The concept of work-life is widely
known and accepted in many European countries; however, there is little

[Haworth co-indexing entry note]: "A Social Partnership Approach to Work-Life Balance in the Euro-
pean Union–The Irish Experience." Quinlan, Maurice. Co-published simultaneously in *Journal of Workplace
Behavioral Health* (The Haworth Press, Inc.) Vol. 20, No. 3/4, 2005, pp. 381-394; and: *The Integration of
Employee Assistance, Work/Life, and Wellness Services* (ed: Mark Attridge, Patricia A. Herlihy, and R. Paul
Maiden) The Haworth Press, Inc., 2005, pp. 381-394. Single or multiple copies of this article are available for
a fee from The Haworth Document Delivery Service [1-800-HAWORTH, 9:00 a.m. - 5:00 p.m. (EST).
E-mail address: docdelivery@haworthpress.com].

Available online at http://www.haworthpress.com/web/JWBH
© 2005 by The Haworth Press, Inc. All rights reserved.
doi:10.1300/J490v20n03_10

evidence of research specifically on the integration of EAPs and work-life programmes. This article will look at one EU country, Ireland, and outline the history and development of EAPs and work-life and present case studies of Irish companies who have developed work-life programmes. *[Article copies available for a fee from The Haworth Document Delivery Service: 1-800-HAWORTH. E-mail address: <docdelivery@haworthpress.com> Website: <http://www.HaworthPress.com> © 2005 by The Haworth Press, Inc. All rights reserved.]*

KEYWORDS. Separate work-life, cultural dimensions, European Union, legal mandates, social partnership

INTRODUCTION

Employee Assistance Programmes

Employee assistance programmes (EAPs) and work-life programmes have developed and evolved in separate directions in Ireland. The first Occupational Alcoholism Programme (OAP) in Ireland was developed in 1973 by The Electricity Supply Board (ESB), Ireland's National Power Company. This was an internal programme serviced by a new grade of professional Staff Services Officers. The second stage of EAP development was by US multinationals who influenced their Irish divisions in establishing internal EAPs provided by Occupational Health Nurses. The third stage was the development of internal EAPs in all government departments provided by welfare and employee assistance officers.

In the early 1980s external EAP providers in the United Kingdom extended contracts into Ireland. The original providers included ICAS, PPC, ACCOR Services The Validum Group, and Dovedale Counselling. A recent development has been the growth of Irish EAP providers. Major Irish-based health insurers VHI and BUPA (UK Subsidary) and many other regional providers are now providing services to a developing market.

In May of 2001 a chapter of the Employee Assistance Professionals Association (EAPA) was established in Ireland as one of the largest outside of the US. There are existing chapters in the United Kingdom, and Greece. A new chapter is forming in Finland and individual EA professionals are providing services in many other European countries such as the Netherlands and Spain.

Work-Life

The concept of work-life balance is not new to Irish business. In 1990 a group of spouses with partners who were members of the Irish Management Institute (IMI) presented a case study at the annual EAP conference in Waterford, Ireland, and told delegates how they formed a Spouse Support Group to examine the impact on the family of absent partners. The Employment Equality Agency (now the Equality Authority) introduced a report on Family Friendly Initiatives in the Workplace (Fisher, 1996). This report defined family friendly initiatives as flexible working, leave arrangements, work breaks, and other initiatives including childcare support and EAPs.

Equal opportunities were now a major issue and the absence of child care facilities were seen as a barrier to females developing their outside the home. The government and the EU established and funded the Equal Opportunities Childcare Programme 2000-2006 with total funding of €436.7 million. Since April 2000 €227.2 million has been committed to supporting 52,000 child care slots through grant assistance including 26,000 newly created child care slots.

The Irish economy was expanding at a 10% annual growth rate in the late 1990s and labour shortages became a serious factor in Irish business. Employers sought to retain skilled workers by becoming employers of choice and offered work-life balance programmes as an incentive.

The Programme for Prosperity and Fairness (A Social Partnership Agreement which includes Government, Employers and Social Partners) established a National Framework Committee for Family Friendly Policies. In the same programme it was agreed that there would be development and expansion of child care facilities and financial incentives were available to provide:

- Capital grants for community-based child care facilities.
- Grants towards staffing costs for community-based child care services.
- Training supports.
- Local child care networks.
- A capital grant scheme for independent child care service providers.

Social Partnership, EAPs, and Work-Life

In 1987 economic growth was very low in Ireland and the government established a social partnership approach to managing the economy. The main partners included the government, employers, trade unions, farmers, the community and voluntary sectors. In return for pay moderation and a no strike clause the government and unions agreed to a partnership approach, giving the unions the opportunity to discuss health care, education, and housing as part of national wage agreements. Local partnership groups were established at enterprise level and influenced the setting up of EAPs and work-life programmes. Negotiation on a new national agreement the Programme for Prosperity and Fairness was formally launched in November 1999 and resulted in the development of a National Framework Committee for the development of family friendly policies at the level of enterprise. A budget of 1.9 million Euro was allocated for this purpose. The objective of this agreement was to support and facilitate the development of family friendly policies which were designed to enhance the opportunity to reconcile work and family life and contribute to the effective and efficient operation of the enterprise.

The European Union, Ireland, and the United States

Ireland held the rotating six month Presidency of the EU in 2004 and 10 new member states from the former eastern block countries joined the existing 15 member states in Dublin on the 1st of May 2004 to bring the total EU population to 450 million. The goal of the EU is to be the world's largest economy by 2010 and applicant members such as Romania, Bulgaria, Macedonia, Turkey, and Croatia will increase the population to approximately 650 million. This will create one of the largest global trading blocks. The EU is engaged in a process called harmonisation of standards, currencies and laws. The EU issues directives which is the most important legislative instrument used by the Union. Its purpose is to create a uniform or whole EU approach to an issue such as labour law while still respecting the traditions and needs of member states. In other words directives harmonise the law across the EU and iron out inconsistencies so that as far as possible the same conditions exist for all citizens in all member states. With those directives the EU has a strong a powerful influence on all its members. The EU employment guidelines in 1999 detailed the importance of designing, implementing and promoting family friendly policies.

There is a strong influence on Ireland as a member state from the EU and another from the United States from Foreign Direct Investment (FDI). Ireland is the number one location in Europe for health care and pharmaceutical companies such as Abbot, Boston Scientific, and Johnson and Johnson. It also has a key information and communications technology investment from companies such as Intel, Dell, and IBM. It is one of the most successful economies in Europe with a total working population of 1.7 million and with the second highest GDP after Luxemburg at €25,100 per capita. Current growth rate stands at 4.2%, inflation at 2% and unemployment at 4.5%. According to the Trans-Atlantic Business Dialogue in 2003 US companies invested 2.5 times more in Ireland than they did in China. The vision for the future is that Ireland will develop from an industrial economy to a knowledge-based economy and that all new business parks will include a family friendly resource centre for child care.

Evolution Of Employee Assistance Programmes

Welfare services were provided in the 1950s by major Irish organisations such as Guinness (now Diagio) who had a designated medical centre for its employees and dependants. Social workers were also employed in what was described as "from the womb to the tomb" services. Many government departments also employed welfare officers.

Following the economic boom of the 1960s Irish business was experiencing excessive levels of absenteeism which was identified as having been caused by excessive drinking described as the "the Monday morning syndrome." There was concern by the Irish Congress of Trade Unions (ICTU) for its members and in 1972 at their annual conference the following motion was proposed:

> Recognising that alcoholism in Ireland is an increasing social problem, that it has a serious cause of loss of work hours in industry and potential source of industrial strive, conference instructs the Executive Council to enter into early negotiations with the Federated Union of Employers (FUE) with a view to establish agreed principles and procedures in the treatment of workers who are victims.

In 1969 the Electricity Supply Board (ESB), Ireland's National Power Company, were reeling from a bruising recommendation of the Fogarty report which was strongly critical of its management style (Fogarty, 1969). Recommendations contained in that report was that personnel specialists should be appointed. In 1973 the ESB introduced a programme to deal with alcohol-related problems for their entire workforce. This initiative had the full support of the trade unions and is recognised as the first programme of its kind in Europe and provided a model for other semi-state and public bodies.

In the early 1980s US multinationals introduced broad-brush EAPs into their Irish and European divisions, but by 1985 there was a decline in companies introducing programmes. As the recession deepened there was a major focus in business on reducing numbers and employee welfare was afforded a low priority. The Health Safety and Welfare Work Act was enacted in 1989 in Ireland. The initial focus of the Act was on workplace physical hazards but later it embraced areas such as work stress, critical incident stress, violence, and workplace bullying.

This Act established that employers have a duty of care to protect employee health from all work-related stress. The act is currently being reviewed and the Health, Safety and Welfare at Work Bill 2004 proposes that employee drug testing would be introduced for those under the influence of an intoxicant (defined as alcohol and drugs).

By 1993 the welfare officers in the government departments established the Association of Welfare and Employee Assistance Counsellors (AWEAC) and in May 2000 a decision was taken to establish a chapter of the Employee Assistance Professional Association (EAPA). This was formally established in May of 2001. In May 2002 a group of seven EA professionals in Ireland undertook the advisement process to prepare for the CEAPI exam. Another Irish group formed and three were successful in 2003.

The current driving forces in EAP development include Employer's Duty of Care for work stress, critical incident stress, violence at work, workplace bullying, harassment, and sexual harassment. Emerging issues include employee drug testing, work-life balance and certification of EA professionals.

Development of Work-Life Programmes in Ireland

The Programme for Prosperity and Fairness (national agreement) and the Irish National Development Plan developed the concept of partnership with the social partners. This was the sixth in a series of national agreements and is credited with Ireland's phenomenal growth rate of 10% GNP in the years 1997 to 2002. Partnership groups exist in many companies and provide a forum for discussion and development of mutually acceptable programmes such as work-life.

The National Framework Committee for the development of Family Friendly Policies which was established under the Programme for Prosperity and Fairness organised a series of national seminars to promote the development of family friendly working arrangements in the workplace. The Framework Committee members included the Irish Business and Employer's Confederation (IBEC), the Irish Congress of Trade Unions (ICTU), and the Equality Authority. Funded by the committee, IBEC developed a new work-life balance training module and organised a national roundtable on work-life which took place in November 2002. A new guideline and toolkit for trade unions on family friendly working/work-life balance was designed by ICTU and this group also provided training for a three-day training course which is being delivered to union members.

The Equality Authority introduced the first family friendly workplace day on Thursday, 1st March 2001. Workplaces were encouraged to have activities to mark that day and it is now an annual event. The Authority also funded consultants to assist business in establishing Work-life Programmes. The National Framework Committee also commissioned research on flexible working "Off the Treadmill–Achieving Work-life Balance" and surveyed 912 employers in the public and private sectors (Drew, 2003). The survey also examined longer hours and overtime and found that longer working was common for 86% of senior managers and professionals, 61% of junior managers and professionals, 30% of other non-manual workers, and 30% of manual workers.

The survey also found benefits of flexible working for employers as employee satisfaction, recruitment, retention, improved productivity, reduced turnover and improved reputation. More than half of all organisations surveyed saw positive benefits. The survey also found that the most common child care arrangement is provided by a relative followed by after school or child minder. Average child care costs were €128 per child per week.

According to the survey the patterns and trends and demand for work-life balance will continue. This will be influenced by the following: heterogeneity of the work force, diversity of working time, economic conditions, demographic change, information communication technology, and public verses private sector adoption of work-life.

"Family Friendly" Employment Legislation

Irish employers are obliged to comply with five main employment laws which impact on work-life balance. Failure to do so may lead to employees to seek redress with the enforcement agencies such as the Equality Authority.

The laws are as follows;

- Maternity Protection Act 1994
- Adoptive Leave Act 1995
- Organisation of Working Time Act 1997
- Parental Leave 1998 Act (Including Force Majeure)
- Carers Leave Act 2001

Pending Legislation includes;

- Maternity Protection (Amendment) Bill
- Adoptive Leave (Amendment) Bill
- Working Group on Parental Leave (National Framework Committee)

The following is a brief summary of the legislation:

Maternity Protection Act of 1994 entitles a pregnant employee to up to 18 consecutive weeks of maternity leave.

Adoptive Leave Act 1995 entitles an adopting female or a single male who is adopting to a minimum of 14 consecutive weeks of adoptive leave from work beginning on the day of placement of the child and up to 8 weeks additional adoptive leave.

Organisation of Working Time Act of 1997 implemented the EU Working Time Directive into Irish law. Effective April 1999 all full-time employees are entitled to 20 days paid annual leave. The act also contains a list of nine public holidays for which an employee is entitled (in addition to annual leave) to receive a paid day of leave. The Act also imposes an average maximum 48-hour working week. The normal averaging period is four months, but this can be extended up to 12 months by collective agreement in certain circumstances. The Act also imposes provisions in relation to weekly, and daily, rest periods, Sunday working and night working.

Parental Leave Act of 1998 enforces an EU Directive on parental leave. The two main purposes of the act (1) are to provide for a new entitlement for men and women to avail of unpaid leave from employment to enable them to take care of their young children. This provides for the manner in which parental leave may be taken–either as a continuous block of 14 weeks or, with agreement of the employer, broken up over a period of time. The employment rights of the employee are protected while s/he is on parental leave and the employee has the right to return to work after such an absence. (2) It provides for limited paid leave (force majeure leave) to enable employees to deal with family emergencies resulting from injury or illness of a family member.

The Act provides that employees are entitled to force majeure leave provided it does not exceed 3 days in any 12 consecutive months, or 5 days in any 36 consecutive months.

Carer's Leave Act of 2001 provides for a new entitlement for an employee to avail of unpaid leave from his/her employment to enable him/her to personally provide full-time care and attention for a person who is in need of such care. The period of leave to which an employee is entitled is subject to a maximum of 65 weeks in respect of any one care recipient (hereafter referred to as a "relevant person"). The minimum statutory entitlement is 13 weeks.

The remainder of the article will examine two case studies to demonstrate the practical implementation of the partnership approach to work-life programmes. The first will outline a case study by a private manufacturing company and the second a consortium approach by six commercial semi-state government organisations.

CASE STUDY NO. 1:
ANDERSON IRELAND–
PARTNERSHIP APPROACH TO WORK-LIFE

Anderson an Austrian company manufacturing high quality fashion and solid silver jewelry established a subsidiary in Ireland. The subsidiary has now operated for 25 years and employs 250 staff–72% female and 28% male. The company is unionised and negotiation rights are vested in one union SIPTU.

The company has a favourable history of industrial relations and both management and union have attempted to resolve any differences in a non-confrontational way. The culture is informal and an open door policy exists to all members of management. A joint union communications forum has been in place for many over a number of years and has served to promote a partnership between labour and management.

Anderson Ireland had existing work-life initiatives such as child care, elder care, and compliance with statutory requirements. The focus on work-life development now was to introduce flexible working hours. The first stage was identifying the needs of the company and employees and to select suitable arrangements. Best practice was researched and a set of proposals were generated and offered, briefing sessions were then conducted with all employees and served as a useful purpose in ascertaining the reactions of people to the initiative. Concern was expressed by those who did not wish to change their existing arrangement and they were assured by stressing that access to the programme was voluntary. In the event that the flexible hours were not suitable then employees could opt out.

Business Case for Work-Life Balance

Anderson identified the following goals as part of their business plan.

- Achieve a high degree of flexibility in responding to marketing demands.
- Retain trained and contented workers in a tightening labour market.
- Prevent increased costs and develop realistic and practical programmes.

Extending Flexible Working

Questionnaires that were returned as a result of a briefing session were summarised and employees expressed interest in the following areas:

- Shorter week–interest was mainly in a four-day week
- Shorter days–considerable interest but diversity as to the most suitable hours
- Additional time off at own expense including one day, one week and periods of one to three months

Programme Initiative

The programme was introduced on a trial basis with an agreement that it would be reviewed at the end of six months. From a total workforce of 250 workers, 69 employees (66 women and 3 men) took advantage of the flexible work hours.

Initiative	Total	Male	Female
Shorter days	31	1	30
Shorter week	24	0	24
Condensed week	10	2	8
Job sharing	4	0	4
Total	**69**	**3**	**66**

CASE STUDY NO. 2:
CONSORTIUM APPROACH TO WORK-LIFE DEVELOPMENT

Work-life Balance Network (WLBN) is a project funded under the European Union Equal Community Initiative Programme. The aim of the Network is to explore work-life balance (WLB) policies and promote models of good practice in constituent organisations which are currently facing a period of significant change.

Constituent members of the consortium are drawn from the Civil Service (Office of the Civil Service and Local Appointments Commissioners), The Semi-States (An Post, Dublin Bus and Irish Rail), a Municipal Authority (Dublin City Council), one private company (Eircom) and the social partners Irish Business Employers Confederation (IBEC) and Irish Congress of Trade Unions (ICTU). There is a total employee population of 30,000 in the six member companies. The project is funded by both the European Union and the Irish Government and with €1 million each and has been in operation for three years.

The development stage which commenced in 2001 lasted for a period of six months. This was followed in 2002 by the implementation phase. Currently the project is in the middle stage and is focused on creating structures is the six member companies. The project is also establishing work-life balance partnership groups with 10 to 15 members in each company, research and planning the business case, and the creation of a diagnostic pack and CD ROM.

As the WLBN project progresses and products are developed, the level of activity and (to a lesser extent) the impact of the project overall is more easily quantified. The following is a summary of some of the key statistics gathered from an analysis of the data and information recorded between May 2002 and May 2004.

- Number of organisations requesting and receiving information: Approx. 171[1]
- Range of organisations included private, public/semi-state, community and voluntary and professional/membership organisations, employing between 1 and over 20,000 employees
- Total indirect beneficiaries–i.e., potentially benefiting from contact/information provided–(conservative estimate): 150,000-200,000[2]
- The range of dissemination activities included launch of the Diagnostic Tool, radio interviews, stand at Equal Helix Event; IBEC Retail, IT and Banking Roundtable, and Executive Breakfast Brief-

ing; NWHB Event; Shop Stewards' Training; 'Best Places to Work' Conference; NCPP Consultation Seminar on the Workplace of the Future; the National Framework Committee on Worklife Balance; and seven radio interviews

- Approximately 700 hard copies of the Diagnostic Tool (Manual and/ or CD ROM) were distributed to the following groups: IBEC Round Tables and Management Breakfast Briefing, ICTU Women's Talent Bank Seminar, ICTU Women's Conference, 'Ireland's Great Places to Work' Conference, 'Tipping the Scales' EU Presidency Conference (Letterkenny), EQUAL national and North-South events, and the EQUAL European Thematic Group (workshops on 'Reconciliation and Desegregation' and 'Gender Mainstreaming')
- Approximately WLBN 5,500 key rings and 55 bags distributed
- Website hits: 670 in total, 95 for Diagnostic Tool
- Articles in the *Irish Times*, the *Irish Independent*, the *Irish Examiner*, and *IRN*
- Approximately 100 hours (14 days) spent on dissemination activities at central project level

Training of Consortium Members

An analysis of data gathered to mid June 2004 shows that the situation regarding the training of managers, indoor and outdoor staff in consortium member organisations, in terms of approximate hours, can be summarised as follows:

	Female	Male	Total
Lower Management	212	65	277
Middle Management	716	302	1,018
Senior Management	147	212	359
Other Management	181	491	672
Sub-Total Management	**1,256**	**1,070**	**2,326 (55%)**
Indoor Staff	315	278	593
Outdoor Staff	8	88	96
Sub-Total Staff	**323**	**366**	**689 (16%)**
Union Representative	442	427	869
Union Official	9	163	172
Union Shop Steward	-	158	158
Sub-Total Union	**451**	**748**	**1,199 (29%)**
GRAND TOTAL	**2,030 (48%)**	**2,184 (52%)**	**4,214 (100%)**

CONCLUSIONS

This article set out to outline the different approach to EAPs and work-life in Europe as compared with the US by looking at the experience of one EU member state. In the past the US version of EAPs was imported and similar questions have been asked in Europe regarding the development of EAPs as a commodity and the misrepresentation as employee counselling. The effectiveness of EAPs in becoming a management tool for preventing, identifying and resolving poor performance caused by personal or external employee issues is also under question.

There are two types of work-life services now being developed, the first is a commodity model and the second is an indigenous or home grown programme. In Ireland the latter is funded by the government and supported by business and the Trades Unions. The intention is to integrate work-life programmes into the mainstream of organisations rather than just providing an external commodity service.

The background to the Social Partnership approach to work-life development and the two case studies have demonstrated the unique approach to work-life development in Ireland and there is an opportunity for global EA professionals to learn from that experience.

The Employee Assistance Professional Association (EAPA) has developed a strategic plan for global development and this will present many challenges and opportunities to those who wish to work in a European setting. Cultural literacy will be a key skill required to understand the many different cultures, approaches, and employment laws.

Adapting the Certified Employee Assistance Professional International (CEAP I) Credential to include those employment laws will ensure that those who provide services will meet all of the requirements.

Employers and trade unions in Ireland are providing training on work-life balance and this concerted effort of the government and social partners will develop programmes in all public sectors. Adoption of these services in private companies will be much slower. At the conference Taking Stock and Looking to the Future of Work-life Balance held in Dublin in November 2003 John Fitzgerald of the Economic and Social Research Unit (ESRI) outlined forecasts on the changing Irish demographics. These will include an ageing population and a decreasing birth rate that will cause serious labour and skills shortages in the future. As Ireland moves to a knowledge-based economy some labour shortages will be met by immigrant workers. Organisations may also see the value in working with the work-life balance of their human capital as a key to operating a successful business.

NOTES

1. e.g., personal, 'phone or e-mail/Web contact with ETS personnel, including EQUAL HELIX Event, launch of Diagnostic, IBEC Roundtables, NWHB Event, Shop Stewards' Training, 'Best Places to Work' Conference, etc.

2. Based on the number of employees in the organisations that requested information from ETS and that gave details of their organisation size; also includes people trained (e.g., Shop Stewards' Training Course on WLB).

REFERENCES

Carmichael, J. (2001) *A Union Perspective on Family Friendly Work-life Balance Policies,* Presented to IBEC National Roundtable on Family Friendly Work-life Balance Policies, 28th September.

Commission on the Family 1998–Final Report to the Minister for Social, Community, and Family Affairs.

Drew, E. (2001) *Off the Treadmill Achieving Work-life Balance,* Published by the National Framework Committee for Family Friendly Policies.

Fisher, H. (2000) *Investing in People–Family Friendly Arrangements in Small or Medium Sized Business.*

Fisher, H. (1996) *Introducing Family Friendly Initiatives in the Workplace* (Employment Equality Agency).

Fitzgerald, J. (2003) The Labour Force to 2020 Implications for Life Style presented to the conference *"Taking Stock and Looking to the Future of the Work-life Balance Programme,"* Thursday 27th November, Dublin, Ireland.

FitzPatrick, N. (2001) Education and Training Services Trust Ltd. Interview 1st September.

Griffin, T. & O'Flaherty, N. (2002) Presented to 2nd Annual Work-life Seminar Work-life Balance in a Changing Economic Environment, Friday 18th October 2002 at Butler House Kilkenny.

National Childcare Strategy. (1999) *Report on the Partnership 2000 expert working group on childcare*–Government Publications, Molesworth Street, Dublin 2.

Programme for Prosperity and Fairness. (2001 National Agreement) Government Publications postal trade section, 4-5 Harcourt Street, Dublin 2.

Quinlan, M. (1999) Presented to the 20th Annual EAP Conference–*Improving Working Life, Developing Family Friendly Initiatives* at the Stakis Hotel Dublin, Ireland, 29th and 30th September 1999.

Ryan, F. (2001), IDA Ireland-Vision 2010 Presented to IBEC National Roundtable on *Family Friendly Work-life Balance Policies,* 28th September 2001.

Strengthening Families for Life (May 1998) *Final report to the Minister for Social, Community and Family Affairs.*

Sustaining Progress 2003-2005, (National Agreement) Government Publications, Postal Trade Section, 4-5 Harcourt Road, Dublin 2.

Web Address *www.worklifebalance.ie*

A CRITICAL ANALYSIS AND FUTURE PERSPECTIVES OF INTEGRATION

Chapter 21

A Commentary on the Integration of EAPs: Some Cautionary Notes from Past and Present

Paul M. Roman

SUMMARY. This article addresses the notion of integration–past and present. The author discusses his earlier experiences and research in the field when the dominant model of service delivery was occupational alcoholism programs and counselors of the day sought to integrate these programs into the personnel management function as a means of more effectively serving the employee and the employer. This article also reviews the evolution of this earlier model into employee assistance programs and points out the success and continued growth of these pro-

[Haworth co-indexing entry note]: "A Commentary on the Integration of EAPs: Some Cautionary Notes from Past and Present." Roman, Paul M. Co-published simultaneously in *Journal of Workplace Behavioral Health* (The Haworth Press, Inc.) Vol. 20, No. 3/4, 2005, pp. 395-406; and: *The Integration of Employee Assistance, Work/Life, and Wellness Services* (ed: Mark Attridge, Patricia A. Herlihy, and R. Paul Maiden) The Haworth Press, Inc., 2005, pp. 395-406. Single or multiple copies of this article are available for a fee from The Haworth Document Delivery Service [1-800-HAWORTH, 9:00 a.m. - 5:00 p.m. (EST). E-mail address: docdelivery@haworthpress.com].

Available online at http://www.haworthpress.com/web/JWBH
© 2005 by The Haworth Press, Inc. All rights reserved.
doi:10.1300/J490v20n03_11

grams was the direct result of empirical research that demonstrated the cost-effectiveness of EAPs. The author reminds the reader to be mindful of the need to maintain the core technology ascribed to EAPs as the range of workplace human service programs continues to expand. Lastly, the author reiterates the necessity of empirical research to demonstrate the value of adding of work-life and wellness services to the broadening scope of programs aimed at maximizing human capital. *[Article copies available for a fee from The Haworth Document Delivery Service: 1-800-HAWORTH. E-mail address: <docdelivery@haworthpress.com> Website: <http://www.HaworthPress.com> © 2005 by The Haworth Press, Inc. All rights reserved.]*

KEYWORDS. Employee assistance, core technology, integration, empirical research

INTRODUCTION

Integration is a multifaceted concept, as I shall attempt to demonstrate in this chapter. Integration with related programming based in or directed at the workplace is clearly a critical issue at this point in history for EAPs and for those engaged in the delivery of EA services. I have been asked to offer a commentary on these matters, using the excellent set of articles in this collection as the context.

My relevant credentials for this assignment are my earlier research on EAPs which led to the formulation of EA core technology in the mid-1980s, my efforts at remaining a friendly critic and outsider to the EA community (although for a brief period I was a card-carrying CEAP as a symbolic reward for being a charter member of the Employee Assistance Certification Commission) and my sheer durability in having stuck around this field for a good number of years.

My major interest is research about EAPs, and doubtless, the integration topic offers a number of opportunities for creative and significant research. My first point centers on an anecdote based in the world of research.

MY FIRST EAP EXPERIENCE

I have strained my memory to date to my first experience in EA-related research and have come up with 1966, a full 39 years ago. I was a Cornell graduate research assistant in a data collection that was centered on evaluating a training program on alcoholism for union shop stewards employed in Consolidated Edison, the electric power provider to metropolitan New York City. This study was funded by the Smithers Foundation, and directed by Professor Harrison M. Trice, with whom I was in the early stages of developing a mentoring relationship.

At that time, Professor Trice was directing a number of studies of supervisory and steward training where the main data collection eventually involved a fairly complex experimental design. Subjects (from Con Ed and other employment settings) were randomized into groups that did and did not receive the training. The research design was adequate to tease out the different effects of receiving the training and being exposed to the data collection instruments, which were centered on the extent of knowledge of the topics being delivered in the training.

Among the findings, published in a distinguished research journal (I was not a co-author), was that training had significant effects on changing attitudes toward dealing with alcoholic employees, but just being questioned about these issues also had significant but lesser effects on attitude change in the desired direction.

These findings, while important and hopefully interesting as well as cautionary, are not the pivotal point that can be drawn from the anecdote. There are several other implications relevant to the subject at hand, integration.

IMPLICATIONS FOR INTEGRATION

First, in 1966 Con Ed, a major American corporation, was not only contributing its employees' time to the project, but was a partner in the research in terms of desiring to learn the results of the study. Con Ed's representative was the late S. Charles Franco, MD, the corporate medical director, under whose supervision the company's employee alcoholism program operated. Dr. Franco came to Cornell frequently during the course of the study to deal with logistics and examine the findings. Given Dr. Franco's status and the company's commitment, it is easy to infer that the program for employees was well integrated into company policy, and into a respected organizational unit, the Medical Department.

Second, along with about 25 other major companies, by 1966, Con Ed had made a management-level commitment to address employee alcohol problems, and had adopted a mechanism to accomplish the task. The program was internally integrated, a term I am using to describe that the parts of the program clearly fit together with one another and the program's role and relationships with other organizational units was clear.

There was no vagueness or ambiguity about the Con Ed program's mission and how its effectiveness should be measured. There was no shifting of the program from month to month or year to year to different types of employee or organizational issues. The program's operatives had no pretense to having the ability to provide "organizational consultation" in areas of interest or concern that popped up among managers from time to time. There was no question about the name or the identity of the program. The program's outreach was primarily to supervisors and shop stewards, and its internal design was geared to solving employee problems that came to the attention of these individuals, but the important point is that employees in these roles were the gatekeepers to the program, not the individual employee who perceived a problem or was "nudged" toward the program by a co-worker.

Third, there was another dimension of integration that is evident from this anecdote. The Con Ed program had joint support from union and management in its design and operation. Save for the three articles centered on international observations, there is scarce mention of organized labor or unions in the remainder of the volume. If we are to assume that at least part of the mandate (perhaps only a tiny sliver) of EAPs, work-life and wellness/health promotion programs is to improve the lives of employed persons, then how can organizations whose prime concern is employee welfare be overlooked, or "talked around" as if they were invisible?

It is clear of course that less than a fifth of the American workforce is unionized, but translating that the percentage into a real number produces an impressive figure. Coupled with the fact that unionized occupations tend to have some of the highest risks for developing serious work-related problems such as alcohol or drug dependence, it seems difficult to justify dismissing or ignoring this segment of the workforce. It is also recognized that within their largest occupational association, the Employee Assistance Professionals Association (EAPA), those involved in EA work from labor and non-labor bases have demonstrated great difficulty in being able to work together. Hopefully these experiences have not encouraged the apparent blind eye being turned toward the role of organized labor in workplace interventions directed toward employees' lives.

Fourth, the anecdote is centered in something that, to me, is increasingly foreign to both the worlds of EAP and work-life programming. That something is research, and specifically research that meets standards of scientific integrity. The diminution of research on these work-place interventions reflects a complex set of reasons. These include a lack of leadership interest in research at the top within a sequence of cohorts of leaders (hopefully not descriptive of the present!), reaching its nadir when an executive director of EAPA was willing to put into print that research gave her a headache. At the other end of the spectrum, there appears to be little interest and no demand for research among those who elect or otherwise choose their leadership.

THE ROLE OF RESEARCH IN CREATING A PROFESSION

Research seems to be poorly understood. It is my impression that most people working in EA today tend to view research in terms of how it may directly affect them relative to an issue they are dealing with now. Asked to name "research questions" of interest to them, individual EA specialists often cite very narrow issues that affect their day-to-day operations. From what I am told, there is apparently an abundance of data about EA dynamics and outcomes on shelves and in file drawers held by organizations and individuals as proprietary information. If data are not shared or shareable, they can hardly constitute research. I would like to able to say that there are answers to many important questions nested in these proprietary studies, but who knows? Without its exposure and evaluation in an objective public forum, we have no idea of the value of this private information. Given the wide variation in training and ethical standards among those who typically perform contract research that cannot be shared, I have a fair degree of certainty that much of this information may actually be of little value to the broader community.

The research to which I refer is community property, and it should be viewed as valuable community property. Empirical research leads to evidence-based practice, and the latter cannot be generated without the former. Looking around and trying to tease out the ingredients of "excellent" programs and then referring to these as "best practices" is educated guesswork. Research is what leads to textbooks, which in turn define the scope of "practice" of a particular field. The core of a textbook is the review of research on the field's practices and the derivation of principles of practice from them. We have no textbooks in EA work, and I know of none in work-life programming. Wellness/health promotion programs are closer to having an evidence base, some of which is compiled in basic textbooks, but it has a much broader base of information from which to draw, as well as technologies that are used in many other settings than the workplace.

Textbooks are the basis for formal coursework and training, which leads to a curriculum, which would be expected to include internships and fieldwork. Both the courses and fieldwork are graded. The distribution of grades leads to some who fail and must re-take the portions of the curriculum that they fail or leave the particular endeavor for something else. This is the core of how a legitimate and recognized profession emerges. Ignoring these steps and self-labeling through calling oneself or one's group a profession is possibly another way to achieve this status, but the foundations for legitimacy are shaky at best.

RESEARCH AND EVIDENCE-BASED PRACTICE

How does this relate to integration? I argue that a core of evidence that defines effective practice principles recorded in textbooks is what integrates a field. From this base, practitioners have a stake in ongoing research that specifies or extends the principles of practice. These are key ingredients in describing a profession. A profession creates its boundaries through its steadily growing and changing database as practice improves from knowledge. A dynamic in this process that is critical is "service to science," namely a flow of feedback about practice and the refining of research issues from practitioners to scientists. Too often science is isolated from practice and thus cannot serve it. Often scientists do not want to mingle with practitioners.

Evidence-based practices do not appear overnight. Their development takes decades, but it requires a partnership between a group of interested scientists and a supportive practitioner community. One of the key ingredients of this support is for practitioners to provide researchers with access to research sites and to data. This assures the possibility of representative sampling, and generalizable findings. Another key ingredient is significant funding, usually from a Federal source where grants tend to be much larger than those typically available from private foundations. This creates another need, namely for a Federal "patron" organization who will incorporate into its portfolio studies related to a particular field of practice.

Up until about 10 years ago, this dynamic was at work in the EA field. Researchers who focused on EA topics typically spent of lot of time mingling with practitioners, and there was a high degree of mutual respect. A base of knowledge was beginning to grow. Research was supported by the National Institute on Alcohol Abuse and Alcoholism (NIAAA), with a few additional studies funded by the National Institute on Drug Abuse (NIDA). Especially exciting was the possibility of linking research questions with broader questions being studied in management and labor research, and attracting a new cadre of researchers into this pursuit. An especially exciting development was EAPA's funding of the *Journal of Employee Assistance Research* that was to be the vehicle for publishing, for the entire EAPA membership, databased research, as well as attracting databased studies from closely related areas that had direct implications for EA practice.

This development was in some ways the beginning of the end. EAPA hired its first executive director with no background in EA work (the first of several such executive directors). This occurred during a period of considerable financial turmoil at EAPA, and one of this director's first decisions was to close down the Journal. This occurred after three issues had been published. Somewhat simultaneously, officials at NIAAA and NIDA who had been key supporters of EA-related research retired or moved on to other jobs. After a relatively short period, EA-related research studies essentially disappeared from the portfolios of NIAAA and NIDA, and such research has not been considered a priority at these institutes since.

Thus, from my perspective, the process of integration whereby the field would derive its solidarity and its identity from a set of evidence-based practices stalled out about a decade ago. As I relate back to my anecdote about my EA beginnings at Cornell, it is clear that progress has been very, very slow on building the stage that Harrison Trice was trying to contribute to by providing evidence-based data about supervisory training.

We have some "sterling" research projects that have been reported, and that provide examples for what is needed for evidence-based practice. Like the study in which I was involved, each of these includes an experimental or quasi-experimental design where there are multiple groups of subjects, each of which has been selected to a manner to create equivalence in the characteristics that might affect the outcome of the study. One group receives a controlled intervention and comparison groups receive other combinations of the intervention, with the intervention withheld from at least one group.

These "sterling" projects include Trice and Beyer's controlled analysis of the effects of constructive confrontation, Walsh's experiment on differential treatment effects on employees with alcohol problems whose treatment was managed through EAP structures, Foote and Erfurt's verification of the effectiveness of sustained follow-up linked to EAP services, Googins, Schneider and Cohen's experiments with different approaches to supervisory training, and Bennett's recent demonstration of an effective model of workplace-based reduction/prevention of employee alcohol use/problems.

These studies are not mentioned to belittle the large bulk of survey and observational studies related to EA and work-life programs, but we can learn things through experimental designs that cannot be learned in other ways. The natural settings of workplaces frequently require adaptation of classic experimental procedures, but it is usually clear whether the results of a study are based on the best "rigor" that can be used in a particular setting.

This leads me directly to the conclusion that if EA work is going to move toward establishing a firm identity and with that, an identifiable utility to employers, it needs to turn its attention to research. Goals should be set to move the field toward being grounded in evidence-based practice. The decade-long "vacation" should be declared over. I honestly do not know if this is possible, given what appears to be the diffuseness of EA practice, the willingness to continue to extend this practice in multiple directions, and in some quarters the dominance of commercial considerations. While the dichotomy is not a clean one, there needs to be a distinction between those whose goals are primarily entrepreneurial versus those whose goals are primarily professional. The needs of these two groups are certainly different. Perhaps there is a core of those who are committed to what EA can do for employees with problems that impact their jobs, including substance abuse, who could form a genuine profession within what is currently, in its diffuse, boundary-less, and multiple forms, an occupation.

WHAT DO WE KNOW NOW?

While not always successful, I attempt to temper my comments about the EA world with the fact that no one really knows what is going on out there. This lack of information is reflected in the fact that the last national survey of EAPs was completed about a decade ago, and that survey did not collect any information on the kinds of problems that were addressed by EAPs, a core issue of concern to many today. Thus, data collection from nationally representative samples of EAPs and/or EAP service providers is badly needed in order to obtain a profile of the different types of EAPs, their patterns of service provision, and the composition of their caseloads.

Such a survey would also offer the opportunity to address the issues that are the concern of this volume. Within a nationally representative sample, what patterns of integration, cooperation, communication and cross-referral are found among EAPs, work-life and wellness/health promotion programs? To me, this would be an essential first step toward examining the merits of different degrees and patterns of integration. The case study chapters in this volume offer a number of excellent leads as to the manner in which a survey would address the important issues representing and surrounding integration among these three types of programs.

To me, this would only be the first step before any kind of recommendations about the merits of integration could be considered. The next step would be to use the survey data to identify different configurations of "integration" and then do an in-depth uniform data collection to measure differences in selected outcome variables. The comparison group would be organizations where the three types of programs indicate no integration whatsoever. Ideally, but unlikely, a final step would be an actual "clinical trial" where carefully controlled models of integration were introduced into randomized worksites and outcomes measured across a no-intervention control group.

This may sound pretentious and even ridiculous to some, but it seems to me a great deal is at stake here, namely the unique identity of the EAP work. While the materials in this volume certainly offer some solid descriptive information, warnings, and positive notes about integration, this is a slender reed upon which to base such a vital decision. My most basic concern is that there is no survey data and virtually no real idea about the empirical reality of patterns of integration or the absence thereof.

Perhaps at this point I should become realistic and assume that few if any will follow or perhaps even consider all of this sage advice about clarifying EA work by moving it toward evidence-based practice. My sentiments about the various suggestions for moving toward integration are not positive, largely because I feel the EA house is in such disorder we are hardly ready to start inviting in roommates.

AN EXAMPLE FROM SUBSTANCE ABUSE TREATMENT

In the research that I have been conducting on the organization of substance abuse treatment services, based on representative national samples, there may be a parallel circumstance worth some examination. As most are aware, many substance abuse clients enter treatment in a pretty broken-down condition, without work, family, or a consistent dwelling unit, and often with physical and psychological disorders, to say nothing of legal and financial problems. Led by the work of Dr. Tom McLellan and his colleagues at the University of Pennsylvania, it has long been recognized that if these other problems are not addressed, relapse to substance abuse is almost inevitable despite the progress in coping with addiction that is observed in treatment.

It would therefore follow that in order to better serve their clients, treatment programs are integrating their basic treatment services with the range of other services that clients need, as listed above. This is not exactly what is happening. Relatively few treatment programs actually move to add these services to their treatment programs so that clients can enjoy one-stop shopping. Rather the issue is approached as a matter of service coordination and follow-through, finding agencies in the community that can effectively provide these services to the types of clients that are attracted to a particular treatment program. Telling a client to go to this service rarely is effective, so follow-through is necessary, making referrals formally and often–through contractual or reciprocal arrangements that the treatment program may have with a particular service provider.

Through this process, the integrity of the treatment program is maintained, and the treatment specialists do what they do best, namely provide substance abuse treatment rather than attempting to provide ancillary services. At the same time, there is not a move to put all the services under one roof unless they can be distinctively separated.

This is not to suggest that there is a particular brilliance in the treatment community that is lacking in the EA, work-life and health promotion/wellness communities. What drives this process of coordination rather than integration is the external forces of funding streams that in turn translate into organizational survival. And it is organizational survival and identity that EAPs risk losing that is the greatest threat of suggested moves toward integration with one or both of the other two types of workplace programming.

RISKS OF "INTEGRATION" FOR EAPs

The risk of EAPs' losing identity and disappearing as a distinctive technology is high because of the extent to which the current identity has drifted so far into ambiguity. Decision-makers in workplaces have a weak understanding of what constitutes an EAP, and their awareness may be limited to whatever the current EA vendor or benefits broker tells them. To some extent, it can be argued that some vendors and brokers are barriers to workplace understanding about EAPs, their proper roles, and the value that they can bring to the organization proactively. The greatest threat to moving toward professionalism is packaging and providing services according to the customer's dictates, and this is the fundamental (and critical) strategy of the entrepreneurial side of the EA house. The kinds of checks and balances that could exist between those with professional and those with entrepreneurial orientations are simply not to be found, and the end result is a lack of education of the consumer/decision-maker in the workplace.

Finally, there is a distinctive difference between the basics of EA (perhaps only in its original "classic" form) and work-life and health promotion/wellness programs. The essence of first establishing an EAP in a workplace was a set of written policy and procedures. The purpose of these written documents was to provide an opportunity for employee (union) involvement but more importantly to insure that the intervention would be provided fairly and within the context of employees' and employers' rights. The key was the employee's responsibility to conform to job performance and job attendance standards and the employer could not intervene beyond performance and attendance issues.

Despite the negative connotations of the term, bureaucracy is essentially designed to assure even, fair, and predictable treatment of people who are interacting with an organizational structure. The classic EAP follows a bureaucratic model in that it is governed by rules, and the rules are accessible to anyone who may be affected by their implementation.

By contrast, there is much about work-life and health promotion/wellness programs that is open-ended. We conducted a comparative study of the structures of workplace wellness programs and EAPs in the early 1990s, and found a significantly higher level of uniformity across a national sample of EAPs as compared to a national sample of wellness programs. Neither work-life nor health promotion/wellness programs are based on written policies and procedures.

While they are seemingly benign, many aspects of both of these programs appear to reflect the values of the employer or the individuals operating the program. They do not include the potentially clear-cut guidelines of job performance measurement as a basis for intervention. In a nutshell, they do not offer the kinds of bureaucratic protections present in a classic EAP. As another of our studies established in examining self-referrals, the implied "free will decision" of the self-referral is almost never the case, but instead the employee is urged or pressured by significant others to enter a workplace program.

A last word on integration: Some years back I wrote several pieces on the integration of EAPs into workplaces. The key idea at that time was to assure that all stakeholders in the workplace were well educated about the EAP, and that the EAP had an organizational placement that assured its long-term survival beyond the career of a particular individual who was in charge. The ultimate goal was to create a sense of ownership of the EAP among key actors in the organization. A pillar of integration was to remain distinctive and identifiable. One of my warnings was to avoid intermingling the EAP with other similar functions in the organization. It is ironic how the years have transformed the meaning of integration.

Chapter 22

Perspectives on the Future of Integration

Patricia A. Herlihy

SUMMARY. Thomas Friedman's political analysis of *The Lexus and the Olive Tree* (2000) is used to frame the discussion of the future of integration in the EAP, Work-life and Wellness field. Many claim that for progress to occur, one needs to understand history. Friedman, however, pushes the reader further to focus on understanding the constant interplay and tension between present day advances and past traditions. This article briefly reviews one of the early attempts at comprehensive benefit services in the United States–Welfare Capitalism as a means to understand the beginnings of some of these endeavors. In addition early research conducted by Lawrence and Lorsch on organizational integration and differentiation are briefly reviewed as a conceptual framework to ground the discussion of future trends in the field of integration. Finally, some closing thoughts are offered that raise both questions on areas requiring further investigation on the topic of integration, as well as a challenge to professionals regarding what role they would like to take regarding the future of these services. *[Article copies available for a fee from The Haworth Document Delivery Service: 1-800-HAWORTH. E-mail address: <docdelivery@haworthpress.com> Website: <http://www.HaworthPress.com> © 2005 by The Haworth Press, Inc. All rights reserved.]*

KEYWORDS. Organizational integration, relational capital, employee benefit services, employee assistance, work-life and wellness programs

[Haworth co-indexing entry note]: "Perspectives on the Future of Integration." Herlihy, Patricia A. Co-published simultaneously in *Journal of Workplace Behavioral Health* (The Haworth Press, Inc.) Vol. 20, No. 3/4, 2005, pp. 407-417; and: *The Integration of Employee Assistance, Work/Life, and Wellness Services* (ed: Mark Attridge, Patricia A. Herlihy, and R. Paul Maiden) The Haworth Press, Inc., 2005, pp. 407-417. Single or multiple copies of this article are available for a fee from The Haworth Document Delivery Service [1-800-HAWORTH, 9:00 a.m. - 5:00 p.m. (EST). E-mail address: docdelivery@haworthpress.com].

Available online at http://www.haworthpress.com/web/JWBH
© 2005 by The Haworth Press, Inc. All rights reserved.
doi:10.1300/J490v20n03_12

Particularity and separability are infirmities of the mind, not characteristics of the universe.

–Dee Hock, 1999

INTRODUCTION

The principal analogy in Thomas Friedman's *The Lexus and the Olive* Tree (2000) is the juxtaposition of time enduring opposites. His basic argument is that "globalization . . . has replaced the old Cold War System . . . (and has) . . . its own rules and logic that today directly or indirectly influence the politics, environment, geopolitics and economies of virtually every country in the world." Alas, the world is made up of far more than microchips and markets and this is where Friedman's comparison of the Lexus, the symbol for technology, and the Olive Tree, the symbol for ancient forces, cultures and people, surfaces. The author contends that "world affairs today can only be explained as the interaction with what is as new as an Internet web site and what is as old as a gnarled olive tree on the banks of the river Jordan" (p. 30).

Friedman's political analysis is quite appropriate for the business world, particularly in regards to benefit services. Many claim that for progress to occur, one needs to understand history. Friedman, however, pushes the reader further to focus on understanding the constant interplay and tension between present day advances and past traditions. The collection of articles in this volume on Integration of EAP, W/L, and Wellness Programs focuses on present practices regarding the integration of services, with trends pointing to what the future may hold. While several articles present a context for appreciating the conceptual richness of programmatic organizational integration, Friedman's insistence for considering the contextual picture of where we have come from and where we are headed may add needed insight to the discussion of the future of integration of services. This article briefly reviews one of the early attempts at comprehensive benefit services in the United States, and then moves onto present day thoughts. Next, the discussion section briefly reviews a useful conceptual framework for the study of integration, and then discusses Friedman's metaphor as it relates to the integration movement. Finally, some closing thoughts are offered on what current trends tell us about the future of integrated efforts in the benefits arena. But first, let's set the context for the historical review.

Historically, at least in the United States, the emphasis for business success has been on the procurement and retention of productive workers. Many historians have written extensively about the dilemma of companies seeking to increase productivity (Mintz and Kellogg, 1988; Kett, 1983; Kanter, 1977; Janson, 1935; Fehlant, 1904). However, it is Stewart Brandes' (1976) *American Welfare Capitalism* that seems most relevant today to the issue of integration of benefit services in organizations.

HISTORICAL BACKGROUND

One of the earliest attempts at creating a comprehensive benefits program occurred in the late 1800s and was referred to as Welfare Capitalism. Brandes (1976) defined this term to indicate "any service provided for the comfort or improvement of employees which was neither a necessity of the industry or required by law." During the period of the Industrial Revolution (1860-1930), the U.S. experienced an explosive growth from the inventions in many arenas: invention and diffusion of electricity, the steam and gasoline engines, the railroad for transportation and distribution of goods, and the telegraph for communication. These discoveries transformed and revolutionized all aspects of American society. The Industrial Revolution propelled the U.S. from an agricultural society to a world class manufacturing leader in the space of a few decades (Googins, 1991).

Factory life typified the shift from rural farm work to urban employment and the workplace became defined by the factory. Factories began employing large numbers of people and the expressions "workday" and "work habits" were introduced. With the search for efficiencies came the birth of the assembly line, a term synonymous with the monotonous, repetitive nature of shift work. Although the assembly line was a boon for production, Brandes notes that it was also a time of rising unhappiness amongst workers, and an accompanying increase in malingering, drinking, absenteeism, and even acts of pure sabotage of production efforts. Strikes were clearly the most ominous and visible sign of the troubled times between employees and management. Between 1880 and 1900, nearly 23,000 strikes affected more than 117,000 establishments. Companies acquired guns, tear gas, and police power to deal with the frequent strikes. Bloodshed on both sides was inevitable. During the great railroad strike of 1877, hundreds of people were wounded and many killed (Brandes, 1976). Management and labor seemed on a collision course threatening the economic progress Americans had come to value so highly.

Business leaders eventually learned that wages, while necessary, were not sufficient to maintain a stable workforce in the factories. Workers needed to be housed, fed, socialized to urban living, and properly educated for the industrial society. Many firms responded by establishing company restaurants and stores. The U.S. Steel Company once owned more than 28,000 houses for their employees (Brandes, 1976). Schools were established for employees and their children. By 1900 various U.S. firms operated every form of school short of college. Toddlers could attend the company kindergarten, children the company grammar school, and even some company high schools were available.

Welfare Capitalism was perceived by some as an attempt by the corporate sector to "co-opt" the employee and their family into the belief that they were all one big happy family. For example, the Endicott Johnson Company gave new employees a booklet entitled "E. J. Workers' First Lesson in the Square Deal." The booklet summarized the services and benefits available to employees and their families and boldly declared: "You have now joined the Happy Family" (Zahavi, 1988).

Many things have changed and evolved in the employee benefits arena since Welfare Capitalism; however, some feel they have stayed the same. During the Golden Age of the 1950s a clearer separation arose between family and work. Husbands were busy commuting back and forth to work while housewives/mothers managed the home front. And all the while, corporate America continued efforts to socialize the family into the norms of the firm. Books were written to inform "corporate wives" how they should respond in social situations (Whyte, 1956). And General Motors conveyed the clear message that what was "Good for the Company" was also good for the family. The not so subtle message was that it was the family's role to be ever ready to bend, sway and adapt to what the company needed for operational growth and efficiency (Googins, 1991). The almighty "Transfer" was one very pervasive method in which the family learned they had to bend to the whims of corporate America. Atlas Van Lines reported that the typical corporate manager moved fourteen times during his career in one organization (Mintz, 1988).

More recently Laura Nash (1994) coined the term "Nanny Corporation," in accusing companies of devising benefits merely to keep workers on the job for longer hours each day. Some of these benefits such as "hot meals," concierge services, organizing children's birthday parties, and academic tutoring are very reminiscent of the old Welfare Capitalism days. The question that continues to surface in today's marketplace is what is the goal of employers regarding the scope of employee benefits and what is the most efficient and effective way of prioritizing them.

PRESENT DAY

Today's organizations interact in a complex milieu of evolving economic and social forces. Since the late 1980s dire reports have surfaced about the nations' education system and its inability to produce people with the proper skills and abilities to meet the needs of today's marketplace (Nation at Risk, 1983). In addition, current reports of an aging workforce and a lagging birth rate have others concerned about the country's ability to meet workforce needs in the future (Burud, 2004). Globalization has also changed the face of business such that a diminishing number of products and companies are purely American. Everyone is competing with everyone else around the world at any given moment in time. Technological innovations are also changing the face of what used to be considered "work." Robert Reich (2004) describes three categories of workers in today's changing society: routine production workers, people who deliver in-person attention-giving services, and symbolic-analytic workers. Reich further points out that it is the symbolic-analytic worker who creates and designs the content of every consumer product and service in the current marketplace.

There is an increasing need for this group of skilled workers in today's society and they are quite different from the skills needed during the days of Welfare Capitalism. Given the need to both recruit and retain skilled workers, it is more important than ever for employers and employees to build up what Reich refers to as "relational capital." Reich coined the term to define: "the cumulative experience of people in the organization in dealing with their customers and clients–understanding their needs and developing those relationships." From his vantage point, the true sources of productivity and success in any organization critically depend on people understanding the needs and capacities of the other people around them. Employees are looking for a sense of whether their employers take into account who they are as individuals while allowing for events that arise in their private lives as well as their work lives. According to Reich, it is this sense of affinity that allows a company to build relational capital and be successful in today's fast-paced competitive global market.

Bringing the conversation to a more concrete and specific level, one can examine current marketplace practices by reviewing employment surveys conducted over the last 40 years. In 1969, the Department of Labor funded three national studies of the United States workforce as part of the *Quality of Employment Survey* (Bond, 2002). The last of these three surveys was conducted in 1977 and was the first one to address the personal lives of employees as well as their work lives (Quinn, 1979). A hiatus occurred in the collection of national workforce data until the early 1990s when the Families and Work Institute began a series of studies entitled the *National Study of the Changing Workforce* (NSCW). To date, three surveys were completed in 1992, 1997, and 2002; each with an average sample size of 3500 workers. The samples surveyed have included wage, salaried and self-employed workers. The most recent 2002 survey incorporated questions from the 1977 study and thus affords the reader an historical lens to compare changes and shifts over time.

The NSCW 2002 results demonstrate that there has been a significant increase in employee sense of "interference between job and family life" since the 1977 survey. Researchers explain this increased spillover between work and home life as arising mainly from increased work demands in today's fast-paced society (Bond, 2002, p. 45). A complimentary reason for this shift is the substantial increase in the number of dual earner couples. In 1977, approximately 66% of the married workforce lived in dual earning relationships. In 2002 that number had increased to 78%. Another interesting finding is the increase in number of hours worked. All workers, couples and single earners, report an increase in the number of hours worked from 70 hours a week in 1977 to 82 hours a week in 2002. The increase for dual earner couples with children has increased from 81 hours a week in 1977 to 91 hours a week in 2002. Clearly, today's couples have less time away from their job responsibilities than they did in 1977 (Bond, 2002).

An important finding from the NCWF 2002 study that relates to the field of employee benefits focuses on the relationship between cyclic spillover from work to home and back to work. If an employee's work environment has negative effects, spillover onto an employee's personal life, this has a direct effect on the worker's attitude toward their job and employer. Employees will be less satisfied with their jobs, less committed to their employers, and less likely to be retained. The NCWF study clearly indicates that in today's world, work and family are inextricably linked. And if there are problems in one arena, either work or home life, then there will likely be resulting problems in the other arena.

All of the above background material addresses historical efforts and current concerns, now we need to turn to the actual discussion of integration. What does organizational integration mean and how has history affected the delivery of employee benefit services?

DISCUSSION

As mentioned in an earlier article the conceptual study of "organizational integration" originated back in the early 1960s when two Harvard Professors, Paul Lawrence and Jay Lorsch, conducted an industrial research study on collaboration (1967). These researchers were aligned with the "contingency" school of organizational theory, but their work focused specifically on refining the concepts of integration and differentiation particularly from the perspective of functional managers. Lawrence and Lorsch posed the question of "what kind of organization does it take to effectively deal with various economic and market conditions." They contributed to the refinement of the concepts of integration and differentiation and characterized them as normal adaptational responses over time within organizations. The term differentiation refers to the "difference in cognitive and emotional orientation among managers in different functional units." Integration, on the other hand, is defined as "the quality of the state of collaboration that exists among departments that are required to achieve unity of effort by the demands of the environment (Lawrence and Lorsch, 1967, p. 11).

As firms grow and adapt to new internal and external requirements, they differentiate into specialized functions. For the system to be viable and operate smoothly these separate parts must be fine tuned with appropriate operational structures, coordinating processes and reward mechanisms that integrate the company together into a functioning whole. In considering how best to achieve this integration, the specific demands and marketplace opportunities as assessed from the organization's environment must be taken into account. The researchers acknowledge an ongoing tension between the need for differentiation as new products or services emerge, and the need for integration as new demands arise for coordination from within the firm or from the external marketplace.

The question now becomes how to integrate Friedman's analogy about the contextual tensions of yesterday and today, with Lawrence and Lorsch's conceptual model of organizational integration. Both acknowledge ongoing tensions. Friedman's refers to the tension between the past and the present while Lawrence and Lorsch address the interplay between developing new products and then integrating them into a cohesive and adaptive system. Addressing the historical piece first, it is interesting that in the late 1890s and around the turn of the 20th century, employers understood the reciprocal benefit of taking steps to care for their employees as a way to obtain productive contributions from their time at work. Many have criticized the underpinnings of Welfare Capitalism as being too paternalistic a movement for our country. The more important issue is that as the country changed from an agricultural society to an industrial one, caretaking moved away from a solely family focus to a role shared by employers. These phenomena continued until the Depression. Brandes (1976) attributed the Depression as starting the demise of Welfare Capitalism. Yet it is fascinating historically that this was also the time when Franklin Delano Roosevelt ushered in the New Deal. The new policies and resulting programs, including Social Security, moved the care of our nation's citizens under a government umbrella. A similar path has been taken on the international level. Many of these benefits were socially and government driven as is illustrated in several of the international contributions to this edition of articles.

In borrowing from Lawrence and Lorsch's work it is interesting to review the history of EAP, W/L and Wellness Programs from a differentiated lens and postulate whether there is readiness to move towards a more integrated model of service delivery. As mentioned in an earlier article, OAPs were the precursor to EAPs and evolved in the early 1940s from employers' need to procure productive workers. The Work/Family field arose in earnest in the early 1970s when a significant increase arose in the number of women entering the workforce. Although some early fitness programs arose about this time, it was not until the 1990s that the Wellness field truly made an appearance in the benefits arena. As each new benefit/product evolved there appeared to be a "silo" effect or a differentiated model of service delivery as the uncertainties associated with new experimental services were tested. Each specialty area was initially housed in different departments and, quite frequently, with little interchange between the programs. Today, the conceptual question is whether corporate culture believes that the most effective and efficient way to deliver these benefits services is through an integrated structure, or whether global competition is driving cost cutting to the detriment of their employee and the breadth and depth of the services needed. As Friedman reminds us it is important during this discovery period to take history and the prevailing norms of both the various professions and the industries into consideration as this evolutionary adaptation unfolds. The bottom line question becomes what is the most organizationally efficient way for employers to deliver benefit services while effectively meeting the needs of its employees.

Today's world and marketplace are an order of magnitude more complex than the early days of the Industrial Revolution. As Reich pointed out, the level and range of skills needed by workers has changed dramatically. What has remained constant is an attitude of employers realizing the competitive importance of providing a culture that attracts and retains talent over time. This quid pro quo approach is pragmatic not paternalistic. Instead it acknowledges that people lead lives with a dual focus on their work and on their personal lives. Now let's turn our attention to the future.

THOUGHTS ON FUTURE DIRECTIONS

Will integration of EAP, Work-life and Wellness services be the wave of the future? With survey predictions reporting that 62% of the marketplace will be providing integrated services by 2007, organizational integration of benefit services is already a documented trend. But numerous important questions remain unanswered. What is the operational definition of integration? What organizations might best utilize an integrated approach versus a differentiated one for service delivery? How does one measure effective integration? Are there stages or linear phases to integration? Can an integrated approach be more cost efficient without introducing detrimental effects such as a decrease in quality of service? Is an integrated approach more or less effective than a differentiated model, and how does one measure and evaluate that difference? What is the decision-making process concerning the evolvement of an integrated program? And how can that be measured? And finally, what are the barriers to an integrated approach to service delivery? Roman, in a previous article in this volume, outlines the research agenda needed to address some of these concerns, but as he points out, the field needs both financial support and interest in conducting this level of empirical studies.

Throughout this collection of articles the reader has learned about organizations which have been successful across various levels while following an integrated approach to service delivery. Other articles raise legitimate questions as to the extent and long-term viability of this approach unless there is a change in mindset about the notion of collaboration and sharing of domain knowledge across professional groups. In our competitive world the notion of collaboration is not always a natural occurrence. As in Friedman's metaphor of the Olive Tree, cultural and professional norms that have developed over time need to be considered in the ongoing tensions for adaptation and change in the face of current environmental demands. The ongoing march of progress and adaptation in the face of an increasingly complex, fast-paced, and fiercely competitive global marketplace may not wait for cultural and professional norms to catch up with current demands. Companies need to be progressive about experimenting with viable solutions to jointly meet the needs of the marketplace and their employees. Rigorous research is needed to contribute guidance about the choices for effective and efficient programs. And the professionals who deliver these services need to grapple with whether they want to be in the forefront of these particular organizational decisions or merely reacting to competitive external market demands.

REFERENCES

Bond, James, Thompson, Cynthia, Galinsky, Ellen and Prottas, David. (2002). Highlights of the National Study of the Changing Workforce. NY: Families and Work Institute.

Burud, Sandra and Tumolo, Marie. (2004). *Leveraging the New Human Capital*. Palo Alto, CA: Davies Black Publishing.

Fehlant, August. (1904). *A Century of Drink Reform in the US*. Cincinnati: Jennings and Graham Publishers.

Friedman, Thomas. (2000). *The Lexus and the Olive Tree*. New York: Random House.

Googins, Bradley. (1991). *Work/Family Conflict: Private Lives–Public Responses*. NY: Auburn House.

Hock, Dee. (1999). *Birth of the Chaordic Age*. San Francisco: Berrett–Koehler Publishers, Inc.

Janson, Charles. (1935). *The Stranger in American 1793-1806*. NY: Press of the Pioneers.

Kanter, Rosabett. (1977). *Work and Family in the US: A Critical Review and Agenda for Research and Policy*. NY: Russell Sage Foundation.

Kett, Joseph. (1983). The stages of life, 1790-1840. In the *American Family in Social Historical Perspective*. (3rd edition), edited by Michael Gordan. NY: St. Martin's Press.

Mintz, S. and Kellogg, S. (1988). *Domestic Revolution: A Social History of the American Family Life*. NY: The Free Press.

Nash, Laura. (1994). The Nanny Corporation. *Across the Board*. July/August.

Quinn, R. and Staines, G. (1979). The Quality of Employment Survey. Ann Arbor, MI, Institute for Social Research. University of Michigan.

Reich, Robert. (2003) *Designing the Future*–Keynote Address at the Alliance for Work-life Professionals Conference in Orlando, Florida.

The U.S. Department of Education's National Commission on Excellence in Education published the report, A Nation At Risk, in 1983.

Whyte, William. (1956). *The Organizational Man*. NY: Simon and Schuster.

Zahavi, Gerald. (1988). *Workers, Managers and Welfare Capitalism: The Shoeworkers and Tanners of Endicott Johnson, 1890-1950*. Urbana: University of Illinois Press.

APPENDIX

Resources in the EAP, Work/Life and Wellness Fields

LITERATURE

American Journal of Public Health
www.healthpromotionjournal.com

Journal of Occupational and Environmental Medicine (JOEM)
www.joem.org

Work & Family Connection News Brief
www.workfamily.com

Work-Family Research Newsletter
http://www.bc.edu/bc_org/avp/wfnetwork/newsletter/

[Haworth co-indexing entry note]: "Resources in the EAP, Work/Life and Wellness Fields." Co-published simultaneously in *Journal of Workplace Behavioral Health* (The Haworth Press, Inc.) Vol. 20, No. 3/4, 2005, pp. 419-424; and: *The Integration of Employee Assistance, Work/Life, and Wellness Services* (ed: Mark Attridge, Patricia A. Herlihy, and R. Paul Maiden) The Haworth Press, Inc., 2005, pp. 419-424. Single or multiple copies of this article are available for a fee from The Haworth Document Delivery Service [1-800-HAWORTH, 9:00 a.m. - 5:00 p.m. (EST). E-mail address: docdelivery@haworthpress.com].

Available online at http://www.haworthpress.com/web/JWBH
© 2005 by The Haworth Press, Inc. All rights reserved.
doi:10.1300/J490v20n03_13

Sloan Work and Family Research Network at Boston College
www.bc.edu/wfnetwork

Work Life Today
www.worklifetoday.com

PROFESSIONAL ORGANIZATIONS

Alliance for Work/Life Progress
www.awlp.org

College and Universities Work and Family Organization
www.cuwfa.org

Employee Assistance Professionals Association
www.*eapassn.org*

Employee Assistance Roundtable
http://*earoundtable.org*

Employee Assistance Society of North America
www.easna.org

National Council on Family Relations
ncfr.org

The Society of Human Resource Management
www.shrm.org

WELCOA–Wellness Councils of America
www.welcoa.org

World@Work
www.worldatwork.org

ORGANIZATIONS/CONFERENCES

American College of Sports Medicine (ACSM; home of the defunct Association for Worksite Health Promotion, AWHP)
www.acsm.org

Boston College Center on Work and Family
www.bc.edu/centers/cwf/

Health Enhancement Research Organization (HERO)
www.the-hero.org/

Health, Work & Wellness Institute (Canadian Group)
www.healthworkandwellness.com

Institute for Health and Productivity Management (IHPM)
www.ihpm.org

Midwest Business Group on Health (MBGH)
www.mbgh.org

National Business Group on Health (NBGH; previously Washington
Business Group on Health)
www.wbgh.org

National Wellness Institute (home of the National Wellness Conference
in Stevens Point, WI, USA)
www.nationalwellness.org

OCCUPATIONAL HEALTH ARENA

Association of Societies for Occupational Safety and Health (ASOSH)
(International-South African)
www.asosh.org/

International Occupational Hygiene Association
www.ioha.net/

International Commission on Occupational Health
www.icoh.org.sg/

American College of Occupational and Environmental Medicine
www.acoem.org/

UNITED STATES GOVERNMENT AGENCIES

U.S. Department of Health and Human Services Substance Abuse and Mental Health Services Administration (SAMHSA) Workplace Services
http://workplace.samhsa.gov/

U.S. Department of Health and Human Services National Institute for Occupational Safety and Health (NIOSH)
www.cdc.gov/niosh/homepage.html

U.S. Department of Labor
Occupational Safety & Health Administration (OSHA)
www.osha.gov/

UNITED STATES REGIONAL WORK/FAMILY ORGANIZATIONS

Boston, MA
New England Work and Family Association (NEWFA)
www.bc.edu/newfa

Purdue University, IN
Midwestern Work-Family Association (MWFA)
www.cfs.purdue.edu/CFF

San Diego, CA
Work-Life Coalition of San Diego
www.worklifesandiego.org

San Francisco, CA
One Small Step
www.onesmallstep.org

EUROPEAN UNION RESOURCES IN THE EAP AND WORK/LIFE

Projects

Work-Life Balance Network, Education and Training Services Trust Ltd
E-mail: *euprojects@etst.ie*

National Flexi-Work Partnership Work-Life Balance Project–Men in Childcare
E-mail: *mfdavis@tcd.ie*

Work and Family in the eWork Era
E-mail: *iosbooks@iospress.com*

Web Sites

Equality Authority
www.worklifebalance.ie

European Foundation for Working and Living
www.eurofound.ie

Chartered Institute of Personnel and Development, UK
www.cipd.co.uk

Employers for Work Life Balance, UK
www.cipd.co.uk

EAP Institute e-mail: *eapinstitute@eircom.net*

Irish

National Childcare Strategy. (1999) *Report on the Partnership 2000 expert working group on childcare*–Government Publications, Molesworth Street, Dublin 2.

Investing in People–Family Friendly Arrangements in Small or Medium Sized Business (2000)
www.equality.ie

Family-Friendly/Work-Life Balance Policies, Irish Business and Employers Confederation (2000)
www.ibec.ie

Balancing Your Life (2003)
www.theliffeypress.com

Shift Working and Family Friendly Policies–A study of practices in four Organisations in Ireland, Published by the National Framework Committee for Family Friendly Policies (2003)
E-mail: *mary_Dooley@entemp.ie*

Off the Treadmill Achieving Work Life Balance, Published by the National Framework Committee for Family Friendly Policies
E-mail: *mary_Dooley@entemp.ie*

AUSTRALIAN RESOURCES

The Employee Assistance Professionals Association of Australia (EAPAA)
www.eapaa.org.au

The Employee Assistance Professionals Association (Australia) (EAPA)
www.eap.com.au

Work/Life Association of Australia
www.worklifeassociation.org

ACCREDITATION ORGANIZATIONS

Council on Accreditation for Children and Family Services (COA)
www.coanet.org/front3/index.cfm

Council on Accreditation of Rehabilitation Facilities (CARF)
www.carf.org/default.aspx

Index

Page numbers in *italics* designate figures; page numbers followed by the letter "t" designate tables. *See also* cross-references designate related topics or more detailed subentries.

Absenteeism, 15,34,193,199-200
Academic research, 39
Academic settings, 105-181
    Johns Hopkins University Faculty
      and Staff Assistance
      Program, 123-142
    University of Arizona Life & Work
      Connections, 105-121
    University of California–Berkeley
      death response program,
      143-157
Access
    employee, 194
    Voice Over Internet Protocol,
      197-198,238
Accreditation organizations, 424
Administrative gains, 192-193
Adoptive Leave Act of 1993 (Ireland),
    388
Aerobics (Cooper), 71
Alcoholics Anonymous, 9
Alcoholism, recognition as disease, 9
Alliance of Work-life Progress.
    See AWP
Ambivalence, conflict of, 133
American Medical Association, 9
American Psychology Society, 39
America Online (AOL), 48
Anthrax attack, 319
Anxiety, 132-133
Assess/refer model, 41,230
Association for Labor-Management
    Administrators and

Consultants on Alcoholism
    (MACA), 70
Attitudes, employee and preparedness,
    167-168
Attridge, Mark, xv, xvii, xxxi, xxxii,
    31-55,67-93
Attridge EAP Value Triad,
    46,46-47,334
Australia, 351-366
    case study: BSS Corporate
      Psychology Services,
      357-358
    case study: private sector wellness
      program, 358-369
    case study: public sector
      occupational health and
      safety, 360-361
    conclusions, 361-363
    evolution of EAP programs,
      353-354
    future directions, 363-364
    industrial climate and EAPs,
      352-353
    integration experiences, 356-361
    lack of understanding of EAPs,
      362-363
    perspectives on integration,
      355-356
Australian Council of Trade Unions,
    353
Australian resources, 424
AWP
    categories of focus, 12

© 2005 by The Haworth Press, Inc. All rights reserved.

definition of work-life
effectiveness, 3

Barriers to integration, 312-313
Barriers to preparedness, 166-168
Baxter HealthCare, 13
Beer, Stephanie, 367-380,xvii
Beidel, Bernard E., xvii-xviii, 281-306
Bidgood, Rick, xviii, 219-242
Birkland, Adib S., xviii, 325-350
Birkland, Stephen P., xviii, 325-350
Blair, Brenda R., xviii-xix, xxxi, 1-29
Blood pressure screening, 71
Boston University Center on Work and
Family, 72-73
Boudewyn, Arne, 219-242,xix
Bowen, Murray, resiliency concept,
110-111
Bragen, Ronnie, xix, 183-201
British Association for Counselling
and Psychotherapy study,
370
Brown, David F., xix, 351-366
Brundtland Report, 5-6
Business, factors in success of, 3-4
Business continuity, 178t
disaster consequence management,
159-181
Business Value Triad model, *46,*
46-47,*334*

Call centers, Fairview Alive program,
270
Carer's Leave Act of 2001 (Ireland),
389
Case studies
Anderson Ireland, 389-390
Australia, 356-361
BSS Corporate Psychology
Services (Australia), 357-358
Flight Centre (Australia), 358-360
Ireland, 389-392

Johns Hopkins University Faculty
and Staff Assistance
Program, 135-141
KPMG, 190-192
occupational health and safety
(Australia), 360-361
Pfizer, 63-64
Redlands Shire Council (Australia),
360-361
substance abuse, 403-404
University of Arizona
Life & Work Connections,
116-120
Work-life Balance Network
(Ireland), 391-392
Worksite Wellness Heart Health
Screenings (U. Arizona),
114-115
Ceridian, 183-201
background, 184-185
challenges, 195-197
communications, 195
employee advantages, 193-194
Employee Advisory Resources
program, 185
employer's gains, 192-193
future directions, 198-200
growth of, 185-186
health education programs, 188
human resources outsourcing, 199
instant messaging, 198
KPMG case example, 190-192
linking programs, 188
measured results, *189,*189-190
new modes of access, 197-200
Partnership Group and, 185
personalization, 194
staying current, 195
supportive social environment
programs, 188
Voice Over Internet Protocol,
197-198
Web services, 186-187
Website design, 196
wellness programs, 187-188

Certified Employee Assistance
Professional International
(CEAP) credential, 393
Change models, 17-19
Chevron/Texaco, 171
Childcare, 11
Collateral services, 95-104. *See also*
Expert survey
Commodization, 64-65
Communication
challenges of, 195
in disaster events, 172-173
Motorola wellness program,
214-215
in preparedness, 169t
Community sustainability, 13
Complementarity, 131-132
Comprehensive Alcohol Abuse and
Alcoholism Prevention,
Treatment, and Rehabilitation
Act (Hughes Act), 9,284
Conceptual models, 1-29
background and principles, 2-3
conclusions, 26
finding commonalities, 22-25
global perspective, 16-17
history and current situations, 9-14
principles of progress, 25-26
services and service delivery
systems, 17-19,*18*
societal factors, 3-7
workplace impact, 7-9
Confidentiality, 237,314,362
Conflict of ambivalence, 133
Consolidated Edison, 395-406
Consulting firms, 60
development of, 70
human capital and, 38-39
Continuity
business, 178t
human, 178t
Control Data Corporation, 184-185.
See also Ceridian
Cooper, Kenneth, 71
Corporate culture, 223

Corporate security, silo effect in, 167
Corporate silos, 167,356
Costs, 32-35
disability, 33-34
human capital and, 36-37
medical, 32
mental health, 33
organizational risks, 35
turnover, 35
Watson Wyatt Human Capital
Index, 37-38
workers compensation, 34
workplace performance, 34-35
Counterproductive work behavior,
337-341
Critical analysis, 395-406
author's first experience, 396-397
case example: substance abuse,
403-404
Consolidated Edison alcoholism
program, 397-399
current status, 402-403
research and professionalism,
399-400
risks of integration for EAPs,
404-406
Critical Incident Stress Management,
118-120
Fairview Alive program, 271
Minnesota state government, 344
New Jersey State Police program,
293-294
Wells Fargo program, 230-231
Critical issues, 48-50
Cultural awareness, 5
Culture
commonalities and, 24-25
organizational, 149,*149*
Culture change, 13

Data sources, 49-50
Death
University of California–Berkeley
program, 143-157

workplace, 144-145
Delowery, Mark, xix, 307-323
Demographic trends, business costs
    and, 36-37
Depression, 170,314
    case example, 135
    cost of, 33
    early detection, 193
    employer cost of, 199-200
    Fairview Alive program, 273-274
    Minnesota state government
        awareness project, 335
    Wells Fargo program, 232-233
Differentiation, 110-111
Disability, costs of, 33-34
Disaster behaviors, 163,178t
Disaster Consequence Management,
    159-181. *See also* Critical
        Incident Stress Management
    background and principles, 160-161
    barriers to preparedness, 166-168
    èvent communication, 173-174
    future directions, 176-178
    integrated approach in, 168-171
    language of, 177-178,178t
    personnel locator planning, 165
    population level approach, 162-163
    post-event evaluation, 174-175
    pre-event education, 172-173
    preparedness role of workplace,
        161-162
    psychological behavioral
        implications, 163-165
    refugee populations and, 175
Disease management initiatives, 100
Disease model, 100,129
Distress responses, 165
DuPont company, 171

EAPA
    Australia, 354,363
    core functions and standards list, 10
    definition of employee assistance, 3
    research projects, 74-81

Ecological studies, 5-6
Education
    Fairview Alive program, 270
    Motorola wellness program, 209
    for preparedness, 169t, 172-174
    vendor programs, 188
Eischen, Barbara D., xix-xx. 263-279
Employee advantages
    Ceridian programs, 193-194
    easier access, 194
Employee assistance, definition, 3
(The) Employee Assistance Handbook
    (Oher), 294-295
Employee Assistance Professionals
    Association. *See* EAPA
Employee Assistance Programs
    (EAPs)
    concerns about diffusion of,
        98-100,99
    definition, 124
    effectiveness and outcomes, 40-41
    essence of, 11
    executives' knowledge of, 99-100
    external vs. internal, 170
    Fairview Alive, 271
    historical background, 70-72
    history, xxx-xxxi
    history and current situation, 9-11
    literature review, 40-41
    mental health and, 40-41
    prevalence and use, 40
    social stigma and, 100,255-256,314
Employee benefits, 45
Employee metrics, 150,*150*
Employer advantages, 44-45
    administrative, 192-193
    Ceridian programs, 192-193
    early detection, 193
    return on investment, 193
Endicott Johnson Company, 410
Erfurt, Jack, 69
Ernst & Young hybrid model, 243-262
    Americas People Team (Human
        Resources), 245
    background, 245

conclusions, 259-260
consensus formation, 248-250
decision guide and contracting,
    251-252,251t
future directions, 258-259
impetus for integration, 245-248
program growth and enhancement,
    257
program implementation, 254-255
program maintenance, 257-258
services offered, 250,250t
vendor identification and selection,
    250-251
vendor perspectives: selection,
    252-254,253t
vendor perspectives: strengths and
    liabilities, 255-257
European Community, 376-377
European Network for Workplace
    Health Promotion, 377
European Union, United Kingdom and,
    384-385
European Union resources, 422-424
Irish, 423-424
projects, 422-423
Web sites, 423
Evaluation, 291-294
of disaster response, 174-175
in preparedness, 169t
Evidence-based practice,
    400-402
Expert survey, 95-104
concerns about core EAP diffusion,
    98-100,99
implications of integration,
    103-104
integration with work-life,
    100-102
interview guide, 97-98
rationale to integrate, 102-103
sampling, 96-97
External service providers, 183-201.
    See also Vendors
External vs. internal employee assistance
    programs (EAPs), 170

Fairview Alive program, 48,263-279
background and principles, 264-265
call center, 270
Critical Incident Stress
    Management, 271
depression initiatives, 273-274
discussion, 277-278
EAP team, 267
education activities, 270
Employee Assistance Program, 271
employee benefits team, 267
employee occupational health team,
    267
evaluation, 274-276
health care costs and, 276
health management team, 267
Health Risk Assessment, 268
history of integration, 265-266
integration process, 271-272
new employee health kits, 268-270
outcomes, 276-277
participation, 272-273,275-276
Population Health Management
    principles, 268
preventive health offerings, 270
services offered, 268-271,269
Soul Journey campaign, 274
staff team, 266-268
vendor partners, 267-268
Web-based services, 270
workers' compensation and,
    276-277
Families and Work Institute
studies by, 412-413
work-life program evolution, 12-13
Family, services to, 70
Family systems, 4
Fasbinder, Betsy, xx, 219-242
Fear, as barrier to preparedness, 168
Federal Occupational Health,
    307-323
agencies served, 312
background and principles, 308-309
barriers to/benefits of integration,
    312-313

client outcomes: employee
    assistance program, 316-317
client outcomes: smoking cessation,
    317-318
conclusions, 320
crisis management, 319
customer satisfaction, 314-315
evaluation, 314-315
feedback on, 314
funding, 310
Global Assessment of Functioning,
    316
organizational integration, 310-312
point-of-service integration,
    313-314
program enhancements/future
    directions, 319-320
range of services, 309-315
satisfaction survey results,
    315-316,315t
specific integration efforts, 318-319
First Interstate Bancorp, 221-222. *See
    also* Wells Fargo program
Fitness of employees, preparedness
    measures and, 167-168
Fitness programs, Motorola, 208-209
Foote, Andrea, 69
Ford Motor Company study, 69
Fortune 500 EAP survey, 40
Franco, S. Charles, M.D., 397
Friedman, Thomas,
    407,408-409,413-415,416
Fullerton, Carol S., xx, 159-181
Future perspectives, 407-417
    comments on, 415-416
    discussion, 413-415
    historical background and, 409-411
    present day and, 411-413

General Motors, 410
Gestalt theory, 129-131
Global Burden of Disease study, 33.
    See also Brundtland Report
Globalization, 4-5,408,411

Global perspective, 16-17
Gold, Daniel B., xx-xxi, 263-279
Gornick, Mary Ellen, xxi, xxxi, 1-29
Goya, Bruce, xxi, 143-157
Great Depression, 414
Grief, 343-344
    University of California–Berkeley
        death response program,
        143-157
Grossmeier, Jessica, xxi-xxii, 263-279
Guilt, 132-133

Health, social ecology of, 107-109
Health and productivity management
    (HPM), 57-65
    commodization, 64-65
    costs, 32-35
    definition, 3,59-60
    developing support for, 60-61
    health care system and, 64
    history and current status, 14-16
    implementation, 62
    Integration Continuum, 62
    Pfizer case study, 63-64
    program design, 61-62
    solutions-oriented approach, 8-9
    specific programs, 15-16
    "wake-up call" for, 58-59
Health and wellness, vendor
        interviews, 87
Healthcare claims records, as data
        source, 49
Healthcare costs, 33,199-200
    United Kingdom, 375-376
Health education programs, 188
Health promotion and wellness,
        literature review, 42-44
Health Risk Appraisals (HRAs),
        14,43,268
Healthy People reports, 72,187-188
Heart attacks, 3
Heirich, Max, 69
Herlihy, Patricia A., xv, xxii, xxxii,
        67-93

HERO studies, 33
Hertenstein, Edward, xxii, xxxii,
    95-104,
Historical aspects, xxix-xxxi, 409-411
History
    Employee Assistance Programs
        (EAPs), 9-11,70
    wellness programs, 71-72
    work-life programs, 71
H.J. Heinz company, xxix
Hoffman, Carol, xxii-xxiii, 143-157
Holbrook, Jean, xxiii, 183-201
Hoskinson, Linda, xxiii, 367-380
Hostility, workplace, 338-339. *See also*
    Violence
Hughes Act (Comprehensive Alcohol
    Abuse and Alcoholism
    Prevention, Treatment, and
    Rehabilitation Act), 9,284
Human Affairs International, 70
Human capital, 38-39
    business costs and, 36-37
    as concept, 59
    workplace programs as driver of,
        39-44
Human Capital (Davenport), 38-39
Human Capital Index, 37-38
Human continuity, 178t
Human resources outsourcing, 199
Hybrid models, 243-279
    Ernst & Young, 243-262
    Fairview Alive program, 263-279
Hypertension, 20,71

IHP definition of health and
    productivity management, 3
IHPM, origins and growth of, 39
ILO Convention 156 on Workers with
    Family Responsibilities, 353
Individual/work environment nexus,
    22
Industrial Revolution, 409
Industrial social services, xxix-xxx.
    See also Welfare capitalism

Influenza vaccine shortage, 108
Infrastructure, organizational, 149,*150*
Instant messaging, 198
Institute for Health and Productivity.
    See IHP
Institute of Medicine, preparedness
    report, 161-162
Institution of Occupational Safety and
    Health (European
    Community), 377
Integrated Benefits Institute (IBI),
    39,60
Integrated value models, 45-48,*46*
Integrated Workplace Resiliency
    Model, 159-181. *See also*
    Disaster Consequence
    Management
Integration. *See also* Health and
    productivity management
    advantages: employees, 45
    advantages: employers, 44-45
    barriers to, 312-313
    challenges of, 289-291
    conceptual framework for,
        1-29,284-287,285t. *See also*
        Conceptual framework
    critical analysis, 395-406
    definition, 3,282-283
    of disaster preparedness, 168-171
    employer attitudes, 100
    evaluation, 291-294
    expert survey, 95-104
    failure rate, 103
    global perspective, 16-17
    hybrid models, 243-279
    internal programs, 203-242
    key variables, 21
    literature review, 31-55,44-48
    New Jersey State Police study,
        281-306. *See also*
        Organizational placement
    opportunities for, 290t
    organizational structures for, 103
    partners and functions, 296t
    potential risks of, 300-302

price pressure and, 21
public sector, 281-349
research on, 67-93
risks of, 404-406
societal factors in, 3-7
traditions behind, 287-288
U.S. efforts, 19-22
workplace death response,
    143-157
Integration Continuum, 62
Interaction, strategic, 23-24
Interactive Voice Reponse,
    187-198,238
Internal programs, 203-242
Motorola, 203-218
Wells Fargo, 219-242
International Labour Organization,
    mental health symposium
    (2003), 164
International perspectives, 351-394
Australia, 351-366
European Community, 376-377
Ireland, 381-394
United Kingdom, 367-380
International Survey of EAP,
    Work-life, and Wellness
    Vendors, pilot survey, 80-83
Internet. *See* Web-based services
Ireland, 381-394
Adoptive Leave Act of 1993,388
Association of Welfare and
    Employee Assistance
    Councilors (AWEAC), 386
Carer's Leave Act of 2001,389
case study: Anderson Ireland,
    389-390
case study: Work-life Balance
    Network, 391-392
Certified Employee Assistance
    Professional International
    (CEAP) credential, 393
conclusions, 393
Employer's Duty of Care, 386
Employment Equality Agency, 383
Equality Authority, 387

Equal Opportunities Childcare
    Programme –2006,383
European Union and United States
    and, 384-385
evolution of EAP programmes,
    385-386
"family friendly" employment
    legislation, 387-389
Irish Business and Employers'
    Confederation, 387
Irish Congress of Trade Unions,
    387
Irish National Development Plan,
    386
Maternity Protection Act of
    1994,388
National Framework Committee for
    Development of Family
    Friendly Policies, 387
Organization of Working Time Act
    of 1997,388
Parental Leave Act of
    1998,388-389
Programme for Prosperity and
    Fairness, 383,386
social partnerships, EAPs, and
    work-life, 383-384
work-life programs, 383,386-387
Irish Congress of Trade Unions, 387
Irish resources, 423-424

Job performance. *See* Work
    performance
Johns Hopkins University Faculty and
    Staff Assistance Program,
    123-142
background and principles,
    125-129,*126,127*
case example: individual, 135-137
case example: supervisory, 137-139
case example: system, 138-141
complementarity and, 131-132
conclusions, 141-142
institutional culture and, 126

organizational structure, *126,*
126-127,*127*
paradigms, 129-131
psychodynamic theory and,
131-134

Keegan, Kate, xxiii, 243-262
Kelly, Brian, xxiii, 183-201
Kirk, Andrea K., xxiv, 351-366

Language, 289-291
of disaster consequence
management, 177-178,178t
Wells Fargo program, 234-235
Lawrence, Paul, 68-69,413-415
Lesch, Nancy K., xxiv, 203-218
Leveraging the New Human Capital
(Burud & Tumolo), 36-37
(The) Lexus and the Olive Tree
(Friedman), 407,408-409,
413-415,416
Literature review, 31-55
conclusions, 50-51
costs and HPM, 32-35
critical issues, 48-50
data sources, 49-50
health promotion and wellness,
42-44
integrated value models, 45-48,
46
integration, 44-48
mental health and EAPs, 40-41
model programs, 47
research design limitations, 50
success factors, 47-48
work-life programs, 41-42
Lorsch, Jay, 68-69,413-415

Macy's Department of Social Services,
xxx
Maiden, R. Paul, xv-xvi

Managed behavioral health care,
10,19-20
Managed mental health care, 70
Maternity Protection Act of 1994
(Ireland), 388
Medical costs. *See* Healthcare costs
Medicine
shift to health focus, 3
stress research, 3
Mental health, 40-41
Mental health costs, 33
Mental health/substance abuse, Wells
Fargo program, 229-230
Metrics, 23,302-303
employee measurements, 150,*150*
objective vs. subjective, 148-151
Mind/body interaction, 20-21
Minnesota state government, 325-350
background and principles, 326
challenges, 333-334
conceptual model, *329,*329-331,*330*
counterproductive work behavior,
337-341
Critical Incident Stress
Management, 344
data collection, 334-335
Depression Awareness Project, 335
employee questionnaire, *350*
evolution of services, 342-343
future directions, 346
goals, 333
grief and loss program, 343-344
health care costs, 331-332
Health Risk Management program,
332-333
history of organization, 326-328
job performance, 336-337
lessons learned, 344-346
management evaluation initiative,
343
organizational costs and
productivity, 341-344
program algorithm, *349*
theoretical orientation, 328-329,*329*
training and development, 344

utility measures, 339-342,340t
work withdrawal, 337
Model programs, 47
    disease management as, 100
Morgan Stanley company, 173
MOSAIC project, 377
Motorola wellness program, 203-218
    background and principles, 204-205
    Club One, 210-211
    communication and marketing,
        214-215
    decentralized predecessors, 211-212
    education and awareness, 209
    fitness and recreation, 208-209
    future directions, 215-217
    Healthy Workplace 2010 elements,
        218
    participation, 213
    pedometer walking program,
        212-213
    Practice Leadership Team, 210
    prevention and screening, 208
    program development and delivery,
        208
    program history, design, and
        definition, 205-208
    resilience tools, 209-210
    Web services, 209-210
    work-life and, 213-214
Mulvihill, Michael D., xxiv, xxxi

Nanny corporation, 410-411
National Institute for Occupational
        Safety and Health (NIOSH),
        309
National Institute on Alcohol Abuse
        and Alcoholism, 70
National Registry of Effective
        Programs, 47
National Study of EAP and Work/
        Family Programs, 67-93
    historical background, 70-72
National Study of the Changing
        Workforce, 13-14,20,412-413

National Survey of EAP and Work/
        Family Programs 1994,72-73
National Survey of EAP and Work-life
        Professionals 2001,74-81
    professional identity, 7-78
    sampling, 75-76,76
    services provided, 77-78,78,79t
Natural disasters
    business costs and, 35
    Ernst & Young hybrid model and,
        257
New Deal, 414
New Jersey State Police study,
        291-304
    conclusions, 303-304
    consultation skills evaluation,
        296-297
    critical incident stress response
        management, 293-294
    evaluation, 291-294
    guidelines derived from, 299-300
    measures, 302-303
    opportunities for integration,
        294-295
    organizational knowledge, 297
    organization contacts and guides,
        298-299
    participation, 292
    potential risks of integration,
        300-302
    September 11 and, 295
    training, 297-298
Norwest Corporation, 222-223. *See
        also* Wells Fargo program
Nurse phone lines, 43. *See also* Call
        centers
    Fairview Alive program, 270-271

Obesity, pedometer walking program,
        212-213
Objective vs. subjective measures,
        148-151
Occupational Alcoholism Programs
        (OAPs), 9,70,288-289,414

Consolidated Edison, 397-399
  history, xxx, xxxi
Occupational health departments, 8-9
Occupational medical departments, 16
Oklahoma City bombing, 319
Organizational barriers, to
  preparedness, 166t
Organizational culture, 149,*149*
Organizational health resources, 421
Organizational infrastructure, 149,*150*
Organizational placement, 281-306
  challenges of, 289-291
  conceptual framework,
    284-287,285t
  consultation skills evaluation,
    296-297
  guidelines, 299-300
  language issues, 289-291
  organization contacts and guides,
    298-299
  partners and functions, 296t
  traditions behind, 287-288
Organizational risks, 35
Organizational structure, 103
  Johns Hopkins University Faculty
    and Staff Assistance
    Program, *126,*126-127,*127*
Organization of Working Time Act of
  1997 (Ireland), 388
Organizations/conferences, 420-421
Outsourcing, human resources, 199
Overlaps, 17-19

Paid Time Off records, 34
Paradigms (Gestalt theory), 129-131
Parental Leave Act of 1998 (Ireland),
  388-389
Participation (utilization), 292
  Australian experience, 362
  Fairview Alive program,
    272-273,275-276
  United Kingdom, 373
(The) Partnership Group, 185. *See also*
  Ceridian

Pedometer walking program,
  Motorola, 212-213
Perception, Gestalt theory of, 130-131
Perceptual priming, 130-131
Personalization, 194
Personnel Performance Consultants,
  70
Pfizer program, 63-64
Pharmaceutical use, costs and, 33
Phone services
  integrated call centers, 102-103
  work-life and, 102
Platinum Book, 49-50
Population health, 162-163
Population Health Management, 268
Population level approach, 162-163
Predictive modeling, 15,60-61
Preparedness, 178t
  barriers to, 166-168
  behavioral issues in, 164-165
  disaster consequence management,
    159-181
  Institute of Medicine report,
    161-162
  Wells Fargo program, 230-231
Present day, 411-413
Presenteeism, 15,34-35,59,
  199-200
Priming, perceptual, 130-131
Productivity, 22-23
Professional identity, 76
Professional organizations, 29,420
Program design, 61-62
Psychoanalysis, defined, 131
Psychodynamic theory, 131-132
Public sector
  Austrialian occupational health and
    safety, 360-361
  Federal Occupational Health,
    307-323
  Minnesota state government,
    325-350
  New Jersey State Police study,
    291-304
Pullman Coach Car company, xxix

Quality assurance, Wells Fargo
    program, 237
Quality of Employment Survey (U.S.
    Dept. of Labor), 412
Quinlan, Maurice, xxiv-xxv, 381-394

Recorla, Rick, 172
Redundancy, 166
Relaxation response, 3
Reliability, 167
Research. *See also* Literature review
    academic, 39
    avenues for, 104
    clinical effectiveness and medical
        cost-offset, 41
    by consulting companies, 38-39
    effectiveness and outcomes, 40-41
    evidence-based practice and,
        400-402
    Harvard study, 68-69
    professionalism and, 399-400
    shortcomings of, 103-104
Resiliency, 111,178t
    disaster preparedness and, 167-168
    Motorola wellness program,
        209-210
    Workplace Resiliency Model,
        168,169t
Resources, 29,419-424
    accreditation organizations, 424
    Australian, 424
    European Union, 422-424
    Irish, 423-424
    literature, 419-420
    organizational health, 421
    organizations/conferences, 420-421
    professional organizations, 420
    United Kingdom and Europe, 379
    U.S. Government agencies, 422
    U.S. regional work/family
        organizations, 422
Risk management, 116
Risks, organizational, 35
Roman, Paul M., xxv, xxxii, 395-406

Roosevelt, Franklin Delano, 414
3 R's of preparedness, 166-168

Sampling
    expert survey, 96-97
    National Survey of EAP and
        Work-life Professionals
        2001,75-76,*76*
    vendors, 81,*81,84*,85
Schnarch, David, resiliency concept,
    110-111
Security, Wells Fargo program,
    228-229
Self-assessment, Web-based, 187
Self-criticism, 133-134
Self-report measures, as data source,
    49-50
September 11,2001 (9/11),
    295,319. *See also* Disaster
    consequence management
Service configurations, 10
Service delivery, United Kingdom,
    372
Service providers, external, 183-201.
    See also Vendors
Services and service delivery systems,
    17-19,*18*. *See also* Vendors
Services provided
    EAPA 2001 survey, 77-78,*78,79*t
    in-depth interviews, 85-87,86t
Sharar, David A., xxv, xxxii, 95-104
Short-term disability, 35. *See also*
        Absenteeism; Presenteeism
Siegel, Everett, xxv
Smoking cessation, 17,317-318
Social ecology of health, 107-109
Social stigma, 100,255-256,314
Societal factors, 3-7
    business, 3-4
    cultural awareness, 5
    ecological studies, 5-6
    globalization, 4-5
    medicine, 3
    social work, 4

Societal trends, business costs and, 36-37
Society for Human Resources Management
Benefits Survey, 40
(SHRM) Retention Practices Survey, 35
Solutions-oriented approach, 8-9
Spillover, 108-109
Splitting, perceptual, 132
Stephenson, Diane, xxv-xxvi, 307-323
Strategic interaction, 23-24
Stress response, 3
Subjective vs. objective measures, 148-151
Substance abuse, 403-404. *See* Occupational Alcoholism Programs
Success factors, 47-48
Supportive social environment programs, 188
Swihart, David L., xxvi, 105-121
Systems theory, 107-109,129-130
Terrorism
business costs and, 35
disaster consequence management, 159-181
employee consequences, 170-171
mental health impact greater in, 165
objectives of, 163
September 11,2001 (9/11), 295
societal fault lines and, 175
World Trade Center 1993 attack, 164
World Trade Center 2001 attack (9/11), 163-164
Thompson, Darci A., xxvi, 105-121
Total rewards concept, 7-8
Towers Perrin company, 38-39
Training, New Jersey State Police study, 297-298
Troubled employee/troubled supervisor, 9-10
Turner, Sandra, xxvi, 243-262
Turnover costs, 35

Union movement, xxx, 409-410
Australia, 353
United Kingdom, 367-380
background, 368
challenges, 375-376
conclusions, 378
funding, 368-370
healthcare costs, 375-376
level of service integration, 371-372
market penetration, 373-374
methodology, 370-371
participation, 373
resources, 379
service delivery, 372
services offered, 372-373
trends, 374-375
working hours as issue, 369
University of Arizona Life & Work Connections, 105-121
adaptations of theoretical base, 112-113
advantages, 115-116
background and principles, 106-107
case application, 116-120
challenges, 115
differentiation and, 110-111
life cycle/work cycle and, 111-112
model for, *113,*113-114
philosophical base, 107-112
resiliency and, 111
social ecology of health and, 107-109
strategic and tactical services, 113
synergy and, 109
systems theory and, 107-109
whole-person view in, 109-110
Worksite Wellness Heart Health Screenings, 114-115
University of Arizona Loss Prevention Program, 116
University of Arizona workplace shooting, 117-120
University of California–Berkeley death response program
background and principles, 145-146

beyond EAP and work-life,
146-147
program features, 152-154
program integration model,
147-152,*149,150,151*
Program Integration Model and,
154-156,*155*
Web services, 154
University of California–Berkeley
program, 143-157
University of Michigan Industrial
Relations Center study, 69
Ursano, Robert J., xxvi-xxvii, 159-181
U.S. Department of Health and Human
Services, 72,309. *See also*
Federal Occupational Health
U.S. Department of Labor *Quality of
Employment Survey*, 412
U.S. Public Health Service, 309
U.S. regional work/family
organizations, 422
Utility measures, 339-342,340t
Utilization. *See* Participation

Vendors, 183-201
business models, 81-83
Ceridian, 183-201
company size, 89
conclusions, 89-90,*90*
descriptive characteristics, 82t
future directions, 90-92
future predictions,
83,87-88,*88,*198-200
health and wellness services, 87
in-depth interviews (2003), 83-89
KPMG case example, 190-192
measured results, *189,*189-190
pilot survey (2002), 80-83
qualitative comments, 88-89
quality vs. cost, 89
sampling, 81,*81,84,*85
services provided, 85-87,86t
Web-based services, 88,186-187
wellness programs, 187-188

Vineburgh, Nancy T., xxvii, 159-181
Violence
risk assessment, 339
Wells Fargo program, 228-229
Violence-Free Workplace Training, 229
Voice Over Internet Protocol,
197-198,238

Watson Wyatt Human Capital Index,
37-38
Web-based services, 88
Ceridian, 186-187
Fairview Alive program, 270
instant messaging and, 198
Interactive Voice Reponse,
197-198,238
Motorola wellness program,
209-210
site design, 196
Voice Over Internet Protocol,
197-198
University of California–Berkeley
death response program, 154
Wells Fargo program, 233-234
work-life and, 102
Web sites, European Union, 423
Weiner, Michael, xxvii, 243-262
Welfare Capitalism,
409,410-411,411,414
Welfare secretaries, xxix
Wellness Councils of America
(WELCOA), 47-48
Wellness programs, 43
Australia, 358-360
Ceridian, 187-188
history, 71-72
Motorola, 203-218
Wells Fargo program, 219-242
access, 226,227
brand conformity, 236
business liaison service, 226
business model, 225-226
call center, 225-226
Coach on Call, 238-239

communications/support materials, 233-234
complex case management, 231
conclusion, 241
confidentiality, 237
consultant support, 238-239
consultant teams (service groups), 227
corporate background, 220-221
corporate culture and, 223-224, 234-235
corporate initiatives, 232-233
cost neutrality, 229
critical incident response/ preparedness, 230-231
Employee Assistance Counseling terminology, 234
Enterprise Incident Management Team, 232
Immediate Service Consultants, 226-227
Interactive Voice Reponse survey, 238
Learning and Development function, 240
mental health/substance abuse benefits, 229-230
People as Competitive Advantage core value, 223
program strategy, 221-225
quality assurance, 237
services marketing, 228
services offered, 228-239
staff qualifications, 234
staff recruitment and training, 239
standards of style, 234-247
structure, 225-227
struggles, 239-241
technology orientation, 236
threat management and security consultation, 228-229
value added, 240
Violence-Free Workplace Training, 229
Web-based services, 233-234
work trauma fund, 232

Welsaeth, Lars, 164
WFD (Work/Family Directions), 185. *See also* Ceridian
Whole-person philosophy, 109-110
Women's movement, 11
Workers compensation, 34
Work/Family Directions (WFD), 185. *See also* Ceridian
Working hours issue, 13,369
Work-life programs
    AWLP categories of focus, 12
    definition, 3
    experts' view of integration, 100-102
    Families and Work Institute steps, 12-13
    historical background, 71
    history and current state, 11-14
    Ireland, 383,386-387
    literature review, 41-42
    Motorola wellness program, 213-214
    phone services, 102
    Web services, 102
Work performance, 22-23,34-35
    measured results, *189*,189-190
    Minnesota state government, 336-337
Workplace hostility, 338-339
Workplace outcomes, as data source, 49
Workplace Resiliency Model, 168,169t
    barriers to preparedness and, 171-175
    event phase, 173-174
    post-event phase, 174-175
    pre-event phase, 172-174
Worksite Wellness Heart Health Screenings (U. Arizona), 114-115
Work withdrawal, 337
World Trade Center
    1993 attack, 164
    2001 attack (9/11), 163-164,170-171,295,319
WorldWide Guidelines for EAPs, 377